Java Programming

FOR THE INTERNET

A GUIDE TO CREATING DYNAMIC,
INTERACTIVE INTERNET APPLICATIONS

Java Programming

FOR THE INTERNET

A GUIDE TO CREATING DYNAMIC,
INTERACTIVE INTERNET APPLICATIONS

VENTANA

MICHAEL D. THOMAS

PRATIK R. PATEL

ALAN D. HUDSON

DONALD A. BALL JR.

Java Programming for the Internet: A Guide to Creating Dynamic, Interactive Internet Applications
Copyright © 1996 by Michael D. Thomas, Pratik R. Patel, Alan D. Hudson & Donald A. Ball Jr.

Library of Congress Cataloging-in-Publication Data
    Java programming for the Internet : a guide to creating dynamic, interactive Internet applications / Michael D. Thomas ...[et al.]. — 1st ed.
        p.   cm.
    Includes index.
    ISBN 1-56604-355-7
    1. Java (Computer program language) 2. Internet (Computer network)   I. Thomas, Michael D.
    QA76.73.J38J38 1996
    005.2—dc20   96-10856
                                                            CIP

First Edition 9 8 7 6 5 4 3 2
Printed in the United States of America

Ventana Communications Group, Inc.
P.O. Box 13964
Research Triangle Park, NC 27709-3964
919/544-9404
FAX 919/544-9472

Limits of Liability and Disclaimer of Warranty
The authors and publisher of this book have used their best efforts in preparing the book and the programs contained in it. These efforts include the development, research and testing of the theories and programs to determine their effectiveness. The authors and publisher make no warranty of any kind, expressed or implied, with regard to these programs or the documentation contained in this book.

    The authors and publisher shall not be liable in the event of incidental or consequential damages in connection with, or arising out of, the furnishing, performance or use of the programs, associated instructions and/or claims of productivity gains.

Trademarks
Trademarked names appear throughout this book, and on the accompanying compact disk or floppy disk (if applicable). Rather than list the names and entities that own the trademarks or insert a trademark symbol with each mention of the trademarked name, the publisher states that it is using the names only for editorial purposes and to the benefit of the trademark owner with no intention of infringing upon that trademark.

President/CEO
Josef Woodman

**Vice President of
Content Development**
Karen A. Bluestein

Production Manager
John Cotterman

**Technology Operations
Manager**
Kerry L. B. Foster

**Product Marketing
Manager**
Diane Lennox

Art Director
Marcia Webb

Acquisitions Editor
Sherri Morningstar

Developmental Editor
Lynn Jaluvka

Project Editor
Judy Flynn

Assistant Editor
J. J. Hohn

**Technical Director,
Multimedia**
Dan Brown

Technical Consultant
Jonathan Magid

Desktop Publisher
Patrick Berry

Proofreaders
Elizabeth Dickens
Heather Grattan
Sandra Manheimer

Indexer
Sherry Massey

About the Authors

Michael D. Thomas, Mary Jo's boy, has been programming in Java since before its release in May 1995. He has extensive experience with the perl, C, and C++ languages, and as an experienced Web site developer, has often hammered his head against the limitations of Common Gateway Interface (CGI) programming. He holds a Bachelor of Science degree in Computer Science from the University of North Carolina. Mike lives in Chapel Hill and can be reached at mdthomas@vmedia.com.

Pratik R. Patel, also of Chapel Hill, works in the Duke University/University of North Carolina at Chapel Hill Medical Informatics research program. He is currently developing an interactive Web resource for breast cancer and decision-support applications for the World Wide Web.

Alan D. Hudson of Raleigh is a consultant for Internet-based applications. He also writes library automation software for public and private libraries.

Donald A. Ball Jr. manages SunSITE UNC, one of the world's largest Web and FTP archives, and Educom's Edupage mailing list. He is currently an undergraduate math major at the University of North Carolina at Chapel Hill.

Acknowledgments

This book was a real team effort. Much of the credit should go to Lynn Jaluvka, Patrick Berry, J. J. Hohn, Dan Brown, and the rest of the Ventana team for taking up the slack in the project. Sherri Morningstar's unbounded patience helped get us through the hard times. And special thanks go to Jonathan Magid for his excellent technical advice.

Of course, we must thank the creators of the Java language itself. Without these visionaries, the exciting world of Java development wouldn't exist! Similarly, the contributions made to the newsgroup comp.lang.java have been essential to the creation of this manuscript.

Donald A. Ball Jr.: My sincerest thanks go to Paul Jones for bringing me into the world of SunSITE, Judd Knott for his unending patience while I struggled with the book, and to the rest of the SunSITE team for picking up my slack. Thanks also go to Jonathan Magid for getting me into this mess to begin with. My deepest thanks go to my family for everything, to my good friend Steve for keeping me relaxed, and most of all to Michelle for understanding.

Alan D. Hudson: Thanks, first and foremost, to Carol Simons for her unpaid and abundant support; to Jon Magid for acting as a sounding board and pin cushion; and to Mike Dodds for a little rest & relaxation, advice, and plain companionship at odd hours.

Pratik R. Patel: First and foremost, thanks to Krishna, Mom, and Dad for their continuous support, to Cap'n J. Mirrow for being a good friend, and to the rest of the Medical Informatics folks at UNC for support and much stimulating discussion.

Michael D. Thomas: Thanks to Cabrini and my family for their support during this project. Also, much credit should go to the University of North Carolina administrators—Tom Black of the Registrar's Office; John T. Jones of Student Stores; Paul Jones, formerly of Sunsite; Judd Knott of Sunsite; and Roger Nelsen of the General Alumni Association—who gave me the opportunity to gain hands-on experience with Internet development while pursuing my degree.

Contents

Introduction

Java is a powerful new programming language developed by Sun Microsystems. Originally conceived for use with interactive television, Java became of great interest to the Internet community when Sun released HotJava, a Web browser that could run small embedded Java programs, called *applets*, inside World Wide Web pages. Shortly thereafter, support for Java applets was added to Netscape Navigator 2.0, arguably the most popular Web browser in existence. Now, embedded Java applets are becoming *de rigueur* for high-profile Web sites.

Java is notable not only because Java applets can be run inside Web pages, but also because it is a powerful and easy-to-use object-oriented language. The Java language handles many of the mundane yet complex problems that programmers generally encounter when developing robust applications. Java supports multiprocessing with its thread classes and automatically performs garbage collection, freeing memory that is no longer being used in the background. The Java Application Programming Interface (API), included with the Java Developers Kit provided by Sun, gives programmers platform-independent access to essential tools for programming complex Internet applications, such as network sockets and a graphical windowing system.

Java makes the ideal of platform independence a reality. Java applets can run on any machine that can run a Java-capable Web browser, and stand-alone Java programs can be compiled to platform-independent bytecode. This bytecode can then be run on any machine with a Java interpreter. Java is the first popular high-level programming language to be truly platform independent.

About This Book

In recent months, Java has been hyped to the point of becoming a buzzword. But Java is still very much a mystery, even to professional programmers and Web developers. Part of the reason for this mystery is that, while Java is a programming language, most Java development is tied to the Web. Programmers and Web designers alike often assume that Java is yet another way to make clever Web pages.

Though this assumption is true, *Java Programming for the Internet* is designed to teach you how to use Java for purposes far beyond jazzing up your home page. Our hope is that Web designers can use this book to greatly expand the functionality of their Web sites, and that programmers will learn how to utilize the Web as a programming platform.

Java is, first and foremost, a new programming language. We spend the first four chapters introducing you to the design of the language, how it improves on previous languages, and the syntax and semantics of Java. From there, we focus our attention on applets and study them almost exclusively for the rest of the book. In Section IV, we expand our applets so that they can converse with the network. By showing you how to both communicate with existing Internet servers and create your own, we demonstrate how applets can act as the front end to true distributed programs.

To wrap up the book, we offer four Java programming tutorials in which we take a project from start to finish. We designed these to mirror real-world projects that you may wish to pursue. By demonstrating how to use Java for life-sized projects, we hope that the concepts discussed earlier in the book will come together for you.

CD-ROM & Online Companion

Our book is supplemented by a Companion CD-ROM and an Online Companion Web site. The CD-ROM provides the Java Developers Kit (JDK) for Windows 95/NT and Macintosh; the UNIX JDK can be found on the Online Companion. In addition, the CD-ROM contains all of the code examples from the book, as well as a number of sample applets and utilities.

The Online Companion (http://www.vmedia.com/java.html) keeps you up-to-date with the Java world. Because the Java language is still in its adolescence, no book about Java can be considered completely current even a month after its release. But through the Online Companion, we can keep you current with changes in the language, new developments in compilers and programming environments, and general Java news.

Hardware & Software Requirements

You can develop Java applets and programs on any machine that has a Java compiler. Sun has released a complete JDK for the following platforms:

- Microsoft Windows 95 & Windows NT
- Sun Solaris 2
- Apple Macintosh

In addition to these platforms, publicly supported compilers are available for some UNIX variants, including Linux, which is a free UNIX-compatible operating system for Intel x86 and DEC Alpha computers.

You can run Java applets in Netscape Navigator 2.0, a popular Web browser available on most platforms. At the time of this writing, Sun's Web browser, HotJava browser, which was packaged with the alpha version of the JDK, is not compatible with the current version of the Java language. Thus, it isn't of any use in developing applets.

What's Inside

Here's a brief description of what each chapter has to offer:

Section I: Introducing Java

Chapter 1, "The World Wide Web & Java," introduces you to the fundamental concepts underlying the Java language.

Chapter 2, "Java Programming Basics," helps you install the Java Developers Kit on your computer and get your first applet and stand-alone program running.

Section II: Java Applet Essentials

Chapter 3, "Object Orientation in Java," contains an introduction to the fundamentals of designing programs in object-oriented languages, and explains how object orientation is realized in Java. Readers already familiar with object-oriented design may wish to skip to the Java-specific material.

Chapter 4, "Syntax & Semantics," covers the syntax and semantics of the Java language in detail. The syntax of Java is very similar to the C programming language, so readers comfortable with C and C++ may wish to skim this chapter. However, we recommend that all readers new to Java see the sections entitled "Arrays" and "Exceptions."

Chapter 5, "How Applets Work," teaches you the essentials of programming interactive Java applets. This chapter is designed to get you coding as quickly as possible.

Chapter 6, "Discovering the Application Programming Interface," details many of the useful classes provided in the Java API, like Vectors and Hashtables.

Chapter 7, "Basic User Interface," describes the basic elements of the Java API's Abstract Windowing Toolkit (AWT), such as checkboxes, buttons, scrollbars, and lists. This toolkit makes it easy to create an attractive, functional user interface for your Java applets and programs.

Section III: Advanced Java Programming

Chapter 8, "Advanced User Interface," describes the advanced elements of the AWT, including dialogs, frames, menus, and the JDK's ready-made layout managers.

Chapter 9, "Graphics & Images," goes beyond the user interface aspect of the AWT and shows you how to draw your own pictures in Java, at the pixel level and using graphics primitives.

Chapter 10, "Advanced Program Design," describes how to create packages of Java classes and interfaces that can be reused for other projects and how to crash-proof your code with exception handling.

Chapter 11, "Advanced Threading," thoroughly explains the mechanisms of Java's threads and explores some of the issues encountered in programming with multiple threads.

Chapter 12, "Programming Beyond the Applet Model" discusses ways to get beyond some of the limitations of Java applets by writing stand-alone Java applications and by integrating platform-specific native methods in your programs.

Section IV: Java & the Network

Chapter 13, "Networking With Sockets & Streams," shows you how to open connections to other networked computers and introduces you to Java's input/output classes.

Chapter 14, "Networking With URLs," describes how to access networked resources by using URLs in your Java programs.

Chapter 15, "Writing Java Servers," diverges briefly from the book's applet focus and explains how to build stand-alone Java servers.

Section V: Internet Applications by Example

Section V contains the book's four tutorial chapters:

Chapter 16, "Interactive Animation: An Advertising Applet," demonstrates how to create a highly configurable interactive animation applet.

Chapter 17, "Interfacing With CGI: The Java Store," walks you through the process of developing a Java applet designed for use as a virtual store.

Chapter 18, "Interfacing With Non-HTTP Servers: A Chess Client," walks you through the development of a client for the Internet Chess Server.

Chapter 19, "Writing Your Own Servers: A Meeting Scheduler," finishes up the tutorials by describing and implementing a client-server scheduling system in Java.

Appendices

Appendix A, "About the Online Companion," describes the supplementary resources to this book that are available on the Online Companion.

Appendix B, "About the Companion CD-ROM," tells how to use the Companion CD-ROM to this book and describes its contents.

Conventions Used in This Book

As we said previously, the CD contains code examples from the text. When you are reading the text and would like to play around with one of the code examples, look above the code fragment to see what example it is. You will see an example number, such as "Example 2-7a." On the CD, you will find this particular code example in the Chapter 2, Example2-7 directory (Chapter2/ Example2-7). The lowercase letter at the end has no significance when you are looking up the code example on the CD—it's there so you can keep track of where you are in the text.

When we discuss a particular class or object, we refer to it by its proper name and, therefore, capitalize the first letter, as in "the String class" or "the String." However, when we describe conceptually what a string is, we use all lowercase letters.

Moving On

Now that you know what we're trying to do with this book, it's time for us to deliver. We hope you have fun as you delve into the world of Java programming.

Introducing Java

1

The World Wide Web & Java

Few programming languages generate the kind of interest that Java has, but then few languages redefine, as Java does, what programs are and what programmers can do. While the programs of other languages are confined to a particular platform, Java is platform independent. While you must always virus scan normal software that you download from the Internet—or put your trust in the company or person who wrote it—the Java language is designed for writing programs that can be downloaded and run safely.

Before Java, software always came in a shrink-wrapped box. You had to give it a permanent home on your hard drive, put it on speaking terms with your network, and upgrade it again and again. Java programs can come on a wire for cordial visits. When you are done with them, they disappear. They are always up-to-date and they have no problem talking to the network.

In addition to platform independence and strong networking capabilities, Java offers the benefits of object orientation and multithreading. These capabilities allow your code to more closely model the real-world problems you are trying to solve. The language is also dynamic: small pieces of Java code are assembled at runtime into the program, rather than being assembled at the time you write the code.

On the Internet these days, there's no lack of hype about Java, and a lot of it sounds like what we've just said. But you will find that there is substance behind the hype. Parts of Java are, admittedly, still in rough draft form, but we believe that the more you learn about Java, the more you will like it.

A lot of the current excitement has been generated by applets— small programs that can be embedded into Web pages. But Java isn't just a means that ends in a clever Web page. First and foremost, it is a powerful, general, platform-independent programming language. Before you finish this book, you may find yourself writing stand-alone applications in Java purely because you don't have to port your Java code from platform to platform. And applets themselves are far more powerful than Web page dressings.

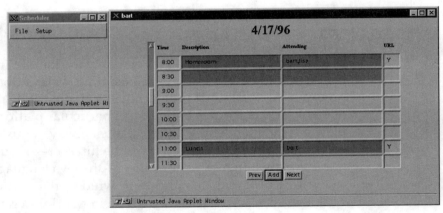

Figure 1-1: *Java Meeting Scheduler Applet.*

For example, Figure 1-1 shows an applet we develop fully in the last chapter of this book. It is your standard meeting scheduler, with a few very powerful twists. You and your colleagues can schedule meetings through your Java-capable Web browsers. You needn't be in the same local area network, on the same platform, or even in the same country— the only requirement is that you are connected to the Internet.

JAVA-CAPABLE WEB BROWSERS

At the time of this writing, Netscape Communications Corporation offers the only full-featured Java-capable Web browser. We give details for downloading Netscape Navigator 2.0 for personal use in Chapter 2. For a current list of Java-capable Web browsers, please visit the Online Companion at http://www.vmedia.com/java.html. We will keep you up-to-date on the best and most stable Java-capable Web browsers for your needs.

In this book, our aim is to build applications that are distributed across the Internet and use the Web as a programming platform. Besides the meeting scheduler, we'll show you how to hook up to servers on the Web by writing a client for the Internet Chess Server, how to start your own store, and how to write highly configurable, interactive applets. Along the way, we'll cover the basics you need to write powerful stand-alone applications and any applet that you could dream up.

In this chapter, we start off by examining how all Java programs are run and why these characteristics are advantageous for network computing. Next, we focus on applets and how they are changing the Web. To back up our claim that Java is good for more than just cute Web pages, we briefly look at the history of Java. Then, we examine the features of Java that make it an easy-to-use, easy-to-learn, general programming language.

How Java Programs Run

The Java language is object-oriented, threaded, dynamic, and all that, but these aspects aren't what sets it apart as the best language available for networking. What makes the difference is how Java programs are executed. Java programs are executed inside *virtual machines* that sit inside the computer on which they are running.

A Java program has no contact with the actual computer; it only knows about the virtual machine. This arrangement has several important implications.

First, as we noted earlier, Java programs are platform-independent. Have you ever had to develop for multiple operating systems? Chances are that you didn't do it for pleasure. When you were done, you probably knew a lot more nuances of the various platforms than you really cared to. When you write a Java program and compile it, it is ready to run on any computer that contains the Java virtual machine. In a sense, you are just writing for one platform, the virtual machine.

LANGUAGE PLATFORM INDEPENDENCE VS. PROGRAM PLATFORM INDEPENDENCE
Although we can accurately say that Java is a platform-independent language, this description doesn't completely do Java justice. For instance, ANSI C is a platform-independent language, but it is not *program* platform independent —you have to compile your programs for each and every platform. Also, ANSI C leaves the size and internal storage format for data and functions to whatever is most convenient for the native platform— all these things are strictly defined for Java. Just one more advantage!

Second, the virtual machine decides what Java programs can and can't do. Programs written in compiled languages, like C or C++, are run directly by the operating system. Therefore, they have direct access to all of the system's resources, including memory and the file system.

Since Java programs are run from within the virtual machine, the people who create the virtual machine get to decide what a program can and can't do. The environment that is created for Java programs is called the *runtime environment*. The virtual machine acts as a firewall between the host computer and the Java program. A Java program never accesses your computer's input and output devices, file system, or even memory. Instead, it asks the virtual machine to access it.

When we run applets, we are downloading them into a virtual machine that prohibits access to the file system entirely. Like all virtual machines that run Java programs, it only allows indirect access to the system resources, which is why we can trust applets not to delete our files or propagate viruses.

Java's runtime architecture also allows Java programs to assemble themselves at runtime. Suppose someone only uses a very small percentage of a program you wrote. Wouldn't it be nice to load the most important parts of the program into memory, and only load the bulky, seldom-used parts if they are needed? Java programs can do that, through a process called *dynamic binding*.

If you're only loading your programs from the hard drive, and your computer is nice and fast, dynamic binding isn't really that important. But when you are downloading programs from the Internet, the biggest factor in program speed is going to be the rate of network transfer. Your Java programs can quickly download the parts they need to get started, and then download the other parts as they begin to run. Dynamic binding also makes Java code easier to maintain, as we will see later in this chapter.

FUNCTIONALITY IN THE VIRTUAL MACHINE

The virtual machine contains a lot of basic functionality that goes beyond the demands of its role as a firewall—such as string manipulation tools, graphics and user interface routines, basic data structures, and mathematical functionality. To use it, you just need to learn about the Application Programming Interface, which we discuss in Chapter 6. The existence of the API means that even the most complicated applets will rarely be bigger than 100 kilobytes after compilation.

Java's runtime environment solves several basic problems of Internet programming. Since the Internet consists of many different platforms, it is beneficial to be able to write platform-independent programs. Java programs can be expected to do no more than the virtual machine allows. And finally, the runtime environment allows us to write programs that can download and start executing speedily.

The Applet Model

All Java programs need a virtual machine in which to run. A special type of Java program, called an *applet*, is run in a virtual machine inside Java-capable Web browsers such as Netscape Navigator 2.0. This virtual machine has been adapted so that applets can't damage the computer to which they are downloaded.

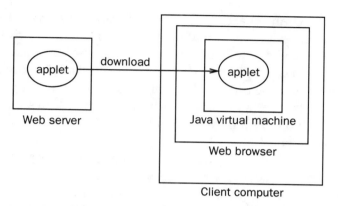

Figure 1-2: *How applets are run.*

Notice that the applet in Figure 1-2 is run on the client computer. Before Java, most Web-related programs had to be run on the Web server machine. The client side execution of applets is a major breakthrough for Web programming. Before Java, Web pages were static. Now that applets can be embedded in Web pages, they can be interactive. They can also talk back to the machine they come from and can be parts of larger systems.

As we progress through each chapter, we'll explore more and more of the possibilities of applets. But first, lets take a high-level view of applets and how they work.

The Applet Runtime Environment

As we have said, the applet virtual machine, or runtime environment, exists inside a Web browser. It is built to run applets—and only applets. In the course of running the applet, it acts as a firewall between the local computer and the applet. Like all runtime environments, it services memory requests and controls access to input and output devices.

But that role as firewall is much more important for the applet runtime environment than it is for the standard runtime environment. For instance, we don't want an applet to download and have access to our local file system. The Java language itself doesn't prohibit access to the file system. If we want to, we can write a Java program that deletes our entire hard drive. If we run it, then we have to expect the consequences—just as if we wrote and ran a C program to do it, or if we just told the operating system to wipe out the drive directly. But even though we can write a Java program that has access to the file system, we certainly don't want applets to download from the Internet and wipe out our drive.

So our applet runtime environment needs to protect the file system. We'll cover how it does this, and things applets *can't* do, first. Protecting the file system prevents much of the potential damage from viruses, but not quite enough. We still need to make sure that our applets are downloaded in a safe manner—we'll cover that second.

What Applets Can't Do

It's possible to write completely valid Java code that could delete the entire file system. So why can't a hacker with evil intentions just stick this code into an applet, embed the applet in a Web page, and tell potential victims to check it out? Well, he can, but when the applet downloads to his victims' Web browsers, the applet will crash, never touching the local file system. The reason is simple: the applet runtime environment doesn't know how to access the file system.

APPLET SECURITY UPDATES

The next few pages describe the reasons why, in theory, applets can't harm a host computer. Though the theory is sound, and we currently know of no cases in which hackers have done damage via applets, Sun is investigating some holes in applet security as this book goes to press. For updates on applet security issues, check the Online Companion at http://www.vmedia.com/java.html.

This is why the runtime architecture of Java is so powerful. The creators of the runtime environment have the final say as to what a program can or can't do. For instance, if they don't want Java programs to print out offensive words, they can keep it from happening. Less prudently, but more importantly, the runtime environment can determine what files, if any, Java programs are allowed to access, what input and output devices they can deal with, and any other effects a program can have on the system.

Like all Java runtime environments, the applet runtime environment doesn't allow direct access to memory. A Java program can only deal with the memory the runtime environment hands to it, and even then it is limited in exactly what it can do with that memory.

The Safe Downloading of Applets

So far, we have seen that applets don't have access to the local system's memory or to its files. However, a hacker has still another chance, when the applet downloads, to overcome any obstacles that might be in the way. The applet runtime environment performs two more steps to ensure that applets aren't trying to do anything destructive.

First, it verifies the .class file that is being downloaded. The .class file contains extra information that guarantees that the program is following all of Java's rules. The applet runtime environment carefully scrutinizes the .class file to make sure that information is there. If it didn't do that, a hacker with an in-depth knowledge of a particular platform could get access to the system's memory.

Second, it loads the Java program into its own memory space. Why is this important? If it isn't loaded into its own memory space, a hacker could replace part of the runtime environment with his own functionality! Then, he could use that class to access the file system or to do a number of other devious things.

Hype, Hope & History

On May 23, 1995, Sun Microsystems formally released Java to the world as an Internet programming language. But Java wasn't part of a long range plan to solve the problems of Internet programming. Nor was it a quick hack to capitalize on the popularity of the Web. Java originated as part of a consumer electronics project that was started in 1990, years before the Web or the Internet gained widespread popularity. Let's look at the origins of Java and how the lessons the originators learned from dealing with consumer electronics affected the language we know today.

MORE JAVA HISTORY

Links to general information about Java, including articles about its history and future, can be found on the Online Companion. One of these links is the primary source for the history we present here. Written by Michael O'Connell for Sun World Online, that history can be found at: http://www.sun.com/sunworldonline/swol-07-1995/swol-07-java.html.

George Gilder also wrote an enlightening article about Java for Forbes ASAP, entitled "The Coming Software Shift." This and other articles by Gilder can be found at: http://www.seas.upenn.edu/~gaj1/ggindex.html. Check this page often—Gilder is very good at explaining emerging technologies.

The intent of the consumer electronics project was not to create a network-ready language. It was to build a network out of all the small computers you use every day, such as the chips in your VCR, television, and microwave. In 1990, Sun saw this as an emerging market and to explore its opportunities, it created a *skunkworks*—a separate, nearly autonomous division—within Sun Microsystems.

In the early 1980s, a similar skunkworks was created within IBM to explore personal computing, and it created the IBM PC. Sun's consumer electronics skunkworks, code-named "Green," didn't revolutionize consumer electronics in the way IBM's skunkworks changed the microcomputing landscape forever. Two years after its inception, it lost out on a bid to get into the interactive television market, and shortly thereafter it dissolved. In the words of Java creator James Gosling (as quoted in the Sun World Online article we cited earlier), they discovered that the "consumer electronics market wasn't real. People had hyped things beyond reason."

But despite this hindsight revelation, they fulfilled their mission as a skunkworks. Separated from the corporate bureaucracy, but with the resources of a large company available to them, a talented group of computer professionals was able to intensely study and solve the problems of networking appliances. They were technically, if not commercially, successful.

Part of that technical success was a computer language named Oak that was designed to work in appliances. In 1995, Sun realized that this language could provide solutions to Internet programming. Unfortunately, somebody else had already trademarked the name Oak, so they renamed it Java.

Lessons Learned From Consumer Electronics

Unbeknownst to the team, the problems that they were attacking in the domain of consumer electronics would be the same problems the tremendous growth of the Web would reveal about the Internet. Until the Web became popular, the Internet was mostly used to connect research centers and universities. Though it was a vast and time-tested network, it wasn't ready for widespread consumer and business use. Let's see how some of the challenges of consumer electronics are also found on the Internet.

Architectural Heterogeneity

Your coffee maker and your television both have microchips, but it is highly unlikely that they are the same type. The Green team couldn't build its system with a particular type of architecture in mind. As the Web introduced Macs and PCs to the Internet, this same problem would emerge. For its network of household appliances, the Green team had to solve this problem up front.

Real-time Software Portability

Not only did the language of the network need to be portable across various platforms, but the programs written in those languages also needed to be runnable on a variety of platforms. Before Java, Internet programmers solved this by compiling different programs for each architecture. For instance, there were separate Mosaic browsers for Mac, Windows, and the various flavors of UNIX.

The Green team couldn't take this approach for two reasons. First, the number of possible platforms was directly related to the number of possible appliances; porting code for each platform would be too time-consuming. Second, consumers aren't going to put up with incompatibility problems. Though personal computer users accept software upgrades as a matter of course, coffee machine users just want their coffee. Neither appliance users nor manufacturers would put up with the difficulties that are a matter of course in the sphere of personal computing.

The solution? All Java programs are run inside the virtual machine we talked about earlier. The virtual machine is layered on top of the microprocessor, so that the Java programs don't have to be concerned about what platform they are running on. Of course, this solution is also directly applicable to Internet programming.

Simplicity & Compactness

Your coffee machine may contain a little computer, but it isn't a Pentium or PowerPC chip with tons of RAM! For their system to work, it had to be designed to function in very small spaces. The Green team solved this problem by keeping the virtual machine small—in the range of kilobytes, not megabytes—and simple. Keeping the virtual machine simple meant also keeping the language simple. Though the software that can be built with Java is quite complex, the language itself is very straightforward. The Green team had to keep the core of the language separated from what could be done with its functionality.

Inherent Software Downloadability

Appliances don't have hard drives, either. The software to run in all those appliances had to be stored elsewhere, and only stored by the appliance's computer when absolutely necessary—at runtime. Thus, Java evolved as a language of the network, not the computer.

Network Safety

Once you start bouncing software over a network, you have to be concerned with what harm the software might cause to a host. The Green team was developing the environment in which to develop software; not the software itself. Since the software was ultimately going to be developed by third parties, they had to ensure that a piece of code couldn't be downloaded to an appliance and effectively destroy it. This is identical to the worries computer users have about software downloaded over the Internet. We don't want viruses to erase our hard drives!

Before Java, these problems were solved by checking downloaded programs for viruses. The Green team adopted a much more direct solution—incapacitate the programs from doing any harm in the first place. They accomplished this by letting the virtual machine determine what downloaded software could and couldn't do. As we described earlier, this solution is why we can be confident that our computers won't be harmed by Java applets we download from the Web.

Java Meets the Web

Quite by coincidence, the Green team solved the problems of Internet programming. The Java language was architecture-neutral and safe for networks, and by the time Web started to take off, it was functional. In 1994, Sun realized that their aborted foray into the consumer electronics market had produced a valuable product—Java.

At the time of Java's development, the Internet was the domain of workstations and supercomputers. Only computer engineers and scientists had any interest in it, and if they wanted to use it, they had to have a pretty thorough knowledge of the UNIX operating system. For the millions of users sitting behind the graphical user interfaces of their Macs and Windows machines, the Internet, and its huge capacity for information storing and communication, was completely foreign. In April 1993, the first graphical Web browser, NCSA Mosaic 1.0, was released, and the Internet was added to the buzzword lexicon.

The Green team created a Web browser named HotJava, and released it to the Internet in the spring of 1995. As a Web browser, HotJava was clunky in many ways. It didn't support all of the latest HTML extensions, and it was quite slow. But it had a powerful feature that had no precedent on the Web; it supported *executable content*. Unlike other Web browsers, it could download small Java programs called applets and run them inside the browser. It ran them in a virtual machine, the same scenario originally intended for your appliances.

Within weeks of the formal release of Java, the maker of the most popular Web browsers, Netscape Communications Corporation, announced support of Java and Java applets. Netscape licensed Java from Sun and began work on incorporating a Java virtual machine into its next line of browsers, Netscape Navigator 2.0. Early versions of these browsers were released in October 1995, thus making Java applets accessible to a much wider range of Web surfers than HotJava was able to. In the meantime, Sun had made improvements to the Java language, changes that included making applets easier to program. Sun released version 1.0 of Java in January 1996.

Since the early HotJava days, Sun has made the inner workings of Java freely available to the Internet community. This helps encourage the porting of the virtual machine to the various platforms of the Internet, including the platforms of Sun's many competitors in the workstation market. Sun's strategy is puzzling to many industry observers. Why invest millions in a technology and then give it away?

Bill Joy, one of the founders of Sun, framed the answer this way in the Forbes ASAP article we cited earlier: "Most of the bright people don't work for you—no matter who you are. You need a strategy that allows for innovation occurring elsewhere." Java is Sun's attempt to make the Internet a level playing field, where hackers like us provide the innovative software. To do this, they are even willing to give control of the Java language specification to a standards body eventually.

What does Sun stand to gain? As one of the major vendors of high-end Web servers, it gains as the market for Web servers grows. There aren't any guarantees here for Sun. The company still has to compete and still has to make good products. It's a cocky strategy, one that most computer companies don't have the confidence to adopt.

Sun is also developing pioneering computers for Java programs to run on, including the Internet appliance, a simple computer costing a few hundred dollars which will function as a hardware Web client. There is also talk of Java's becoming the tool that will move interactive television from the snake-oil shelf to the living room. Java may yet return to its roots—consumer electronics.

All this means that the Java skills you learn today will probably serve you well in whatever path the Information Superhighway takes. In many ways, the Internet is quite lucky to have Java. The Web was ripe for a scripting language of some sort. The first halfway decent one to come along would probably have become a standard, even if it wasn't platform independent, safe for the network, and completely open to third-party development. Instead, we got a language that is close to being custom-designed for the Internet. Now, let's look more closely at Java and the features that you will soon come to love.

Why You Will Love Java

We hope our discussion of Java's history has reassured you about its future. Now, let's examine what actually emerged from the vaporware of consumer electronics. Our buzzword density is going to be pretty high over the next few pages, but we'll try to stay well below the acceptable standards of hype. But Java isn't perfect—we will also point out some of its weaknesses along the way.

The Best of the Old & New

Probably one of the most feared phrases in computerese is "legacy systems." As changes in the world of computers take place at a dizzying pace, it's sometimes hard to comprehend that we are moving into the third decade of widespread computing. Unfortunately, the early programming languages had to follow the rules of what is, today, primitive computing. They will probably go down in intellectual history as significant turning points, but they have also propagated problems that existed in those early computing environments. Despite our blazing processors and tons of system resources, the ghosts of those early computers continue to haunt our programming languages.

This is the demand of backward compatibility, but Java doesn't answer the call. Because it was developed from scratch, it doesn't have to be able to compile on computers only found in museums. We could compare some of the "features" of older programming languages to the human appendix; it no longer serves a purpose and can become infected. If we were to design a new revolutionary species, we could drop it out of the plan. However, if we take an evolutionary approach—as language designers often do to ensure backward compatibility—we would be stuck with it.

Java is revolutionary in the sense it avoids incorporating the problems of decades of computing for the sake of backward compatibility. At the same time, it doesn't demand that we learn tons of esoteric new concepts. Java represents a synthesis of many programming languages that came before it. It borrows the time-tested concepts of previous languages, but eliminates the problems that would be required for backward compatibility's sake.

The same reasoning can be applied to the creation of programming languages. There is a lot of wisdom stored in their 30-year evolution. Luckily, the creators of Java didn't go too far adrift in the design. For instance, the basic syntax is pretty much the same as the C programming language. In fact, Java has the basics of most languages—types, variables, and subroutines.

Java isn't about radically changing the way people are supposed to think and adding tons of exotic features. Mostly, Java is a simplified C++, with some additions from other languages. The arcana inherited from those 1960s era computers is gone, along with C++ "features" that are hard to learn and make code harder to maintain. In the words of Bill Joy, quoted in Forbes ASAP, "What we have taken away is mind-boggling complexity." Let's look at some of the complexity and arcana of C++ that has been left out of Java. The next few pages will certainly make more sense if you have C or C++ experience. But, as we do throughout the book, we have attempted to describe the differences between C++ and Java so that anyone with some programming background can understand.

No Preprocessor

For those of you not familiar with C and C++, the preprocessor performs global substitutions on your code before it goes to a compiler. This results in the compiler seeing an entirely different set of code than is written, and the person responsible for maintaining that code has to figure out what the preprocessor is doing. The designers of Java saw the preprocessor as performing magic on your code, so they discarded it.

No Makefiles & Library Linking Worries

When you program in C or C++, often one of the biggest challenges is creating your Makefile, a small program that tells the compiler how to build your executable file. Usually your source code is spread across many files and requires the use of libraries of code that have already been compiled. The purpose of the Makefile is to make sure that all the right information is fed to the preprocessor, that source code that hasn't changed isn't compiled needlessly, and that the library is linked in correctly.

Java takes care of the Makefile's first purpose by not having a preprocessor. The manifestation of the second purpose is built directly into the compiler. If you have a bunch of source code files in your project and you only change one, the compiler won't bother to update the ones that haven't changed.

The last problem is taken care of because Java is a *dynamic* language. The virtual machine links Java programs together at runtime, thus eliminating the need to link to libraries at compile time. We will look at this property of Java shortly, in the section entitled "Dynamic."

No Direct Memory Access or Pointer Arithmetic

In C and C++, a *pointer* is an integer that represents a memory address on the computer. When you use pointers in C or C++ programs, you are actually telling the computer to look at that specific memory address and deal with whatever resides there. If you want, you can perform arithmetic on the memory address and then tell the computer to act on whatever is there.

This is part of C's heritage as a systems programming language. When you are doing very low-level programming for a particular platform, it is valuable. But for high-level programming, it's bad programming practice and usually leads to confusing code. Because it represents bad programming style and can lead to unsafe programs, Java doesn't have direct memory access or pointer arithmetic.

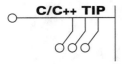

C/C++ TIP

If you're an experienced programmer, you may be wondering how useful a language can be without direct memory access. Although Java doesn't allow you to directly access memory, it does have reference variables that play the same role as C and C++ pointers— you can make a linked-list or a stack, for instance. The difference is that you can't access the memory address directly or cast the memory address to an integer.

No Operator Overloading

Many programming languages allow the programmer to define what some of the operators—like the + sign—mean in relation to certain data types. They define the meaning with a subroutine that is called whenever the operator is seen, which is called *operator overloading*. Here's an example where SetA and SetB are a programmer-defined type representing a set of integers:

```
SetA=SetA+SetB;
```

What is the programmer attempting to do here? We don't really know. We would have to ask the programmer, who is probably doing something intuitive, like adding together each value of the two vectors. But ultimately, the overloaded operator raises more questions than it answers: What happens if one vector has more numbers than another? As people who are trying to understand this code, we are not helped by operator overloading. We still have to look at the subroutine defining the actions of the overloaded operator to know what is going on. Also, the language has to be more complex to allow operator overloading. Because operator overloading inhibits the readability of the source code and makes the language more complex, Java's designers declined to put it in.

No Multiple Inheritance

For those of you who don't have a background in object-oriented programming, the concept of inheritance will be easier to understand after reading Chapter 3. For now, we'll look at what you may think of as a childish example—complete with children. Let's assume we have a society in which every family has only one parent, and the children in one family do things in the following way: If they have learned how to do something themselves, they do it their way; if not, they ask their parent. In turn, if the parent doesn't know how to do something, he or she asks his/her parent. This is a very simple model of single inheritance. Each child can only inherit properties from one parent, who in turn can only inherit from one parent.

In multiple inheritance, the child can inherit ways of doing things from multiple parents. This makes the life of our child more complicated. Different parents could define differently how the child should perform a certain action, or the child could have inherited from the same parent twice. Even without these ambiguities occurring, the child would have to ask all of the parents involved in order to figure out how to do something.

When we program in object-oriented languages, modules within our programs can inherit ways of doing things just like the child in our example. When a language allows multiple inheritance, it must be more complex because the problems become more complicated. Why do any languages use multiple inheritance? We will discuss this in depth in Chapter 3, but the short answer is that our modules need to take on the characteristics of more than one parent. As we will see, Java supports this design concept without complicating the entire language with multiple inheritance.

Object Orientation

We've stated that Java is good partly because it is new. One of the most important advantages of starting from the ground up is that Java was created to be an object-oriented language. Since object orientation is perhaps the most popular trend in modern software development, we can put a check in the buzzword column for Java. But before we proceed down our buzzword checklist, let's look briefly at what object orientation is and how Java implements it.

To understand the importance of object orientation, it helps to remember a simple fact: computers don't think the way we do. They store 1s and 0s in registers. The antithesis of intuition is assembly language—a very narrow way to view the problems of the universe. Computers live in a world so simple that it's difficult for us to comprehend it, and our world is too complicated for computers to grasp. Something mechanically simple, such as adding a thousand numbers together, can take us an hour, while computer scientists are still trying to teach computers how to write grammatically correct sentences.

In our early interactions with computers, we had to play by their rules. As computer research progressed, computer languages were developed that allowed us more sanity when telling our computers what to do. The first major breakthrough was procedural languages. Instead of just passing the computer a long list of very simple instructions, procedural languages allowed us to build a short list that could be called again and again—a subroutine. With subroutines, we could represent discrete blocks of action that we could relate to, like finding the minimum value of a set of values. We are able to build on subroutines in the creation of our program.

Object orientation gives us a level of abstraction about the actions of our programs. Still, it is quite distant from how we intuitively attack problems. Try to visualize the following directive: "Go to the store, get milk, go home." We have directed you to perform three actions, but chances are that your first step in thinking about the problem is thinking about the nouns, not the verbs, of our directive. For instance, you don't want to get milk that's sour, and you don't want to waste time going to a store that doesn't have milk. If we were to ask you how you planned to attack the problem, you may say, "Starting from my current location, I am going to use an available source of transportation and proceed to a store that sells milk, buy milk that isn't sour, and proceed to the place where I live."

The crux of our milk-buying problem has to do with the properties of the objects involved—the milk, the store, and even the house. Procedural languages force us to focus entirely on the actions involved in solving the problem. Object-oriented languages allow us to solve our problem by defining objects. Instead of thinking about checking each carton of milk to see if any are sour, we can think about milk having the condition of being sour. Table 1-1 illustrates each object in our problem, the information inherent to it, and the questions we would wish to ask it.

Object	Data	Questions
Transportation	Range	What stores are in range?
Milk	Expiration date	How long until expired?
	Price	How expensive is the milk?
Store	Location	Does this store have milk?
House	Location	Is the store within range of transportation?
	Owner	Is this my house?

Table 1-1: *Objects of our problem.*

In Java, we can write our program by creating a representation of each of these objects. As you will see in Chapter 3, our objects can very closely model the approach we took in Table 1-1. We still write subroutines. For instance, to code our example above, we would write subroutines to answer all of the questions in the third column and to set the values in the second column. The difference is that all of our subroutines are associated to an object. This is the point of object-oriented languages—to describe our problems for the computer to solve in terms that we would naturally use.

Unfortunately, object orientation often fails to achieve this enlightened goal. The reasons are many, but let's generalize three of them. First, object orientation is a still maturing methodology. Some early attempts at implementing object-oriented languages led to such levels of abstraction that mere mortals were lost. Second, procedural languages force programmers to think procedurally. As B. L. Whorf once said, "Language shapes the way we think, and determines what we can think about." Even though an object-oriented approach more closely models most real-world problems, many programmers will prefer the more familiar approach learned for procedural languages. The computer language has shaped the problem solving process!

But perhaps most importantly, the advance of object orientation has been impaired by *hybrid* object-oriented languages; languages that are both procedural and object oriented. C++ is the chief culprit here, with Object Pascal close on its heels. Hybrid languages make it particularly easy for the object-oriented programmer to routinely create code that is not object oriented. Since they can still write procedural programs, they probably will, throwing in objects occasionally when they feel daring. Also, hybrid languages introduce tons of special cases that pure object-oriented languages eliminate. They not only make it easier for people not to adopt an object-oriented methodology, they make it harder to use object-oriented features in the first place!

Java works to solve all three of the problems listed here. As we mentioned before, it is a synthesis of languages that preceded it, and it solves many of the problems exposed by the early object-oriented languages. It solves the latter two problems by being completely object oriented. This eliminates the complexity of hybrid languages, while forcing procedural programmers to use object-orient programming.

Network Ready

Java was developed from the start to be a language of the network. We have already looked at a couple of advantages this gives us that involve the virtual machine. The virtual machine keeps programs from harming the computer they are downloaded to, allows programs to download quickly, and runs the programs so that they aren't dependent on the underlying operating system.

These advantages are inherent to the Java language. In day-to-day programming, we never have to worry about them. But since Java was born to be networked, we have an extensive set of functionality included in the API to allow us to converse with the Internet. Using the API, we can use high level abstractions like Uniform Resource Locators (URLs) or communicate on very low levels by just passing packets back and forth.

Because the networking support is so strong, we can write applets that communicate back to the computer they came from in ways we define. In fact, this is exactly what we do with our meeting scheduler, the applet and server we develop in Chapter 19. The applet downloads via the HyperText Transfer Protocol (HTTP). But HTTP is really only meant for retrieving information, not communication. So the client applet then opens a connection with the schedule server on the Web server machine. All of the actual communication occurs on that connection.

We didn't put encrypted data transfer into our scheduler system, but if you wanted to, you could. If you figure out a better way to compress video, just write an applet that knows how to interpret the compression and a server that knows how to transfer the video. Instead of having to write a massive client program and then convince people to install it, you can just write an applet that downloads to their Web browsers and becomes the client. The API gives you the ability to define your own way of transferring data, while the platform independence and safety inherent to the language means that you can get client programs to the users' computers.

Dynamic

A C or C++ program, when compiled, is a monolithic file of machine instructions. For large programs, the size of this executable file can be measured in megabytes, such as Microsoft's Word for Windows 6.0, which is 3.2 megabytes. But when you develop a truly massive project, you usually use code that others have written previously. The original source code is compiled and stored in a library. When a program is compiled, the new source code that has been written is linked to this existing library, and the whole image is dumped into a big executable file.

But what if a bug is found somewhere in the library, or for some other reason you want to change one of the modules? Then you get to relink each and every program that uses that library. Java programs don't have this problem because they assemble themselves at runtime, as we discussed in the first part of this chapter. This means that the modules exist independently of the programs into which they are compiled.

Threaded

Have you ever wanted to be in two places at the same time? If you have, then multithreaded programming is for you. Like object orientation, threads are abstractions designed to make your life as a programmer easier. Their purpose is to allow you to easily describe sets of actions that happen concurrently.

Let's say you write a program to draw a circle on the screen that starts in the middle and grows out. It takes you days to figure out how to do it. When you're all done, your program could be condensed to the following pseudocode:

```
//pseudocode, not Java!!
set_center
set_the_color
radius=1
do {
  draw_circle(radius)
  radius=radius+1
  }
while (radius<final_circle_size)
```

You show your program to your boss, who is ecstatic, but now asks you to make the program draw two circles on the screen at the same time. Back to the drawing board! After a couple of weeks, you come back with a program that could be represented as follows:

```
//pseudocode, not Java!!
set_center_for_Circle1
set_center_for_Circle2
set_color_for_Circle1
set_color_for_Circle2
Circle1_radius=1
Circle2_radius=1
do{
   if (Circle1_radius<final_circle1_size)
     draw_circle1(Circle1_radius)
   if (Circle2_radius<final_circle2_size)
     draw_circle2(Circle2_radius)
   if (Circle1_radius<final_circle1_size)
     Circle1_radius=Circle1_radius+1
   if (Circle2_radius<final_circle2_size)
     Circle2_radius=Circle2_radius+1
   }
_ while (Circle1_radius<final_circle1_size
       AND
          Circle2_radius<final_circle2_size)
```

If you look at the pseudocode above, you'll see that all we are doing is repeating each instruction for circle 1 to circle 2. This repetition is something very mechanical that a computer can do well, and it is also what threading is all about. Instead of having to write new code to draw the second circle, we can make our first example a thread. Then, we can run two threads at the same time. The processor would run an instruction first from one thread, and then another.

If you have been looking at the applets on the Web, you've probably seen threads in action in the animations that are dressing up so many Web pages these days. In Chapter 5, "How Applets Work," we'll show you how to use threads to easily create your own animated applets. In Chapter 11, "Advanced Threading," we'll cover how to pass information back and forth between multiple threads.

Moving On

Now that we have introduced you to Java and applets, the real fun begins. In the next chapter we'll install the Java Developers Kit (JDK) and write a couple of basic programs. After your first experiences as a Java programmer, we'll look at Java's object orientation in Chapter 3 and then fully explain its syntax and semantics in Chapter 4. With those basics down, we'll walk you through all of the steps of writing simple applets in Chapter 5. From there, we're off—exploring the API, writing applets with powerful user interfaces, and creating applets that converse with other programs on the Internet.

2

Java Programming Basics

Java has stirred up a lot of excitement in the programming world. So let's get ready to join the excitement. By the end of this chapter, you will have written your first Java programs. Our aim is to provide an overview of the basic structure of a Java program while walking you through the process of writing, compiling, and running your code. Hopefully, through this process, you will start to see the similarities and differences between Java and any other programming languages you have used.

First, we get the Java compiler and runtime environment installed on your computer. We test the installation the best way we know how—by writing a Java program. We next look at Java program structure and at the way Java programs run. Finally, we introduce applet basics and demonstrate how to put your applets up on the Web for all to see.

We attack Java pretty furiously this chapter, but don't be too concerned if all your questions about Java aren't answered in the next few pages. By Chapter 5, "How Applets Work," we will have elaborated on all of the material we cover here. In the next few pages, you will gain a basis to start your exploration of Java—and you will have written several simple Java programs to boot!

GETTING THE EXAMPLE FILES

Throughout this book, an "Example" caption above a source code example indicates that we have provided the files to make that example come alive. Windows 95 and Macintosh users can find the files on the Companion CD-ROM; UNIX users can find them on the Online Companion at http://www.vmedia.com/java.html. There, you will find links to the examples.

Getting Started

Your first step to becoming a Java programmer is installing the Java compiler and the Java runtime environment on your system. These are contained in the Java Developers Kit (JDK), which Sun Microsystems has made freely available. Version 1.01 of the JDK is available on the Companion CD-ROM (for Mac and Windows 95/NT users) and on the Online Companion (for UNIX users). As new versions of the JDK are released, we will make them available for download from the Online Companion. Before you install the JDK from the CD, you may want to check the Online Companion to make sure you are installing the latest version.

THIRD-PARTY JAVA PROGRAMMING ENVIRONMENTS

Many software vendors, such as Borland and Symantec, have Java programming environments in the works. All these vendors have promised graphical user interfaces that will be more user friendly than the JDK. Of course, you have to pay for these. Since you might not have one of these products, we cover the JDK exclusively in this book. As new Java programming environments make it to market, we will review them on the Online Companion.

Once you make the decision to install from the CD or the Online Companion, you need to install the JDK onto your file system. From the CD, you will just copy the files over; from the Online Companion, you will download the JDK and uncompress it. Please refer to the appropriate appendix (Appendix A, "About the Online Companion," or Appendix B, "About the Companion CD-ROM") to learn how to accomplish this for your particular platform. Once you figure out the nitty-gritty of file moving for your machine, you are ready to install the JDK. In the following sections, we've provided recipes for each of the platforms to which Java has been ported at press time. As new ports are completed, check the Online Companion for those installations.

Windows 95/NT Installation

Before you proceed with the following directions, place all of the files of the JDK on your hard drive by copying them over from the CD. When you copy the files, place them in the directory of your choice. In that same directory, you must set an environment variable, CLASSPATH, so that the Java compiler can find the auxiliary classes it needs to compile your Java programs and the program you are currently writing. If you put the distribution in the directory C:\JAVA, you would set the CLASSPATH variable as follows from the DOS shell prompt:

```
C:> SET CLASSPATH=.;C:\JAVA\LIB
```

You should probably enter this into your AUTOEXEC.BAT file. You will also want to include the Java tools in your path. If you placed the distribution in the C:\JAVA directory, you'll find all of the necessary tools in C:\JAVA\BIN. Add this to the PATH environment variable in your AUTOEXEC.BAT.

With the environment variables set, you are ready to start programming. Of course, this means picking a text editor. About the only requirement for the text editor is that it will save your files as plain text and that you can give the files a .java extension. It is preferable that your chosen text editor also be fast, since you can't format your text with different fonts. For example, using Microsoft Word 7.0 would be a poor choice. The ideal text editor will also do basic syntax checking as you program. If you have a C++ programming environment already installed, try using its text editor.

Power PC Macintosh

Once you uncompress the files from your file system, your JDK is ready to go. Please refer to Appendix A or Appendix B for instructions about moving the files from the CD or Online Companion and uncompressing them. The JDK for Macintosh that is on the CD can be used only for applets. Remember our description in Chapter 1 of how Java programs are run inside a virtual machine, and applets are run inside a special type of virtual machine that keeps them from harming your computer? At press time, only the virtual machine that runs applets had been ported to the Macintosh platform. This means that you need to use the appletviewer to run many of the simple programs in this chapter to demonstrate basic Java concepts. To run these programs, do the following:

- Click on the appletviewer icon in the top level of your uncompressed JDK distribution.

- Click on index.html. This will run an applet called ProgramRunnerApplet.java, which will, in turn run the simple programs as they were run from the command line on a UNIX or Windows machine.

Eventually, you will be able to run stand-alone programs on the Macintosh. For now, you can use the appletviewer to follow along with the examples.

But before you can run any Java code, you need to write it. For this you need to choose a text editor. The only requirement is that it can save your file as plain text. It helps if it can also do on-the-fly syntax checking. If you already have a C++ programming environment installed, try using its text editor for creating your source code.

UNIX

Before you proceed with the following directions, place all of the files of the JDK on your hard drive. This means you'll have to download the distribution from the Online Companion. Please refer to Appendix A for directions on how to do this.

When you copy the files to your file system, place them in the directory of your choice. In the same directory, you must set an environment variable, CLASSPATH, so that the Java compiler can find the auxiliary classes it needs to compile your Java programs and the program you are currently writing. Suppose you put the distribution in the directory /usr/local/java. Then, from the C shell prompt, you would set the CLASSPATH variable as described in Table 2-1 for the various UNIX shells (you should probably enter this in your .login file).

Shell	Command
C shell	prompt>setenv CLASSPATH /usr/local/java:.
Bourne shell	prompt>CLASSPATH=/usr/local/java:. prompt>export CLASSPATH
Korn shell	prompt>export CLASSPATH=/usr/local/java:.
bash	prompt>export CLASSPATH=/usr/local/java:.

Table 2-1: *Setting the CLASSPATH environment variable.*

You will also want to include the Java tools in your path. If you placed the distribution in the /usr/local/java directory, you'll find all of the necessary tools in /usr/local/java/bin. Add this to the PATH environment variable in your .login.

Your next step is choosing a text editor. Emacs, vi, and pico will all do fine.

Your First Java Program

Now let's see if your installation was successful. Like all the example code in the book, you can find the code for Example 2-1 on the CD-ROM and Online Companion (see the "Getting the Example Files" sidebar). We suggest that Mac users point the appletviewer at /Chapter2/Example1/appleProgram.html on the CD. If you're not on a Mac, just type it in this time, so you can start deciding whether or not you are happy with your text editor.

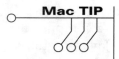

Mac TIP

Macintosh users should wait until later in this chapter, when we are writing applets, before trying out your chosen text editor.

Example 2-1: Simple Hello Java program—OurPrimaryClass.java.

```java
import java.util.*;

public class OurPrimaryClass {

public final static void main(String S[]) {
        System.out.println("Hello, Java!");
        Date d=new Date();
        System.out.println("Date: "+d.toString());
                }
        }
```

After you type this in, save the file as OurPrimaryClass.java. Any time you write a public class, you need to save it in a file of the same name. We explain exactly what a public class is later on in the chapter. First, let's compile the code using the Java compiler, javac. UNIX and Windows users, you can do this from your command line as follows:

```
javac OurPrimaryClass.java
```

Mac users should just click on the Java compiler icon, and then open the OurPrimaryClass.java file for compiling.

If you get any errors, make sure that you made no typing errors, or simply copy it over from the CD or Online Companion. If you still have problems, make sure that:

※ Your system knows where javac is. UNIX and Windows users, make sure that javac is in your path. Mac users don't need to worry about this.

※ Make sure that javac can find the rest of the JDK. For UNIX and Windows users, this means setting the CLASSPATH environment variable as described above. Mac users don't need to worry about this.

Assuming that all went well, you are ready to run our program. UNIX and Windows users can do this by typing:

```
java OurPrimaryClass
```

This invokes the java runtime environment, which takes OurPrimaryClass and executes the method main. The output should be:

```
Hello, Java!
```

followed by today's date. If you get an error instead of this output, then the runtime environment is probably having trouble finding the file OurPrimaryClass.class—the file javac produced. UNIX and Windows users should make sure that CLASSPATH includes the current directory.

Macintosh users should run this example as an applet, as we described previously.

Passing Command Line Parameters

Those of us not using a Macintosh for development can also pass command line parameters to our simple program. That is where String S[] comes in. Let's rewrite our main method so that it will print out everything that is passed to it from the command line:

Example 2-2: Main method that deals with parameters.

```
public class PrintCommandLineParameters {
public final static void main(String S[] ) {
  System.out.println("Hello, Java!");
  System.out.println("Here is what was passed to me:");

  for(int i=0;i<S.length;i++)
        System.out.println(S[i]);
  }
}
```

Our program will now print out any command line parameters we pass to it. If we invoke our program as follows:

```
java PrintCommandLineParameters parameter1 parameter2
parameter3 parameter4
```

it will produce the following output:

```
Hello, Java!
Here is what was passed to me:
parameter1
parameter2
parameter3
parameter4
```

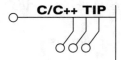

C/C++ TIP

The main method is analogous to the main function required in C and C++ programs.

Simple Text Output

You probably figured out by now that System.out.println is the key to writing output back to the screen. For simple programs, System.out.println lets us generate output very easily. When we start writing applets, we're going to see how to produce graphical, rather than text only, output. For now, let's look at the basics of using System.out.println.

As we have already seen, if we pass System.out.println characters enclosed in quotation marks, it will print the characters, followed by a new line. We can also have it print out the value of a variable, either alone or with a string enclosed in quotation marks:

Example 2-3: Using System.out.println.

```java
public class PrintlnExample {

public static void main(String ARGV[]) {

    System.out.println("This example demonstrates the use");
    System.out.println("of System.out.println");
    System.out.println("\nYou can output variables values");
    System.out.println("like the value of an integer:\n");

    int i=4;
    System.out.println("variable i="+i);
    System.out.println(i);
    }


}
```

Java Program Anatomy

You have written a simple Java program. Now let's take a look at what is actually happening. We're going to expand on our primaryClass program to include the basic building blocks that all Java programs have in common.

Again, we won't promise that you will understand all of Java in the next few pages. We cover Java's object-oriented features in the next chapter and discuss in detail the syntax of the language in Chapter 4. In this chapter, we want to develop a basic understanding of what a Java program is. It is important to note that the programs we are going to develop in this section aren't applets. (We write a "Hello, Applet!" applet towards the end of this chapter.) However, our discussion here is applicable to applets, which are the fundamental elements of all Java programs, whether we run them from the command line or within a Web page.

Structure Overview

All Java programs have four basic building blocks: *classes*, *methods*, *variables*, and *packages*. Regardless of your programming background, you are most likely familiar with methods, which are subroutines, and variables, which are data. Classes, on the other hand, are the basis of object orientation. To keep things simple for now, we just say that a class is a unit that contains variables and methods. Packages contain classes and aid the compiler in locating the classes that are needed to compile our code. We will also see in Chapter 3, "Object Orientation in Java," that classes contained in a package have a special relationship with one another. For now, though, let's just think of a package as a set of classes. The program we wrote to check the JDK installation has all of the parts we describe here.

These are the parts that are apparent in every Java program. However, Java programs can have other entities that we aren't going to describe in depth yet. But, in order to give you an overview, Table 2-2 outlines the other building blocks. Although these aren't required for every Java program, they are necessary for many that we will be writing.

Entity	Purpose	Where Covered
Interfaces	Allow "polymorphism."	Polymorphism and Interfaces are discussed in Chapter 3.
Exceptions	Allow for easier error handling.	Chapter 4.
Threads	Used to concurrently execute different blocks of code.	Introduced in Chapter 5; discussed in depth in Chapter 10.

Table 2-2: *Java entities not covered in this chapter.*

A Java program can have any number of classes, but there is always one class that has a special relationship with the runtime environment. It is always the first of our classes that the Java runtime recognizes. We call this class the *primary class*. In Example 2-1, it was called OurPrimaryClass. The driving characteristic of a primary class is that it has one or more preset methods that must be defined in the class.

When we run a program from the command line, as we did with Example 2-1, there is only one special method that we need to define—main. When we write our simple applets later on in this chapter, we will see that there are several methods that we need to define in the primary class of an applet.

Now let's look at each of the essential building blocks—variables, methods, classes, and packages—in more depth.

Variables

You have seen variables before. They are just boxes in which data is kept. Java's variables, like variables in most programming languages, are of specific *types*. The type of a variable determines what kind of information can be stored in it. For instance, a variable of type int is used for storing integers. Let's use a variable of this type in an example:

Example 2-4: Using a variable.

```java
public class UsesInt {
public static void main(String S[]) {
        int i=4;
        System.out.println("Value of i="+i);
        }
}
```

Here we have used the assignment operator = to give *i* the value of 4, and then we output it via System.out.println. The type we are using, int, belongs to one of the two major groupings of types found in Java—the *primitive types*. The other major grouping is called *reference types*, which includes programmer-defined types and array types. The primitive types are your standard, run-of-the-mill types that represent numeric values, single characters, and boolean (true/false) values. Reference types, on the other hand, are dynamic. We outline the major differences between the two groupings in Table 2-3.

Characteristic	Primitive Types	Reference Types
Defined by Java Language?	Yes	No
Predefined Memory Requirement?	Yes	No
Memory Must Be Allocated At Runtime For The Variable?	No	Yes

Table 2-3: *Primitive vs. reference types.*

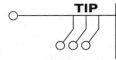
TIP

Primitive and reference types also differ in the way they are passed as parameters to methods. Primitive variables are passed by value, while reference variables are passed by reference. If this description doesn't brighten any light bulbs for you, don't worry —we cover this in the "Methods" section later in this chapter.

In day-to-day programming, the most important difference between primitive types and reference types is shown in the last column of Table 2-3: memory must be allocated at runtime for a reference variable. With reference types, we need to explicitly request memory for the variable before we put anything in it because the runtime environment doesn't know how much memory is necessary. Let's consider an example that illustrates this, remembering that all arrays are reference types—notice the commented lines that start with //:

Example 2-5: Primitive and reference variables.

```java
public class Variables {

public static void main(String ARGV[]) {

int myPrimitive;
//a variable of a primitive type
int myReference[];
//a variable of a reference type

myPrimitive=1;
//we can go ahead and put something in our primitive
//variable...

myReference=new int[3];
//but we need to allocate memory for our reference variable
//first...

myReference[0]=0;
myReference[1]=1;
myReference[2]=2;

//now we can put stuff into it.

    }

}
```

Since ints are primitive types, the runtime environment knows exactly how much space they require—in the case of ints, 4 bytes. But when we declare that we want an array of ints, the runtime environment doesn't know how much space we want. Before we can put anything in myReference, we have to request some memory space for the variable. We do this with the *new* operator; it requests the appropriate memory from the runtime environment.

Note that variables of array types and programmer-defined types "point" to a space in memory where the real meat of the variable actually resides, while variables of the primitive types are contained entirely in presized boxes.

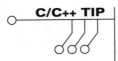
C/C++ TIP

As you can see, reference types are quite similar to pointers in C/C++. There are a couple of key differences. First, using reference types, you can't access and manipulate the memory address directly. And second, since you can't get at the memory address, there is no such thing as pointer arithmetic in Java.

Primitive Types

First, let's look at primitive types such as the int type we used in our earlier code example. This is one of the eight *primitive types* of the Java language. A primitive type is a type that is defined by the Java language itself. Table 2-4 lists the primitive types of Java.

Type	Size in Bytes	Inclusive Range	Example Values
int	4 bytes	-2147483648 to 2147483647	200000, -200000
short	2 bytes	-32768 to 32767	30000, -30000
byte	1 byte	-128 to 127	100, -100
long	8 bytes	-9223372036854775808 to 9223720368547775807	1000, -1000
float	4 bytes	dependent on precision	40.327
double	8 bytes	dependent on precision	4000000.327
boolean	1 bit	true, false	true, false
char	4 bytes	all unicode characters	

Table 2-4: *Primitive types of the Java language.*

The first six types in our table are the numeric primitives. You can use the +, −, *, and / operators with them for addition, subtraction, multiplication, and division. We provide a complete discussion of the syntax of dealing with the numeric types in Chapter 4. By and large, you will find it identical to the C programming language. Let's go on to the boolean type, a type that many programming languages don't explicitly have. Here's how we assign to a boolean variable:

Example 2-6: Assign to a boolean.

```
boolean truth=true;
System.out.println(truth);
boolean fallacy=false;
System.out.println(fallacy);
truth=(1==1);
fallacy=(1==0);
System.out.println(truth);
System.out.println(fallacy);
```

If we put this code fragment inside the main method from Example 2-1, we get the following output:

```
true
false
true
false
```

As you can see, boolean variables can be assigned the result of a comparison operation. In Java, the !, !=, and == operators play the same role with boolean variables that they play with ints in C. As with the rest of the primitive types, we discuss the syntax and semantics of the boolean type fully in Chapter 4.

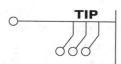

TIP

Often throughout the book, we give example code fragments like the one above. They won't actually compile by themselves, but if we wrote a whole program to demonstrate the concept, it would be hard to discern what we were actually trying to prove. However, we have put all of our code fragments within compilable programs on the CD.

Reference Types

As we've already said, reference types differ from primitive types in that they aren't defined explicitly by the Java language and thus their memory requirements are unknown. We have already looked at one grouping of reference types, Java's arrays. Array types exist for every other type in Java, including programmer-defined types, which are used much more often in Java than any other type.

Before we look at reference types, we need to know a little of the pertinent vocabulary. When we allocate memory for a reference type with the new operator, we are *instantiating* the reference type. Thereafter, the variable is an *instantiation*, or *instance*, of the particular reference type.

"Exactly what hair are you trying to split here," you may be wondering. The problem is that we can't just declare a reference variable and start putting data into it. We have to ask the runtime environment for some memory, and the runtime environment has to record that we have activated a variable of that particular reference type. That's a mouthful, so we just call the process instantiation. Then, once we instantiate the type, the target variable is qualitatively different—now we can put data into it. To indicate that the reference variable is now available for stuffing, we say that it is an instance.

Now let's look at our programmer-defined types. Then, we will examine arrays a little more closely.

Programmer-Defined Types

Most languages support type definition—in C, you can define types with a struct, while in Pascal you do it with records. In Java, we can define types with *classes*, which we touch on here, or *interfaces*, which we save for Chapter 3, "Object Orientation in Java."

At the simplest level, classes are similar to structs and records in that you can use them to store and access a collection of data. But classes can include methods as well as data. We can define a type called "MyType" as follows: the public keyword that precedes the declarations is an access modifier—it means that our members are accessible from outside the class. We examine the access modifiers a little later in this chapter.

Example 2-7a: Defining a type.

```
class MyType {
   public int myDataMember=4;
   public void myMethodMember() {
      System.out.println("I'm a member!");
      System.out.println("myData="+myDataMember);}
   }
```

You probably noticed that this example is very much like the Java *programs* we have been writing. Actually, classes play double duty in the Java language. In the programs that we have been writing, they play an organizational role.

Classes also can be used to define types. Variables of types defined by classes are called *objects*, *instantiations*, or *instances*, of a particular class. We create, or instantiate, an object with the *new* operator and access its members with the dot (.) operator:

Example 2-7b: Instantiating an object.

```
public class RunMe {

public static void  main(String ARGV[]) {

   MyType Mine=new MyType();
   int i=Mine.myDataMember;
   Mine.myMethodMember();
   }
}
```

Example 2-7 shows us the three things we can do with an object; create it, access one of its data members, and access one of its functional members. Here, the third line of code calls the myMethodMember method, which prints out:

```
I'm a member!
myData=4
```

MyType

Since ~~myDataType~~ is a reference type, we use the *new* operator. It allocates some memory for our object. We can also define some other stuff to happen when our class is instantiated by defining a constructor. Here is a constructor for ~~myDataType~~ that just lets us know the class has been instantiated: *MyType*

Example 2-8a: A constructor that verifies instantiation.

```java
public class MyType {

int myDataMember=0;

public MyType() {
   System.out.println("Instantiation in process!");}

}
```

We can also use constructors to initialize the values of data members. This constructor will set the value of myDataMember to the integer that is passed:

Example 2-8b: A constructor that initializes values of data members.

```java
public MyType(int val) {
   System.out.println("setting myDataMember="+val);
   myDataMember=val;}
```

Assuming that we have both of these constructors defined in our myDataType class, let's look at another short program that uses both of them:

Example 2-8c: A program that uses both constructors.

```java
public class RunMe {

public static void main(String ARGV[]) {
   MyType instance1=new MyType();
   MyType instance2=new MyType(100);
   }
}
```

Now, our output will be:

```
Instantiation in progress!
I'm a member!
myDataType=4        my DataMember = 4
setting myDataType=100    setting my DataMember = 100
I'm a member!
myDataType=100        my DataMember = 100
```

PREDEFINED PROGRAMMER-DEFINED TYPES

One important thing to remember about programmer-defined types is that you don't always have to be the programmer who defined it. Included in the JDK are dozens of ready-to-use classes that we can use in our programs. In fact, a large part of learning Java is knowing how to use these classes that are already defined for you. These ready-to-use classes are included in the Application Programming Interface (API). We explore the API in Chapter 6.

The String Type

We've discussed primitive types and programmer-defined types. Now we need to look at a special type that is a hybrid of the two—the *String type*. The String is primarily a programmer-defined type: it is defined by the String class, and it contains methods and variables. The hybridization happens when you assign to String variables:

```
String myString="Hello!";
```

"What's so strange about that," you may ask. Indeed, it's the most intuitive way possible to create strings. We also have the convenience of using the + operator for concatenation:

```
int myInt=4;
String anotherString=myString+"myInt is "+myInt;
```

The value of anotherString will be "Hello! myInt is 4". But because anotherString is an object, we can access the method members of the String class. For instance, it is easy to extract the first five characters of the anotherString:

```
String helloString=anotherString.substring(5);
```

The problem here is that we are instantiating our Strings without using the *new* operator. From a day-to-day programming standpoint, this isn't problematic. Since we use strings so much, it is very convenient. But as you start programming in Java, you need to understand that Strings are special—the String is the only programmer-defined type that can be instantiated without using the *new* operator.

Array Types

Array types define an array—an ordered set of like variables. Array types exist for all of the types in Java, including programmer-defined types. We can also have arrays of arrays, or multidimensional arrays—we leave that discussion for Chapter 4, "Syntax & Semantics." Basically, if we can create a variable of some type, we can create an array of variables of that type. However, creation of Java arrays is a little strange in that it requires the *new* operator:

Example 2-9a: Allocating space for arrays

```
int myIntArray[];.
myIntArray=new int[3];

myType myObjectArray[];
myObjectArray=new myType[3];
```

The *new* operator tells the runtime environment to allocate space for the array. As you can see, you don't have to declare the size of the array when you create the array variable. Once you create the array with the *new* operator, the array works the same as the arrays of C or Pascal:

Example 2-9b: Assigning to arrays

```
myIntArray[0]=0;.
myIntArray[1]=1;
```

```
myIntArray[2]=2;

myObjectArray[0]=new myType();
myObjectArray[1]=new myType();
myObjectArray[2]=new myType();

myObjectArray[0].myDataMember=0;
myObjectArray[1].myDataMember=1;
myObjectArray[2].myDataMember=2;
```

Java's arrays are beneficial for three reasons. First, as we have already seen, we don't have to set the size of the array as we declare it. Second, every Java array is a variable, so we can pass it as a parameter to a method and return it. We will look at this advantage of arrays when we look at methods in the next section. And third, we can easily find out how big an array is. For instance, the following code fragment will display the size of the array we defined above:

Example 2-9c: Getting the length of an array.

```
int len=myIntArray.length;
System.out.println("Length of myIntArray="+len);
```

Methods

A method in Java is a subroutine—similar to the functions of C and Pascal. Methods have a return type and can take parameters.

For ease of demonstration, we are going to declare all of our methods *static*. The static modifier declares that the method will have a particular type of behavior within our object-oriented program (more on this later).

Our first concern is syntactical: the modifiers precede the return type, which precedes the method name and parameter list. The method body is enclosed in brackets:

```
<method modifiers> return type method name (<parameters>) {
    method body
 }
```

The method body can contain variable declarations and statements. We aren't restrained to declaring all of our variables before any statements, as we would be in C.

With the syntax out of the way, we first look at how methods return data. Then, we examine how we can pass data—or parameters—to our methods. Lastly, we look at a feature of Java's methods called *method overloading*, which allows us to give the same name to several different methods that differ in the parameters that they take.

Return types

All methods must specify a return type. The void return type of our main method in earlier examples is a special return type that means the method doesn't return a type. Methods that specify void as their return type are like Pascal's procedures. For methods that have another return type, we need to have a return statement. Our return type can be any of the types we described in the Variables section—any of the primitive types or any type we define with a class. Here we give examples of void methods and methods that have a return type:

Example 2-10: Calling methods.

```
public class MethodExamples{

static void voidMethod() {
   System.out.println("I am a void method");
   }

static int returnInt() {
   int i=4;
   System.out.println("returning 4");
   return i;}

static public final void main(String S[]) {
   System.out.println("Hello, methods!");
   System.out.println("Calling a void method");
   voidMethod();
   int ans=returnInt();
```

```
System.out.print("method says -");
System.out.println(ans);
  }
}
```

Note that we are calling our methods in much the same way that we would call them using a non-object-oriented language. This is true because a static method is calling other static methods within the same class. It's also true when nonstatic, or dynamic, methods call other dynamic methods. Things change when dynamic methods call static methods, or vice-versa, and when we are calling methods from another class. We explain all of this in the next section.

Parameter Passing

Let's move on to parameter passing. We can pass variables of any type—including types we define with classes—and arrays of any type. However, variables of primitive types act differently than variables of reference types do when passed to a method. We examine primitive variables first.

All primitive variables are passed to methods *by value*. This means that a copy of the variable is made when it is passed to the method. If we manipulate the variable inside the method, the original isn't affected—only the copy. Let's illustrate this with an example:

Example 2-11: Primitive parameter passing.

```
class ParameterExample {

static int addFour(int i) {
    i=i+4;
    System.out.println("local copy of i="+i);
    return i;}

public final static void main(String S[]) {
    System.out.println("Hello, parameter passing!");
    int i=10;
    System.out.print("Original value of i="+i);
```

```
int j=addFour(i);
System.out.println("value of j="+j);

System.out.println("Current value of i="+i);
}

}
```

When we run our program, we get the following output:

```
Hello, parameter passing!
Original value of i=10
value of j=14
Current value of i=10
```

The value *i* does not change, though we added 4 to *i* in the addFour method. However, reference variables are changed if they are manipulated within a method. Consider an example with an array of integers:

Example 2-12: Passing reference variable as a parameter.

```
public class ReferenceParameterExample {
static void changeArray(int referenceVariable[]) {
    referenceVariable[2]=100;}

public static void main(String ARGV[]) {
    int anArray[]=new int[3];
    anArray[2]=10;
    System.out.println("anArray[2]=");
    System.out.println(anArray[2]);
    changeArray(anArray);
    System.out.println(anArray[2]);}

}
```

The output of our program will be:

```
anArray[2]=
10
100
```

When we pass a reference variable to a method, we are directly altering what that variable refers to—in this case, an array of ints.

STRINGS & PARAMETER PASSING

Though the String is a programmer-defined type, it does not follow the rules of reference types when passed as a parameter. Instead, String variables act like primitive types. When a String is passed into a method, you are actually working with a copy. Changes to the String inside the method will not affect the original that you passed in.

Method Overloading

Have you ever had to write two subroutines that perform essentially the same function, but take different sets of parameters? Java allows you to give the same name to several methods that differ in the types of parameters they take. For instance, let's say we have a method that compares two integers:

Example 2-13a: Comparing two numbers.

```java
public static String compareNums(int i, int j) {
if (i==j) {
   return "Numbers "+i+" and "+j+" are equal";}
if (i>j) {
   return "Number "+i+" greater than "+j;}

return "Number "+j+" greater than"+ i;
  }
```

Then we decide that instead of just comparing two numbers, we would like to compare three. It would be clumsy to define a new method with a name like compareThreeNums—luckily, we don't have to:

Example 2-13b: Overloading a method with additional parameters.

```java
public static String compareNums(int i, int j, int k){
String S=compareNums(i,j);
S=S+"\n";
S=S+compareNums(i,k);
return S;}
```

As long as the list of parameters is different, we can overload the method compareNums as many times as we would like. This is especially convenient when we want to perform the same action on different types of variables. As we will see in Chapter 4, we can't pass double variables into methods expecting ints. However, we can overload our method so that it accepts doubles or any other type:

Example 2-13c: Overloading a method with different types of parameters.

```java
public static String compareNums(double i, double j) {
if (i==j) {
  return "Numbers "+i+" and "+j+" are equal";}
if (i>j) {
  return "Number "+i+" greater than "+j;}

return "Number "+j+" greater than"+ i;
}
```

Method overloading is very convenient when we call our method. Instead of having to remember several different method names, we just have to remember one name. The compiler figures out which method should actually execute:

Example 2-13d: Calling overloaded methods.

```java
public static void main(String ARGV[]) {

  int a=3;
  int b=4;
  int c=5;
  double d=3.3;
  double e=4.4;
```

```
String S=compareNums(a,b);
System.out.println(S);
S=compareNums(a,b,c);
System.out.println(S);
S=compareNums(d,e,f);          // f has not been defined.
System.out.println(S);

}
```

Classes

Now, we can finally start filling in some of the gaps in our discussion by explaining classes. When we first introduced classes, we said that classes contain variables and methods. This is true enough, as you probably noticed in the primary classes that we have been writing. But classes also form the basis of Java's object orientation, and we look at them in that light now.

Static vs. Dynamic Members

When we were looking at variables, we saw how classes could define types. Now let's demystify the static modifier we've been using for our methods. So far, we have just been using it on methods, so we explain what it means as a method modifier first. The static modifier can also be used with variables, but then it has a different meaning.

You may have noticed the absence of the static modifier in the methods that we have been writing here. This is because they are *dynamic* methods, which is the default. Dynamic methods and variables are members of objects—we can access them through an object variable. Static methods, on the other hand, can't be part of objects. Table 2-5 lists the syntax for calling dynamic methods versus static methods.

Method Type	Modifier	Syntax
Dynamic	none (the default)	<object>.<method name>(<parameter list>)
Static	static	<class name>.<method name>(<parameter list>)

Table 2-5: *Dynamic vs. static syntax.*

We illustrate this with an example:

Example 2-14a: Static vs. dynamic methods.

```java
public class StaticVsDynamic {
        int i=0;

        public static void staticMethod(int j) {
            System.out.println("A static method");
            System.out.println("j="+j);
            }

//dynamic methods

        public void setInt(int k) {
            i=k;
            System.out.println("setting i to "+k);
            }

        public int returnInt() {
            return i;}


    }
```

This example class has a static method and a dynamic method. The static method doesn't know about the dynamic members setInt, returnInt, and *i*. Here is a primary class that illustrates the differing syntax for calling static and dynamic methods:

Example 2-14b: Calling static and dynamic methods.

```java
public class RunMe {

    public static void main(String S[]) {
    int i=0;

    StaticVsDynamic.staticMethod(10);
    //don't need to construct an object to call a static method

    StaticVsDynamic A=new StaticVsDynamic();
    //must instantiate before calling dynamic method

    A.setInt(20);
    System.out.println("A.i = "+A.returnInt());

    }
}
```

STATIC MODIFIER & THE MAIN METHOD

Now we can make sense out of the static modifier that is always present in main method declarations. When we type "java primaryClass," the java runtime environment loads primaryClass into memory as a type. Then, it simply calls the main method by saying "primaryClass.main(S)," where S is an array of all of the command line parameters.

We can also use the static modifier in conjunction with variables. The syntax for accessing the variable is basically the same:

```
<class name>.<variable name>
```

Since all methods and variables must be contained in a class, the static modifier is used to describe methods and variables that don't function as part of an object. They are more or less equivalent to the subroutines and global variables of a non-object-oriented language, except that we need to know the class that contains them in order to call them.

Member Access

We can control how our methods and variables are accessed in Java. So far, all of our class members have been public. The public modifier specifies that we can change our variables from any point in our program. We can limit the access of methods and variables with the access modifiers listed in Table 2-6.

Modifier	Description
Public	Member is accessible from outside the class.
Private	Member is accessible only from inside the class.
Protected	Public inside a package; private outside.

Table 2-6: *Access modifiers.*

In addition to these three, there is one more access modifier we discuss in Chapter 3, named *private protected.* The purpose of the access modifiers is to keep objects from interacting with class members they shouldn't mess with. It may seem that we are personifying our code. After all, the programmer has the ultimate control over what a program is doing. This is true, but the modifiers give us a way to guarantee that an object is going to behave the way we've programmed it to. If someone else uses our code, or if we use it at some later date when we have forgotten its nuances, we know that it will still work. We ensure this by allowing only certain parts of a class to be used by other classes.

WHAT ABOUT PUBLIC CLASSES?

Throughout this chapter, we have been declaring our classes public. This means that they can be accessed by classes outside of their package. Unlike methods and variables, classes are either public or not public. The other three access modifiers can't be applied to classes.

This concept is called "data hiding," and it plays an important role in our discussion of object orientation in Chapter 3. For now, we illustrate this concept with a simple example. Suppose we are writing a class that keeps track of how much money a store is taking in and how many customers it has had. There are any number of other things we might want to keep track of, such as what we sold and when we sold it, but let's keep it simple for now. Here's our code:

Example 2-15: Private vs. public members.

```java
public class SaleProcessor {
    private int Revenue=0;
    private int numSales=0;

public void recordSale(int newRevenue) {
    Revenue=Revenue+newRevenue;
    numSales=numSales+1;}

public int getRevenue() {
    return Revenue;}

public int getNumSales() {
    return numSales;}
}
```

Every time a customer buys ~~record Sale~~ something, the payment is processed with the ~~ringUpCustomer~~ record Sale method, which guarantees that the revenue is increased appropriately and that the customer tally is incremented. By not allowing direct access to these variables, we can better ensure their accuracy.

Class Inheritance

We have seen how modifiers make our classes more dependable because we can ensure that only certain methods and variables can be accessed from outside the class. *Inheritance* makes our classes reusable by allowing us to extend classes that have already been written by adding new functionality. Our new class will have all of the members of the original class, plus any we want to add.

Let's consider the SaleProcessor class we developed in Example 2-15. Our boss says, "This is great! But I need a cash register class that tracks the bills in the register." We already have a start with the SaleProcessor class—object-oriented programming allows us to expand upon it. To keep things simple, we ignore coins, bills over $10, and making change:

Example 2-16: Inheritance.

```java
class CashRegister extends SaleProcessor{

private int Ones=0;
private int Fives=0;
private int Tens=0;

CashRegister(int startOnes, int startFives, int startTens){
   Ones=startOnes;
   Fives=startFives;
   Tens=startTens;}

public void sellToCustomer(int newOnes, int newFives, int
newTens) {
   int thisSum=0;
   Ones=Ones+newOnes;
   thisSum=newOnes;
   Fives=Fives+newFives;
   thisSum=thisSum+(newFives*5);
   Tens=Tens+newTens;
   thisSum=thisSum+(newTens*10);
   recordSale(thisSum); // in class SaleProcessor
   }

public int numOnes() {return Ones;}

public int numFives() {return Fives;}

public int numTens() {return Tens;}

}
```

CONSTRUCTORS & INHERITANCE

In the code segment above, we have defined a constructor in the subclass. As we said earlier, all classes in Java have a "default" constructor that takes no parameters. This isn't magical—in fact, all classes in Java extend a special class called Object by default. The Object class defines our default constructor.

Because we extend the **S**aleProcessor class, we can build on that code instead of rewriting it. The ease of code reuse like this is one of the key advantages of object-oriented programming languages.

Packages

We have now covered the core of the Java language. You've seen that classes are the key building block of any Java program. Compared to classes, packages are very utilitarian. They simply contain classes and two of the other entities of Java we haven't discussed yet—exceptions and interfaces. Beyond this, they allow us to define members that are protected; they are public to classes within the same package, while private to those classes outside of the package.

Let's look at packages as containers first. In this sense, they play a very simple, though fundamental, role: they give the compiler a way to find the classes we need to compile our code. You know the System.out.println method we've been using to write output so far? Well, System is actually a class contained in the package java.lang, along with String. We use the import statement to access these classes. In our first example, we used this import statement to access the Date class.

```
import java.util.*;.;
```

The wildcard character at the end tells the compiler to import all of the classes in the java.date package. This is one of several packages included in the API, which we discuss in detail in Chapter 6, "Discovering the Application Programming Interface."

The java compiler implicitly defines a package for classes in the current directory and implicitly imports it. This is why we haven't had to explicitly place the classes that we've written into a package. If we want to explicitly place them into a package, the mechanics are simple:

Example 2-17: Package example.

```
package simplePackage;
class SimpleClass1 {
        public void pubMethod() {
            System.out.println("This is a public method");}
        protected void protectedMethod() {
                System.out.println("This is a protected
method");}
            }
```

This puts our class simpleClass1 into simplePackage. We can put other classes into this package by putting the statement "package simplePackage;" at the top of the file. Other classes that we put into simplePackage will be able to access the method protectedMethod, while classes that aren't part of simplePackage will not be able to.

The Java Runtime Environment

We still have a few chapters to go before you will understand all of the nuances of the Java language, but hopefully you have a good understanding of the basic structure. Before we begin to write our first applet, let's look at the runtime environment closely. As you may remember from Chapter 1, "The World Wide Web & Java," Java programs are run inside a virtual machine. What the program does know about is the *runtime environment* supplied to it by the virtual machine. As a language, Java has quite a few features that make it a delight for the programmer, including object orientation, built-in error handling, and threading. But what really sets Java apart is its platform independence, and this is entirely due to the structure of a runtime environment. Let's look at how the runtime environment affects our lives as programmers.

The Compilation & Execution Process

Java is a semi-compiled language. Unlike compiled languages, the Java compiler does not create a file that is ready to execute on our system. Instead, it creates a file that the Java runtime environment can run. This means that you can write and compile a Java program on one platform, move it to another platform, and it will work the same.

The .class file that the Java file creates contains bytecodes. *Bytecodes* are instructions for the Java runtime environment—similar to the machine instructions that a compiled C program contains. But instead of the operating system executing machine instructions, the Java runtime environment translates the bytecodes. When a program needs more memory, or access to an input/output device (the keyboard or monitor, for example), the runtime environment will service the request. The program itself, however, never has direct access to the system. In this way, the Java runtime environment acts as a firewall between a Java program and the system. This buffer is especially important in conjunction with applets—you wouldn't want to be reading a Web page while an applet embedded in the page deletes your hard drive!

DEFINITION OF BYTECODES

We aren't going to linger on bytecodes for too long. Suffice it to say that our Java source code is translated into bytecodes, which are then translated by the Java runtime environment. Indeed, the bytecodes compose a language itself, though not one in which we would directly write programs.

You may be wondering, "Well, if the Java runtime environment is translating those bytecodes, shouldn't we be calling Java a translated language, like Perl or BASIC?" True, the .class file is translated, like Perl or BASIC source code. But Java is much faster than these languages because it is easier for a computer to translate bytecodes than human-readable perl and BASIC source code.

In a sense, a .class file is a compressed version of a .java file; compressed in such a way that it is easy for the Java runtime environment to run it. However, the .class file is not optimally compressed. If we were guaranteed that every .class file was generated by javac, or some other Java compiler that followed all of the rules, then we would find that our .class files have more information than is strictly necessary. This information is used to ensure that the bytecodes aren't trying to "trick" the Java runtime environment.

What kind of trick might this be? It would be something that would violate the runtime environment's role as protector of the local system. The Java compiler forces us to write code that doesn't try to trick the runtime environment, but a malicious hacker could write a program directly in bytecodes. The runtime environment requires the .class files it runs to have enough extra information so that a maliciously written file couldn't get around the restrictions of the Java language itself. As we shall see, this is one of three ways that the runtime environment that runs applets guarantees that applets don't harm the computer they are running on.

Even with the extra information contained within the bytecodes, our Java programs still run faster than those written in strictly translated languages such as Perl or BASIC. But the speed still lags behind programs that are compiled for the local machine, such as C and C++ programs. Luckily, help is on the way in the form of Just In Time (JIT) compiling. What JIT compiling does is compile—instead of translate—the bytecodes into machine language as the code is running. Once a code segment has run once, it is compiled to machine language. Subsequent executions will be as fast as if the code segment were compiled. Our Java programs will take an initial performance hit while the bytecodes are being compiled, but afterward, our code will run as fast as if it were compiled for the local platform.

KEEPING AN EYE ON JIT

At the time of this writing, JIT compilers are just being released. However, they haven't entered the mainstream of the Java programming world yet. They haven't been ported to all supported platforms, and they have yet to be incorporated into a Web browser. But Sun Microsystems is driving the push to realize JIT compiling all across the Java world. Check the Online Companion for updated information about JIT compilers.

Though the days of JIT compiling are just around the bend, you needn't worry that you'll have to change your code. Since JIT compiling is implemented as part of the runtime environment, it will simply result in faster executing code.

Garbage Collection

If you want to speak intelligently about Java development, you need to understand the architectural aspects of the Java runtime environment discussed in the previous section. But the structure of the runtime environment isn't something we need to concern ourselves with every time we sit down to program. The fact that our .class file is being run inside a virtual machine doesn't affect how we write our code—as long as it does what we want, we don't care whether it is compiled, semi-compiled, translated, or conjured into reality by magic.

The runtime environment performs one essential function that *does* affect how we write our code: garbage collection. Indeed, garbage collection makes our lives as programmers much easier. You probably guessed that the garbage collection the Java runtime environment performs has nothing at all to do with those candy wrappers, soda cans, and coffee cups that gather about any worthwhile coder's workstation. No, the garbage that is collected is made up of the variables within our program that are no longer needed.

Have you ever experienced a "memory leak"? Memory leaks occur when a program asks for a lot of memory from the operating system but never gives it back. After a while (sometimes a very short while) the amount of memory that is requested exceeds what the operating system has available, and your program crashes. Often, it takes the whole computer with it!

Memory leaks clearly result from a programmer's error, but they can be devilishly hard to find. All you have to do is request that memory be allocated and then forget to give it back. To find the cause of the leak, you must look at every place in your code where you allocate memory and make sure you are throwing the memory away. In programs that are thousands of lines long, this can be very, very time consuming.

In Java, we never have to worry about this. First, the only time our programs can ask for memory while running is when we make an assignment to an object variable or create an array. This is done implicitly—we weren't leaving some vital step out of all of those examples we have had you type in this chapter! Also, garbage collection keeps us from freeing memory twice or writing to memory we have already freed.

When we make an assignment, the runtime environment puts a marker on the memory block that has been allocated. If we have created an object or array for local use inside a code block, a method body, for example, then the memory it was taking up will be given back to the operating system when the code block concludes. This process is called "collecting the garbage." But if we pass that variable on for use by the rest of our program (by either returning it from the method or making it part of an object or array passed in as a parameter), then it won't deallocate the memory.

"But," you may say, "you promised that garbage collection would have some relevance to me, the programmer." Well, it does. First, you don't have to worry about memory leaks, because the runtime environment keeps track of how your program is using memory. So garbage collection kills off memory you don't need anymore.

While garbage collection clearly identifies garbage, it also doesn't throw away memory that isn't garbage. Let's consider an example that has cost many beginning C programmers hours of debugging time and handfuls of hair:

```
public char * thisWontWork() {
    char localArray[6];
    strcpy(localArray,"hello");
    return localArray;}
```

Supposedly, this function creates a character array, fills it with "hello", and returns it. Unfortunately, this isn't quite what happens. Since we declared localArray within this function, the memory it takes is killed off at the conclusion of the function, despite the fact that we return localArray! But the story gets worse. If we try to print out localArray as soon as the function returns, it's usually still there because the memory hasn't been overwritten yet. But eventually, the memory *will* get overwritten, and it will take just long enough so that we think an entirely different part of our program is causing the error!

Because Java's garbage collection tracks our variables dynamically, we don't need to worry about encountering this problem. Let's consider the equivalent Java code:

```
public char[] thisWillWork {
    char localArray[6];
    localArray={'h','e','l','l','o'};
    return localArray;}
```

The garbage collector notices that localArray is being returned and is, thus, still being used. It will only deallocate localArray when there is no variable assigned to it or when the program ends.

Creating Java Applets

So now you have trudged through the basics of the Java language and the Java runtime environment. It's time for the fun stuff—applets!

Because applets are embedded in Web pages, applet development has a few more twists and turns than the usual program development cycle. Hopefully, by the end of this section, you will have adapted to the process of coding and running your own applets. You will then be prepared to attack Chapter 5, "How Applets Work," and join the scores of applet writers who are waking up the Web.

Your First Applet

Let's dive right in and write our first applet. Crack open your favorite text editor and type along with me:

Example 2-18a: Your first applet.

```java
import java.applet.*;
import java.awt.*;

public class FirstApplet extends Applet {
 public void paint(Graphics g) {
    g.drawString("Hello, Applets!",50,50);}
}
```

You'll notice that this program is quite different from the programs we have been writing. We will dissect it in a moment—first, let's get it running. Just follow this recipe:

1. Compile the class.

2. Embed the applet into a Web page. Crack open that text editor again and create the following file:

Example 2-18b: Web page for FirstApplet.

```html
<APPLET CODE=FirstApplet.class WIDTH=200 height=200>
You aren't using a Java capable web browser.
Consider visiting <a href="http://
www.netscape.com">Netscape</a> and download
Netscape 2.0
</APPLET>
```

You can save it under any name you choose as long as it ends with .html. The text between the <APPLET...> and </APPLET> tags is displayed to Web browsers that don't know how to run applets.

3. Find a program called "appletviewer" in the JDK distribution. For UNIX and Windows users, it can be found in the bin directory. If you added this directory to your path as described earlier in this chapter, you will be able to simply type "appletviewer" in the next step. Mac users will find it in the top level of the JDK.

4. Use the appletviewer to open up the .html page you just created. UNIX and Windows users should give the .html filename just created as a command line parameter. Mac users can just start the appletviewer, pull down the File menu option, and choose Open.

You should see something similar to Figure 2-1

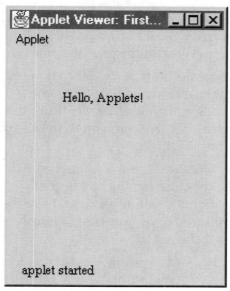

Figure 2-1: *Your first applet.*

Note that we aren't using a Java-capable Web browser to look at our applet at this stage. Neither the appletviewer nor Netscape Navigator 2.0 is smart enough to recognize that we have recompiled our code. In either case, each time we change our code, we have to quit the program that is running our applet and start it up again. The appletviewer is a much smaller program and tends to be quicker to start up. Therefore, you'll probably find it preferable to use the appletviewer during the development cycle.

Applet Anatomy

Now that you have written your first applet, let's look at its anatomy. The class we just wrote is still a primary class, though it is quite different from the primary classes we wrote at the beginning of the chapter. Previously, we had defined only one method—main. Here, we have defined two. As we will see in Chapter 5, "How Applets Work," there are several more methods we need to define to create interesting effects like animation.

The key to understanding applet programming is understanding the basics of our primary class. Let's note a couple of differences between this primary class and the ones we were writing earlier:

- None of our methods are static. Since none of our methods are static, our class is instantiated at some point. A quick scan of our code concludes that we didn't instantiate it. Instead, the runtime environment of the Web browser instantiates our class.

- Our primary class extends a class named Applet. The Applet class, contained in the java.applet package, defines the functionality that our applets can have. What are commonly referred to as "applets" are, technically speaking, Applet subclasses.

- We can tell that both of our methods executed, but we didn't call either of them from within our code. In the same way that the Java runtime environment looked for the main method in our classes before, the applet runtime environment executes methods in our Applet subclass.

Within this last observation is the key to understanding applet anatomy. Previously, the runtime environment called the main method, from which our entire program ran. When the browser's runtime environment starts our program, it first calls the init method, but as we observed, the entire program is *not* run out of the init method. How does our paint method get called? Whenever the screen needs to get painted, the paint method is called. If you cover up the Web browser with another window and then uncover it, the paint method will be called again.

The Applet class has a large number of methods that are called in response to user actions, such as moving the mouse or touching certain keys on the keyboard. We describe all of these in greater detail in Chapter 5. For now we demonstrate the mouseDown method, which is called every time the first mouse button is clicked within the applet's space. We use it to write "Hello, Applet!" at the position where the mouse is clicked:

Example 2-19: An applet that interacts with the mouse.

```java
import java.applet.*;
import java.awt.*;

public class SecondApplet extends Applet {
    int curX=50;
    int curY=50;

    public boolean mouseDown(Event e, int x, int y) {
        curX=x;
        curY=y;
        repaint();
        return true;}

public void paint(Graphics g) {
    g.drawString("Hello, Applets!",curX,curY);}
}
```

Notice that we are now making a call to repaint in mouseDown. The repaint method tells the runtime environment to update the screen. It does this by passing the screen, in the form of a Graphics object, to our paint method. After we click the mouse in the lower right-hand corner, our applet will look like Figure 2-2.

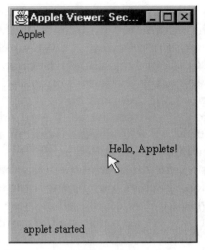

Figure 2-2: *Interactive applet.*

Besides the fact that the runtime environment calls any method of a variety of methods when necessary, the primary class for applets behaves the same as the primary classes we built earlier. We can define new methods—rather than just override the ones defined in the Applet class—and we can instantiate new classes.

Putting Applets on the Web

So far, we have been using the appletviewer to run our applets locally. Now we are going to talk about making your applets available to the world via the World Wide Web.

Probably the most important ingredient is access to a Web server. We need to move our .class files and the .html files in which the applet is embedded into the space from which your web documents are served. If you program on the same machine from which you'll be serving your applets, you probably just need to move your files from one directory to another. If your Web server resides on a different machine than the one you work on, you will need to move them onto that machine.

You should probably talk to your webmaster for details about moving the files into Web space. Regarding the two examples we wrote earlier, a total of four files, you just need to make sure that the .class file is in the same directory as the .html file that references it. Then, just point your Web browser to the .html file. The appletviewer can also load applets from the Internet—instead of telling it to open a file, tell it to open a URL.

Our .class file for the SecondApplet.html page we wrote needed to be in the same directory as the secondApplet.html file. If we want, though, our .class file can reside elsewhere within the Web space of the server. We can control this with the CODEBASE parameter of the Applet tag. Here is an example .html file that contains the CODEBASE attribute.

Example 2-20: Using the CODEBASE attribute.

```
<APPLET CODE=ProgramRunnerApplet.class CODEBASE="class.dir"
WIDTH=300 HEIGHT=150>
You aren't using a Java capable web browser.
Consider visiting <a href="http://www.netscape.com"> Netscape
</a> and download Netscape 2.0
</APPLET>
```

In this case, SecondApplet.class needs to be in the directory, class_dir, below the directory that contains our example .html file. The value for CODEBASE can also be an absolute path, but it will be absolute to the top of the Web space. In addition to the CODEBASE attribute, there are several others that you can use inside the APPLET tag to customize the appearance and behavior of your applet. These are summarized in Table 2-7.

Attribute	Meaning	Required?
CODE	The compiled applet—should be a .class file.	Yes
WIDTH	The width in pixels that the applet will take up on the Web page.	Yes
HEIGHT	The height in pixels that the applet will take up on the Web page.	Yes
CODEBASE	A directory on the Web server in which to look for the .class file specified by CODE.	No
ALT	Specifies alternate text to display in case the browser understands the APPLET tag but does not support Java. There are currently no Web browsers that would display the text.	No
NAME	Gives a name to the applet—other applets on the page can look it up by name.	No
ALIGN	Determines how the applet will be aligned on the page.	No
VSPACE	Sets a vertical margin, described in pixels, around the applet.	No
HSPACE	Sets a horizontal margin, described in pixels, around the applet.	No

Table 2-7: *Attributes of the APPLET tag.*

In addition to these attributes, we can also pass information into an applet using the <PARAM...> tag. Any number of PARAM tags can reside between the <APPLET...> and </APPLET> tags. Inside the PARAM tag you can specify a NAME and a VALUE. The applet is able to look up these pairs while it's running. In Chapter 5, we develop several applets that make use of the PARAM tag. Here is the how the Web page looks for one of these examples:

Example 2-21: Using the PARAM tag.

```
<APPLET CODE="AnimatedCursorApplet.class" HEIGHT=250
WIDTH=250>
<PARAM NAME="CURSORFILE0" VALUE="images/anim0.gif">
```

```
<PARAM NAME="CURSORFILE1" VALUE="images/anim1.gif">
<PARAM NAME="CURSORFILE2" VALUE="images/anim2.gif">
<PARAM NAME="CURSORFILE3" VALUE="images/anim3.gif">
<PARAM NAME="CURSORFILE4" VALUE="images/anim4.gif">
<PARAM NAME="CURSORFILE5" VALUE="images/anim5.gif">
</APPLET>
```

This particular applet uses the name-value pairs to get images for an animation, but it is entirely up to the individual applets how to interpret them. Of course, applets don't have to look at them at all.

Automatically Documenting Your Code

Documenting your code is always very important. A tool included in the JDK, javadoc, creates Web pages based on your documented source code. It creates the Web page by looking for special comments within your source code. Here is an example:

Example 2-22: Automatic documentation.

```
/** I wrote a class. I even documented it!
 *   I documented it using javadoc.
 */
class documentedClass {
/** Now I am going to document this variable.
    * It's an int!
      * I love documenting!
 */
public int documentedVariable;
/** How about a documented method!
 * This is a method that takes a String as a parameter.
 *It doesn't do anything with it—I'm just documenting for fun.
 * But if it did—oh boy—I would tell you all about it!*/
public void documentedMethod(String x) {
   System.out.println("Documented method");}
  }
```

Then, we can run javadoc on our code by typing:

```
javadoc -d <API directory> documentedClass.java
```

Where <API directory> is the directory in which the rest of the documentation for the Application Programming Interface resides.

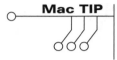

Mac TIP

No javadoc tool exists in the Macintosh JDK at the time of this writing.

Javadoc will output an html file, documentClass.html. In Figure 2-3, we pointed the Web browser at the file.

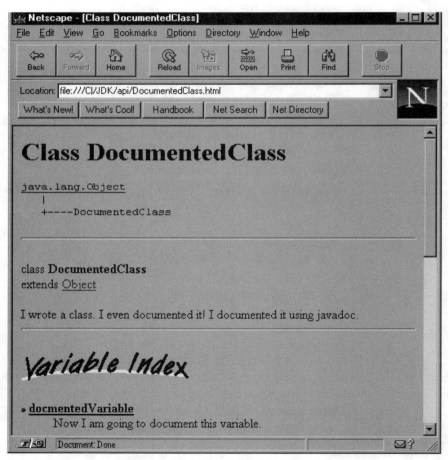

Figure 2-3: *Documentation with Javadoc.*

As you can see, our comments are placed in a Web page. Notice that our String parameter is hyperlinked; the link goes to documentation about the String class. All class parameters are hyperlinked, and all comments that start with /** are written into the Web page. If you want to place a link to some class, you can do this with @see tag, followed by the name of the class. This will set a link to that particular class. You can also include regular HTML tags within the comments.

Moving On

Now you have a feel for the basics of the Java language and the programming environment. In Chapter 3, we explore the principles of object-oriented programming, and how they are expressed in Java, in more depth.

Java Applet Essentials

3

Object Orientation in Java

In the preceding chapter, we touched on Java's object-oriented features when we talked about variables and classes. Object-oriented programming (OOP) is such a fundamental part of the Java language that we had to introduce some of the concepts even when writing very simple Java programs. Before we go any further, let's explore object orientation in more detail.

We start off with a general explanation of what object orientation really is and why Java is a better language because of it. We also introduce some terminology that describes the conventions of the classes we touched on in Chapter 2, "Java Programming Basics." With a better understanding of what object orientation is—and, yes, a little more technobabble—we can then review what we covered in Chapter 2 with a new eye. Finally, we delve into some advanced object-oriented features of the Java language.

Advantages of Object Orientation

Object orientation is possibly the most popular buzz phrase in all of computing. Like all buzz phrases, there are a ton of different interpretations of what it actually means. In Chapter 1, we described the definition that is generally agreed upon: Object orientation is a methodology that makes our problems easier to solve. But that definition describes the "product" that a thousand stress management books, video tapes, and courses try to sell us. Before we chant the mantra of object orientation, let's use what we learned from Chapter 2 and iron down a programming-level definition.

Classes are the real nuts and bolts of object orientation. As you'll remember, a class describes a type that contains both subroutines (or methods) and data. Since a class describes a type, we can create variables that contain both methods and variables. Such variables are *objects*. Objects differ from the variables of procedural programming languages because they can define how data can be changed. Subroutines in object-oriented languages differ from their counterparts in procedural languages in that they have a set of data (the data members defined in the same class) which they can change but that other methods can't.

This definition describes the implementation of the methodology of object orientation from the programmer's point of view. Now, we can begin to discuss why this is advantageous to the programmer. Before we go on, take a look at Table 3-1 for a quick review of some Java terms that are related to object orientation.

Term	Definition
Package	A unit that contains the entities of the Java language, including classes.
Class	A definition of a data type that contains data and subroutines.
Method	The Java name for subroutine instantiation.
Construction	The creation of a class into a variable; occurs at runtime.
Instance, object, instantiation	A variable of a class type that has been instantiated.
Access modifier	Describes what set of classes can have access to a member of a class. The access modifier is also used to indicate that a class can be accessed from outside its package.

Table 3-1: *Key Java terms pertaining to object orientation.*

WHAT ABOUT STATIC?

You may have noticed that Table 3-1 does not include the *static* keyword that we described in Chapter 2, "Java Programming Basics." Though object orientation has many benefits, there are times when a simple subroutine doesn't need to be closely bound to any particular set of data. Likewise, you may wish to define a variable that will always have the same value, and there is no reason to go to the trouble of instantiating an object just to get to it. For cases like this, when object orientation serves no benefit, the static modifier is provided. Since such cases fall outside the realm of the object-oriented methodology, we don't cover the static methods and variables in this chapter.

Data Hiding

Remember the private access modifier we were using in Chapter 2? When we declare a variable private, we are practicing *data hiding*. We are hiding the data (the variable) from all of the subroutines in our program except those defined in the same class. When does it make sense to hide data? Let's consider a paradox that often arises in procedural programming.

If you've ever taken an introductory programming class, at some point your instructor probably told you not to make variables global (that is, accessible from any subroutine in your program). If a variable is global and a bug develops relating to that variable, it becomes very hard to track down precisely which subroutine is causing the bug. Somebody maintaining your program—buggy or not—will have a tough time figuring out what is happening to that variable.

Fair enough. But what if you write a program that has, say, eight subroutines, and four of them use the same variable. In accordance with the taboo against global variables, you obligingly pass it among the four methods that use it. But this is really just a workaround to avoid declaring a variable global. What you really want is for the variable to be global for those four subroutines that use it.

In Java, we just slap that variable into a class, declare it private, and throw those four methods in along with it. When somebody else looks at our code, or when we look at it long after we have forgotten how it actually works, we know that those four methods are the only ones in the program that are allowed to work with the variable.

Encapsulation

In the process of hiding data, we implicitly describe a relationship between the variable and the methods contained in the same class. If a method outside of the class wants to alter the variable, it has to do so by calling one of the methods defined in the class. This relationship between the members of a class is a concept called *encapsulation*, which is closely related to data hiding.

Let's consider the value of encapsulation when we are dealing with a single variable. Suppose the variable is an integer, and the purpose of one of our subroutines is to print out that number of blank lines. If we were writing this in a procedural language, we would be obligated to check to make sure that the integer isn't a negative number. If we encapsulate the subroutine and the variable in a class, we don't need to check to see if it's negative. Since only the methods within the class are allowed to alter the value, we just write all of our methods so that none of them ever sets the integer to a negative value:

```
public class printLines {
private int linesToPrint=0;

public void printSomeLines() {
   for (int i=0;i<=linesToPrint;i++) {
   System.out.println("");}
   }

public void setLinesToPrint(int j) {
   if (j>0) {
   linesToPrint=j;}
      }
   }
```

Since the only way the value can be changed is through the setLinesToPrint method, we only have to check for negativity there. So we save a few lines of code. The advantages are much more apparent when we have several variables contained in our class.

Let's switch back to procedural language mode to see why. Previously, we described a scenario in which there was a single variable that many subroutines did business with. Let's expand on this and say the variable is an array, and you need to keep track of a position in the array. Thus, every time you pass the array, you must pass an index variable, too. Then, the program gets more complicated, and every time you pass this particular array, you also need to pass along an entirely different array and its index.

We now have a set of data that is entwined—each member of the set has a relationship with all of the other members. This means that in a procedural language, each subroutine that deals with any member of the set is responsible for the upkeep of that relationship. Since each subroutine is simply acting on the data, it's hard to discern how the relationship is being maintained. If the relationship is breaking down at some point, determining which particular action is messing it up will be hard—just like in human relationships!

Since our personal lives are well beyond the scope of this text, let's concentrate on how object orientation helps us to maintain the relationships within our programs. Let's look at a simple example. Suppose we have an array of characters. Our challenge is to start at some position in the array and swap the character that is already there with some other character. The next time we need to do a replacement, we start at the next position in the array. The following class will do the trick:

```java
public class replaceChars {

    private char myArray[];
    private int curPos=0;

    public replaceChars(char someArray[]) {
        myArray=someArray; }
```

```java
public boolean replaceNextChar(char c, char d) {
    if (newPositionSet(c)) {
        myArray[curPos]=d;

        return true;}
    else {return false;}
}

private boolean newPositionSet(char c) {
    int i=curPos;
    while (i<myArray.length) {
        if (c==myArray[i]) {
            curPos=i;
            return true;}
        else {i++;}
        }
    return false;
    }

public boolean atEnd() {
    return(curPos==myArray.length-1);}
    //subtract 1 because positions in an array
    //start at zero
    }
```

We were able to solve our problem completely in a few lines of code. Also, notice that our newPositionSet method is marked private. This goes back to the concept of data hiding. Instead of hiding data, we are hiding a method that changes the data. Presumably, we don't want the position to be changed unless a character has been replaced.

Now, consider the difficulties involved in solving our problem using a procedural language. First, we can't hide our data or any helper subroutines. This means that we must always check and make sure that our curPos variable is in range. Second, we have no straightforward way to keep track of our current position in the array.

The simple challenge we solved above isn't impossible in procedural languages. However, our class has the advantage that

it is actually a type definition. When we encapsulate our methods
and variables into a class, we are really encapsulating our solution. Since our solution is a type, it's easy to reuse our solution—
we just instantiate another variable:

```
replaceChars solution1=new replaceChars("Java is great!")
replaceChars solution2=new replaceChars("I want to learn more
java!");

while (!soulution1.atEnd())
  {solution1.replaceNextChar('a','x');}
while (!solution2.atEnd())
  {solution2.replaceNextChar('o','y');}
```

Once we define methods that interact correctly with a set of
data, we needn't worry about the details of our code. If we tried to
solve our simple problem using a procedural language, we would
always have to maintain the relationship between our position
integer and the array. If we wanted to perform our operation on
multiple arrays, the complexity would be compounded. Our
object-oriented approach allows us to use our code at a higher
level of abstraction.

Of course, abstraction isn't new with OOP. Procedural languages define sets of action in subroutines, and the subroutines
are thus reusable. Also, simple data types like integers are just
abstractions of how bits are stored in the computer's memory.
Object orientation simply takes this abstraction to a new level. It
marries the abstractions of data types and subroutines, so that the
relationship between data and action can also be reused.

Reusability via Inheritance

Once we solve a problem by encapsulating methods and variables, we can easily deploy our solution over and over again in
our programs. But what if we find ourselves faced with a new
problem that is very much like one we have already solved?
Object orientation also has a feature, *inheritance*, that allows us to
reuse already-coded solutions when solving new, similar problems.

Let's see inheritance in action. In the code fragment of the preceding section, we call replaceNextChar for the same two characters again and again. Wouldn't it be nice if we could do this using one of the methods in the replaceChar class? We could just add it to the class and recompile. But let's say somebody else is already using the original replaceChar class. Now we have to maintain two classes of the same name, which will probably cause confusion down the road. Instead, we can create a new class that inherits the characteristics of our replaceNextChar class:

```
class betterReplaceNextChar extends ReplaceNextChar{

    public int replaceAllChars(char c, char d) {
    int i=0;
    while(!atEnd()) {
       replaceNextChar(c,d);
       i++;}
    return i;}

}
```

Now we have a new class that has all of the methods of the ReplaceNextChar class, plus the one additional method we have defined here. We have been able to encapsulate the solution to a new problem by extending the class. As we saw when we wrote our first applet in Chapter 2, inheritance is a very important concept in Java programming. We explore it more fully a bit later in this chapter.

Maintainability

Throughout our discussion, we have repeatedly mentioned that object-oriented code is easier to maintain. But what exactly does code maintenance mean? After all, once the code compiles, it will presumably work forever—it's not like we're building bridges that will eventually suffer from metal fatigue. Software, however, is expected to adjust to its environment in ways that physical structures aren't expected to.

For instance, a program that was originally designed to keep track of payroll needs to be updated to take care of health care benefits. Or, a networking system originally designed to just broadcast messages to neighboring machines now needs to listen for updates from a server on Wall Street. We could make a very lengthy list of examples, but our premise is that software lives in a world of infinite and ever-changing complexity. Problems arise that the original programmer didn't foresee, or new demands are placed on the system. Rarely does a production computer program go unchanged for more than a few years. When it is changed, someone new may be making the changes, or the original programmer may have long ago forgotten the intricacies of the program. In either case, whoever is making the changes would prefer not to start from scratch. Modern programming languages must provide features that ensure programs' maintainers that the programs can be easily modified to meet new needs.

This is the underlying goal of object-oriented languages, and all of the features we have mentioned support this goal in some way. For instance, reusability directly implies maintainability. If someone can reuse code we have written to solve new problems, it will be easier to grow the program to deal with new circumstances. Additionally, the code itself is easier to understand. When we employ data hiding by declaring a variable private inside a class, any Java-fluent programmer will know that only the methods in that class are able to alter that variable. Likewise, the encapsulation of methods and variables makes it easy to discern the relationship between data and action in our programs.

Encapsulation also makes it easier to add features to the program. As long as a class works as it is supposed to, someone trying to add features to our programs won't have to figure out the underlying details. All they need to know is how to use the public methods and constructors.

There's another implicit advantage of encapsulation. Since other objects in the program can only interface with a given object through its public methods and constructors, the private parts of the system and the code making up the public methods and constructors can be changed without breaking the entire system.

Why is this advantageous? Let's consider the problem of the year 2000. As the millennium approaches, a lot of specialist programmers are going to make up to $500 per hour making sure that institutional computers don't misinterpret the turn of the century. Why? There are tons of mission-critical programs that won't correctly interpret the new millennium because they use only two digits to store the year. This means that your bank may start thinking that you are –73 years old, or a phone call from the East Coast to the West Coast starting at 11:59, December 31, 1999, could be logged as taking 99 years!

The problem is hard to fix because these programs predate object orientation. Written in procedural languages, each has its own individual way of comparing two dates. Those high-flying specialists are going to be sifting through tons and tons of individual subroutines, looking for places where dates were compared incorrectly. Let's consider how an object-oriented approach would eliminate this problem. Below is the Year class, in which we deliberately messed up the comparison. (So our example doesn't make us look like complete idiots, let's just say our original intention was to store the Year in as little space as possible.)

```java
public  class Year {
   private byte decadeDigit;
   private byte yearDigit;

   public Year(int thisYear) {
      byte yearsSince1900=(byte)thisYear-1900;
      decadeDigit=yearsSince1900/10;
      yearDigit=yearsSince1900-(decadeDigit*10);}

   public int getYear() {
      return decadeDigit*yearDigit;}

//Other methods

}
```

We go on to build dozens of systems that rely on this class to store the date, and other programmers use it, too. Then one day in

December of 1999, we realize what boneheads we are. Time to call in the $500-an-hour consultant? Of course not! All we have to do is rewrite the implementation of the class. As long as we don't change the public method declarations, everything in all of those systems will still work correctly:

```java
public class Year {

    private byte centuryDigit;
    private byte decadeDigit;
    private byte yearDigit;

    public Year(int thisYear) {
        centuryDigit=(byte)thisYear/100;
        int lastTwo=thisYear-(centuryDigit*100);
        decadeDigit=(byte)lastTwo/10;
        yearDigit=(byte)(lastTwo-(decadeDigit*10));
    }

    public int getYear() {
        return decadeDigit*yearDigit*centuryDigit;}

//Other methods
}
```

Now, we're set until the year 12799, and some hack wasn't paid $500 an hour to fix our code!

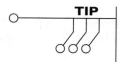

TIP *Java's API, which we discuss at length in Chapter 6, contains a Date class that won't break at the turn of the century.*

Java Object Specifics

We have illuminated the concepts underlying some of the code we were writing in Chapter 2, and, we hope, convinced you that they are sound advantages of the Java languages. Now, we're going to focus on how these features actually work in practice.

Java's Class Hierarchy

When we use the term *class hierarchy,* we are describing what happens when we use inheritance. Let's say we have three classes; call them Mom, Son, and Daughter. The Son and Daughter classes inherit from Mom. Our code would look as follows:

```
class Mom {
//declarations, definitions
}

class Son extends Mom {
//declarations, definitions
}

class Daughter extends Mom {
//declarations, definitions
}
```

We just created a class hierarchy! Just like an organizational hierarchy, it's very easy to visualize.

Table 3-2 lists some terms that we use to describe our hierarchy. Mom is the *base class*—the class on which other classes are based. Son and Daughter are *subclasses* of Mom, and Mom is the *superclass* of Son and Daughter.

Term	Definition
Class hierarchy	A group of classes that are related by inheritance.
Superclass	A class that a certain class extends.
Subclass	A subclass that is extended from a certain class.
Base class	The class in a certain hierarchy that is a super-class of all other classes in the hierarchy.

Table 3-2: *Class hierarchy terminology.*

Now that we have some vocabulary to work with, we can talk specifically about class hierarchies in Java. First, all classes in Java have exactly one direct superclass. As we discussed in Chapter 1, this characteristic of the Java language is known, in object-oriented parlance, as *single inheritance*. Of course, a class can have more than one superclass. Mom and Daughter, for example, could both be superclasses of another class, Granddaughter.

"But wait," you may be wondering, "if all classes have exactly one direct superclass, what is Mom's superclass?" The class hierarchy we describe here is actually a subset of a huge class hierarchy that contains every single class ever written in Java. Figure 3-1 illustrates how the small class hierarchy we developed fits in with this much larger hierarchy. At the top of this class sits a special class named the Object class.

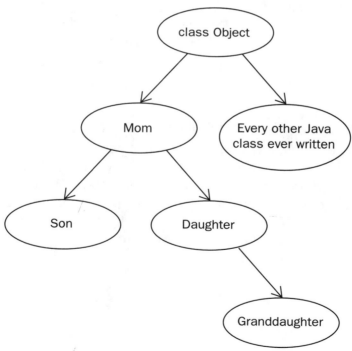

Figure 3-1: *How our class hierarchy fits in with the entire Java hierarchy.*

When we declare a class, if we don't explicitly specify that it extends some other class, the Java compiler assumes we are extending the Object class. Thus, the following definition for our Mom class is exactly equivalent to the definition we gave earlier:

```
class Mom extends Object {
//declarations,definitions
}
```

So why is this global, all-encompassing class hierarchy a good thing? Since all classes inherit from the Object class, we know that we can call the methods of the Object class.

The Object class's methods include methods that determine equality and that allow all Java classes to use Java's multithreaded features. Also, we never have to worry about combining different hierarchies, because all hierarchies are simply subsets of the global Java hierarchy. And finally, class hierarchy guarantees that every class has a superclass; we'll see the importance of this in Chapter 6, when we look at the object container classes.

WHAT'S IN THE GLOBAL CLASS HIERARCHY?

As we said, any and every Java class ever written is in the global hierarchy. More important, you have a very valuable chunk of that hierarchy in your Java Developers Kit. It's called the Applications Programming Interface (API), and it includes classes such as the base applet class, the String class, networking classes, windowing classes, and utility classes, as well as other neat stuff. In Chapter 6, we explore the API in depth.

Special Variables

Each class in Java has three predefined variables we can use: null, this, and super. The first two are of type Object. In short, *null* represents a nonexistent object and *this* points to the same instance. *Super* is a special variable that allows access to the methods defined by the superclass. Let's examine each of them in turn.

Null Variable

In Chapter 2, "Java Programming Basics," we explained that a class needs to be instantiated before it can be used. Before it is instantiated, it has the value of the null variable, and we say that the object is null. When an object is null, we aren't allowed to access any of its members because there hasn't been an object created for them to be associated with. If we try to access members before they are created, we run the risk of causing a NullPointerException, which will halt our program. The following method runs that risk because it takes a ReplaceNextChar object as a parameter and uses it without checking to see if it is null:

```
public void someMethod(ReplaceChars A) {
A.replaceNextChar('a','b');}
```

The following code, which calls someMethod, will generate a NullPointerException because ReplaceNextChar hasn't been constructed:

```
ReplaceChars B;
someMethod(B);
```

To keep our programs from crashing, we must check objects to make sure they aren't null before we attempt to use them. This rewritten someMethod checks to make sure that *A* isn't null before attempting to access one of its members:

```
public void someMethod(replaceChars A) {
   if (A==null) {
      System.out.println("A is null!!!");}
   else {
      A.replaceNextChar('a','b');
}
```

This Variable

Sometimes you'll need to pass a reference to the current object to another routine. You can do so by simply passing the variable *this*. Let's say that our Son and Daughter classes define a constructor that takes a Mom variable in its constructor. The *this* variable allows the Son and Daughter to keep track of Mom by storing a reference to her in a private variable:

```
public class Son {
    Mom myMommy;

public Son(Mom mommy) {
    myMommy=mommy;}
//methods }

public class Daughter {
  Mom myMommy;
public Daughter(Mom mommy) {
    myMommy=mommy;}
```

When Mom constructs her Sons and Daughters, she needs to pass a reference of herself to their constructors. She does this using the *this* variable:

```
public class Mom {
    Son firstSon;
    Son secondSon;
    Daughter firstDaughter;
    Daughter secondDaughter;

public Mom() {
    firstSon=new Son(this);
    secondSon=new Son(this);
    firstDaughter=new Daughter(this);
    secondDaughter=new Daughter(this);}

//other methods}
```

If we construct Mom with:

```
Mom BigMama=new Mom();
```

then Figure 3-2 will represent the relationships of our family.

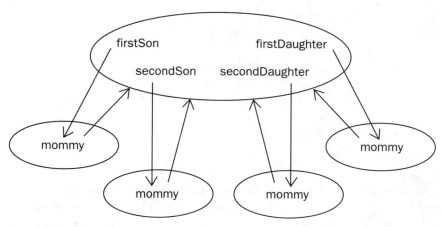

Figure 3-2: *BigMama's family.*

Super Variable

You'll often need to access a parent's implementation of a method that you have overridden. Suppose that you implemented a constructor that was defined in your parent class. Maybe you wanted to initialize a few variables private to the new class, and now you want to call your parent's constructor. This is where the *super* variable is useful. In the following example, we define a class that overrides its parent constructor and then calls it using the super variable.

Think back to our Mom, Son, and Daughter hierarchy. Let's say Mom defines a method that cleans up a room, called cleanUpRoom. Son is supposed to clean up the room exactly as Mom has defined, after which he needs to print out, "Cleaned up my room!" Since Mom has defined the method for cleaning up the room, Son can call it using the super variable and then perform the additional action of printing out the message:

```java
public class Mom {
//declarations, constructors
public void cleanUpRoom() {
//code for cleaning up room}
//other methods}
}
```

```
public class Son {
//variables, constructors

public void cleanUpRoom() {
   super.cleanUpRoom();
   System.out.println("Cleaned up my room!!");}

//other methods
}
```

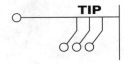

TIP

Be careful not to think of the super variable as pointing to a completely separate object. You need not instantiate the superclass to use the super variable. It's really just a way to run the methods and constructors that were defined in the superclass.

Constructors, like methods, can also use the super variable, as in this example:

```
public class SuperClass {
   private int onlyInt;

   public SuperClass(int i) {
   onlyInt=i;}

public int getOnlyInt() {
   return onlyInt;}
}
```

Our subclass can reuse the code we have already written in our constructor by using the super variable:

```
public class SubClass extends SuperClass {
private int anotherInt;

public SubClass(int i, int j) {
   super(i);
   anotherInt=j;}

public int getAnotherInt() {
   return anotherInt;}
}
```

There are two important restrictions on using the super variable to access the constructors of the superclass. First, you can only use it in this way inside a constructor. Second, it must be the very first statement inside a constructor.

Class Instantiation

We've been instantiating classes since Chapter 2. When we use the *new* operator, we are bringing our class to life as an object and assigning it to a variable. Now, let's look at some issues about instantiation we haven't covered yet.

When we first started instantiating classes, we used the default constructor that takes no parameters:

```
someClass A=new someClass();
```

Then, we showed that we can pass variables to the constructor. What we haven't taken advantage of is *constructor overloading*, in which a class defines multiple constructors with differing parameter lists. Since constructors are really just a special type of method, constructor overloading works like the method overloading discussed in Chapter 2. The class we define below utilizes constructor overloading:

```
public class Box {
    int boxWidth;
    int boxLength;
    int boxHeight;

public Box(int i) {
    boxWidth=i;
    boxLength=i;
    boxHeight=i;}

public Box(int i, int j) {
    boxWidth=i;
    boxLength=i;
    boxHeight=j;}
```

```
public Box(int i,int j, int k) {
   boxWidth=i;
   boxLength=j;
   boxHeight=k;}


//other methods
}
```

In the section of code above, we have a class that describes a box. If we are only passed one parameter for the constructor, we assume that a cube is desired. If we are passed two, we assume that the base is square and that the second integer describes the height of the box. When passed all three, we use each of them in describing the box. Overloading constructors allows us to give the users of our class multiple ways to create the class.

When we declare a variable and don't initialize it to a particular value, Java assigns a value for us. Above, our variables were initialized to zero. Generally, you want to make sure that each constructor assigns values for each of the variables in the class. Data encapsulation depends on the data being valid, and doesn't work very well if you don't initialize the value.

But this creates an interesting predicament—we can't expect constructors defined in the superclass to properly initialize variables defined in the subclass. Java resolves this difficulty by having a different set of rules for constructor inheritance than it does for method inheritance and variable inheritance. If you define a constructor, any constructor, Java ignores all constructors in the superclass.

WHAT HAPPENS WHEN AN OBJECT ISN'T NEEDED ANYMORE?
As we discussed in Chapter 2, Java is a garbage-collected language. Since it keeps track of when memory needs to be freed, the need for a deconstructor is greatly reduced. However, Java does provide a method, called *finalize*, that is run when the garbage collector reallocates the memory. By defining it, you can describe a set of actions you want to take place when the garbage collector detects that the variable isn't being used anymore.

Be careful using the finalize method—it may not be called until the program ends, and you can't predict the order in which objects that are no longer in use will be reclaimed.

Access Rules

When we were discussing the advantages of data hiding, we introduced the private modifier. The private modifier only allows a variable or a method to be accessed from within the class, while the public modifier makes a member accessible from anywhere. There are three other modifiers that affect the object-oriented nature of members of a class: protected, private protected, and final. We've listed them in order of familiarity — protected is closest in behavior to the public and private modifiers that we've been using, and final is furthest from what we are used to. Thus, let's start by looking at protected.

The Protected Modifier

The *protected modifier* lets us make class members public to only a certain set of classes—the ones that are in the same *package*. We place a class into a package with a statement at the top of the file:

```
package somePackage;
```

If we don't explicitly put a class in a specific package, it's placed into a default package with all classes defined in the current directory.

TRAP

If you don't explicitly modify a method or variable, the compiler assumes you want it to be protected. However, if you later decide you want to put it in its own package, members that had previously been accessible from classes in the same working directory won't be accessible anymore. It's always a better idea to explicitly modify class members.

The Private Protected Modifier

The *private protected modifier* represents a more narrow accessibility than the protected modifier, but wider accessibility than private. A private protected member can be accessed only by the subclasses of a class. While the other access modifiers we've used fit into the concept of data hiding, the private protected modifier has the most important implications when we are considering class inheritance.

Let's say we declare a variable or a method as private in a particular class. If we subclass this class, the subclass can't access the private members if the superclass isn't in the subclass. As we explain in the next section, it's often advantageous to develop a base class that is really just a placeholder—you expect it to have several subclasses. In such a case, it's much more convenient to use the private protected modifier instead of the private modifier so that the subclasses don't have to do all of their real work through the public methods of the superclass.

Putting Inheritance to Work

We have looked at much of what is under the hood of Java's object orientation. Hopefully, you are now comfortable with two key concepts of object orientation, data hiding and encapsulation, and how to use them in Java. We've introduced inheritance. Now let's look at the mechanism of inheritance in greater depth. In this section, we demonstrate how you can become a more efficient programmer by using inheritance to form class hierarchies. Java provides us with abstract classes and methods to help us out in structuring class hierarchies.

Structuring Class Hierarchies

When we discussed reusability earlier in this chapter, we showed you that inheritance allows us to build on classes that have already been written. But our example showed only one part of reusing code. Reusability is only one advantage of inheritance. Using inheritance, we can lay out the key modules of our program in an intelligent manner.

Consider the scenario we used to introduce object orientation in Chapter 1, "The World Wide Web & Java." As you may recall, we looked at the simple problem, "go to the store and get milk," and showed how to think about it in terms of object orientation. Let's look at one of the components of the problem, the carton of milk.

Suppose we are coding up the entire system. We could write a class that describes the milk. But there are several different types of milk, such as lowfat and chocolate. And if all types of milk were grouped together as a unit, that unit would be only one of many dairy products. Thus, we could create a class hierarchy such as the one shown in Figure 3-3.

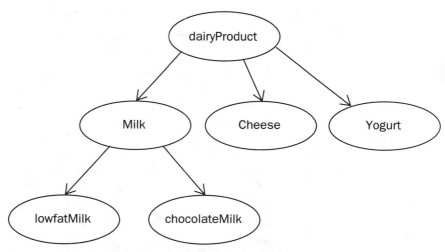

Figure 3-3: *Class hierarchy of dairy products.*

Luckily, this is more than just an exercise in critical thinking. Java allows us to instantiate a subclass and then *cast* it so that it acts like a variable of the superclass. This is very valuable if we only care about one general aspect defined at the top of the class hierarchy, such as whether a dairy product is going to go sour this week. Let's say that our dairyProduct class has a method that will tell us this:

```
public class dairyProduct {

//variables, constructors

    public boolean sourThisWeek() {
       //appropriate code}

    //other methods
    public void putOnSale() {
       //code for putting a dairy product
       //on sale

    }
```

This is where casting comes in. If we already have a variable of, say, lowfatMilkType, we can cast it to be a variable of type dairyProduct:

```
lowfatMilk M=new lowfatMilk();
dairyProduct D=M;
if (D.sourThisWeek()) {
  System.out.println("Don't buy");}
```

What's the advantage of this? Let's say our store manager wants to check to see which cartons of milk are going to go sour this week. The ones that are will be put on sale. He can just pass all of his lowfatMilk, Milk, Cheese, and Yogurt objects to the following method:

```
public void dumpSourGoods(dairyGood d) {
   if (d.sourThisWeek()) {
     d.putOnSale();}
   }
```

If we hadn't created a structured class hierarchy in the first place, we would have to write a different method for each type of dairy product.

Abstract Classes & Methods

In the previous example, we created a class hierarchy to make our code more useful in its system. But our dairyProduct class has methods that have no body. When we wrote it above, we just said they would be overridden in the subclasses. However, somebody looking at our code may not understand that this is our intention. Java provides as with the abstract modifier to help us with this situation.

When we use the abstract modifier with methods, all subclasses have to override the abstract method. This is how we would make abstract methods for our dairyProduct class:

```
public class dairyProduct {

//variables, constructors

public abstract boolean sourThisWeek();

//other methods
public abstract void putOnSale();
}
```

The dairyProduct class can still be instantiated—the abstract methods just can't be accessed via a dairyProduct instance. However, we can also use the abstract modifier to describe that we don't want a class to be directly instantiated:

```
public abstract myAbstractClass {
//code
}
```

When we define a class as abstract, we can put regular methods and variables in it. When we subclass the abstract class, it inherits all of the members of the abstract class according to the same inheritance rules we have already described.

Polymorphism & Java's Interfaces

When we covered the advantages of object orientation, we stuck with the concepts we could easily explain based on what we learned about Java in Chapter 2, "Java Programming Basics." Now we are going to introduce the concept of polymorphism and how a Java structural mechanism, interfaces, allows you to employ it in your code.

Polymorphism is the process by which we are able to make the same method call on a group of objects, with each object responding to the method call in different ways. We have already dealt with polymorphism in our example about dairyGoods. For instance, the methods putOnSale and sourThisWeek are defined in all of the classes in the hierarchy. We are free to call these methods on any of the objects—as we did when we put all nearly sour dairy goods on sale—and each different class defines how its instantiations will actually will react.

However, polymorphism is somewhat limited. We are only guaranteed that the classes in the same hierarchy will contain the methods defined in the top class. Many times, some of the subclasses may need to have methods that the entire hierarchy doesn't have. For instance, since milk and yogurt are liquid, we may want a method cleanUpSpill in case they tumble. But it would be silly to define a method for the cheese class describing how to clean up a cheese spill. Also, many products in the store that aren't dairy products can spill.

A well structured class hierarchy doesn't solve this predicament. Even if we have a class, storeGood, that sits above all classes defining products in our store, it wouldn't make sense to define a cleanUpSpill method at the top, because so many goods in the store can't spill. What is needed, and is supplied by Java, is a way to define a set of methods that are implemented by some classes in the hierarchy, but not all. This structure is called an *interface*.

Let's start exploring interfaces by defining one for our liquid products that may spill:

```
interface spillable {

  public void cleanUpSpill();

  public boolean hasBeenSpilled();
}
```

As you can see, the methods are defined in the same way we define abstract methods. Indeed, they are abstract—they have to be defined inside a class that implements the interface. Also, notice that we don't have any variables or constructors. These aren't allowed in an interface because an interface is just a set of abstract methods. Here's how we use an interface in our class Milk:

```
public class Milk extends dairyProduct
   implements Spillable {
     //variables, constructors

   public boolean hasBeenSpilled {
     //appropriate code}
   public void cleanUpSpill {
     //appropriate code}

   //other methods
   }
```

The key here is the keyword *implements*. It designates that class Milk defines the methods in the interface Spillable. Of course, if we have an instance of the Milk class, we can call the hasBeenSpilled and cleanUpSpill methods. The advantage of interfaces is that, like classes, they are data types. Although we can't instantiate them directly, we can represent them as variables:

```
class Milk M=new Milk();
Spillable S=(Spillable)M;
if (S.hasBeenSpilled())
   {S.cleanUpSpill();}
```

Therefore, we can access all of the methods having to do with spilling through the Spillable data type, without having to define the methods in a base class for all products, spillable or not spillable, in the store.

We're also allowed to implement more than one interface in a class. For instance, we could write a Perishable interface that would describe all products that may spoil. Our Milk class implements both of them with the following class declaration:

```
public class Milk implements Spillable, Perishable {
//class definition
}
```

In actuality, it would be better to implement the Perishable interface at the dairyGoods level, since all dairy goods are perishable. Not to worry—subclasses inherit the interfaces their superclasses implement.

Conceptual Summary & Example

We covered a lot of concepts in this chapter. You learned why OOP techniques are helpful in general, and how to declare and use objects and apply fundamental OOP practices, such as inheritance and overloading, in Java. Arrays were introduced to show what objects could do for the language itself. Let's wrap up the chapter with Table 3-3, which summarizes the OOP concepts, and an example that employs them all.

Concept	Description
Class	A type describing some data and a group of functions that act on this data.
Object, instance, instantiation	A variable of a class type after instantiation of the class has taken place.
Data hiding	The practice of making a variable hidden from other objects. Data hiding typically makes it easier to change underlying data structures.
Encapsulation	Grouping like functions and data into one package.

Concept	Description
Access modifiers	Statements that describe what classes can access the variables or methods defined in a class.
Instantiation	Creating an object from a class. Instantiation creates an *instance* of the class.
Constructor	A bit of initialization code called when a class is instantiated.
Class hierarchy	A multitiered diagram showing the relationships between classes.
Inheritance	Creating a new class by extending the functionality of another class.
Superclass	A class that is inherited from a particular class.
Subclass	A class that inherits from a particular class.
Method overriding	Redefining methods in the subclass that have already been defined in the superclass.

Table 3-3: *OOP concepts and vocabulary.*

In order to summarize these concepts in a program, let's introduce a small classes hierarchy. These groups of objects are going to implement a low-level graphics system. Suppose our client has asked us to create a painting program. She would like to be able to move picture elements around as whole objects. The first demo will include primitive shapes, but the final project could include many complicated shapes and bitmaps. If we can get a demo copy to her by next week, we get the contract; otherwise, we'll be stuck manning the technical support lines for another six months. Dreadful thought, so let's get this demo up and running!

The fact that we don't know all the shapes to be implemented makes our task harder. We will have to incorporate our knowledge of OOP techniques and make our code as extensible as possible. One of our most powerful tools is inheritance. If we design our object hierarchy right, it will be a snap to add any number of new shapes.

Remember our discussion of interfaces? We use interfaces to make a group of objects conform to a standard set of features. We will need this ability to implement our paint program. Each shape must be able to handle a few important routines. Primarily, we need each shape to be able to show itself on the screen, hide itself from view, and change its location. With this basic set of operations, we can create a simple paint program. Let's call this interface Shape. The definition for Shape is:

```java
interface Shape {

    public void show();
    public void hide();
}
```

In order for a new shape to be added to the paint program, the paint program will have to implement only these routines. The rest of the routines will be handled by other objects in our hierarchy. This object will be responsible for keeping track of a shape's position. Any code we wish to share between shapes will be stored in this class. We call this class BaseShape; it is defined below. Notice that it is abstract and contains abstract methods:

```java
class abstract BaseShape {
    protected int x,y;

    public void setPos(int newX, int newY) {
        x = newX;
        y = newY;
    }
}
```

We now have a common interface for each shape and a base class to inherit from. Any method that needs to be implemented in all shapes will be placed in the interface. All common code between shapes goes in the baseShape class. The final piece of coding is to implement the individual shapes and a small demo paint program.

The following shows the implementations of a few shapes, namely, a rectangle and a circle. Each shape may need extra data elements and methods to implement its particular picture. In order to follow good data hiding practices, we declare these variables and methods as private:

```java
class Rectangle extends BaseShape implements Shape {

    private int len, width;

    Rectangle(int x, int y, int Len, int Width) {
        setPos(x,y);
        len = Len;
        width = Width;
    }

    public void show() {
        System.out.println("Rectangle(" + x + "," + y + ")");
        System.out.println("Length=" + len + ", Width=" +
width);

    }

    public void hide() {}
}

class Circle extends BaseShape implements Shape {

    private int radius;

    Circle(int x1, int y1, int Radius) {
        setPos(x1,y1);
        radius = Radius;
    }

    public void show() {
        System.out.println("Circle(" + x + "," + y + ")");
        System.out.println("Radius=" + radius);

    }

    public void hide() {}
}
```

The last piece to be coded is the paint program itself. Imagine how you might go about coding a paint program. Since we want to keep each shape separate, we must have a way to store individual components. The combination of these shapes will form some picture. The advantage to this is that we can easily move or copy elements of a picture to different places. To do this, we need a way to store the elements of the picture.

We have something of a problem here. What type of data structure can we use to hold many different types of objects? The simplest would be an array. Arrays in Java allow you to hold any type of data. The data could be a simple type like an integer, a more complex type like an object, or, as in this case, an interface, which is a programmer-defined type. We declare an array that will hold objects that implement the interface *shape*. This lets us call any of the defined shape methods without knowing exactly what type of object it is. We can keep creating new shapes without having to change our paint program. This is a great improvement on procedural-based languages!

```java
class testShapes {

public static void main(String ARGV[]) {

    Shape shapeList[] = new Shape[2];
    int i;

    shapeList[0] = new Rectangle(0,0,5,5);
    shapeList[1] = new Circle(7,7,4);

    for(i=0, i<2, i++) {
       shapeList[i].show();

       }

    }

}
```

There we have it—a simple program that implements the basics of our paint program. Add to this a little graphics code, and we have ourselves a usable and extensible paint program. When the client comes back and asks for changes to the original program, we'll be ready. This framework provides a base to implement an ever-improving paint program. No more technical support for us—we got the contract!

Moving On

Hopefully, you now have a good grasp of the key concepts of object orientation and how Java uses them. In the next chapter, we'll spend some time covering the syntax of the language. Although some of this will be a review, other parts will be entirely new to you. With a strong conceptual understanding of the language, we hope that when we get to the nitty-gritty—writing Java applications and applets—you'll be ready to get down to business.

4

Syntax & Semantics

Since Java is based largely upon the C/C++ class of languages, those familiar with these languages will find this chapter mostly a review. The designers of Java had a simple objective: They wanted a language that was close to C/C++, one that carried that language's strengths into the realm of Internet and Intranet programming. But to use it as intended, Java had to resolve weaknesses of C/C++ in the areas of security, portability, and maintenance. They also added multiple threading and exception handling to make Internet programming easier. Thus, the differences between C/C++ and Java generally fall into these categories.

Most of the information in this chapter was culled from the *Java Language Specification* for release 1.0. Java is still changing, so you can expect changes in future versions. The language design still incorporates some unused keywords, for example, and Sun has already mentioned some possible changes and additions to the language. The Online Companion for this book will be updated as these changes occur.

Although this chapter is meant to serve as a reference that you can turn to again and again during programming, it does provide important basic information about Java. We recommend that you at least scan this chapter before proceeding to the rest of the book. Be sure to read the sections on Arrays and Exceptions carefully. Java handles Arrays and Exceptions in ways you might not expect based on your knowledge of other languages. The concept of Exceptions, in particular, is a key concept that is used throughout the book.

In this chapter, we discuss Java syntax for the following elements, in this order:

- Identifiers and Unicode
- Keywords
- Data types
- Primitive data types
- Primitive data type conversion
- Variable declaration
- Operators
- Packages
- Classes
- Reference variables type conversion
- Interfaces
- Arrays
- Control flow
- Exceptions

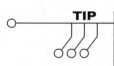

TIP *Check out the Online Companion for this book at http://www.vmedia.com/java.html for the latest updates to the Java language.*

Identifiers & Unicode

Identifier is the technical term for what we use to name elements in our programs. Anything we create in our Java programs—be it a variable, method, or class—is named using an identifier. Identifiers are composed of a sequence of Unicode characters. "Unicode? Never heard of it," you might say. The truth of the matter is that after this chapter, you may never hear of it again.

Java was designed to be portable, not only across computer platforms, but also across national barriers. Multilanguage support has become a hot topic as companies race to access global markets. Currently, most computer programs are written in English. A programmer in a non–English-speaking country is forced to program in a foreign language. Computers are already foreign to many people; adding another level of complexity can make learning to program even harder. This is where Unicode comes in.

Unicode has been developed by the Unicode Consortium and was first publicly released in 1990. It is designed to encode most modern and historic languages. Each character is stored in 16 bits. Most users are probably familiar with the ASCII character set, which uses 7 bits to define each character. Unicode uses the extra bits to add many language-specific characters and to provide diacritics. Diacritics are symbols used to show how a word is accented. Many non-English languages use diacritics. Java programs are written in Unicode, and all strings and characters are stored as 16-bit Unicode characters.

Will you have to learn a new character set? The answer is no. Rest assured that Unicode will not greatly affect your programming. If you program in English, you can continue programming as you already do. The Java compiler will convert any ASCII file into an equivalent Unicode file. Furthermore, your source files won't be affected by the change to Unicode.

Sun's decision to use Unicode has no significant effect on the average programmer. Certain items may take up more memory—specifically, all strings will be twice as large. This might seem bad, but remember that Java is not designed to be superefficient in speed or memory. It's designed to make Internet programming easier and to make programs portable. These advantages make the extra memory requirements somewhat inconsequential. Be aware that characters take up more space, but don't stress over the fact. When you move on to internationalizing your product, you'll stop cursing and soon begin to sing.

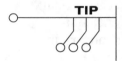

TIP

If you would like more information on Unicode, point your Web browser to http://unicode.org. Here you will find information about the Unicode standard, how to get hard copies of the standard, and membership information for the organization.

Comments

Java supports C-style comments and adds a new style for automatically creating online documentation. It doesn't matter which commenting style you use; they will all have the same effect. Any information specified by commenting characters will not be processed by the compiler.

The common C-style comments are as follows:

- /* text */
  All enclosed text is ignored. This can span multiple lines.

- // text
  All text following // to the end of the line will be ignored.

Java has added a third commenting style, which is used in automatic program documentation. These comments are processed by javadoc, a program supplied with the Java language that creates Web pages describing your code. The comments supplied in this new format are included in the Web pages. Comments used in automatic documentation use the following format:

```
/** text */
```

This documents a coming variable or method.

Every language designer is faced with decisions about comment nesting and other compiler issues. It seems that each language handles comments in its own way, and Java is no exception. The rules dealing with comments are as follows:

- Comments cannot be nested.

- Comments cannot occur within string or character literals.

- The notations /* and */ have no special meaning inside // comments.

- The notation // has no special meaning in comments beginning with /* or /**.

One example will serve to explain what all these rules mean. The following will be treated as one legal comment:

```
/* Normal Comment with // /* /** characters inside.  It ends
here */
```

Keywords

Every language has a group of words that the compiler reserves for its own use. These *keywords* cannot be used as identifiers in your programs. Table 4-1 lists the keywords reserved for the Java compiler. Those items marked with an asterisk are reserved for future use. Some, such as const and goto, are reserved for better error messages, and others indicate concepts that Sun may include in later versions of the language.

Java Keywords				
abstract	do	implements	package	throw
boolean	double	import	private	throws
break	else	*inner	protected	transient
byte	extends	instanceof	public	try
case	final	int	*rest	*var
*cast	finally	interface	return	void
catch	float	long	short	volatile
char	for	native	static	while
class	*future	new	super	
*const	*generic	null	switch	
continue	*goto	operator	synchronized	
default	if	*outer	this	

Table 4-1: *At the time of this printing, items marked with an asterisk are reserved for future use.*

Data Types

A variable can be one of four kinds of data types: classes, interfaces, arrays, and primitive types. At compile time, the compiler classifies each variable as either a reference or a primitive value. A *reference* is a pointer to some object. Classes, interfaces, and arrays are stored as references. *Primitive types* are data types that include integers, floating point numbers, characters, and booleans. Primitive data types are stored directly; their size is easily determined and never changes.

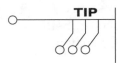

TIP   *For information on primitive types, see the next section, "Primitive Data Types." For information about the reference types, see the sections, "Classes & Interfaces" and "Arrays."*

Primitive Data Types

Primitive types are the heart of any programming language. They are the types the compiler specifically knows about; every element of a user-defined type can be decomposed to a primitive type. They are building blocks that will be required in all but the simplest program. Let's explore each primitive type and see what the Java language is made of.

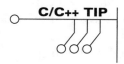

C/C++ TIP *The Java designers have already defined the sizes for each data type. There are no machine-dependent sizes for a type as in C and C++, so there is no need for a sizeof function. Finally, a glimmer of hope for true portability!*

Integers

An *integer* is a whole number with no fractional value. It can be modified only in whole increments. Most computer operations are done on integer values. The integer type is further identified by its size. A Java integer can range from 8 bits to 64 bits. The type of integer you use determines its minimum and maximum values. Java doesn't support unsigned types, so you may need to use a type you don't ordinarily use. Table 4-2 shows characteristics of each integer type.

Name	Size (bits)	Minimum	Maximum
byte	8	–128	127
short	16	–32768	32767
int	32	–2147483648	2147483647
long	64	–9223372036854775808	9223372036854775807

Table 4-2: *Integer types.*

Integer literals can be represented in a program in one of three bases: You can enter them in base 10 decimal, base 16 hexadecimal, or base 8 octal. All numbers are assumed to be in decimal unless otherwise specified. All literals are of the type int, unless you cast them to other values or end them in the letter *l*, meaning "long."

A hexadecimal digit can range from 0 to 15. A digit in a decimal system ranges from 0 to 9. To represent the numbers from 10 to 15 in one digit, a letter is used. The letters *a* through *f* represent 10 through 15 respectively. Hexadecimal numbers are used frequently to specify large numbers or to represent binary coded values. Since each digit can represent 16 possible values, a large number can be written in a more compact form.

Take, for example, the number 32767, represented in the decimal system. This is the largest value possible for a short. It would be represented in hexadecimal by 0x7FFF. Any time you wish to use a hexadecimal number, you must preface it with 0x. The case of the letters is not significant.

An octal digit ranges from 0 to 7. A number in the octal system is specified by a leading zero followed by zero or more octal digits. For instance, 32767 in decimal would be represented as 077777 in octal. The leading zero tells the compiler to expect an octal number.

Integers exhibit a property called *wrapping*. If you try to increment or decrement an integer so that it overflows or underflows, the number will wrap. Consider a byte with a value of 127. If you increment this byte by 1, its value will be –128. That's right—the number went from the largest positive to the smallest negative number. The reverse would happen if you subtracted 1 from –128. Know what range of numbers you want to support, and choose an integer of the appropriate size.

Floating Points

Java implements single and double precision floating point numbers as specified in *IEEE Standard for Binary Floating-Point Arithmetic*. Two forms are supported: a float and a double. A *float* is a 32-bit single precision floating point number. A *double* is stored in 64 bits and is a double precision number.

In addition to storing a value, a floating point can have a few specially defined states: negative infinity, negative zero, positive zero, positive infinity, and not-a-number (NaN). Since these values are defined by the Java language, you can check for them in your code. Generally, they will only occur in special situations—for example, when zero is divided by zero. The result is specified as NaN and can be explicitly checked for. Error checking is much easier when the language supports these states.

All floating point literals are assumed to be of type double unless otherwise specified. To make a number a 16-bit float, follow it with the letter *f*. This will tell the compiler that you want this literal stored as a float. Since Java enforces type checking, you will have to do this to initialize a floating point variable.

The following code fragment will generate a compiler error due to a type mismatch:

```
float num = 1.0;
```

Since all floating point literals are assumed to be doubles, you need to specify that this is a float literal by placing an *f* after the value. The corrected code from above is:

```
float num = 1.0f;
```

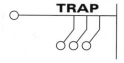

TRAP

One cautionary note about floating points: using them in control statements can be confusing. Two floating point numbers can be equal for many decimal places, but if they are not exactly equal, they will cause bugs by not evaluating as equal. Comparing floats in an if statement or using a floating pointer variable as a loop counter is a sure way to decrease speed and create subtle bugs.

Characters

Characters are implemented using the Unicode standard (see "Identifiers & Unicode" earlier in this chapter), meaning that each character is stored in 16 bits. Unicode allows you to store many different nonprinting or foreign characters. To specify a character

literal, you can use either a normal character or a Unicode escape sequence. In either method, you'll need to enclose the value in a pair of single quotes.

Unicode escape sequences can be specified using two methods. The first format will be familiar to C/C++ programmers. You can specify commonly used escape sequences by a backslash (\) followed by a letter from Table 4-3.

Escape	Function	Unicode
\b	Backspace	\u0008
\t	Horizontal Tab	\u0009
\n	Linefeed	\u000a
\f	Form Feed	\u000c
\r	Carriage Return	\u000d
\"	Double Quote	\u0022
\'	Single Quote	\u0027
\\	Backslash	\u005c

Table 4-3: *Unicode escape sequences.*

You can also specify escape sequences typing **\u** followed by a four-digit hexadecimal number (the specific Unicode number assigned for the character you want). The number can range from \u0000 to \u00ff. A few examples of character literals are:

- 'a'—The character *a*.
- '\n'—Escape shorthand for linefeed.
- '\\'—Escape shorthand for backslash.
- '\u0042'—Unicode escape sequence.

Booleans

Booleans are variables that have two states: true or false. The only way to assign a value to a boolean variable is with the literals, true and false. Unlike with C, you cannot assign integers to a boolean.

To simulate C's automatic type conversion, you can compare the integer to 0. The C language states that 0 is false and all other values are true. In converting the integer *i* to a boolean, you might use the following Java code:

```
int i;
boolean b;

b = (i != 0);
```

Here, we are using the not-equals operator to see if *i* is equal to zero. The parentheses are required for the expression to evaluate in the proper order.

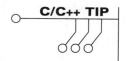

C/C++ TIP

Booleans are an important concept in Java. There are many language constructs, such as loops and if statements, that accept only boolean expressions. They are easy to understand, but if you are used to C-style expressions, booleans may take some getting used to.

Primitive Data Type Conversion

Converting between two primitive data types is a common practice. The trick to converting one variable to another is making sure you understand what is going on. If you're not careful, you might lose information or get a result you were not expecting.

Java enforces strict type checking. The compiler will not automatically convert from one type to another. You need to explicitly convert to another type by using a mechanism called a *type cast*, which will tell the compiler to convert from one type to another.

In Java, type casts are done the same way they are done in C/C++. You specify a type name by enclosing it in parentheses. If the type conversion is supported, the result of the computation or assignment will be the typed value. Suppose you have two variables, shortVar and intVar (shortVar is of type short; intVar is of type int). There are two possible type conversions between these types:

```
short shortVar=0;
int intVar=0;

intVar = shortVar;
shortVar = intVar;  // Incompatible type for equals
```

When this code is compiled, assigning shortVar to intVar results in an incompatible type error. You are trying to assign a larger variable (intVar, of type int) to a smaller variable (shortVar, of type short). This type of conversion is called a *narrowing conversion*, in which you try to convert to a type that contains fewer bits than the original. When performing a narrowing conversion, you may lose magnitude or precision information. Java makes you explicitly state that you understand this may happen: you must type cast all narrowing conversions. This is another case in which the Java language tries to force good programming conventions. Any time you lose bits, for instance, by converting from a long (64 bits) to an int (32 bits), you must make an intelligent decision about handling the lost magnitude information. If you are sure that the long won't be too large, use a cast; otherwise, you'll need to write some code to inform the user of the lost magnitude information.

The code we presented above can be made to work by adding a type cast. The correct code would be:

```
short shortVar=0;
int intVar=0;

intVar = shortVar;
shortVar = (short) intVar;
```

The compiler will now allow you to make the assignment. The integer, intVar, will be converted to a short by dropping the high-order bits while preserving the sign of the number. In this case, we are going from a 32-bit integer to a 16-bit short. The upper 16 bits will be lost.

Table 4-4 shows the possible primitive type conversions in Java. An entry of *C* means that you must use an explicit cast, or you will get a compiler error. An *L* means that you may lose magnitude or precision in the conversion. An *X* means this type of conversion is not allowed in Java.

Original Type	Destination Type							
	byte	short	int	long	float	double	char	boolean
byte							C	X
short	C, L						C	X
int	C, L	C, L					C, L	X
long	C, L	C, L	C, L		C, L	C	C, L	X
float	C, L	C, L	C, L	C, L			C, L	X
double	C, L	C, L	C, L	C, L	C, L		C, L	X
char	C, L	C	C	C	C	C		X
boolean	X	X	X	X	X	X	X	

Table 4-4: *Primitive type conversions.* C *means you must use an explicit cast;* L *means that you may lose magnitude or precision;* X *means Java doesn't permit this type of conversion.*

Floating Point to Integer

When converting from a floating point number to any integer type, you will lose all fractional information. Java truncates the value by rounding toward zero. It will then convert the resulting integer by dropping or adding bits as needed.

Double to Floating Point

A conversion from a double to a float will round according to IEEE 754 round-to-nearest mode. Values that have too large a magnitude will result in either positive or negative infinity. NaN (Not a Number) will always convert to NaN.

Boolean to or from Any Type

No type may be converted to or from a boolean variable. If you want to convert from an integer to a boolean or a boolean to a string, you must manually convert these values. You might use the following code:

```
boolean bool;
int i=15;
String st=null;

if (i == 0) bool = false; else bool = true;
if (bool) st = "true"; else st = "false";
```

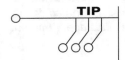

TIP

For information about converting reference data types *(classes, interfaces, and arrays), see "Objects" later in this chapter.*

Variable Declaration

A *variable* in Java can be a primitive type, an object, or an interface. Variables may be created in any position that would be appropriate for a statement. Any variable declaration can be followed by an initialization statement, which sets an initial value for the variable.

As we've seen in earlier examples, defining a variable is an easy task. Let's define and initialize some Java variables:

```
int i=42;
String st="Hello World";
float pi=3.14f;
boolean cont;
```

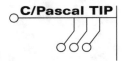

C/Pascal TIP

Notice that we said a variable can be created in any position that is appropriate for a statement. It isn't necessary to put your variable declarations first—you can put them where you use the variable.

Scoping

Every variable declaration has a *lifetime*, or *scope*, that is based on where the variable is declared. When you place a block of code within curly braces {}, you have defined a new *scoping level*. The scoping level determines when a variable is deallocated and where it is accessible. A variable is only accessible if it was declared in the current scope block or declared by one of its parents.

When you leave a scoping level, any variables declared in that block become inaccessible. They may or may not become deallocated, since the rules for deallocation are a little more complex than those for accessibility. When a variable is declared, it has space allocated for it. When the current scope block is ended, the variable is available for deallocation. It's up to the garbage collector to decide when a variable is actually deallocated. This will happen only when there are no more references to the variable. So, for primitive data types, deallocation will occur when the scope block ends. For reference variables, it might be sometime later.

Scoping rules are easier to understand if you think of them as branches on a tree—each new block creates a new branch in the tree. The more levels of blocks there are, the taller the tree will be. Let's take a piece of code and draw its scoping tree:

```
class foo {
    int cnt;

    public void test1 {
        int num;
    }

    public void test2 {

        for(int cnt=0; cnt < 5; cnt++) {
            System.out.println(cnt);
        }
    }
}
```

Figure 4-1 shows the scoping tree for the preceding code.

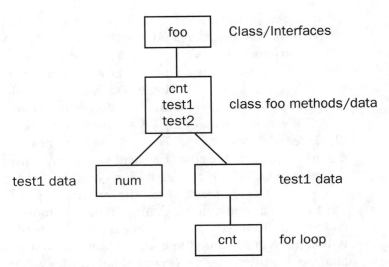

Figure 4-1: *Scoping tree.*

Notice that each new block creates a new scoping entry. We start at the package level, where all the classes and interfaces are declared. At the next level, we have the class variables and the method names for the class. Each class method starts its own scoping level, and its local variables are defined there. Notice, in particular, the case of the method test2: It has no local variables declared in the first scope, but the *for* loop creates a new scope and defines a variable called cnt. This variable shadows the previous declaration of cnt on the class level.

For non-C programmers, the *for* loop may be new. We will explain *for* loops and many other loop constructions in the "Control Flow" section later in this chapter.

Having multiple levels of scoping creates the ability to *shadow*, or hide, other variables. Let's say you created a class variable cnt. Then, in a method for the class, you also created a variable cnt. The new variable would shadow, or hide, the existence of the class variable cnt. Any references in the method to cnt would be to the newly created local variable. To access the class variable cnt, you would use a predefined class variable called *this*. The *this* variable is just a reference to the class. Any time you need to access a shadowed variable, use the *this* variable to point to the shadowed class variable. In our example, we could access the class variable cnt in the following way:

```
this.cnt = 4;
```

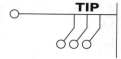

TIP

As a general rule, it's best to avoid shadowing a variable. If you must shadow it, you will have to live without the class declaration or use the this *variable to access it.*

Variable Naming

A variable name must start with a letter. It can be of unlimited length and consist of letters, digits, and any punctuation character except the period. A variable cannot duplicate any other identifiers on the same level of scoping. This means that you can't have a variable with the same name as:

❧ a label;

❧ another variable defined on the same level; or

❧ a parameter to a method.

If you're using the Unicode character set to provide foreign language support, then you need to be aware of how Java handles character comparisons. An identifier will be equal to another if it has the exact same sequence of Unicode characters. This means that a Latin capital A (\u0041) is distinct from a Greek capital A (\u0391) and all other representations of the letter A. It follows, then, that the Java language is case-sensitive—a capital A has a different value then a lowercase a.

Operators

Java supports a wide range of *operators*. An operator is a symbol used to perform a particular function on one or more variables. Some common operators are plus (+), minus (–), and equals (=).

Operators are classified by the number of arguments they accept. Some operators, such as minus, have different meanings based on whether they have one or two operands.

.	[]	()		
++	—	!	~	instanceof
*	/	%		
+	-			
<<	>>	>>>		
<	>	<=	>=	
==	!=			
&				
^				
&&				
||				
?:				
=	op=			
,				

Table 4-5: *Operator precedence. The order of precedence is from top to bottom. Items in the same row are of equal precedence.*

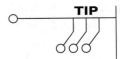
TIP

The operator op= is shorthand for the a class of equality operators. An example is +=.

An *expression* is a combination of operators and operands. The evaluation of an expression is governed by a set of precedence rules. To say that one operator has precedence over another means that it will be evaluated first. A common example from grade school mathematics is the difference between addition and multiplication. We can scan the expression x = 2 + 4 * 3 and know that x equals 14, not 18. The multiplication operator is evaluated before the plus operator.

For complicated expressions, you are better off just using parentheses to denote the order of operations. Not only will you be sure it's correct, but other programmers will appreciate your clarity. Table 4-5 is provided to answer questions of precedence. Items that appear on the same line are of equal precedence and will be evaluated from left to right.

Operators That Act on Numbers

Operators that act on numbers fall into two categories: *unary* operators, which act on one variable, and *binary* operators, which act on two. The binary operators can be further divided into those that compute a numerical result and those that are used to compare values.

The result of an operator will always be of the same type as the largest operand. Let's say that we are adding two numbers—one a short, the other a long. The result of the addition would be a long. Table 4-6 shows how this works. Notice that the smallest result returned for integers is an int. Any number added to a floating point number will be a float or double. Now that we know what the resultant type will be, let's examine the unary operators.

Type 1	Type2	Resultant
byte	byte	int
byte	short	int
byte	int	int
byte	long	long
short	short	int
short	int	int
short	long	long
int	int	int
int	long	long
int	float	float
int	double	double
float	float	float
float	double	double

Table 4-6: *Operator resultant.*

Unary Operators

A *unary* operator takes one operand as its parameter. The operation is performed, and the result is placed in the operand. The resulting type will always be the same as the original type, and there is no chance of a loss of precision or magnitude. Table 4-7 lists the unary operators in Java.

Operator	Description
–	Unary Minus
+	Unary Plus
~	Bitwise Complement
++	Increment
—	Decrement

Table 4-7: *Unary operators.*

Some possible unary expressions are:

- i++
- -i
- ~i

Unary Minus & Plus   The *unary minus* operator (–) is used to change the sign of a number. A negative number becomes positive, and a positive number becomes negative. The unary plus operator actually performs no work. It is there for completeness.

Integer negation can be thought of as subtraction from zero. This holds true for all but the largest negative numbers; unary minus has no effect on these numbers. The reason for this is that the negative numbers have one more value than the positive numbers. To illustrate this, let's look at a piece of code. It will output a possibly unexpected result of –128:

```
byte i=-128;

System.out.println(-i);
```

When dealing with floating point numbers, there are a few extra considerations. A number with the value of NaN will still be NaN afterward. Positive and negative zero will do as expected and change sign. This also holds true with positive and negative infinity.

Bitwise Complement   The *bitwise complement* operator only works on integer type variables. It looks at an integer on the bit level, where it changes 0s to 1s and 1s to 0s. If you were performing this operation on a variable named x, then ~x would be equivalent to (–x) – 1. Those not familiar with bit-level manipulations may have never seen this operator. It is more commonly used when looking at a variable as a collection of separate bits than as a complete number. This operator will flip each bit. If you have an integer that represents the value 0, then its complement would be 65535.

Increment & Decrement   The *increment* and *decrement* operators are shorthand for adding and subtracting 1. They can be placed either before or after a variable. The placement determines whether it is a prefix or a postfix operator.

A prefix operator will return the value of its operand after evaluating the expression. A postfix operator returns the operand and then performs the evaluation. Let's look at a piece of code to see this concept in action:

```
int i=0;
int j=0;

System.out.println(++i);
System.out.println(j++);
```

The output of this program will be 1 and then 0. In the first print statement, we've used a prefix operator. The variable *i* will be incremented, and then it will be printed. In the second case, the variable *j* will be printed and then incremented. Note that in both cases, *i* and *j* will be equal to 1 at the end.

Binary Operators

The *binary* operators take two operands, perform an operation, and return a result. The result is the same type as the largest operand. Adding a byte and an int will result in an int. The operation will not affect the variables involved. We can divide the binary operators into those that compute some numerical value and those that compare two numbers. Those that compute numerical results are listed in Table 4-8.

Operator	Description
+	Addition
-	Subtraction
*	Multiplication
/	Division
%	Modulus
&	Bitwise AND
|	Bitwise OR
^	Bitwise XOR
<<	Signed Left Shift
>>	Signed Right Shift
>>>	Unsigned Right Shift
op=	Combination assignment and operation

Table 4-8: *Binary computation operators.*

Additive Operators   The *additive* operators are + and –. If either operand is a floating point number, they will both be treated as floating points. Any integer types besides a long will be converted to an int. This means that the additive operators will never return a byte or short value. To assign the result to a byte or short, you'll have to use an explicit cast.

Java follows IEEE rules for floating point addition and subtraction. This does what you expect, but you might need to check the *Java Language Specification* for information on how Java handles special cases, such as adding two infinite numbers.

Multiplicative Operators   The *multiplicative* operators are *, /, and %.
They convert operands in a manner similar to that of the additive
operators. Operations on integers are associative, except for
operations on floating point numbers. For example, imagine we
have two floating point numbers. One is positive 1; the other is the
largest representable positive number:

```
float one = 1f;
float max = 2^24e104;
```

Given this setup, the following expression would not be true:

one + max − one == max − one + one

In the first case, we are adding 1 to the largest representable
float. This will cause an overflow, and the result of that sub-
expression will be positive infinity. Subtracting 1 from infinity still
produces infinity, so the result of the left-hand expression is
positive infinity. The right-hand expression subtracts 1 from the
max, then adds 1, yielding a value of max.

The remainder (%), or *modulus*, operator is defined such that
(a/b) * b + (a%b) = a. This operator does what you expect—it
gives you a positive result when the dividend is positive and a
negative result when a negative operand is used. The result is
always less than the magnitude of the divisor.

An example of the modulus operator and its behavior is:

```
int i=10;
int j=4;
int k=-4;

System.out.println(i % j); // = 2
System.out.println(i % k); // = -2
```

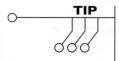

TIP

*The behavior of the Java modulus operator is different than specified
by IEEE 754. If you want to use that definition, you can access it
from the math library as Math.IEEEremainder.*

Bitwise Operators The *bitwise* operators are used to perform operations concerned with how a number is represented in bits. They only make sense when dealing with integer numbers. Floating point numbers are not simple encodings of bits; therefore the bitwise operations would not make sense on floating points. It is common practice to use the bitwise operators and the and (&) , or (|), and xor (^) operators to check individual bits of an integer.

Let's assume we are using each bit of a byte to store a flag. We can store eight flags—one for each bit. In the following code, we'll show you some common bit-manipulation operations:

```
byte flags=0xff;    // Initialize to 11111111
byte mask=0xfe;     // Set mask to    11111110

flags = flags & mask; // Set position 8
flags = flags | mask;  // Clear position 8
flags = flags ^ mask;  // = 00000001
```

C/C++ PROGRAMMERS
Java does not support bit fields. You can either use the java.util.BitSet class or use bit masks to access individual bits.

Shift Operators Java supports three *shift* operators—left shift (<<), right shift (>>), and the unsigned right shift (>>>). The form for all shift operations is a shift expression, the shift operator, and the distance to shift. The shift expression must be an integer type. If you want to perform a shift operation on a floating point number, you'll have to perform an explicit conversion.

The signed shift operators will preserve the sign on the operand. The unsigned right-shift operator will use zero-extension. (*Zero-extension* means that it will replace each shifted position with a zero, ignoring the sign bit.) Shifting by a value of zero is allowed, but it serves no purpose.

Using the shift operators, we can perform an easy integer division by 2. A right shift will cause a loss of 1 bit. Right-shifting by 1 is equivalent to dividing the number by 2. For odd numbers, this operation will round down:

```
int i = 128; // This is 10000001 in binary

i = i >> 1;  // Now this is 10000000 or 64
```

Combination Assignment Operators   Some operators can be combined into a combination shorthand that does the operation and then assigns the result to the operand. The operators that can be combined in this manner are those that perform a numerical computation—that is, all the Java operators except the relational operators (see "Relational Operators" below).

You need to be aware of how operands are loaded when using combination operators. If you change the resultant variable in the combination expression, it will not affect the result. This concept is best shown with a code example:

```
int i =0;

i += ++i;
```

You might think the code would yield a value of 2. The outcome may surprise you. First, *i* is loaded into a register. The expression ++i is calculated, assigned back to *i*, and used as the second operand to the plus operator. When the two operands are added together we get 0, the original value of *i*, and 1. This results in a value of 1.

Relational Operators   In addition to numerical computing operators, there is a group of operators that compare two values. They are *relational* operators—they take two parameters and return a boolean result stating their relationships. The relational operators in Java are described in Table 4-9.

Operator	Description
<	Less than
>	Greater than
<=	Less than or equal to
>=	Greater than or equal to
==	Equal to
!=	Not equal to

Table 4-9: *Relational operators.*

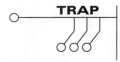

There is a common pitfall when using the relational operators. Invariably, programmers use a single equals sign instead of a double equals sign in a statement. A single equals sign is used to assign one value to another. A double equals sign is used to compare two numbers. Unlike with C/C++, Java will catch this error, but it is much easier not to make the mistake in the first place.

Boolean Operators

Boolean operations are very similar to comparable operations on numbers. All of the boolean operators will return booleans as their result. For a list of the boolean operators in Java, see Table 4-10.

Operator	Description
!	Negation
&	Logical AND
|	Logical OR
^	Logical XOR
&&	Conditional AND
||	Conditional OR
==	Equal to
!=	Not equal to
op=	Combination assignment and operation
?:	Conditional operator

Table 4-10: *Boolean operators.*

The conditional operator is the only ternary operator in the Java language. The operator's format is a:b?c. Expression *a* is evaluated for a boolean result. If it is true, then *b* is returned; if not, *c* is returned. Basically, it is an *if* statement. There are two ways to write a piece of code:

```
int i;
boolean cont=false;

// Conventional if statement
if (cont) i=5;
else i=6;

// Using the short hand
i = (cont:5?6);
```

The above code is setting the value of *i* to either 5 or 6 based on some boolean variable cont. When cont is true, *i* is set to 5; when it is false, *i* is set to 6. The conditional operator gives us a shorthand way to achieve this.

Character Operations

There are no operators that return a character result. Most of the operators we've discussed return an integer type. If you wish to perform an operation on a character, you will have to cast the result back to a character. When a character is an operand to an operator, it will be converted to an int. This is a simple conversion that will not lose any information.

Suppose we wanted to convert a character from uppercase to lowercase. The integer value of the character *A* is 98 in both ASCII and Unicode. A lowercase *a* has a value of 65. If we take an uppercase letter and subtract the difference between 98 and 65, we will get a lowercase letter. Let's use this principle and a bit of Java code to illustrate character operations:

```
char c='B';

c = (char) c - ('A' - 'a');
```

Operators That Act on Objects

Objects in Java support the following operators: =, ==, !=, and instanceof. Generally, operations such as adding two objects together make no sense. The only time this type of operation is allowed is in the special case of string addition.

The assignment operator (=) is used to assign an object pointer to a reference variable. This does not create a copy of the object. Instead, after using the equals operator, the reference variable will point to the operand. When all references to an object go out of scope, the object will become available for garbage collection. Assuming that we have a class called foo, the following code shows the use of the equals operator:

```
foo test = new foo();
foo test2 = null;

test2 = test;
```

In the above code, we have shown the valid uses of the equals operator when dealing with objects. The first line illustrates its use when creating a new instance of an object. The new command returns a reference to a newly created object. In the second line, we assign test2 to null. Test2 now references no object, and any attempt to use test2 will create a NullPointerException. The last line assigns test2 to test. Now both reference variables are pointing to the same object.

Objects support two comparison operators: the equals operator (==) and the not equals operator (!=). These operators test to see whether the objects in question reside in the same place in memory. They don't test each individual component of an object for equality. Two objects with the exact same contents that are different instances will not be equal to each other. For example, we have two instances of some class foo that are defined as follows:

```
foo test = new foo();
foo test2 = new foo();
foo test3 = test;
```

Using these definitions, we can create a table of equality relationships between each reference variable. Table 4-11 will show you which operator, equals or not equals, you would use to get a result of true.

	test	test2	test3
test	==	!=	==
test2	!=	==	!=
test3	==	!=	==

Table 4-11: *Object equality.*

The instanceof operator is used to determine the runtime type of an object. Its use is necessary because you can't determine a reference variable's type at compile time. For example, you might have a situation in which you have a class called shape. A subclass of shape is polygonShape. If you have a variable that holds a shape, how can you tell if it's a polygon? Let's look at a code fragment that would solve the problem:

```
shape shapeHolder;

if (shapeHolder instanceof polygonShape) {
    polygonShape polygon = (polygonShape) shapeHolder;

    // Do something with the polygon
    ...
}
```

In this example, we have some generic shape. If the shape is of a specific type, polygonShape, then we want to perform some operations on it. In order to access the member functions specific to polygonShape, we need to have a reference variable of the correct type.

The type of situation we've just described happens frequently when you are dealing with a data structure that holds objects that are subclasses of a common parent. Suppose we have an object-based paint program, and that we store all of the shapes the user has drawn in a data structure. To print this data, we will need a loop that will traverse our data structure and print each shape. If a particular shape needs special instruction in order to print, we will need to use the instanceof operator.

Operators That Act on Strings

As we explain in the "Strings" section of this chapter, the string class in Java is a hybrid of a primitive type and an object. It looks like an object to the user, but special cases have been included in the compiler for strings, creating a somewhat confusing dichotomy. There are a few pitfalls associated with operations with strings.

We said earlier that objects in Java do not support operators like plus and minus. Generally, these types of operations would make no sense. However, here are some objects (possibly a complex number object) for which it would be handy to have the option. In other languages, it's common to use operator overloading to define the meaning of operations on certain objects. By assigning some meaning to an operator, you can then use standard operators, like the plus operator, to perform operations on objects. But the authors of Java felt this made code harder to read and maintain, so they didn't include it. Their decision on this matter is somewhat controversial.

The most common use for operator overloading is with strings. So as a compromise, the Java authors overloaded the plus operator to include strings. If either operand of the plus operator is a string, the result will be the concatenation of both. If one of the operands is not a string, it will be converted to one. The string created from the operand follows the rules listed in Table 4-12.

Operand	Rule
Null Variables	Any variable whose value is null will result in a string of "null."
Integer	An integer will be converted to a string representing its decimal notation, preceded by a – sign if negative. There will be no leading zeros, and if the value is 0, the string 0 will be returned.
Floating Point	Floating point numbers will be converted to a string in a compact fashion. If it exceeds 10 characters in length, it will be represented in exponential form. If it is negative, it will be preceded by a – sign.
Character	A character will be converted to an equivalent string of length one.
Boolean	The result will either be "true" or "false" based on the boolean's value.
Objects	An objects toString() method will be called.

Table 4-12: *String creation rules.*

Once both operands are strings, the two will be concatenated. Let's look at a few examples that will illustrate this point:

```
String foo = "Hello ";
String bar = "World";
int i = 42;
boolean cont = false;
String result = null;

result = foo + bar;     // = "Hello World"
result = foo + i;       // = "Hello 42"
result = foo + cont;    // = "Hello false"
```

Adding the plus operator seems like a good move—for strings, it makes a lot of sense. But now let's ask ourselves a question: If they changed the plus operator, then what does the minus operator do? The answer is nothing. And what do the == and != operators do? Stumped? Try this piece of code:

```
String foo = "Hello";
String bar = "Hello";

if (foo == bar) System.out.println("Equal");
else System.out.println("Not Equal");
```

The code above will output equal. It makes sense, doesn't it? The two strings are equal, so the equals operator returns true. Let's recall how the equals operator for objects works. It checks to see whether two objects are in the same place in memory, not if their components are equal. Here is another piece of code using the equals operator:

```
class testString {
    String st = "Hello";
}

class testString2 {
    String st = "Hello";
    String st2 = "Hello";

    public static void main(String args[]) {

        testString test = new testString();
        testString2 test2 = new testString2();

        if (test.st == test.st2) System.out.println("Equal");
        else System.out.println("Not Equal");

        if (test.st == test2.st) System.out.println("Equal");
        else System.out.println("Not Equal");
    }
}
```

The output of this code might be bewildering. In the first case, it will return Equal; in the second, it will return Not Equal. This is because internally, the compiler has performed a space optimization. The variables st and st2 have only been allocated one instance between them. Again, it makes sense, since they're the same value. The problem is that this masks how the == operator really works.

You can't use the == operator to compare two strings. You must use the equals method of the string class. Using the class definitions from above, we could rewrite the main method correctly as follows:

```
public static void main(String args[]) {

    testString test = new testString();
    testString2 test2 = new testString2();

    if (test.st.equals(test.st2))
       System.out.println("Equal");
    else
       System.out.println("Not Equal");

    if (test.st.equals(test2.st))
          System.out.println("Equal");
    else
       System.out.println("Not Equal");
  }
}
```

For further discussion of the String class, see "Strings" in this chapter and Chapter 6, "Discovering the Application Programming Interface."

Packages

A *package* is an organizational tool provided with the Java language. Conceptually, a package is a grouping of related classes and interfaces. You are already familiar with a package, namely, java.lang. This package provides most of the functionality of the Java language. The Application Programming Interface (API) classes are grouped together as packages. They comprise a powerful tool that will allow you to make your own code libraries.

A package is stored in one or more source files. Each source file needs to have the package declaration at the top. Only one public class may be placed in each source file. When the source files are compiled, the class files will be placed in directories based on the package name, which is simply the directory path, with dots instead of slashes. Thus, if we wanted to create a package in the directory ventana/awt/shapes, we would use the following package command at the top of each source file:

```
package ventana.awt.shapes;
```

Packages are important for implementing code libraries, and they will be covered in greater detail in Chapter 10, "Advanced Program Design."

Import

Once we have a package, how do we go about accessing its classes and interfaces? One method is to use a class' full name. Let's say we have implemented the shapes package above and it contains two classes, a circle and a rectangle. If we want to create a new instance of the circle class, we can use the following code:

```
ventana.awt.shapes.circle circ = new ventana.awt.shapes();
```

Accessing classes using their full names can be tedious. Java's import statement makes it easier. When you import a package, you gain a shorthand convention for its classes and interfaces. Let's import the circle class from the shapes package and see what we have gained:

```
import ventana.awt.shapes.circle;

class tryShapes {
    public static void main(String args[]) {
        circle circ = new circle();
    }
}
```

This option is significantly easier and requires much less typing. This is how you will access all the code that Java provides you. First you import the packages you want to use, and then you use the short form for the class and interface names.

There is one other shortcut available for dealing with classes. If you're working with a package that has many classes and interfaces, it would be a drag to have to list each class you wanted to use. You can use a form of wildcards in your import statement by specifying, at the end of the statement, an asterisk instead of a class or interface name. This says to import all classes and interfaces into that package. To access all the members of the shapes package, we would use an import statement like this:

```
import ventana.awt.shapes.*;
```

Don't worry about this increasing your code size. It only loads the package's contents into the compiler's symbol table, which is basically a big dictionary the compiler uses to look up references in your program. You can use the long form or the short form. Both are correct, so the choice is yours.

C/C++ Users

The import statement is similar to the C/C++ #include compiler directive. An important distinction is that the import statement generates no code; it is simply a programming convenience. The #include directive is equivalent to pasting the included code into the current source file. Java does not allow this type of operation. You should *inherit* functionality, not copy it.

Classes

We have declared classes in the previous chapters. Now we will cover the nuts and bolts of the syntax. This discussion will introduce you to new material and serve as a reference as you progress to more advanced topics. If the concept of objects is new to you, please read Chapter 3, "Object Orientation in Java." Without an understanding of objects, the rest of this book will make little sense.

The *class* is the fundamental building block for Java programs. It is composed of data and methods. The methods define ways to modify and interact with the encapsulated data. By making one unit contain both the data and the ways to modify it, we increase our code's reusability and make maintenance much easier.

Constructors

In Java, a *constructor* must be called in order to create a new instance of an object. The constructor for a class is a method with the name of the class and no return type. You can have multiple constructors, but they must each have a unique signature, consisting of the number and type of parameters. The names of the parameters make no difference in the constructor's signature. Having two constructors with the same parameter (a String, for instance), but with different names, is not valid. Let's look at a few constructor definitions:

```
class foo {
    foo() {...}              // No parameter constructor
    foo(int n) {...}         // Takes one int parameter
    foo(String s) {...}      // Take a string parameter
}
```

The constructors that each take one parameter are unique because the types are different. You could not have another constructor like foo(int i)— although the name is different, the type is not unique. The types or number of parameters must be unique.

Destructors

Each class may have one *destructor*. The destructor is called when the object is slated for garbage collection, so you can't be sure when the destructor will be called. This is a good place for closing files and releasing network resources. You wouldn't want to get user input or interact with other objects in this code.

The destructor in Java is called *finalize*. It has no return type and takes no parameters. We could add a destructor to our class foo with this code:

```
class foo {
    finalize() {...} // Do some cleanup code
}
```

Class Modifiers

Class declarations can be modified in three different ways—they can be declared abstract, final, or public. The modifiers go before the class keyword. We can specify a class foo with a class modifier in this way:

```
public final class foo {...}
```

A *public* class can be accessed from other packages. If a class is not public, it can only be accessed by the package in which it is declared. You can only declare one public class per package. Therefore, a source file can only contain one public class or interface.

The *final* modifier signifies that the class can't be extended. Some of the classes in the Java API are defined final. For example, the Array and String classes are final because they are hybrid classes. In other words, they are not fully objects, but have support code directly in the compiler. Generally, you want to avoid making a class final because then your class cannot be subclassed. This is not good object-oriented programming and means people will not be able to inherit your functionality. The final modifier is useful when dealing with native methods or other nonportable activities.

By declaring a class abstract, you are telling the compiler that one or more methods will be abstract. An *abstract* method is one that has no code and will be implemented in later subclasses. It can't be instantiated, but it can be extended. Each subclass of the abstract class must instantiate the abstract methods or be declared abstract themselves. This is useful for defining concepts and then allowing specific implementations to follow. A mechanism for declaring a whole class as abstract is called an *interface*. For more on interfaces, check out the "Interfaces" section later in this chapter, and see Chapter 3, "Object Orientation in Java."

The Extends Keyword

Inheritance relationships are created with the *extends* keyword. A class may extend, at most, one class. Hence, multiple inheritance is not explicitly supported. Through the use of interfaces, however, it's possible to mimic some features of multiple inheritance.

All objects in Java have the same parent object called Object. If you don't specify a parent object for a class, it will descend from the class Object by default. To specify a parent for a class, use the extends keyword. If we had already created a class foo, we could create a subclass bar by:

```
class bar extends foo {...}
```

A subclass inherits the methods and variables of a class. You can redefine or shadow a method or variable by creating an identifier with the same name. In order to access the shadowed identifiers, you can use the *super* variable. This variable points to a class's immediate parent. If foo had a method called test, and we shadowed it in bar, we would have to use this mechanism:

```
class bar extends foo {
    void test() {
        super.test(); // Call parents test(foo.test)

        ... // Do more work
    }
}
```

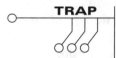

TRAP

When extending a class, you will get a compile-time error if you make a circular inheritance relationship. Class B cannot be a subclass of A if you have already made A a subclass of B.

Implements

A class can implement any number of interfaces. An *interface* is a class whose methods are all abstract. The *implements* keyword is the final component of a class declaration. The complete syntax for a class declaration is:

ClassModifiers class *ClassName* extends *ParentName* implements *InterfaceName* {...}

Everything but the class keyword and ClassName is optional. If a class implements an interface, it needs to provide code for the methods defined in the interface. The only exception to this rule is, if the class is abstract, its "children" are responsible for implementing the interface's methods.

If we had an interface called shapeInterface that had two methods, draw and erase, then we could define a class called shape that implements this interface:

```
class shape implements shapeInterface {
    void draw() {...}
    void erase() {...}
}
```

You can have a class implement multiple interfaces by separating the interfaces with commas. The programmer then must implement all the methods of each interface. If we had two interfaces, say shapeInterface and moveableInterface, then we could define a class, dragDrop, that implements both of these interfaces:

```
class dragDrop implements shapeInterface, moveableInterface
{...}
```

For a conceptual discussion of interfaces, see Chapter 3, "Object Orientation in Java." The syntax for interfaces can be found later in this chapter in the section, "Interfaces."

Variable Modifiers

When defining variables for a class, you can specify certain modifiers. These modifiers affect such things as which classes can access the variables, certain multithreading operations, and whether a variable is static or final. The variable modifiers are public, private, protected, static, final, transient, and volatile.

A variable can be declared public, protected, private protected, or private. A *public* variable can be accessed in the package in which it was declared and by any other packages. It is the least restrictive access modifier.

A *protected* variable in a class *C* is available to classes that are in the same package or that are subclasses of class *C*. This restricts classes outside of the package from accessing the variable, but it allows any subclasses of the class to access it.

If a variable in class C is defined as *private protected*, it can be accessed only from a subclass of C. It can't be accessed by other classes in the same package. So if no other classes in the package need access to a variable, this is the appropriate access modifier to use.

A *private* variable is only accessible by methods of the class in which it is defined. This is the most restrictive access modifier. Subclasses of the class cannot access the private variable.

Here is an example using all four of the access modifiers:

```
class circle {
    public String className;
    protected int x,y;
    private protected float radius;
    private int graphicsID;
}
```

If a variable is declared *static*, there is only one variable of that name for all instances of the object. The variable is allocated at compile-time, so you don't have to instantiate the class to access the variable. This is how the Math class in the java.lang package provides its constant variable PI. We can print this value like so:

```
System.out.println("PI:" + Math.PI);
```

The *final* modifier states that the variable's value cannot be changed. It must contain a variable initializer, and any attempt to modify the variable will result in a compile-time error. The final modifier is usually used to specify a constant. Constants are normally specified as public static final. We could declare a const for some class foo as:

```
class foo {
    public static final int Answer = 42;
}
```

The *transient* and *volatile* modifiers are part of the multithreading modifications to the language. They are primarily used for optimization purposes. A variable that is declared transient is not part of the persistent state of the object. The transient keyword will be used to implement some functions in later versions of the Java language.

A *volatile* variable is a variable that is known to be modified asynchronously. Volatile variables are reloaded and stored to memory after every use. These two modifiers are reserved for future use, but they are currently valid modifiers (for more on volatile variables, see Chapter 11, "Advanced Threading."

Method Modifiers

A method can be modified with the modifiers listed in Table 4-13. The public, protected, and private keywords function like the variable modifiers. They determine which classes can access the methods.

public	protected	private	static
abstract	final	native	synchronized

Table 4-13: *Method modifiers.*

The *static* modifier makes a method accessible even when the class isn't instantiated. A static method is implicitly declared final; therefore, you cannot override a static method. Inside a static method, you can access only members of the class that are also static.

An *abstract method* is one that will be implemented in a later subclass. If you make any method within a class abstract, the class is abstract and can't be instantiated. If all the methods of a class are to be abstract, you might consider defining the class as an interface.

A *final method* is one that cannot be overridden by a subclass. A private method is effectively a final method because it can't be overridden. An optimizing compiler might "inline" the method to increase speed. To "inline" a method is to copy the code to each reference in your program. This trades code space for speed and is a common practice in C++.

The *synchronized* keyword is used to mark a method as needing the class's monitor lock before it can be executed. We discuss synchronization and multithreading in Chapter 11, "Advanced Threading."

Method Overloading

If you wish to write code that handles various parameter types under the same name, you can overload a method. Usually, you overload a class's constructor so that it will accept many kinds of initialization information. You can overload almost any method, be it a constructor or a normal method. However, you cannot overload the class's destructor, since it takes no parameters and you can't control when or how it is called.

To overload a method, make another method, using the same name and return type but different parameters. Each overloaded method must be unique, and uniqueness is determined by the number of parameters and their types. Parameter names do not affect uniqueness. The following code will not compile:

```
class foo {
   foo(int i) {...} // will not compile
   foo(int j) {...} // Same number & type
}
```

The code above tried to have two methods that both take an int as their parameter. You can't have two overloaded methods that have the same number and type of parameters.

One important note about overloading—you need to know what type you are passing into a method. Consider the two methods declared below:

```
class foo {
   foo(int i) {}
   foo(byte j) {}
}
```

This code will compile, but look closely at what you have specified. If you pass a short or long into this method, it won't compile. Java won't perform any type conversions on overloaded methods. As we noted earlier, the lack of explicit type conversion is an important distinction between Java and C/C++.

Reference Variables Type Conversion

All references to objects and interfaces are done through *reference variables*, otherwise known as *pointers*. You may have heard that Java has no pointers, but that's not technically true. Java has no *pointer arithmetic*, but it still has pointers. In order to make Java a safer and more robust language, its designers decided that the only way to change where a reference variable points would be through an assignment statement.

It's easy to define a reference variable. Use the class or interface name you want to contain, but don't call the *new* operator. You can then assign this variable to an object or interface that has already been created. Let's define a reference variable to hold a class called myClass and one to hold an interface called shapes:

```
myClass myRef;
shapes myShapes;
```

There are rules for assigning values to a reference variable. You can always assign a reference variable to other references of the same type. A question arises when you try to assign it to another type, an interface, or an array. In some cases you can do it, in other cases you will need to type cast it, and in still others, it's just not possible. The rules for when Java will automatically convert it for you are somewhat complex. We will give you some guidance, but the Java Language Specification will have to be your ultimate authority on the subject.

If you create a reference variable of class *S*, you can assign the following types to it:

* A class *T* that is the same class as *S* or a subclass of *S*.

* An interface *T*, only if *S* implements *T*.

* An array *T* if *S* is of type Object.

If you create a reference variable of interface S, any assignments to S must implement S. Type consistency must be determined at runtime because a subclass of S might have implemented the interface.

It might be possible to use casts for other assignments. If you use a cast to assign values to reference variables, you may generate runtime errors. Make sure you know what this object will be at runtime; if you're not sure, be certain to catch the CastClassException.

Interfaces

An *interface* is equivalent to a class with all its methods declared abstract and its variables declared static and final. (For definitions of these terms, see "Variables Modifiers" in this chapter.) Every method is left unimplemented, and all variables are constants. Every variable within an interface must contain an initializer, and the variable may not be declared as transient or volatile. An interface's methods may not have the modifiers of final, native, static, or synchronized.

Any class that implements the interface will be responsible for coding the methods. An interface is primarily a conceptual model. It is helpful in the design of object hierarchies. Some code design methodologies design all of the interfaces and classes first, which helps prevent code integration problems. Later, the interfaces are implemented. Designs made in this manner are usually more general and can be more easily extended.

Defining an interface is very similar to defining a class. The major difference is use of the *interface* keyword instead of *class*. We can define an interface called shapeInterface that has two methods, draw and erase, as follows:

```
public interface shapeInterface {
    public void draw();
    public void erase();
}
```

We can now implement several different shapes that use this interface. Later, we'll be able to create data structures that contain variables of the type, shapeInterface. Regardless of the actual shape, we can access the interface's methods. The interface is a powerful design tool, and is especially useful for making code reusable and simpler to understand.

Arrays

An *array* is a hybrid primitive-object type. It looks like an object, but it has special meaning to the compiler. The Array class is declared final, so you will not be able to extend its functionality in an object of your own.

An array is commonly used to store a group of similar information. All items in an array must be of the same compile-time type. If the array is made up of primitive types, they must all be of the same type. If it consists of reference types, they must all point to a similar type.

An array is like an object in that you must use the *new* operator to instantiate each element. In this respect, Java arrays differ from the arrays implemented in most languages. In most languages, each element of the array is already initialized for you.

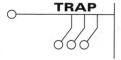

TRAP

Arrays in Java are significantly different from arrays in most languages. It will save you time in the long run to learn a little about them now. Don't assume that they act the same as arrays do in C or Pascal. If you have played with SmallTalk, then you are more familiar with Java-style arrays.

Array Creation

Arrays are initialized using the *new* operator. Think of each element in the array as a separate object. The array itself can be thought of as a container for all the objects, which gives them a common access point.

The simplest type of array is a one-dimensional array of a primitive type—for instance, an int. The code to create and initialize this array is:

```
int nums[] = new int[5];
```

Looking at this declaration, we can see most of the concepts important to declaring arrays. The brackets after the identifier, nums, tell the compiler that nums is an array. The new operator instantiates the new array and calls a constructor for each element. The constructor is of type int, and it can hold five elements. If you keep in mind that you can use constructors to create arrays, you'll have no problem with multidimensional arrays.

Arrays in Java must have at least one dimension specified. The rest can be determined at runtime. To create and initialize a two-dimensional array, we can use the following code:

```java
class tarray {
    public static void main(String args[]) {

        int numsList[][] = new int[2][];

        // Specify second dimension later

        numsList = new int[2][10];

        for(int i=0; i < 10 ;i++) {
            numsList[0][i] = i;
            numsList[1][i] = i;
        }

        for(int i=0; i < 10; i++) {
            System.out.print(numsList[0][i] + " ");
            System.out.println(numsList[1][i]);
        }
    }
}
```

This code creates an array called numsList, in which only one dimension is specified. We can then specify the second dimension. It's important to remember to call a constructor for each element of the array. We can use this feature of the language to create nonrectangular arrays. Take, for instance, the creation of a triangular array:

```
int[][] createArray(int n) {

    int[][] nums = new int[n][];

    for(i=0; i < n; i++) {
        nums[i] = new int[i+1];
    }
    return nums;
}
```

This code will create a triangular array of *n* elements. The first element will have one element, the second will have two elements, and the last will have *n* elements. This type of initialization creates many new applications for arrays. Where once a linked list or other dynamic data structure was needed, we can now use an array.

Array Initialization

Arrays can be initialized at the time of creation by enclosing the desired initial values within braces {}. You need not specify a size—Java will initialize the array to the number of elements specified. You can nest the initializers in order to initialize a multidimensional array.

Let's look at an easy example—a one-dimensional array. We want an array that contains the numbers from 1 to 5. We can initialize it in this manner:

```
int nums[] = {1,2,3,4,5};
```

Initializing a two-dimensional array requires nesting the initializers. We can create an array of arrays that contain an integer pair:

```
int nums[][] = {{1,1},{2,2},{3,3},{4,4},{5,5}};
```

As you've just seen, initializing one- and two-dimensional arrays is easy. You may find it harder to picture the multidimensional array. The syntax is the same; you just need to nest more levels of initializers. In practice, you will end up using loops to initialize multidimensional arrays.

Array Access

An array can be indexed by a byte, short, int, or char value. You cannot index arrays with a long, floating point, or boolean value. If you need to use one of these types, you will have to do an explicit conversion.

Arrays are indexed from zero to the length of the array minus one. You can determine the length of any array by looking at its length variable. We can use this variable to traverse an otherwise unknown length array:

```
long sum(int[] list) {

   long result=0;

   for(int i=0; i < list.length; i++) {
      result = result + list[i];
   }
   return result;
}
```

This code will sum an arbitrary length array of integers. It uses the length variable to determine the upper bounds for the array.

Java provides bounds checking. This means that each access to an array will be checked to make sure it is inside the array. If the index falls outside the array, an ArrayIndexOutOfBoundsException will be generated.

Arrays in Java are powerful, but you will pay for some of this power. Some compilers may optimize for rectangular arrays; others may not. Generally, any array that uses a different size for each element will have a slower access time. Again, you must weigh the benefits of a simple implementation with the loss of speed.

Control Flow

Most computer programs make decisions that affect their flow. The statements that make these decisions are called *control statements*. Among these are the familiar if-then statements and looping statements. All computer languages have control statements, and many of these should be familiar to you. We will cover each one in detail. If you're not a C programmer, you may find the switch statement a worthy addition to your repertoire. Before we go any further, let's summarize the control statements available in Java:

```
if (boolean) statement1;
else statement2;

for(expression; boolean; expression) statement;

while(boolean) statement;

do statement; while(boolean);

break label;
continue label;
return expression;

switch(expression) {
   case value : statement;
   ...
   default : statement;
}
```

If-Else Statement

The most commonly known control statement is the *if-else* statement. An expression is evaluated to generate a boolean result of true or false. A result of true will cause the first statement to be executed; false will cause the else portion to be executed. The else portion is optional: if you don't want to perform any action when the comparison is false, just leave off the else statement. The following is a simple example of the if-else statement:

```
if (done == true) System.out.println("Done");
else System.out.println("Continuing");
```

You can also string multiple if-else statements together. Each if statement will be evaluated until one is true. If none of the if statements is true, then the else statement will be executed. We might use this feature to print different messages based on an integer representing the current temperature in Celsius:

```
int temp;

if (temp < 0) System.out.println("Brr, it's freezing out");
else if (temp > 100) System.out.println("Water boiling?");
else System.out.println("Nice day isn't it!");
```

You may have noticed that only one statement is executed after an if statement. What if you needed to execute multiple statements? Java supports the concept of blocks. A block is a section of code that can be placed anywhere a statement is allowed. It is delineated by braces {}. Let's use this concept in another if-else example:

```
int itemCount;
boolean checkout;

if (itemCount <= 10) {
    System.out.println("Thank you, starting checkout");
    checkout = true;
}
else {
    System.out.println("Maximum 10 items in express lane!");
    checkout = false;
}
```

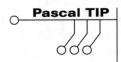
Pascal TIP

In Pascal, blocks are delineated by the begin/end pair. Java has adopted the C/C++ convention of using curly braces.

You need to be aware of one more issue concerning if-else statements—the problem of else statement ambiguities. A question sometimes arises as to which if an else statement belongs to. The following code exhibits this quality:

```
int checkCost, moneySaved;
boolean overDraft;

if (checkCost > moneySaved) // incorrectly coded
    if (overDraft == true)
        System.out.println("Overdraft enabled");
else System.out.println("Item purchased");
```

The example shown above, a simple check processing system, is incorrectly coded. Notice the else statement. It is indented as if it is to be part of the main loop. Unfortunately, this is not how the code will run. It's hard to tell which if statement the else is paired with. Else blocks are always associated with the last if block. If this is not what you want, you should enclose your code into separate blocks; doing so will ensure that the compiler and you know what will be executed. When it's rewritten to use blocks, the code looks like this:

```
int checkCost, moneySaved;
boolean overDraft;

if (checkCost > moneySaved) {
    if (overDraft == true) {
        System.out.println("Overdraft enabled");
    }
}
else System.out.println("Item purchased");
```

Proper use of blocks will make your code easier to read and possibly stop you from making subtle logic bugs. The if-else statement is a useful tool in programming, but you must be careful to clearly pair all if-else pairs.

While & Do-While Statements

The *while* and *do-while* statements are used for two special cases of looping. The while statement is used when you may not want the loop body to be executed. The comparison expression is evaluated before the loop is ever executed. When this expression is false, the

loop is exited. You must change the value of the loop variable inside the loop body; failure to do so will result in an endless loop. As is often the case, we have set a boolean variable someplace in our program, and we now wish to execute a piece of code based on its result. Let's assume we have a function named result, which returns a boolean value telling us whether we should continue:

```java
while( result() ) {
    // Execute some statements
    ...
}
```

This loop will execute until the function result returns false. If it initially returns false, the loop will never be executed. If we want the loop to execute at least once, we can use a do-while loop. This type of loop will execute once, regardless of its comparison expression. Using the same boolean function, result, we can rewrite the above code to execute a minimum of once:

```java
do {
    // Execute some statements
    ...
} while( result() );
```

The while and do-while statements are common loop constructs. Java also supports a loop type called a *for* loop. This new loop type doesn't add any new functionality, but it can make your code easier to read.

For Statement

The *for* statement is a rather powerful looping device. It provides an expression to initialize variables, followed by a comparison expression and then a place to increment or decrement the loop variables. This type of loop is particularly good for counting applications. With the following code, we will print the numeric values 0 to 4:

```java
for(int i=0; i < 5; i++) {
    System.out.println(i);
}
```

The three expressions of the for loop are evaluated at different times. The first expression, or *initialization* segment, is executed once at the beginning of the loop. The second, or *looping*, expression is evaluated before each iteration of the loop, including the first time. The last expression, the *stepping* expression, is executed after the completion of the loop body; this part is typically used to increment or decrement a variable.

There are a few points to be made about the program above. Notice that the initial expression creates a new variable. This is a legal and useful way to create temporary variables. By declaring the variable in the initialization expression, you scope the variable to its lowest level. Declaring a variable close to its use makes its function clearer to another reader. It also makes a portion of code more contained and easier to move around.

The second expression is the comparison expression. The result of this expression must be a boolean value. Unlike with C/C++, you can't have an expression that evaluates to an integer. A common shorthand among C programmers was an expression such as (i), which would evaluate to false when *i* was equal to zero; and true otherwise. But it won't work in Java; you'd have to write the expression as (i != 0). The authors of Java are trying to enforce good programming practices by making everyone's code a little easier to read.

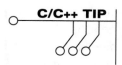

C/C++ TIP

All looping expressions must evaluate to a boolean expression. An expression of an integer type cannot be a comparison expression. Java will not convert an integer to a boolean value.

The last part of a for statement is the looping expression, and it is executed at the end of each loop. Normally, it is used to either increment or decrement the loop variable. Stating each expression at the declaration of the loop makes it easier to understand how many times a loop will execute. The for loop can be made to mimic any other looping construct. To illustrate this, let's create the while loop:

```
boolean cont = true;

...

for(; cont == true;) {
    // Statements that do some work
    ...
    // Logic that sets cont
    ...
}
```

A while statement has a comparison statement, which is checked at the beginning of the loop. If the comparison is false, the loop never executes. By having no initializing or looping expressions, the for loop mimics the while loop. Notice that two semicolons are still used in the for loop. Even though there is no initializing or looping expression, you must provide a place for them.

Break & Continue Statements

Java has done away with the much-derided *goto* statement. Gotos, used mainly to exit loops on some exceptional condition, have largely been abandoned as being needlessly complex. Suppose you have a loop that is usually supposed to execute for 10 repetitions, but on alternate Thursdays it should execute only four times. Should you slip a goto statement in to exit the loop early? Nope—use Java's glorified gotos, called *jump statements*.

Java handles this situation with the *break* and *continue* statements. You can use these statements to exit a loop or method before it would normally exit. The type of statement you employ determines where control is transferred.

The break statement is used to transfer control to the end of a looping construct (for, do, while, or switch). The loop will exit regardless of its comparison value, and the next statement after the loop will execute. We might use a break statement to exit a while loop, which would normally run forever:

```
int i=0;

while(true) {
   System.out.println(i);
   i++;
   if (i > 10) break;
}
```

The above code would print the numbers 0 to 10. Normally, this loop would execute forever because the *while* statement always evaluates to true. The break statement directs the computer to exit the loop when i > 10.

The continue statement is similar to the break statement. The continue statement causes program execution to continue after the last statement in the loop. This is useful when you want to skip some steps of an execution body. We can also use it to avoid a division by zero error:

```
for(int i = -10; i < 10; i++) {
   if (i == 0) continue;
   System.out.println(1/i);

   // Control is transferred to here
}
```

The loop will not process the case where i = 0 when the continue statement is used. In the example above, it's important to note that the looping expression, i++, is executed *after* the continue. If this were not true, the loop would get stuck. Continue statements are often used to skip sections of code that won't work for a particular value.

Both the break and continue statements can use optional labels. In fact, any statement in a Java program can be labeled. To add a label, use the label name, a colon, and then the statement. We could label a loop as follows:

```
loop: for(int i=0; i < 10; i++) {
}
```

The application of labeled loops may not be apparent until you use multiple levels of loops. Imagine a situation in which you are buried several levels deep, and an error occurs. You might then wonder, "Why doesn't Java have a goto statement?" The answer is that the goto statement is not needed. Java handles this situation with two mechanisms: exceptions, which we cover later in this chapter, and labeled jump statements.

A *labeled jump statement* is similar to the goto statement. Take a possible multiple loop situation: You are searching a two-dimensional array for a certain value, say 5. When you find that value, you wish to exit. Labeled jumps allow you to do that:

```java
int i,j;
int nums[][] = new nums[5][5];
boolean found = false;

loop:
    for(i=0; i < 5; i++) {
        for(j=0; j < 5; j++) {
            if (nums[i][j] == 5) {
                found = true;
                break loop;
            }
        }
    }

if (!found) System.out.println("Value not found");
else System.out.println("Value found at " + i + "," + j);
```

This piece of code covers a fair bit of what we have learned in this chapter. It also represents a rather common task. If you are comfortable with this code example, you have a good grasp of such concepts as loops, arrays, operators, and jump statements. If you're new to languages such as C, these programs may be hard to read. C programmers should feel very comfortable with most Java constructs.

Return Statement

Return is a statement, like break and continue, that is used to transfer control. Instead of exiting loops, this statement exits methods. It can also be used to return information, hence its name. A return statement ends execution of a method and returns to where the method was called. Or you can provide a return value, such as an error code or some useful value—perhaps a number raised to some power. We could code a "to the power of N" function as follows:

```
class power {
    public int toN(int base, int n) {

        int result=base;

        for(int i=0; i < n - 1; i++) {
            result = result * base;
        }
        return result;
        // No code after this will be executed
    }
}
```

This code calculates base raised to the *n*th power. It then uses the return statement to deliver the result. Any code following the return statement is not executed. The value you return must be of the same type as the return type of the method. If the method has a void return type, you can just use the keyword *return* followed by a semicolon. The return statement doubles as a function-level goto and a way to return values.

Switch Statement

In older languages, it was common to see large expanses of if-else statements. You may have seen one of these in a menu application. Typically, the user enters a command, and then some code is executed based on the entered value. In large programs, especially programs like word processors, there might be hundreds of possible commands. The switch statement was developed to ease this burden.

A switch statement accepts a char, byte, short, or int as its comparison expression. This value is then looked up in the case statements that follow the switch statement, and the proper code is executed. Let's use our menu example to show a switch statement:

```java
int cmd; // Assume the user has entered a command

switch(cmd) {
   case 1  : System.out.println("Menu item 1");
             break;
   case 2  : System.out.println("Menu item 2");
             break;
   default : System.out.println("Invalid command");
}
```

Each option you want to handle is specified in a case label. The value after the case statement must be of the same type as the switch expression. You can also have a label called default, which is executed if the switch expression is not found.

Notice the use of the break statement. This makes each case distinct. If there is no jump statement—which is commonly a break statement—the execution will continue into other cases. Sometimes this is desired, but other times it's not. You can use this to your advantage by grouping commands together that have similar operations. Just be sure to put in break statements when needed.

Exceptions

The Java language was designed around the C/C++ languages because they are solid languages and have a large user base. Some changes were made to enhance security, reduce bugs, and make maintenance easier, but generally the languages were left alone. Java has been described by its authors as C++ *without* the weaknesses regarding safety and maintenance, but *with* the benefits of threading and exceptions. Because Java is made to work in a networking environment, it needs certain enhancements to gracefully handle a multitude of errors and complications.

Exception handling is required to deal with problems commonly found in networking. Many Net citizens know how frequently a connection can be lost. Your program must be ready to deal with this and other errors at any point in your code. One can imagine having a function that checks the state of the Net connection after every statement. Ludicrous as this sounds, early BBS software had something very similar. Good exception handling is almost impossible without language support, and Java provides this support.

Exceptions are thrown whenever the runtime system doesn't know how to handle a situation. Some common problems are running out of memory, dividing by zero, and accessing null pointers. If you have provided no exception handlers, then the runtime system grinds to a halt. Sometimes you have no way to fix the problem; other times you can fix the problem and continue on with the program. At a minimum, you should try to save any user data and close any files you have open. Either way, Java tries to make you more aware of possible problems. By using exception handling, you can create more robust programs.

The Java designers implemented exception support through the mechanisms of the *try* and *catch* statements. These statements specify blocks of code which direct how an exception will be handled. Basically, you specify a block of code to try and then catch any exceptions that are generated. Consider the simple problem of dividing by zero:

```
int i = 0;

i = i / i;
```

Upon execution of this code, the Java runtime system will generate an exception. The program will end, and an error message will be printed to the screen. Your paying clients will be giving you a call, inconveniently, just as you sit down to dinner. You could have easily avoided this situation. Let's use the try and catch mechanism to catch this arithmetic exception:

```java
int i = 0;

try {
    i = i / i;
}
catch (ArithmeticException e) {
    System.out.println("Caught divide by zero, continuing");
}
```

After a try block, you can specify any number of catch blocks. When an exception is thrown, the runtime system creates an object describing the error. These objects are descended from a class called *Exception*. The Exception objects are then passed on to our exception handlers. If there is no exception handler, the system grinds to a halt. We have caught the arithmetic exception here. But other exceptions would still cause a runtime exception to be generated.

When an exception is generated, the computer looks for catch blocks that might handle it. It looks for the best match first. If it can't find an exact match, it then travels up the inheritance tree for other possible matches. Since the arithmetic exception is a subclass of Exception, it would be picked. This concept is easier to understand with an example. The previous example can be rewritten to handle all errors:

```java
int i = 0;

try {
    i = i / i;
}
catch (ArithmeticException e) {
    System.out.println("Caught divide by zero, continuing");
}
```

```
catch (Exception e) {
    System.out.println("Caught some exception");
    // Perform some cleanup code
    ...
    // Regenerate the exception
    throw(e);
}
```

You may notice a problem in the code above. We have caught an exception, but we don't really know which one we caught. If you don't know how to handle an exception, it's best to let the runtime system handle it. Here, we caught some exception, did the cleanup work we could do, and then passed the error on. If no other error handlers are present, the program will stop—unless somewhere higher up in the code, we have created more error handlers. It's best to handle exceptions as close to the source as possible, but you can handle some errors in very general ways. This code would then be written somewhere else, possibly in the main loop of your program.

The *throw* command takes an object and passes it up the exception chain. You can have multiple levels of try and catch statements. A throw statement ignores the current level of catch statements and tries to find a match. Again, if no match exists, it will generate a runtime exception.

Sometimes you need to execute a piece of code even if an exception is generated. This can be accomplished using a *finally* block. No matter how you leave the block—as you normally do, as an exception, or as a jump statement like break or continue—the finally block will be executed. A skeleton try, catch, finally block would look like this:

```
try {
    // Try some code that might generate an exception
}
finally {
    // Perform any cleanup needed
}
catch (ArithmeticException e) {
    // Handle a divide by zero exception
}
```

The previous skeleton program provides a good framework for dealing with pieces of code that can generate exceptions. Enclose the suspect code in a try block. Perform any cleanup needed in the finally block. Handle any errors that you can safely diffuse, and allow the rest to be passed up the exception chain. Now you have created a well-behaved system that will handle the errors it can, always clean up after itself, and pass on exceptions it can't handle.

Table 4-14 contains a list of common exceptions generated by the runtime system. Most classes in the API will also have their own exceptions. When using a new class, make sure you familiarize yourself with the exceptions it can generate.

Exception	Description
ArithmeticException	An exceptional arithmetic condition has occurred; for example, trying to divide a number by zero.
ArrayIndexOutOfBoundsException	You have an index value that is outside the bounds of the array. Remember that arrays start at 0 and go to N-1 where N is the number of elements.
ArrayStoreException	You have tried to store the wrong type of object in an array. The object must be either the same type, a subclass, or one that implements the interface specified.
CastClassException	An invalid cast has occurred.
InstantiationException	You have tried to instantiate an interface or an abstract class.
NegativeArraySizeException	You have tried to create an array with a negative size.
NullPointerException	You have tried to use a reference variable that has not been initialized or has been set to null.

Exception	Description
NumberFormatException	A value could not be converted to a number. This typically happens when trying to convert a string to a number.
OutOfMemoryError	Even after garbage collection, you have run out of memory. This happens infrequently, but it *is* possible.
SecurityException	You have tried to do something that the security manager doesn't like.
StringIndexOutOfBoundsException	While trying to access a string as an array, you specified an index value outside the length of the string.

Table 4-14: *Common runtime exceptions.*

Moving On

We hope you'll refer back to this chapter whenever you have a syntax question while programming.

Now that we've gotten most of the basics out of the way, it's time for a little fun. In Chapter 5, "How Applets Work," we cover the essentials of programming interactive Java applets. You're about to see how to make your Web pages come alive.

5

How Applets Work

By now you should have a good understanding of the differences between top-down programming and object-oriented programming, along with a healthy appreciation for the syntax and semantics of the Java language. You've got a great idea for a killer applet, and you're ready to start coding. Where do you go from here?

In this chapter, we'll explain the basics of writing applets. We'll start by explaining how to extend the Applet class and describing the important methods to override to get the behavior you want from your applet. We'll show you how to use the methods of the Applet class to get pictures and sound clips from the network. You'll learn how to get parameters from HTML code so your applets can exhibit different behaviors without being recompiled. We'll explain how to make your applet respond to mouse actions and keyboard input. Finally, we'll show you how to make your applets come to life by using threads and teach you how to rid your applets of that annoying flicker.

TIP

This chapter's code example files can be found on the Companion CD-ROM (for Windows 95/NT and Macintosh users) and on the Online Companion (for UNIX users). Visit the Online Companion at http://www.vmedia.com/java.html.

What Is an Applet?

An applet is a nifty class combining elements of a sophisticated graphics window with easy-to-use networking capabilities. It is, in essence, a miniature graphical user interface, like Microsoft Windows or X11, that is guaranteed to have basically the same functionality regardless of the type of computer running it.

Applets are very useful for writing applications on the Internet because they can be embedded in HTML documents and run using Java-enabled Web browsers like Netscape Navigator 2.0. To create your own applets, you extend the Applet class and reference the new class in a Web page. Let's take another look at the Hello World Applet from Chapter 2, "Getting Started With Java."

Example 5-1a: The Hello World Applet.

```
import java.applet.Applet;
import java.awt.Graphics;

public class HelloWorldApplet extends Applet {
   public void init() {
      resize(250,250);
   }
   public void paint(Graphics g) {
      g.drawString("Hello world!",25,25);
   }
}
```

The Hello World Applet extends the Applet class, meaning that all of the methods and variables available to the Applet class are available to our extension of it. Two of these methods are init and paint. We can override these methods, changing their default behavior so they will do what we want. Here's the HTML code for a Web page that embeds the Hello World Applet:

Example 5-1b: The Hello World Web page.

```
<HTML>
<HEAD>
<TITLE>Hello World Applet</TITLE>
</HEAD>
<BODY>
<APPLET CODE="HelloWorldApplet.class" WIDTH=250 HEIGHT=250>
</APPLET>
</BODY>
</HTML>
```

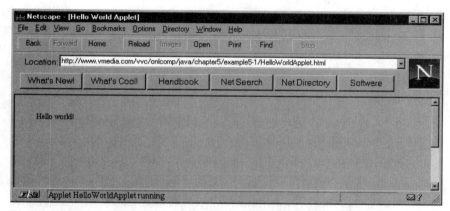

Figure 5-1: *The Hello World Applet running under Netscape Navigator.*

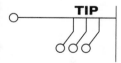

TIP

The APPLET tag has not been incorporated into any existing HTML standards by the World Wide Web Consortium (W3C), the authoritative standards group for the WWW. This syntax is used by Netscape Navigator 2.0 and by Sun's appletviewer, the only Java-capable Web browsers currently in existence. Therefore, it will probably enjoy a pseudostandard existence like that of the other non-HTML compliant markup tags used by Netscape, such as <CENTER> and <BLINK>. The W3C is currently proposing an <INSERT> tag for embedding applications in Web pages; for the latest news on this topic, check out http://www.w3.org/pub/WWW/ TR/WD-insert.html.

The CODE parameter inside the APPLET tag specifies the full URL to the applet's compiled class—here we are assuming that this HTML page is in the same directory as the Hello World class. Notice that we have to tell the Web browser, by using WIDTH and HEIGHT tags, how large the applet will be so that it can lay out the page properly. Under Netscape Navigator 2.0, you can specify 100% for the values of these tags—this will cause the browser to give the applet as much space as it needs initially.

Programming applets in Java is stylistically different than programming applications in other languages. Java code is written largely in an event-driven fashion, similar to hypertext a la the Web instead of the usual linear flow as in traditional text. The run-time environment, your Web browser, acts as an interface between the code and the computer on which the browser is running. Figure 5-2 graphically represents this relationship.

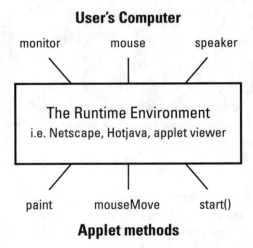

Figure 5-2: *Applets and the runtime environment.*

The runtime environment understands certain applet methods, like paint and mouseMove, and it will call these when it needs to—when the screen needs to be painted or when the mouse has moved. By default, an applet does nothing when these methods are called—it is up to you, the programmer, to override these methods if you want your applet to respond to the corresponding events, such as mouse motion or a request to refresh the graphics display.

THE APPLETCONTEXT INTERFACE

The runtime environment, your Web browser, creates a Java class that implements the AppletContext interface. The AppletContext interface describes several methods by which applets can request resources from the runtime environment— for instance, the getImage and getAudioClip methods (described later in this chapter). The AppletContext class watches for events in the runtime environment and calls the proper methods on the applet to deal with those events. It can be thought of as a bridge between your applet code and the runtime environment. Applets can request a runtime reference to their AppletContext using the getAppletContext method. You will not need to interact with the AppletContext directly unless you want to make several applets talk to one another. We will describe how to do this in Chapter 13, "Networking With Sockets & Streams."

The Stages of an Applet

When a Java-compliant Web browser loads an Applet class, it first allocates memory for the applet and its global variables. Then it runs the applet's init method. (Generally programmers use the init method to initialize global variables, get resources from the network, and set up the user interface.) Next the browser calls the applet's start method. If the portion of the browser containing the applet is visible (which is generally the case when an applet is just being started!), the applet's paint method is called. If the user leaves the page containing the applet, the browser calls the stop method. When the user returns, the start method is called again, as well as the paint method. The following code illustrates what happens when the user leaves the page and then returns:

Example 5-2: The Counting Applet.

```java
import java.applet.*;
import java.awt.*;

public class Count extends Applet {

   int InitCount=0;
   int StartCount=0;
   int StopCount=0;
   int PaintCount=0;

   public void init() {
      resize(250,75);
      InitCount = InitCount + 1;
   }

   public void start() {
      StartCount = StartCount + 1;
   }

   public void stop() {
      StopCount = StopCount + 1;
   }

   public void paint(Graphics g) {
      PaintCount++;
      String Output = new String(
         "Inits: "+InitCount+
         " Starts: "+StartCount+
         " Stops: "+StopCount+
         " Paints: "+PaintCount);
      g.drawString(Output,25,25);
   }
}
```

The applet's output after being loaded is shown in Figure 5-3. The applet has been initialized once, started once, stopped never, and painted at least once.

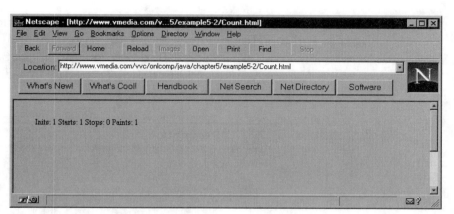

Figure 5-3: *The Counting Applet.*

If you go to another Web page and then come back to this one (without shutting down your Web browser), you see that the applet still has been initialized only once, but has been started twice, stopped once, and painted at least twice. This output is displayed in Figure 5-4.

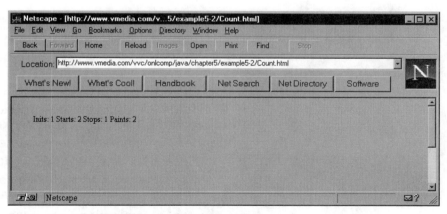

Figure 5-4: *The Counting Applet after a reload.*

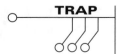

Clicking the Reload button in Netscape Navigator 2.0 causes the applets on the current page to be stopped and started again.

If you obscure the applet by moving another window on top of it, and then bring it back to the foreground by moving the window away again, you'll find that the applet has not been started or stopped again, but that it *has* been painted again. Table 5-1 lists some important Applet methods.

Method	Description
init()	Called once only, when the applet code is first loaded.
start()	Called whenever a Web page containing the applet becomes active in the Web browser.
stop()	Called whenever a Web page containing the applet is no longer active in the Web browser.
destroy()	Called when the applet is explicitly killed.
paint(Graphics g)	Called when the applet needs to redraw its graphics window.

Table 5-1: *Applet stages cheat sheet.*

OVERRIDING THE DESTROY METHOD

Applets can also override the destroy method, which is called after the stop method when the applet is explicitly killed. The destroy method is intended for cleaning up resources that the applet had been using. In practice, this method is seldom overridden because Java cleans up resources for you. Once an applet is killed, all variables in memory lose their runtime references and become subject to garbage collection. The garbage collection routines run in the background and occur when the system deems it necessary, so there is no real need for you to do your own garbage collection. It can be useful to override the destroy method if, for example, you want to make sure the user really wants to kill an applet before doing so.

Security concerns constrain applet design in some respects. Most notably, applets are unable to access a user's local hard drive in any fashion. Thus, any large chunks of data needed by your applets have to be retrieved from a file-serving computer via a network, as we explain in the next section.

Getting Resources

One of the things that has made the World Wide Web so successful is the ease with which authors can add pictures and sound to their Web pages simply by including, in the page's HTML code, the location of the image or sound clip they want to use. It is just as easy and much more powerful to do this using Java. HTML is a document description language; Java is a bona fide programming language. Your Java applets could use images as graphical icons or sprites in an arcade-style game. The following Java applet grabs a picture and a sound clip from the network and displays them:

Example 5-3: Web-capable applet.

```
import java.applet.*;
import java.awt.*;
import java.net.*;

public class WebApplet extends Applet {

   private Image myImage;
   private AudioClip mySound;
   private URL ImageURL;
   private URL SoundURL;

   public void init() {
     resize(250,250);
     try {
       //Bind URLs to the resources
       ImageURL = new URL("http://www.vmedia.com/vvc/onlcomp/
java/chapter5/images/sample.gif");
       SoundURL = new URL("http://www.vmedia.com/vvc/onlcomp/
java/chapter5/sounds/sample.au");
     }
```

```
      //Watch out for bad URLs
      catch (MalformedURLException e) {}
      //Download the picture
      myImage = getImage(ImageURL);
      //Download the audio clip
      mySound = getAudioClip(SoundURL);
   }

   public void start() {
      //Start sound playing in a loop
      mySound.loop();
   }

   public void stop() {
      //Stop playing sound
      mySound.stop();
   }

   public void paint(Graphics g) {
      //Paint the image
      g.drawImage(myImage,0,0,this);
   }

}
```

As you read through this code, you'll see references to three classes that may be unfamiliar to you: java.awt.Image, java.applet.AudioClip, and java.net.URL. These classes, like most classes defined in the Java API, do more or less what their names imply.

Image
The Image class defines a simple, generic, two-dimensional graphics image. The Graphics class (used by the paint method) can draw Images with the drawImage method, as shown in the following example:

```
Image myImage;
myImage = createImage(50,50);
g.drawImage(myImage,0,0,this);
```

The createImage method is defined for the java.awt.Component class, a parent of the Applet class. The createImage method can take two integers as arguments and create an empty new instance of the Image class with the specified size.

The drawImage method takes four parameters: the Image itself, the X and Y coordinates of the Image's new location in the Graphics window, and an ImageObserver. We'll describe the ImageObserver class in detail later in Chapter 9, "Graphics & Images," but for now be sure to always use your applet itself as the ImageObserver when using drawImage.

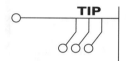

TIP

When you need to explicitly pass your applet as a parameter, you can use the this *keyword, discussed in Chapter 4, "Syntax & Semantics."*

The Applet class uses the getImage(URL) method to grab images from the network. This method is really implemented by the AppletContext (see the sidebar "The AppletContext Interface" earlier in this chapter). Consequently, Java applets can import images of any graphics format that the context supplied by the Web browser can understand. The most common formats are the Graphics Interchange Format (GIF) and Joint Photographic Experts Group (JPEG) format. Images may take a while to download, but we can go ahead and draw the Image in our applet; it will just take a while for the picture to actually appear. If you need finer control over the Images, you can use the Mediatracker class, which is discussed in Chapter 9.

AudioClip

The java.applet.AudioClip class is a high-level representation of a clip of audio data. Three methods are defined in the class: play, loop, and stop. The applet class defines a getAudioClip method that, when given the URL of a sound clip, returns an AudioClip containing that sound. Like the getImage method, the

getAudioClip method is actually implemented by the applet's context; so again, the applet is able to use any sound format that the Web browser directly supports. Here's a short example:

```
AudioClip mySound;
mySound.play();
```

This code plays the sound represented by the given AudioClip. The Applet class defines a method, play(URL), which, when passed a URL that points to an audio clip, plays it. If the audio clip is missing, or in an unsupported format, nothing happens. AudioClips, like Images, can be used as soon as they are instantiated, but it may take some time to actually download and play the sound. While you can use the Mediatracker class to download pictures ahead of time for you, the Mediatracker does not yet support AudioClips.

URL

A URL, or Uniform Resource Locator, is the complete address of an object on the World Wide Web (for example, http://www.vmedia.com/index.html is the address for the home page of the Ventana Online site). The Java language provides a separate class to handle URLs. An instance of the class represents an object on the Web. The URL class will be described completely in Chapter 14, "Networking With URLs," but you can go ahead and start using it now. The easiest way to create a URL object is to use the URL (String) constructor:

```
URL myObject;
myObject = new URL("http://www.vmedia.com/index.html");
```

Unfortunately, this Java code is incomplete. If we tried to compile this code, the Java compiler would complain that we have failed to handle a MalformedURLException. URLs can be very complex, and it's easy to try to create a URL object with a string that looks like, but is not, a URL. If this happens, the URL constructor will fail and notify the applet that the string it tried to parse as a URL is a MalformedURL. We have to be prepared for this contingency and catch the error. The following code accomplishes this:

```
URL myObject;
try {
  myObject = new URL("http://www.vmedia.com/index.html");
  }
catch (MalformedURLException e) {
  //Code here is run if URL is malformed
}
```

We'll be covering exceptions in detail in Chapter 10, "Advanced Program Design," so don't worry if this is unclear. Just remember that when you create a new URL, you have to try to catch the exception. If you're absolutely sure your URL has the proper syntax, you needn't put any code between the second set of braces.

There is another important URL constructor that takes a URL and a String as parameters. The URL indicates a base absolute URL, and the String contains the path to the object relative to the base. For instance, if you supplied http://www.vmedia.com/ourbook/ as the URL and "images/picture.gif" as the String, the new URL would point to http://www.vmedia.com/ourbook/images/picture.gif. If you supplied "/otherbook/index.html" as the String, the new URL would point to http://www.vmedia.com/otherbook/index.html.

This constructor is useful in conjunction with the Applet class's getCodeBase method, which returns the URL of the Applet's class file. You can use getCodeBase and the relative URL constructor to create URLs to objects without specifying a host name. This is especially useful because untrusted applets are not allowed to open network connections to remote hosts, except to the Web server from which the class file was loaded (we'll discuss these restrictions more thoroughly in Chapter 13, "Networking With Sockets & Streams"). So, you need to install the resources you want your applet to use on the same Web server as the applet. When constructing URLs to these resources in your applet, it is easiest and safest to use the getCodeBase method with the relative URL constructor instead of using absolute URLs. Doing so also makes your applet easier to install on a new Web server.

You may have noticed that we have coded some data into our example applet—namely, the URLs of the image and the sound clip. If you're a professional programmer or a computer science professor, you probably noticed this and cringed—by most traditional programming standards, this is a bad thing to do. Whenever you want to change the image or sound clip used by this applet, you'll have to change the code and recompile the class. Fortunately, Java gives you a way to fix this by allowing you to give your applets parameters at runtime that you can use to specify a different image or sound clip.

Getting Parameters

A feature of most good high-level languages is the ability to take arguments from the command line. Programmers use this capability to make it possible for programs to change their behavior based on user input, eliminating the need for a complicated user interface. But Java applets are not run from the command line—they are embedded inside HTML code, and so are their "command line" parameters. Consider the following Web page:

Example 5-4a: A Web page with parameters.

```
<HTML>
<HEAD>
<TITLE>Good Web Applet</TITLE>
</HEAD>
<BODY>
<APPLET CODE="GoodWebApplet.class" WIDTH=250 HEIGHT=250>
<PARAM NAME="IMAGE" VALUE="../images/sample.gif">
<PARAM NAME="SOUND" VALUE="../sounds/sample.au">
</APPLET>
```

We have embedded a variable named IMAGE with the value "../images/sample.gif" in the HTML code shown in Example 5-4a. The applet can access the IMAGE variable using the getParameter method, which takes the name of a parameter variable as its input and returns a String containing the variable's value. The process is the same for the SOUND parameter. All parameters are represented as Strings.

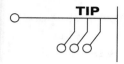

TIP

Chapter 6, "Discovering the Application Programming Inter-face," will teach you how to convert variables of type String to other types—a useful technique, if you want to get a number as a parameter.

Using this new functionality, we can rewrite the init method of our Web-capable applet to make it dataless:

Example 5-4b: A good Web-capable applet.

```
public void init() {
   String ImageParam;
   String SoundParam;
   resize(250,250);
   //Fill in from HTML code
   ImageParam = getParameter("IMAGE");
   SoundParam = getParameter("SOUND");
   try {
      //This is a URL to our class file
      URL me = getCodeBase();
      //Use parameters to grab URLs
      ImageURL = new URL(me,ImageParam);
      SoundURL = new URL(me,SoundParam);
   }
   catch (MalformedURLException e) {}
   myImage = getImage(ImageURL);
   mySound = getAudioClip(SoundURL);
}
```

By allowing the author of the Web page, rather than the pro-grammer, to determine the locations of the picture and sound clip, we have made this applet much more useful. All the author has to do is change the VALUE tag of either parameter to change the image or sound clip used by the applet. When you have an applet feature you want to change frequently, or have some default applet behavior you'd like Web page authors to be able to modify easily, you should use parameters.

As useful as they are, parameters allow applets to interact with users in a very narrow fashion only—the input is via a series of strings written down before the user starts the program. Suppose we want to change the applet's behavior while the applet is running—when the user moves the mouse, or presses a certain key? This capability is essential for writing complex Internet applications, and Java's event handling paradigm makes it easy to accomplish.

Handling User Events

Java applets employ the concept of *events* to handle real-time user interaction and changes in the runtime environment. Events are packets of information generated in response to certain user actions, such as moving the mouse or pressing a key on the keyboard. They also can be generated in response to modifications of the environment—for example, when an applet's window is obscured by another window. The runtime environment watches for events to occur and passes the event information on to another method called an *event handler*. An event handler is a method that is called when a particular event occurs. Many commonly used event handlers are predefined for the Applet class. By default, these handlers do nothing—to use them, just override the appropriate method with your own code. For instance:

```
public boolean mouseMove(Event evt, int x, int y) {
   //Code here is run when the mouse is moved
   return true; //The event has been handled
}
```

Whenever the mouse is moved, the mouseMove method is called. It returns true to indicate that it has handled the event, and that no other object needs to worry about it.

Mouse Events

Three parameters are passed to the mouseMove event handler: the event itself, which is a class containing all of the information needed to uniquely identify an event, and the X and Y coordinates of the event—in this case, the new location of the mouse within the applet. Table 5-2 lists predefined event handlers.

Event Handler	Description
mouseDown(Event,int,int)	The mouse button is pushed. The integer arguments indicate the location of the mouse.
mouseUp(Event,int,int)	The mouse button is released.
mouseMove(Event,int,int)	The mouse is moved.
mouseDrag(Event,int,int)	The mouse is moved while the button is being held down.
mouseEnter(Event,int,int)	The mouse enters the applet.
mouseExit(Event,int,int)	The mouse leaves the applet.
keyDown(Event,int)	A cursor or function key is pressed. The integer argument indicates the particular key (see Table 5-3).
keyUp(Event,int)	A cursor or function key is released.

Table 5-2: *Frequently used predefined event handlers.*

By overriding some of these predefined event handlers, we can write the Cursor Applet, listed below. The Cursor Applet paints an image that follows the mouse around the applet's window. The chasing behavior can be turned off and on by clicking the mouse button:

Example 5-5: Cursor Applet.

```
import java.applet.*;
import java.awt.*;
import java.net.*;

public class CursorApplet extends Applet {
  //The position of the mouse
  private int mouse_x, mouse_y;
  //Do we want to follow the mouse?
  private boolean Follow = true;
  private Image CursorImage;
```

```java
public void init() {
   mouse_x = 125;
   mouse_y = 125;
   resize(250,250);
   String CursorFile = getParameter("CURSORFILE");
   try {
     URL CursorURL = new URL(CursorFile);
     CursorImage = getImage(CursorURL);
   }
   catch (MalformedURLException e) {
     CursorImage = createImage(0,0);
   }
}

public void paint(Graphics g) {
   //A simple border
   g.drawRect(0,0,249,249);
   //Draw cursor at the mouse's location
   g.drawImage(CursorImage,mouse_x,mouse_y,this);
}

public boolean mouseMove(Event evt, int x, int y) {
   if (Follow) {
     //Update our local mouse information
     mouse_x = x;
     mouse_y = y;
     //Redraw the graphics window
     repaint();
   }
   return true;
}
public boolean mouseDown(Event evt, int x, int y) {
   //If it's not one thing...
   if (Follow) {Follow = false;}
   //It's another
   else {Follow = true;}
   return true;
}
}
```

When you check for mouse-down events, you can specify different handling depending on whether the user single-clicks or double-clicks. The Event class defines a variable, clickCount, which is set to 1 for single-clicks and 2 for double-clicks. It will, in fact, be set to the number of clicks the user manages to make before the Event is generated. In practice, only single- and double-clicks are useful. The following code fragment illustrates the use of this variable:

```
public boolean mouseDown(Event evt, int x, int y) {
  if (evt.clickCount==1) {
    //Single-click case
  } elseif (evt.clickCount==2) {
    //Double-click case
  } else {
    //Super-nimble-finger case
  }
  return true;
}
```

This method is called when the mouse button is pressed. If the button is pressed once, the applet enters the single-click case; if the button is pressed twice, the applet enters the double-click case.

Keyboard Events

The keyUp and keyDown methods work in the same way the mouse event methods work, except that they are passed the key's *identifier* rather than the event's coordinates. A key's identifier is an integer that corresponds to that key. Normal typewriter keys have their ASCII values. Java supports many special keys as well, and these are shown in Table 5-3. These special keys are actually defined as static integer variables (constants) for the Event class. Chapter 6, "Discovering the Application Programming Interface," will show you how to convert integers to Strings if you want to display the keyboard input.

The following code fragment checks for arrow key presses:

```
public boolean keyDown(Event evt, int key) {
  switch(key) {
```

```
        case Event.UP:
        case Event.DOWN:
        case Event.LEFT:
        case Event.RIGHT:
        default:
      }
    return true;
  }
```

The keyDown method is called when a key is pressed. The switch statement differentiates between the four arrows and all other keys, and it calls the appropriate section of code for the key in question.

SHIFT, CTRL & META

Events can be handled differently depending on whether or not any of the special masking keys are down when the event occurs. Shift, Control, and Meta are the masking keys in the Java language. The Meta key is equivalent to the Alt key in Microsoft Windows; it can be bound to many different keys under the X11 window system. The Event class provides shiftDown, controlDown, and metaDown methods that return a boolean variable indicating the status of each of the masking keys.

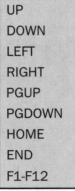

UP
DOWN
LEFT
RIGHT
PGUP
PGDOWN
HOME
END
F1-F12

Table 5-3: *Cursor and function key identifiers.*

Event Handling: What's Really Going On

Here's what is really going on when an event occurs. The AppletContext notices that an event has occurred inside the applet (see the sidebar "The AppletContext Interface" earlier in this chapter). The AppletContext creates a new instance of the Event class, fills in the appropriate parameters so the applet will know what kind of event has happened, and passes the new Event to the applet's handleEvent method. The Event class contains all of the information needed to uniquely identify an event; these event variables are listed in Table 5-4.

Event Variable	Description
public Object target	The component in which the event occurred—for applet writing, this is generally the applet itself.
public long when	The time at which the event happened. The timestamp is a long integer containing the number of milliseconds since 00:00:00, January 1, 1970, GMT. Java provides a method, java.lang.System.currentTimeMillis, that returns this value.
public int id	The type of event (see Table 5-6).
public int x	The X-coordinate of the event.
public int y	The Y-coordinate of the event.
public int key	The key identifier (for special keys, see Table 5-3).
public int modifiers	The state of the masking keys.
public Object arg	An optional argument. This is not used for mouse and keyboard events, but will be of great use when using the graphics widgets provided by the Java API. These are described in Chapter 9, "Graphics & Images."

Table 5-4: *Event variables.*

The handleEvent method checks the type of event and calls the appropriate predefined event handler, passing it the relevant parameters. (A diagram of this process is shown in Figure 5-5.)

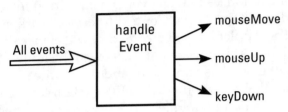

Figure 5-5: *The handleEvent method.*

For example, when the mouse is moved, an Event of type MOUSE_MOVE is constructed and passed to the handleEvent method. This method notes that the Event is a MOUSE_MOVE and calls the mouseMove method, passing to it the Event and its location. It is in fact unnecessary to pass the Event's location as separate parameters because this information is encoded in the Event itself. This is done for the programmer's convenience.

You can override the handleEvent method if you want to be able to handle a large number of different events without overriding each individual method. This may also be useful if you want to handle sequences of events differently. If you do this, remember that the predefined event handlers will not be called unless you call them explicitly in your new handleEvent method. The following example calls a generic mouse event handler for mouse events and passes all other events to the runtime environment:

```
public boolean handleEvent(Event evt) {
    switch (evt.id) {
        case Event.MOUSE MOUSE_DOWN:
        case Event.MOUSE MOUSE_UP:
        case Event.MOUSE MOUSE_MOVE:
        case Event.MOUSE MOUSE_DRAG:
        case Event.MOUSE MOUSE_ENTER:
        case Event.MOUSE MOUSE_EXIT:
    }
}
```

You can generate events in your own code. To do so, simply construct a new instance of the Event class and post it to your applet (event constructors are listed in Table 5-5). Generating events might be useful for writing a macro system that incorporates mouse motion, for example. You could implement a drawing package that, after recording the user drawing a figure, could replicate the figure in other locations. The following code will make your applet think the mouse has moved to a new location:

```
Event FakeEvt;
long time = System.currentTimeMillis();
FakeEvt = new
Event(this,time,MOUSE_MOVE,new_x,new_y,0,0,null);
postEvent(FakeEvt);
```

Event Constructor	Description
Event(Object,long,int, int,int,int,int,Object)	The target component, timestamp, event type, X-coordinate, Y-coordinate, key identifier, modifiers, and argument.
Event(Object, long, int, int, int, int, int)	The target component, timestamp, event type, X-coordinate, Y-coordinate, key identifier, and modifiers.
Event(Object, int, Object)	The target component, event type, and argument.

Table 5-5: *Event constructors.*

A complete list of the event types appears in Table 5-6. The types marked with an asterisk are irrelevant for applets. The SCROLL_ and LIST_ types are used in conjunction with user input components, which will be covered in Chapter 7, "Basic User Interface."

Event Types	
WINDOW_DESTROY	MOUSE_EXIT
WINDOW_EXPOSE	SCROLL_LINE_UP
WINDOW_ICONIFY	SCROLL_LINE_DOWN
WINDOW_DEICONIFY	SCROLL_PAGE_UP
WINDOW_MOVED	SCROLL_PAGE_DOWN
KEY_PRESS	SCROLL_PAGE_ABSOLUTE
KEY_RELEASE	LIST_SELECT
KEY_ACTION	LIST_DESELECT
KEY_ACTION_RELEASE	ACTION_EVENT
MOUSE_DOWN	LOAD_FILE*
MOUSE_UP	SAVE_FILE*
MOUSE_MOVE	GOT_FOCUS
MOUSE_DRAG	LOST_FOCUS
MOUSE_ENTER	

Table 5-6: *The events marked with an asterisk are not used in applets.*

As you can probably guess, much of the code in a good Java applet will be written for methods that run in response to events. But suppose we want some sequence of events to run independently of other events? Specifically, suppose we want our applet to display an animated figure and respond to events at the same time? If we start a loop to display the animation in any of our methods, the method will never complete and the applet will be stuck. Fortunately, Java provides an elegant way out of this trap: *Threads*.

Animation With Threads

Imagine your runtime environment as an office, with a single worker scurrying around inside. This worker is in charge of running the applet's methods in response to various events. Our worker is very methodical; it must wait until each task is complete before going on to the next one. Suppose we want to give the worker a method to run that is so complex or repetitive that it would preclude the worker from doing anything else? The solution in this case is simple—hire a new worker to do the time-consuming job. The new worker is a new Thread.

Threads are different from other classes in that once they are instantiated and begin running, they run independently in the runtime environment of the method that started them. In this respect, they resemble processes in multi-processing operating systems like UNIX. When most methods are called, the program waits until the method has been completely executed before continuing. But when a thread's run method is called (usually when the thread is started), the originating method keeps executing while the thread's run method is running. Figure 5-6 contains flowcharts for a single Thread and for two Threads.

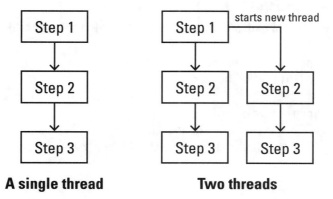

Figure 5-6: *Thread flowchart.*

You can use threads in your Java programs by defining extensions of the Thread class. We'll describe this process in detail in Chapter 11, "Advanced Threading." But for now we'll explain how to allow your applet to use threads. This technique will be useful if, for instance, your applet displays an animated image, but you want the applet to do other things while the animation is playing.

The Runnable Interface

Since the Java language does not allow for multiple inheritance, as discussed in Chapter 3, "Object Orientation in Java," your applet cannot directly extend both the Applet and the Thread classes. You can allow your applet to have a method that runs inside of a thread by using the *Runnable interface*. This interface, like the Thread class, is part of the java.lang package. You can use it this way:

```
class ThreadedApplet extends Applet implements Runnable {
}
```

The Runnable interface tells the compiler that this class will define a run method, and that this method should be executed inside of a thread. The run method is controlled by an instance of the Thread class constructed on the applet itself. Here is how you would use this in practice:

```
class ThreadedApplet extends Applet implements Runnable {

    private Thread engine = null;
    //This will be our thread

    public void init() {
        engine = new Thread(this);
        //This thread now controls our run method
```

```
        }
    public void start() {
        engine.start();
        //This starts the run method
    }
    public void stop() {
        if (engine!=null && engine.isAlive()) {
        //If we need to,
            engine.stop();
            //Stop the run method
        }
    }
    public void run() {
        while (engine.isAlive()) {
            //code here runs until applet stops
        }
    }
}
```

When the applet is initialized, it creates a new thread bound to the applet. When the applet starts, it starts the thread running. The thread executes the code inside the loop in the run method until the applet is stopped.

Simple Thread Methods

The Thread class defines many methods to help you control your threads. We'll cover these in detail in Chapter 11, "Advanced Threading," but Table 5-7 briefly describes the most important methods to remember.

Thread Method	Description
isAlive()	Returns a boolean variable indicating whether the thread is alive or not.
sleep(long)	Asks the thread to sleep for the specified number of milliseconds. This method will throw an InterruptedException if it receives an interrupt signal from another thread. Interrupts are discussed in Chapter 11, "Multi-Threaded Applets."
start()	Starts the thread running.
stop()	Stops the thread running.
suspend()	Temporarily pauses the thread.
resume()	Resumes running after suspension.

Table 5-7: *Common Thread methods.*

Using a thread, we can extend the Cursor Applet (Example 5-5) to display an animated image that follows the cursor, shown in Figure 5-7. We'll modify the applet so that clicking on the mouse button stops and starts the animation, to give the user some control over it.

Example 5-6a: Animated Cursor Applet.

```java
import java.applet.*;
import java.awt.*;
import java.net.*;

//This class has a thread run method
//and will control it through a Thread
//instance constructed on this applet
public class AnimatedCursorApplet extends
Applet implements Runnable {

    private int mouse_x, mouse_y;
    //Array of animation images
    private Image CursorImages[];
```

```java
//Index of the current image
private int CursorIndex = 0;
//This Thread controls the run method
private Thread anim = null;
//Is the animation paused?
private boolean paused = false;

public void init() {
  resize(250,250);
  //Bind the thread instance to the applet
  anim = new Thread(this);
  mouse_x = 125;
  mouse_y = 125;
  //We assume 5 images-for now
  CursorImages = new Image[5];
  int i;
  String CursorParam;
  URL CursorURL;
  //Fill the image array
  for (i=0; i<5; i++) {
    CursorParam = getParameter("CURSORFILE"+i);
    try {
      CursorURL = new URL(CursorParam);
      CursorImages[i] = getImage(CursorURL);
    }
    catch (MalformedURLException e) {
      //Create blank if URL is bad
      CursorImages[i] = createImage(0,0);
    }
  }
}

public void start() {
  //Start the run method
  anim.start();
}
```

```java
public void stop() {
  if (anim!=null && anim.isAlive()) {
    //Stop the run method if necessary
    anim.stop();
  }
}

public void paint(Graphics g) {
  int px, py;
  //Set Cursor to the current image
  Image Cursor = CursorImages[CursorIndex];
  g.drawRect(0,0,249,249);
  //Center the image
  px = mouse_x - Cursor.getWidth(this)/2;
  py = mouse_y - Cursor.getHeight(this)/2;
  g.drawImage(Cursor,px,py,this);
}

public boolean mouseMove(Event evt, int x, int y) {
  mouse_x = x;
  mouse_y = y;
  return true;
}

public boolean mouseDown(Event evt, int x, int y) {
  //If paused, restart the run method
  if (paused) {
    anim.resume();
    paused = false;
  }
  //Otherwise, pause the run method
  else {
    anim.suspend();
    paused = true;
  }
  return true;
}
```

```
    public void run() {
       while (anim!=null) {
          try {
             //Suspend for 50 milliseconds
             anim.sleep(50);
          }
          //In case something wakes us up
          catch (InterruptedException e) {}
          //Move along to the next image
          CursorIndex = CursorIndex + 1;
          if (CursorIndex==5) {
             //Start again at the beginning
             CursorIndex = 0;
          }
          repaint();
       }
    }
}
```

Example 5-6b: Animated Cursor Applet Web page.

```
<HTML><HEAD>
<TITLE>Animated Cursor Applet</TITLE>
</HEAD>
<BODY>
<APPLET CODE="AnimatedCursorApplet.class"
HEIGHT=250 WIDTH=250>
<PARAM NAME="CURSORFILE0" VALUE="../images/anim0.gif">
<PARAM NAME="CURSORFILE1" VALUE="../images/anim1.gif">
<PARAM NAME="CURSORFILE2" VALUE="../images/anim2.gif">
<PARAM NAME="CURSORFILE3" VALUE="../images/anim3.gif">
<PARAM NAME="CURSORFILE4" VALUE="../images/anim4.gif">
</APPLET></BODY></HTML>
```

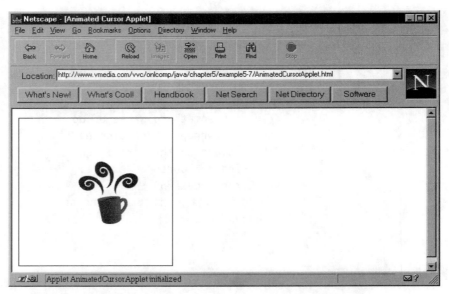

Figure 5-7: *The animated cursor.*

Removing Flicker

Unless you are working on an amazingly superfast graphics work-station, when you view this applet you will notice a flickering that is somewhat annoying. This effect is a result of the applet's efforts to paint the screen faster than the screen can update itself. The classic solution to this problem is a method called *double buffering*. Figure 5-8 contains a diagram of this procedure.

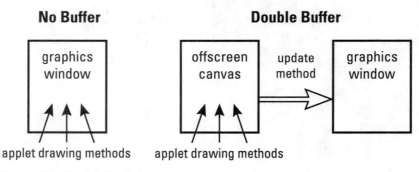

Figure 5-8: *Double buffering.*

When the runtime environment needs to repaint the graphics window—for example, when a window has been obscured, or when the applet has requested that the window be repainted—the applet's context calls the applet's update method and passes it the graphics window's Graphics object. An Applet can request a repaint of its graphics output with the repaint method. The repaint method calls the update method as soon as possible. If the applet calls for another repaint before the update method has been called from the first repaint, the applet is still only updated once. The update method, as defined on the default Applet, simply passes on its Graphics object to the paint method.

Applets can define an offscreen canvas to paint to instead of painting directly to the runtime environment's graphics window. The canvas is an Image; the applet can paint onto the Image by using the Image's getGraphics method. This method returns a Graphics object bound to the Image. The applet can paint to the Image as fast as it cares to. The applet's update method draws the Image onto the applet context's Graphics object instead of allowing the applet to draw onto it. The net effect is to remove flickering caused by overly fast graphics output from an applet.

There is one significant difference between painting to the runtime environment's Graphics object and painting to an Image's Graphics object. The runtime environment's graphics window is cleared and must be repainted in its entirety every time it is updated. An Image will retain things painted onto it unless they are explicitly painted over. If you want to use an Image to paint an animated figure, you must repaint the background around the figure each time you update it, otherwise your figure will leave trails as it moves.

We can add double buffering to our Cursor Applet by using an offscreen Image:

Example 5-7: Flicker-Free Animated Cursor Applet.

```
import java.awt.*;
import java.applet.*;
import java.net.*;
```

```java
public class AnimatedCursorApplet extends Applet implements
Runnable {

  private int mouse_x, mouse_y;
  private Image CursorImages[];
  private int CursorIndex = 0;
  private Thread anim = null;
  private boolean paused = false;
  private Image OffscreenImage;
  //This will be our offscreen canvas
  private Graphics OffscreenGraphics;
  //And this will be our interface to it

  public void init() {
    resize(250,250);
    OffscreenImage = createImage(250,250);
    //Make a new image the same size as us
    OffscreenGraphics = OffscreenImage.getGraphics();
    //Bind our interface to the Image
    anim = new Thread(this);
    mouse_x = 125;
    mouse_y = 125;
    CursorImages = new Image[10];
    int i;
    String CursorParam;
    URL CursorURL;
    for (i=0; i<5; i++) {
      CursorParam = getParameter("CURSORFILE"+i);
      try {
        CursorURL = new URL(CursorParam);
        CursorImages[i] = getImage(CursorURL);
      }
      catch (MalformedURLException e) {
        CursorImages[i] = createImage(0,0);
      }
    }
  }

  public void start() {
    anim.start();
  }
```

```
public void stop() {
  if (anim!=null && anim.isAlive()) {
    anim.stop();
  }
}

public synchronized void update(Graphics g) {
  paint(OffscreenGraphics);
  //Do applet painting to our canvas
  g.drawImage(OffscreenImage,0,0,this);
  //Paint the real graphics window
}

public void paint(Graphics g) {
  int px, py;
  Image Cursor = CursorImages[CursorIndex];
  g.setColor(Color.white);
  g.fillRect(0,0,249,249);
  //Paint over old image
  g.setColor(Color.black);
  g.drawRect(0,0,249,249);
  //Draw the border
  px = mouse_x - Cursor.getWidth(this)/2;
  py = mouse_y - Cursor.getHeight(this)/2;
  g.drawImage(Cursor,px,py,this);
}

public boolean mouseMove(Event evt, int x, int y) {
  mouse_x = x;
  mouse_y = y;
  return true;
}

public boolean mouseDown(Event evt, int x, int y) {
  if (paused) {
    anim.resume();
    paused = false;
  }
  else {
    anim.suspend();
```

```
            paused = true;
        }
        return true;
    }

    public void run() {
        while (anim!=null) {
            try {
                anim.sleep(50);
            }
            catch (InterruptedException e) {}
            CursorIndex = CursorIndex + 1;
            if (CursorIndex==5) {
                CursorIndex = 0;
            }
            repaint();
        }
    }
}
```

Moving On

After reading this chapter, you should be able to code multimedia Java applets. You can now get picture and sound data from the network, get runtime parameters from HTML code, handle user interface events, and bring your applet to life with threads. These methods are necessary for creating applets that incorporate multimedia, but they are not sufficient for writing applets that can interact with the user at a high level, who uses text and other input devices.

By now you should have a good feel for the use of the Java language. The following chapters will discuss the rich hierarchy of classes the Java API provides. These classes and interfaces add useful functionality to the Java language, providing an elegant implementation of, among other things, many of the advanced data structures used by programmers and a complete graphical windowing toolkit. They also are a good example of the power of reusable, extensible objects.

6

Discovering the Application Programming Interface

Using what you learned in the previous chapter, you've probably already joined the Java craze by writing some applets of your own. But Java is much more than an instrument to create animations for your Web pages. By the time you finish this book, you'll be writing applets and applications that utilize a robust windowing environment and talk with the Internet. The secret to your growth from applet coder to Internet programmer is gaining a solid understanding of the *Application Programming Interface* (API).

The API is a huge toolbox of functionality that comes free with the Java Developers Kit. In it you will find string manipulation tools, networking calls, mathematical functionality, and even program workhorses such as hashtables and stacks. Because of this richness, the API provides the foundation for all of our Java endeavors. In fact, we have already been using it! The Applet, URL, Image, String, and System classes are all members of the API. Remember the import statement we were using in the last chapter? Any time we follow it with a token beginning with "java.", we are using the API.

TIP

Most object-oriented programming languages have some form of a class library—a collection of classes that are written in the language and ready to use. If you're accustomed to class libraries, then you can think of the API as Java's class library—the two are identical in concept. However, as you'll see, this isn't technically correct because the Java API also contains Interfaces. We will stick with the term API for the rest of the book.

For almost any program we'd want to write, we can use the API. In fact, the Object class that sits atop the Java class hierarchy is itself a member of the API. A large part of your work in becoming an advanced Java programmer is learning what tools are at your disposal in the API toolbox. This chapter focuses on those parts of the API that will save you tons of work as you start writing more and more applets. It also gives you some background for more advanced topics. For example, when we describe user interfaces in Chapter 7, images in Chapter 9, and networking your applets in Section IV, we are really building on code already contained in the API.

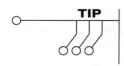

TIP

This chapter's code example files can be found on the Companion CD-ROM (for Windows 95/NT and Macintosh users) and on the Online Companion (for UNIX users). Visit the Online Companion at http://www.vmedia.com/java.hmtl.

API Basics

Most commercial programming languages include something similar to the Java API. While the language specification says how the operators and keywords work together, basic functionality such as input and output are written into the language and included with the compiler. Java is no exception. Those of you familiar with C will probably see a lot of similarity between the standard C libraries that come with any compiler and the Java API. This comparison is quite valid. Without the C libraries, you can do no more than manipulate the basic types, and then you don't have a straightforward way of either inputting or outputting them.

However, the Java API has a few advantages over the standard libraries included with other languages' compilers. First, the API is completely object oriented. So you don't have to mix and match class libraries with the ANSI C libraries as you do when you're working in C/C++. Also, the platform independence of the language means that the API is also platform independent. You never have to worry about libraries on different platforms being incompatible.

Since the API is so easy to use, you'll have little trouble learning the parts that are absolutely necessary. If you really dive in and explore the API, you'll be able to do a lot of basic things without writing your own code. And you'll gain a lot of insight into how to use the object-oriented features of the Java language.

First, you need to understand the structure of the API. Then, we will review just enough Java syntax so that you can use the individual classes and interfaces to their fullest extent.

Structure

The API is a collection of several dozen ready-made classes, interfaces, and exceptions. Within the API, these classes, interfaces, and exceptions are grouped into eight packages: java.applet, java.awt, java.awt.image, java.awt.peer, java.io, java.lang, java.net, and java.util. Table 6-1 briefly describes the purpose of each package.

Package	Description
java.applet	Contains classes and interfaces that enable the applets we wrote in Chapter 5, "How Applets Work."
java.awt	Allows us to write Graphical User Interfaces.
java.awt.peer	Composed wholly of interfaces that allow Java's windowing system to be easily ported across platforms—of no interest to the average programmer.

Package	Description
java.awt.image	Devoted to image creation and manipulation; discussed in Chapter 9, "Graphics & Images."
java.io	Handles raw input and output of the program; discussed in Chapter 11, "Advanced Threading."
java.lang	Contains the core elements of the Java language, such as Object, String, Exception, and Thread.
java.net	Handles interaction with the network. Discussed in Chapter 11, "Advanced Threading" and Chapter 12, "Programming Beyond the Applet Model."
java.util	Contains several utility classes to make your life easier, such as commonly used data structures.

Table 6-1: *Packages of the API.*

As you may remember, a package is a related set of classes and interfaces that are allowed to access one another's protected methods and variables. In many cases, members are contained by a certain package because of design considerations revolving around the *protected* keyword. Other times, a particular member belongs to a particular package because it is most similar in purpose to the other members of that package. As users of the API, we can think of the different packages as families of functionality. Don't be tricked by java.awt.image and java.awt.peer—their members have no special syntactical relationship with java.awt's members. The creators of the Java API just chose those names to demonstrate that members of the two packages are similar in functionality.

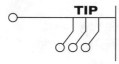

TIP *Subclasses of other API classes aren't necessarily in the same package as their parent. For instance, the Applet class exists in java.applet, but its superclass is in java.awt.*

In day-to-day programming, the package structure is important
to you in two ways. The first has to do with using the import
statement to access a class in the API. Second, you need to be
generally familiar with the contents of the packages because the
Java Developers Kit's online documentation is organized by
packages, as shown in Figure 6-1. Each class, interface, and exception has its own Web page that details all of the public methods
and variables available to you.

After you finish this chapter, give the JDK's online documentation a good surf. As you encounter compile-time bugs in your Java
programs, you'll find the online documentation invaluable for
sorting them out. Throughout the life of this book, we will maintain a link on our Online Companion home page to the most
current online documentation provided by Sun Microsystems.

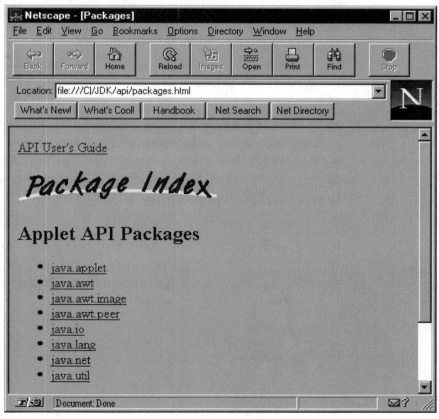

Figure 6-1: *Home page of the JDK online documentation.*

Using the API

The first step to using the API is accessing the packages with the import statement. Once you do this, your learning process is going to take two directions. First, you'll learn how to use the building blocks of Java programming. And because the building blocks are written in Java themselves, as you become proficient in using the API, you will also develop a firm grasp of the principles and syntax of the Java language.

The API is a great hands-on way to learn the specifics of Java because it is already written. You can learn by using what already exists. You may not always agree with the design decisions of the creators of the API, but you will get a good feel for what kind of design decisions arise in Java programming. As you start developing your own classes, interfaces, and packages, you can use the API as a design reference.

Importing Packages

We've been importing packages since Chapter 2, and we described the syntax fully in Chapter 3. As you may remember, you simply say:

```
import <package name>.*;
```

It isn't necessary to import packages—it just makes your code easier to read. If, in Chapter 5, we hadn't imported the package java.applet, we would have had to declare our class as follows:

```
class MyApplet extends java.applet.Applet {
```

For classes that we'll be using a lot, it would become annoying to have to spell out the full name of the class each time.

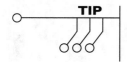

TIP

The java.lang package is so essential that the compiler always imports it.

To make the best use of the import statement, you can use the recipe below. The class that we are going to use for our example is java.util.Date, which is a neat class that allows us to access the current time and date.

1. Determine the package containing the class that you want to use. In this case, it's pretty simple—since the full name of our package is java.util.Date, we know that the package is java.util. Otherwise, we would consult the JDK online documentation to find the appropriate package.

2. Import the class with the import statement. If we are only using the Date class, we could just say:

```
import java.util.Date;
```

Generally, you will find that we use several classes from a single package. In this case, we should use the wildcard to import all of the classes from that package:

```
import java.util.*;
```

3. Now we are ready to use our class to access today's date. Using the import statement is pretty simple. The trap to avoid is importing only the package and not the classes. You fall into this trap with the following import statement:

```
import java.util;
```

This statement doesn't actually import any classes! By adding the wildcard or a class name, we are able to declare variables as follows:

```
Date d;
```

As opposed to:

```
java.util.Date d;
```

With or without the import java.util.*; statement, the latter code is valid. However, this type of declaration is awkward and error prone.

Static vs. Dynamic Methods

You may remember from Chapter 2 that Java methods can be
either static or dynamic. Dynamic methods are much more common—they are associated with an instantiation of a class. Static
methods, on the other hand, are methods that are associated with
a class itself. We know a method is static when the static modifier
is present in its declaration. Figure 6-2 shows a static method
named parse in the java.util.Date class. Note the presence of the
static keyword.

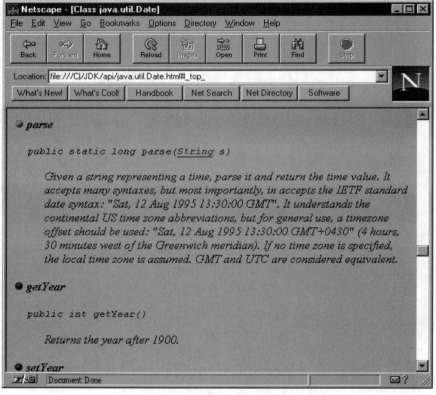

Figure 6-2: *A static method in the Date class.*

When we use a static method such as parse, we don't need to create an instance of the class. Instead, we reference the class, as follows:

```
public long demoStatic(String S) {
   return Date.parse(S);}
```

Many of the methods in the API are static because, even if they were dynamic, they would produce exactly the same result for any instantiation. Therefore, it would be annoying to have to create a variable when we are only interested in a method that takes input and produces output indifferent to the state of the rest of the object.

But this convenience often causes problems for new Java programmers because they will try to access static methods dynamically. It may help if you think of each class as having two separate parts—one that is dynamic, and one that is static. The dynamic part consists of the variables and methods that are part of the class's instantiation—those that aren't modified by the static keyword. In the case of our Date class, this would include methods other than our parse method.

The static variables and methods, on the other hand, are just utilities that belong to a certain class because that class is where you would logically look for them. Let's take the parse method in Date, for example. This method takes a String that is formatted as a Date and returns to you the number of seconds since the Epoch—midnight, January 1, 1970, Greenwich Mean Time.

If you needed such a functionality and started browsing the API online documentation looking for it, you would probably drop in on the Date class. By browsing through the method descriptions of the Date class, you would see that the method you need already exists and you don't need to write it yourself.

Once you see that the method exists, though, determine if it is static. If it is static, you will need to know that:

- You don't need to instantiate an object to use that method.

- You can't access a static method from an instantiated object.

- You access the method with the syntax *<class name>.<method name>*.

Other Modifiers to Consider

As you check the online documentation to see if a method is static, be on the lookout for other method modifiers. We defined all of these modifiers in Chapter 3, "Object Orientation in Java." Here we review them in terms of how they affect us as users of the API:

◈ **Protected**. *Protected* means that the method or variable is available only to other classes in the package. Since we aren't writing classes that will be part of any API package, we should consider these methods off-limits. Don't worry—we'll get to use the protected keyword when designing and implementing our own packages in Chapter 11, "Advanced Threading."

◈ **Final**. The *final* modifier means that the method—or the entire class—can't be subclassed. When we are using classes that are part of the API, this keyword has no meaning to us. However, if we want to subclass an API class to make our own class, we need to take note of the absence or presence of the final modifier.

◈ **Abstract**. If an entire class is abstract, then we may instantiate only its subclasses. If one of the class's members is abstract, then we can only access that member in a subclass that overrides that particular abstract method—this goes back to our discussion of abstract methods and classes in Chapter 3, "Object Orientation in Java." When you see the abstract modifier, remember that all is not as it seems. You should probably look at the tree of the API, which is included in the online documentation, and investigate the subclasses provided by the API. In Figure 6-3, we show the tree for the abstract class java.awt.Component. Understanding the subclasses of this class is a large part of learning Java's Abstract Windowing Toolkit, and we'll investigate them fully in the following two chapters.

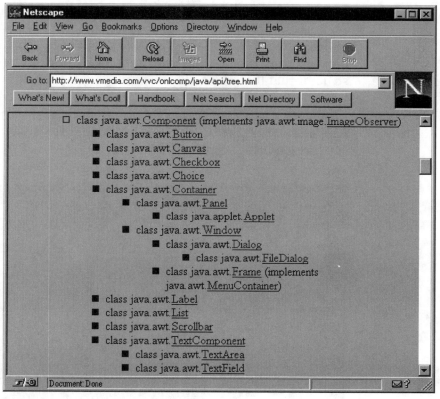

Figure 6-3: *The tree of the API.*

🦋 **Synchronized and native.** These two modifiers have no real importance to users of the API. To review, *synchronized* means that a particular method or variable can't be accessed more than once at any particular time. Synchronization is important for multithreaded programs, as we will see in Chapter 11. But for now, we don't need to worry about it.

The native modifier specifies that the method is actually implemented in a dynamic linked library (DLL) that wasn't written in Java. All native methods are meant to blend seamlessly into code written in Java. Again, we don't need to take special note when we see that a method we would like to use happens to be native. We'll look at native methods in greater detail in Chapter 12, "Programming Beyond the Applet Model."

Exceptions & the API

As you look at the Java online documentation to see what modifiers are present for certain methods, you'll notice that some methods and constructors throw exceptions. We encountered a constructor that throws an exception in Chapter 5, "How Applets Work"—the constructor for the URL class, which is contained in the java.net package. Figure 6-4, the URL class home page, shows us that the constructor that takes a String throws the MalformedURLException.

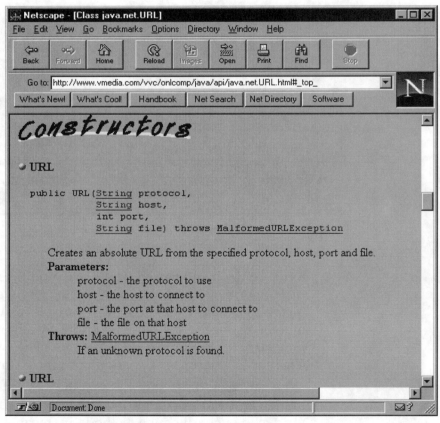

Figure 6-4: *A constructor that throws an exception.*

To use the API effectively, you need to be aware of the exceptions that a method or constructor may throw. We will cover thoroughly how to write your own exception-handling routines in Chapter 10, "Advanced Program Design." For right now, we are just going to present a recipe for dealing with API methods and constructors that throw exceptions. The underlying strategy is presented in a flow chart in Figure 6-5.

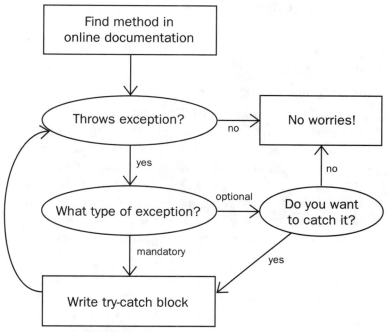

Figure 6-5: *Flow chart for dealing with exception throwers.*

Step 1 is pretty obvious—we first look to the online documentation to see if our method throws an exception. If the *throws* keyword exists in the method or constructor declaration, then we know that we proceed to Step 2—figuring out what kind of exception is being thrown. The simplest way to do this is to click on the exception name, which in the case of our URL constructor is MalformedURLException. Since exceptions are classes in their own right, they have their own home pages.

When we get to the exception's home page, we determine what kind of exception it is; that is, we look to see where it falls as a subclass. If it is a descendant of RuntimeException or Error, then the compiler doesn't force us to use a try-catch block. We then need to think about whether we would like to catch the exception. Usually, there isn't any reason to catch an Error—they are thrown when something goes really wrong, such as running completely out of memory. But there *are* times when we will want to catch runtime exceptions.

WHY CATCH A RUNTIME EXCEPTION?

You may be thinking, "If I'm not forced to catch an exception, I would rather not bother." However, there are many methods in the API that throw runtime exceptions we would like to catch. Later in this chapter, we will look at methods that change Strings into numeric primitive types, such as floats and ints. If the String isn't valid, the runtime exception NumberFormatException is thrown. If we try to turn a String into a number that isn't valid and we *don't* catch it, our program will crash!

If we have to catch an exception, or decide that we want to catch a runtime exception, we write a try-catch block around the method that throws the exception. When we write the try-catch blocks, we must remember to put everything that depends on the normal execution of the method or constructor inside the try block. Also, we must make sure we actually handle the exceptional event in our catch blocks. Though the following applet will compile and will work properly, it's a good example of exception abuse:

```java
import java.applet.*;
class badApplet extends Applet {

Image img;
//variable declarations
```

```
public void init() {
URL imgURL;
//bad idea - should be in try block!
try {
  imgURL=new URL(getParam("image"));
  }
  catch (MalformedURLException e) {}
  //bad idea! We don't do anything in
  //the case of the exception

img=getImage(imgURL);
}
//other methods
}
```

Consider what happens if the parameter, "image", doesn't represent a valid URL. Our catch block doesn't even tell our audience something has gone wrong! Worse yet, we've used imgURL outside of the try-catch block. This means that our program will crash when we attempt to retrieve the image.

The code above is the result of someone's unwillingness to try to handle exceptions well in a program. Since exception handling is often foreign to new Java programmers, they may treat it as an annoyance and do only what's absolutely required. As we will see in Chapter 10, "Advanced Program Design," exception handling is the key to writing bulletproof Java code. We aren't going to discuss it in depth just yet. But as you begin using the API, try not to develop bad exception-handling habits. As you write try-catch blocks, take to heart the following tips:

- If the writer of the method bothered to throw an exception, there is probably a good reason.

- Make sure all code that depends on the method or constructor that throws the exception is contained in the try block. The easiest way to ensure this is to declare any variables that are assigned by the particular method or constructor inside the try block.

◈   Always use your catch blocks to intelligently deal with the circumstances that cause the exception to be thrown. In our badApplet example, we should have alerted the user to the fact that the "image" parameter is invalid. In extreme cases, you may have to terminate execution in the catch block.

The java.lang.Object Class

The java.lang.Object class is the fundamental class of Java. Remember in Chapter 3, "Object Orientation in Java," when we said that all classes are descended from a single class? This is the one! The most important thing about the Object class is that it sits atop the hierarchy. It is not, however, merely an abstraction—it contains several methods and can be instantiated like other classes. Since all classes are descended from the Object class, its methods are present in every other class. Most of the basic methods in Table 6-2, if not all, are usually overridden in the subclasses.

Method	Description	Exceptions Thrown
boolean equals(Object o)	Returns true if o is equivalent to this Object.	None
String toString()	Returns a String that represents information about this Object.	None
Object clone()	Creates a clone of this Object.	CloneNotSupportedException
void finalize()	Called when this object is garbage collected.	Throwable

Table 6-2: *Basic methods of the Object class.*

Although the Object class has other methods, these are the most important ones. The first two are overridden by every class in the API. The clone method is our secret to making new copies of objects. This goes back to our discussion in Chapter 4 about the assignment operator =. Let's recall our example:

```
public void sampleMethod(someClass anObject) {
someClass anotherObject=anObject;}
```

In this case, anotherObject and anObject are really the same—the assignment did not create a new copy. When the clone method is overridden, we can use it to make a copy of an instance:

```
someClass aCopy=anObject.clone();
```

Here, we are assuming that the author of someClass has defined how he wants instances of someClass to be cloned. However, it isn't always a good idea for a class to define a way for objects to clone themselves—we will discuss why in Chapter 10. The writer of a particular class decides whether or not instances of that class can be cloned, and many of the classes in the API are not cloneable. We know that we can use this method when the class, or one of its superclasses, implements the interface cloneable and explicitly overrides the method.

But what about the other methods in the Object class? They are outside the scope of this chapter. Table 6-3 describes what they do and where they are discussed further.

Method	Description	Where Covered
wait, notify, notifyAll	Allows an object to talk to Java threads.	Chapter 11, "Advanced Threading."
hashCode	Allows an object to be used with java.util.Hashtable.	Chapter 10, "Advanced Program Design."
getClass	Used to get runtime information about this object.	Chapter 10, "Advanced Program Design."

Table 6-3: *Other methods of the Object class.*

String Manipulation Tools

As you know, a string is simply a sequence of characters. Virtually all programming languages support strings in some way, and Java is no exception. The String class, whose documentation home page is shown in Figure 6-6, is in the java.lang package and is used to represent strings. This class provides functionality such as conversion to number types, searching and replacing substrings, accessing individual characters, and trimming white space. Chances are that you will use the String class more than any other class in the API, and you need to know its member methods pretty well. In this section, we explore the String class in depth. Also, we look at some other classes in the API that will aid your string manipulation tasks.

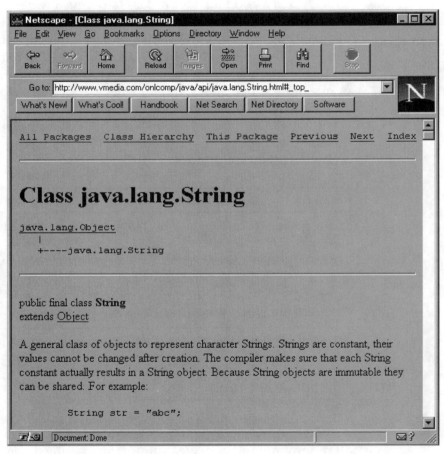

Figure 6-6: *The String class home page.*

Creating Strings

You can create strings in one of two ways:

* Use one of the seven constructors of the String class; or
* Use the = operator.

So far, we have been using the = operator to make Strings. The statement:

```
String S="My string,";
```

is the simplest way to create a String. The + operator can also be used with Strings to make string concatenation easy as shown in Example 6-1:

Example 6-1a: Building Strings from primitive types.

```
String S2="another string";
String S3=S+S2+"and a primitive type: "
int i=4;
S3=S3+i;
```

S3 will now have the value "My string, another string and a primitive type: 4". The + operator works with all of the primitive types. However, the = operator doesn't! The following code fragment won't compile because of the last two statements:

```
int i=4;
String S1=i;
//Won't compile!
String S2=4;
//Won't compile!
```

This limitation is unfortunate, but there is a simple, if slightly ugly, workaround. Just create an empty String and append to it:

Example 6-1b: Assigning primitive types directly to Strings.

```
int i=4;
String S1=""+i;
String S2=""+4;
```

The = operator only works with string literals (anything contained within quotation marks) and other Strings. The + operator will work with string literals, other Strings, and all of the primitive types. Strings can also be constructed using the constructors described in Table 6-4.

Constructor	Creates
String()	An empty string.
String(String S)	A new String that is a copy of S.
String(char charArray[])	A String based on charArray.
String(char charArray[], int offset, int len)	A String based on the subarray, starting at offset and ending after len characters.
String(byte byteArray[], int hibyte)	A String based on byteArray, where hibyte describes the Unicode high byte of each char.
String (byte byteArray[], int hibyte, int offset, int len)	A String based on the subarray, starting at offset and ending after len bytes.

Table 6-4: *String constructors.*

Though the = operator isn't compatible with the primitive types, this is really the only thing that is counter-intuitive about Java String creation. Once we get past the oddities of comparing Strings, you will be ready to use Strings without worry.

Comparing Strings

Now that you know the intricacies of creating Strings, our next step is comparing them. The String class has two methods that will do comparisons for us—the equals method and the compareTo method. The equals method overrides the equals method in the Object class and returns true when the strings are the same, while the compareTo method returns 0 upon equivalence.

Example 6-2a: Comparing Strings with compareTo and equals.

```
if (S1.compareTo(S2)!=0)
   System.out.println("S1 is equivalent to the String S2");
if (S1.equals(S2))
   System.out.println("S1 is equivalent to the String S2");
```

The value returned by compareTo is –1 if S1 is lexigraphically less than S2, and 1 if S1 is lexigraphically greater than S2. *Lexigraphically* is essentially the same as *alphabetically*, as you can see from the example below. The difference is that it extends to digits and other nonalphabetic characters, so that "a113" is lexigraphically greater than "a112". The ordering is determined by the Unicode values.

Example 6-2b: Lexigraphical comparisons with compareTo.

```
S1="alpha";
S2="beta";
if (S1.compareTo(S2)==-1)
   System.out.println("this will always be printed");
if (S2.compareTo(S1)==1)
   System.out.println("this will always be printed");
```

The lexigraphic ordering is derived from the integer values of the Unicode characters. Beginning at the first character, the compareTo method compares each character based on its integer value. When it finds a difference, it returns 1 or –1 as described above. For digits and alphabetic characters, the ordering is pretty intuitive and easy to remember, as we show in Figure 6-7.

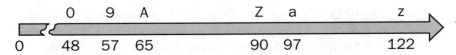

Figure 6-7: *Lexigraphical ordering of digits and alphabetic characters.*

Life gets more complicated when using non-English characters and characters like %, @, !, or *. (Please don't be offended, we aren't trying to curse.) If you find yourself needing to know the value of strange characters not covered in Figure 6-7, the easiest thing to do is just to cast the char to an int and print its value:

```java
public void strangeCharacter(char Strange) {
int val=(int)Strange;
System.out.println("One strange character!");
System.out.println("The char "+Strange+" = "+val);}
```

THE == OPERATOR & STRING COMPARISONS

You may have seen some Java code that compares Strings using the == operator. In simple cases, the == operator works the same for primitive types as it does for Strings. But this usage is not part of the language specification, is compiler dependent, and may not work in some cases. To avoid the possibility of painful and hard-to-find bugs, always use either the equals or compareTo methods.

In addition to the two comparison methods we just examined, there are six others that will compare two Strings in various ways. All of these are summarized in Table 6-5, in order of increasing complexity.

Method	Returns True When:
equalsIgnoreCase(String S)	Instance String equals S, regardless of case.
beginsWith(String S)	Instance String starts with S.
beginsWith(String S,int len)	Instance String starts with the first len characters of S.
endsWith(String S)	Instance String ends with S.
regionMatches(int toffset, String S,int ooffset, int len)	The substring in the instance String, starting at position toffset, matches the substring starting at ooffset, for len characters.
regionMatches(boolean ignoreCase, int toffset, String S, int ooffset, int len)	Same as above regionMatches; ignores case when ignoreCase==true.

Table 6-5: *String comparison methods.*

Most of the string comparison methods are pretty intuitive, but the regionMatches methods need some explanation. The regionMatches methods let you compare any of the substrings in S1 and S2. The first parameter determines the position in the instance string where you want to start your comparison. The second parameter is some other String, with the third parameter being the position at which you want to start in that String. The last parameter is the length of the region. We illustrate the usage of the regionMatches methods in Figure 6-8.

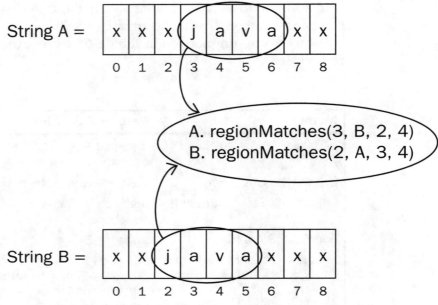

Figure 6-8: *Using the regionMatches methods.*

As you'll see when we start parsing Strings, the two comparison methods are extremely useful. The trick is passing them the right integers as parameters. To get a feel for this, let's think about using them to emulate the startsWith and endsWith methods. The following expression always evaluates to true:

Example 6-3a: Mimicking the startsWith method using regionMatches.

```
String A="some random String";
String B="some";

int lengthB=B.length();
if (A.startsWith(B)==A.regionMatches(0,B,0,lengthB))
    System.out.println("This will always be printed");
```

We can better illustrate how to arrive at the right parameters to pass by making the endsWith method equivalent to the regionMatches method:

Example 6-3b: Mimicking the endsWith method using regionMatches.

```
int lengthB=B.length();
int startA=A.length()-B.length();
if (A.endsWith(B)==A.regionMatches(startA,B,0,lengthB))
    System.out.println("This will always be printed");
```

Dealing With Substrings

We just saw how the String class lets us do comparisons of substrings. We also have many methods for extracting substrings. Let's start with the straightforward substring methods:

```
public String substring(int start)
public String substring(int start, int len)
```

The first method shown above returns a new String that begins at the start position in the character array and contains all the characters past that position. The second method only contains len characters past the start position. The first character of a String is at the 0 position. Here are some examples:

```
String S="0123456789";

String S1=S.substring(0);
String S2=S;
//String S1, S2, and S are all equivalent.

String S4=S.substring(4);
//S4 has the value "456789"

String S5=S.substring(4,3);
//S5 has the value "456"
```

The substring methods alone aren't valuable if you always have to conjure up the parameters to pass to them. This is where the indexOf methods come into play. The indexOf methods allow you to examine a String class for individual characters or Strings and return the array index. The returned integer value can then be passed to the substring methods for extraction or to the regionMatches methods for comparison. Table 6-6 describes the various indexOf methods.

Method Declaration	Parameters	Return Value
int indexOf(char *a*)	*a* is the character to look for.	Index of the first occurrence.
indexOf(char *a*, int *start*)	*a* is the character to look for, *start* is the position at which to begin looking.	Index of the first occurrence of *a* past *start* position.
indexOf(String *S*)	*S* is the String to look for.	Index of the start of the first occurrence of *S*.
indexOf(String *S*, int *start*)	*S* is the String to look for, *start* is where to begin.	Index of the start of the first occurrence of *S* past *start*.

Table 6-6: *The indexOf methods of the String class.*

LASTINDEXOF()
For each indexOf method there is a corresponding lastIndexOf method. As the name implies, the lastIndexOf method begins its search at the end of the String.

Altering Strings

Throughout this chapter, we have been altering Strings with statements such as:

```
String S="some string";
S=S+", more of the string";
S=S.substring(14,4);
//assign substring back to original String
```

Notice that when we do these alterations, we have to assign the results back to the original String. This step is necessary because, once created, an instance of the String can't be altered. So we create a new copy of the string by calling one of the String class methods and then assigning the new copy back to the original variable.

Besides the substring methods, there are four other methods we can use to make alterations. These methods are outlined in Table 6-7. Remember that in each case, a copy of the String is made, the alterations are made on that copy, and the copy is returned. None of the methods in the String class actually alters the String itself—instead, you assign a new copy to either the same variable or a different variable.

Method Usage for String S1	Parameters	Returns
S1.concat(S2)	S2 is the String to be appended to S1.	S1+S2
S1.replace(a,b)	Char b replaces char a.	S1 with occurrences of a replaced by b.
S1.toLowerCase()	None.	S1 with no uppercase letters.
S1.toUpperCase()	None.	S1 with no lowercase letters.
S1.trim()	None.	S1 with no leading or trailing white space.

Table 6-7: *String alteration methods.*

Parsing Strings

We now have all of the tools we need to be able to parse Strings. We can compare substrings and, using the indexOf methods, retrieve certain substrings. But let's say we know that our Strings are going to have several occurrences of the same substring. For instance, a mathematical expression that we need to evaluate may have several occurrences of +. Computer scientists would refer to such a substring as a *delimiter*. In such a case, it's the items between the delimiters that count. These are called *tokens*.

TOKENS, DELIMITERS & COMPILATION

You may have seen the word *token* associated with computer languages. Compilers need to break up a source code file by looking for delimiters like commas and white space. A simple example is the process of understanding the parameter list. The compiler first isolates the characters inside the parentheses. Then, using the comma as a delimiter, it can identify the tokens—individual variable declarations. With these separated out, it can start compiling the rest of a subroutine.

Based on the indexOf and substring methods we have already talked about, you could write some code that could parse out tokens of a String based on a particular delimiter. But it would be a lot of work. Luckily, the java.util package contains the StringTokenizer class, which will break up a given String based on a given delimiter. Figure 6-9 shows the online documentation for StringTokenizer.

Figure 6-9: *StringTokenizer documentation home page.*

Let's say that we are given a String like "3+4+2+7", and we want to compute the sum of the integers. The StringTokenizer class will split up the String based on the + signs, starting from the left:

Example 6-4: Parsing Strings with StringTokenizer.

```
public int getSum(String S) {

int runningSum=0;

StringTokenizer tok=new StringTokenizer(S,"+");
//S is the String to tokenize,
//"+" is the delimiter to split on
```

```
while (tok.hasMoreTokens()) {
String thisToken=tok.getNextToken();
runningSum=Add(thisToken);
}

System.out.println("Total="+runningSum);}

private static int Add(String S) {
  return Integer.parseInt(S)+runningSum;}


}
```

As you can see, this is much simpler than using the indexOf and regionMatches methods to do the same thing. We can reserve the use of indexOf and regionMatches for when we only have to split a given String once. Table 6-8 details the constructors, while Table 6-9 outlines the essential methods you need to use this class effectively.

Constructors	Effect
StringTokenizer(String S, String delim)	Will tokenize S based on delim.
StringTokenizer(String S, String delim, boolean returnDelims)	As above, except if returnDelims==true, delimiters will be returned as tokens.
StringTokenizer(String S)	Will tokenize based on white space ("\t\n\r").

Table 6-8: *The StringTokenizer constructors.*

Method	Returns
String nextToken()	Returns the next token.
String nextToken(String newDelim)	Returns the next token, after switching the delimiter to newDelim.
boolean hasMoreTokens()	Returns true if there are tokens that haven't been returned yet.
int countTokens()	Returns number of tokens in the String.

Table 6-9: *StringTokenizer methods.*

Converting Strings to Other Data Types

We often need to do conversions between Strings and primitive data types such as integers. To convert primitive data types to Strings, we have the valueOf methods. There is a valueOf method for each of the primitive data types, and they all work in the same way. Let's demonstrate int, float, double, boolean, and char:

Example 6-5a: Primitive-to-string conversions.

```
int someInt=1;
String StringInt=String.valueOf(someInt);

float someFloat=9.99f;
String StringAsFloat=String.valueOf(someFloat);
//StringAsFloat has the value of "9.99"
//note the trailing f to distinguish it
//from a double literal.

double someDouble=99999999.99;
String StringAsDouble=String.valueOf(someDouble);
//StringAsDouble has the value of "999999999.99"

boolean someBoolean=true;
String StringAsBoolean=String.valueOf(someBoolean);
//StringAsBoolean has the value of "true"

char someChar='a';
String StringAsChar=String.valueOf(someChar);
//StringAsChar has the value of "a"
```

These methods aren't any different than the workaround we used previously to assign primitive types to Strings by using the + operator and a null String. You may find these methods useful to make your code a bit more understandable. But how do we convert Strings to primitive types? As may be expected, there are static methods available in the API to accomplish this—but they aren't in the String class. Instead, they are contained in the primitive type wrapper classes we will discuss next. Here are examples

of conversions for the numeric primitive types, excluding short and byte:

Example 6-5b: String-to-primitive conversions.

```
String intString="10";
String floatString="10.1f";
String longString="999999999";
String doubleString="999999999.9";

try {
   int i=Integer.parseInt(intString);
   float f=Float.valueOf(floatString).floatValue();
   long l=Long.parseLong(longString);
   double d=Double.valueOf(doubleString).longValue();
   } catch (NumberFormatException e) {
     System.out.println("invalid conversion attempted");}
```

In our example, we don't have to worry about our Strings being invalid because we assign them literally. But in many cases—such as when you are getting input from a user—you need to be prepared in case the Strings aren't properly formatted. NumberFormatException is a runtime exception, so you don't *have* to catch it. But if you don't, your program will certainly crash one day.

This wraps up String-to-numeric primitive conversions, with the exception of byte and short. Remembering that all of the numeric data types can be cast to byte and short, the following fragment will do the trick:

Example 6-6a: String to byte and short.

```
String S="0";

try {
    byte b=Integer.intValue(S);
    //narrowing an int value to byte;
    //information could be lost.
```

```
        short s=Integer.intValue(S);
        //narrowing an int value to short;
        //information could be lost.
        } catch (NumberFormatException) {
          //deal with S being invalid
          //you might need to throw the
          //exception again.
          }
    }
```

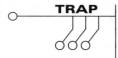

TRAP

In the sample code above for String-to-byte and String-to-short conversions, we are narrowing from one primitive data type to another. If I.intValue() returns a value greater than 256 or less than –255, our byte value will be wrong. Likewise, a value greater than 32768 or less than –32767 will produce an incorrect value for s. The best way to handle these eventualities is by writing your own exception handlers. We'll show you how by expanding on this code fragment in Chapter 10, "Advanced Program Design."

The only primitive types that we haven't covered are boolean and char. Converting to char is trivial—just use the charAt method to return the first character of the String:

```
public char stringToChar(String S) {
return S.charAt(0);}
```

Converting to boolean is more like the numeric conversions. Unfortunately, the valueOf method of the class Boolean doesn't throw an exception when the String doesn't look like a boolean. Rather, it returns true when the String equals "true", and false in all other cases:

Example 6-6b: String to boolean conversions.

```
String truth="true";
String fallicy="false";
String whiteLie="anything else";
String nothingness=null;
```

```
boolean b1=Boolean.valueOf(truth).booleanValue();
// b1==true
boolean b2=Boolean.valueOf(fallicy).booleanValue();
 //b2==false
boolean b3=Boolean.valueOf(whiteLie).booleanValue();
//b3==false
boolean b4=Boolean.valueOf(nothingness).booleanValue();
//b4==false
```

Primitive Type Wrappers

The Java language has a dichotomy between its object-oriented variables and the primitive data types: boolean, char, double, float, int, and long. The classes that we are going to look at now bridge the two worlds. They are Boolean, Char, Double, Float, Integer, and Long. As we saw above, they are needed to allow conversions from Strings to the primitive data types. They are also useful when using the data structures, Vector and Stack, which we will cover in the next section. Additionally, the numeric wrappers, Double, Float, Integer, and Long, are useful when you are doing math—they contain constants that represent maximum, minimum, infinite, and Not-a-Number values. We look at these constants in a later section of this chapter, "Math & the API."

The structures of these "wrapper classes" are all very similar. Each wrapper class is declared *final*, meaning that you can't subclass it to create new classes. Each one can be constructed with either a String or its corresponding primitive data type as the sole parameter. And each one has the methods that interface with its corresponding primitive type. Example 6-7 shows an example of the two types of construction for Integer and Float.

Example 6-7: Primitive type wrapper construction.

```
int i=2;
String intString="3";
Integer I1=new Integer(i);
Integer I2=new Integer(intString);
```

```
float f=2.1f;
String floatString="3.2";
Float F1=new Float(f);
Float F2=new Float(floatString);
```

Object Container Classes

If you have ever taken an advanced Computer Science course, you are probably familiar with hashtables and stacks. If you haven't, then you're lucky; with the Java API, you can reap the benefits of these powerful utilities without experiencing the pain of writing them for a professor! The classes that we cover here are the Java implementations of some of the most powerful data structures of Computer Science. These classes, which we are calling *Object Container classes*, are used to group different types of objects together.

The Object Container classes don't care how many objects you want them to hold, and they provide you with very useful functionalities for placing and retrieving them. The Hashtable class allows you to make key–value pairs of objects and to access the value object based on a comparison to a key. The Vector class is useful when you know that you will need to create multiple instances of the same class, but don't yet know how many. The Stack class allows you to keep track of a set of objects on a "First In, First Out" basis.

PRIMITIVE TYPES & THE OBJECT CONTAINER CLASSES

The primitive types can't be used with the Object Container classes because the Data Structure classes deal exclusively with objects. To put a char, boolean, float, int, or double into one of these Data Structures, first wrap it in its corresponding primitive wrapper.

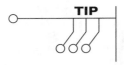

TIP *After you read about the Object Container classes, you will want to use them to manage objects that you have written. To do so properly, you need to override the boolean equals and hashCode method in the Object class. We discuss this in Chapter 10, "Advanced Program Design."*

The Vector Class

Let's start with the simplest data container, the *Vector class*. Don't let the name mislead you—this class is not reserved for complicated scientific and graphical programs. A Java Vector is essentially an expandable array. After you learn the basics of this class, you will find many uses for it. Have you ever needed an array of some data type, but not known how big it needed to be? The Vector class takes care of this. Unlike an array, you can add as many elements as you need to a Vector. When you are done adding elements to a Vector, you can create an array of the correct size and copy all of the elements into it. Table 6-10 outlines the methods we need to accomplish this.

Method	Purpose
void addElement(Object o)	The object o is added.
void insertElementAt(Object o, int i)	Inserts object o at location i. No elements are erased; the size grows by one.
void copyInto(Object someArray[])	All of the elements in the Vector are copied into someArray.
int length()	Returns the number of elements currently in the Vector.

Table 6-10: *Basic Vector methods.*

Let's see this powerful data structure in action. Remember the animation applet from Chapter 4, "Syntax & Semantics?" We used the getParam method of the Applet class to get image URLs from the HTML page. We arbitrarily set the number of images at five. Alternatively, we could have counted the number of images and then created an array of that size. By creating a Vector first, we can add each image as we encounter the corresponding parameter on the HTML page. Now we can write an animation applet that loads any number of images:

Example 6-8: Animated Applet with an arbitrary number of images.

```
public class AnimatedApplet extends Applet implements
Runnable {

private Image imgs[];

public void init() {
    if (getImages()>0) {

        ...
        }

public int getImages() {
    int indx=0;
    Vector imageVec=new Vector();
    while (getParameter("image"+indx)!=null) {
        String S=getParameter("image"+indx);
        try {
        URL U=new URL(getDocumentBase(),S);
        Image im=getImage(U);
        imageVec.addElement(im);
            }
        catch (MalformedURLException e)
        { showStatus(S+"is not a valid URL - skipping"); }

        indx=indx+1;
        }

    imgs=new Image[imageVec.size()];
    imageVec.copyInto(imgs);

    return indx;

}
```

Now we have a way to easily store as many images as we want, but we can still have all of them in an array. If we wanted to, we could just leave them in the Vector. Since we can access the *n*th image using the elementAt method, our Vector is as functional as an array. If we are expecting additional images later on, we should use this approach. But if we aren't expecting new elements, it is usually better to use the copyInto method. At a glance, it is easier to figure out what the program is doing with an array than with a Vector instance. In general, it will also be more efficient from a memory usage standpoint, since you usually have to greatly overestimate the size of the array if you are going to set it up first.

THE COPYINTO METHOD & PROGRAM PERFORMANCE

When using the copyInto method that we describe above, you may use less memory than you otherwise would, but there is a performance concern. When the copyInto method is called, it creates an array and then copies to the array the references to the objects contained in the Vector. If you have a Vector containing N elements, N copy operations must be performed.

The copy operation itself isn't that much of a drain—you aren't making copies of all the objects, just the references to the objects. This means that you are probably only copying a total of N*8 bytes, depending on the implementation of the virtual machine. Of course, for exceptionally large N, this could cause quite a blip in your execution time.

Storing an undefined number of objects is the most powerful use of the Vector class, but you can also use it for other purposes. As Table 6-11 shows, you can make an exact copy of the entire vector, search for particular elements, access elements by their index, and remove all the elements. Notice that you can't remove only part of a vector's elements—this method is an all-or-nothing proposition.

Method	Description
boolean contains(Object o)	Sees if o is in the Vector. Calls o.equals(eachObject) on each element.
int indexOf(Object o)	Returns location of o, or –1 if not in Vector. Uses equals method as above.
int indexOf(Object o, int i)	Same as previous indexOf method, except begins search at the i position.
int lastIndexOf(Object o)	This acts like indexOf(Object o), except the search begins at the last element.
boolean isEmpty()	Returns true if there are no elements.
int removeAllElements()	Removes all elements in the Vector.

Table 6-11: *Additional Vector methods.*

Since the Vector class doesn't have a predetermined size, you may be wondering how efficient it is. Since it's dynamic, we can't expect it to be as efficient as an array—as it grows, it will eventually need to ask for more memory. By default, space for 10 objects is allocated. Each time more space is needed, the internal size of the Vector is doubled. This is important to remember, since you can control how the Vector expands by using the constructors and methods described in Table 6-12. The first constructor Vector(int size), simply creates a Vector of the specified size. If you know you'll have at least 100 elements, go ahead and create a vector of that size. You can change how the Vector grows by passing a value to the second constructor to use as a capacity increment. The Vector will then allocate space for that number of elements each time it needs to grow, instead of always doubling. And you can control the size of the Vector even after it has been instantiated, using the ensureCapacity or the setSize method. The setSize method is a tad dangerous, though; if your Vector is bigger than the size you specify, all of the elements past the index of size will be chopped off. So you'll probably prefer the ensureCapacity method.

Method/Constructor	Description
Vector(int size)	Creates a vector with space for size Objects.
Vector(int size, int inc)	Creates a vector with space for size Objects, and sets capacity increment to inc.
ensureCapacity(int size)	If capacity is less than size, procure enough space for size Objects.
setSize(int size)	Sets to size, possibly deleting end elements.

Table 6-12: *Efficiency and the Vector class.*

There is one property of Vectors that we haven't explicitly talked about: you can put different types of objects in the same Vector. This is possible because the methods of the Vector class that allow you to put elements into your Vectors, insertAt and addElement, take the type Object as their parameter. Since all classes are descended from the Object class, all of our objects can be cast to Objects. All of the Object Container classes share this property—we'll give an example of its usefulness in our discussion about Hashtables.

Hashtables

Just as vectors are great for storing an undefined number of objects, hashtables are great for storing an undefined number of *pairs* of objects. As its name implies, a *hashtable* is a table of data. The table has two columns, as shown in Figure 6-10. One column contains *keys*, and the other contains *elements*. Each key is associated with one, and only one, element. If you attempt to add a key–element pair, and the key is already in the Hashtable, the element is replaced. After you have put some pairs into the Hashtable, you can access their elements by using the associated keys. That is, you can pass the Hashtable some object, and if that object is one of the keys, it returns the associated element. These basic activities can be done with the methods in Table 6-13.

Serge	30
Eric	48
Mike	27
Ed	18
Shammond	29
...	...

Figure 6-10: *A simple Hashtable.*

Method	Description
Object put(Object key, Object element)	Places key–element pair into the hashtable. If key was already in the hashtable, its associated element is returned.
Object get(Object key)	Returns element associated with key.
boolean containsKey(Object key)	Returns true if key is in the table.
Object remove(Object key)	Removes key–element pair from the table.

Table 6-13: *Basic hashtable methods.*

Now let's build the hashtable shown in Figure 6-10. We'll first construct a simple example that doesn't do any error checking and then make it more robust. Since the keys are numbers, we need to use our primitive type wrappers. Pay particular attention to the casting between types in this example. When we are done, we will be able to access a person's age if we know his or her name.

Example 6-9a: Tracking ages with a Hashtable.

```
class ageManager {

private Hashtable H=new Hashtable();
//other variable declarations

void updateAge(String person, int age) {
//person must not be equal to null!!
Integer intWrap=new Integer(age);
  H.put((String)person,(Integer)intWrap);
  }

int getAge(String person) {
  //person must be in the Hashtable!!

  Integer I=(Integer)H.get((String)person);
  return I.intValue();
  }
```

ALL THAT CASTING NONSENSE

If you don't explicitly cast the variables when you put them into a Hashtable, as we've been doing, your code will still compile. The Hashtable will be able to fetch values based on keys because the Object class contains the necessary methods to determine equality. However, your code will be easier to read if you follow the convention of casting variables before putting them into Hashtables.

Basic Hashtable methods will allow us to get our integers in and out of the Hashtable. When we pass the name to our ageManager object, it will return the age. Again, we must create Integers, because Hashtables don't know how to deal with the primitive data types. Now that we see how to move our variables in and out of the hashtable, we can make our methods more robust:

Example 6-9b: A more robust getAge.

```
//class ageManager continued

int getAge(String person) {
//returns:
//person's age if they are in the table
//-1 if person isn't in the table
//-2 if person==null

  if (person==null)
     return -2;
  if (!H.containsKey(person))
     return -1;

   Integer intWrap=(Integer)H.get((String)person);
   return intWrap.intValue(); }
```

Now we need to protect our *put* method from errors and give the caller some information about what happened. Since our put method returns Object, we can return the old value, if there was one. We can use this to figure out whether we are adding a new name–age pair or replacing the age of someone already in our hashtable:

Example 6-9c: Updating ages.

```
int updateAge(String person, int age) {
   //returns: age if changed,
   //-1 if not changed,
   //-2 if person==null
```

```
    if(person==null)
      return -2;

    Integer intWrap=new Integer(age);
    if (H.containsKey((String)person)) {
    intWrap=(Integer)H.put((String)person,
        (Integer)intWrap);
      return intWrap.intValue();}
    else {
    H.put((String)person,(Integer)intWrap);
  return -1;
  }
```

We mentioned that casting is essential for proper hashtable operation; now let's see why it is advantageous. Proper casting allows us to put different types of objects into the same hashtable. When we retrieve them, we can decide what type of object we want. Let's demonstrate this with a very small hashtable in Example 6-10—class Vector is the superclass of Stack.

Example 6-10: Casting and the Hashtable.

```
Vector Vec=giveUsAVector();
Stack St=giveUsAStack();
//Stack is a subclass of Vector
H.put("vec",(Vector)V);
H.put("stack",(Stack)St);
Stack newStack=(Stack)H.get((String)"stack");
Stack newStack2=(Stack)H.get((String)"vec");
```

Here, we have gotten two different Stacks out of our Hashtable, though we only put one in.

```
Hashtable H=new Hashtable();
H.put((String)"stack",(Stack)St);
H.put((String)"
```

We can do the same with the key value we pass to the get method.

This wraps up the core functionality of the hashtable. Table 6-14 outlines the remaining methods defined in the Hashtable class. With what you learned from our discussion and the information in Tables 6-13 and 6-14, you should be able to make great use of the hashtable with API classes. But you aren't ready to hop in and start using it on classes that you create yet. Before you can do that, you need an understanding of the hashCode method, and how it works with Hashtables (we'll cover this in Chapter 10).

Method	Description
void clear()	Clears the hashtable.
Hashtable clone()	Makes a copy of the hashtable.
boolean contains(Object o)	Returns true if o is an element of the hashtable.
boolean isEmpty()	Returns true if the hashtable is empty.
int size()	Returns the size of the hashtable.

Table 6-14: *Other hashtable methods.*

Stacks

If you peek under the hood of any complex software, you will find a *stack* in there somewhere. A stack in Java is simply a stack of objects. You are allowed to access only the top item, and you can add items only to the top. Stacks are most useful for keeping track of a program's past activity. Table 6-15 covers all of the methods of this elegant class.

Method	Description
Object push(Object o)	Pushes o onto the stack.
Object pop()	Pops top item off the stack.
Object peek()	Returns top item without removing it.
boolean empty()	Returns true if the stack is empty.
int search(Object o)	If o is in the stack, returns distance from the top.

Table 6-15: *Methods of the Stack class.*

Stacks are usually buried quite deeply in software, so we are going to have to assume a lot of things for our example. Let's do a simple calculator that has an Undo button. The variable sum is just the running total, while class Operator is a superclass from which the allowed operators are derived. Each operator has an inverse method that will return an instance of its opposing operator. We assume that all error checking is done before the compute method is called:

```
class Calculator {
Double sum=null;
Stack prevActivities;
//other declarations

void compute(Operator op, Double nextValue)
    {sum=op.newValue(op,nextValue);
    prevActivities.push((Operator)op);
    prevActivities.push((Double)nextValue);
    }

boolean undo() {
if (!prevActivities.empty() ){
//We only have to check once, because we always
//push two at a time.

    Double lastValue=(Double)prevActivities.pop();
    Operator lastOp=(Operator)prevActivities.pop();
    sum=op.newValue(lastOp.inverse(),lastValue);

  return true;
    }
else return false; }
    }
```

As you can see, Stacks are a good way to keep track of a user's past actions on a First In First Out basis. Sometimes, you may need to keep track of the user's action on a Last In First Out (LIFO) basis. In this case, you should use a Vector.

Interfaces of the API

As we said in Chapter 3, "Object Orientation in Java," Java's
Interfaces let us use a set of methods of a class without creating an
instance of the class. The Interface declares the methods, and some
class implements these methods. Interfaces play a crucial structural role in the API, and there are two Interfaces in java.util,
Enumeration and Observer, that are especially useful. By learning
the structural role of Interfaces and how to use these two utility
interfaces, you'll be able to use Interfaces to their fullest as you
move on to the other Java packages and design your own.

Structurally Important Interfaces

If you look at the source code for the API's classes, you will often
see Interfaces used in the following way:

```
public class Applet extends Panel {
//the base Applet class
    private AppletStub stub;
public final void setStub(AppletStub stub) {
  this.stub=(AppletStub)stub;
    }
//the rest of the Applet class
  }
```

The code is taken directly from the base Applet class that we
used to write our own applets in Chapter 5, "How Applets Work."
What does this code accomplish? Essentially, it allows the runtime
environment to implement platform-dependent methods defined
in the AppletStub interface. For instance, when you use the
getParameter method, it actually calls stub.getParameter:

```
public String getParameter(String name) {
  return stub.getParameter(name);}
```

In passing the call to the interface stub, the runtime environment has to deal with the issues of retrieving the parameter from the Web browser. Our applets don't have to be concerned at all with what environment in which they are running—the runtime environment passes them a stub and they utilize it.

All of the interfaces in java.applet and java.awt.peer serve this purpose—to keep the classes of the API independent of the environment in which they run. Although these interfaces are important structurally, they are of no real use when we are simply using the API. For instance, unless we are doing something such as writing an environment that will run Applets, we never need to be concerned with AppletStub. When we start developing our own packages in Chapter 10, "Advanced Program Design," we'll want to remember this technique. But for now, don't get lost in the Interfaces of these two packages.

The Enumeration Interface

Unlike the AppletStub Interface, java.util.Enumeration is useful directly in our programs. When API classes such as Vector or Hashtable return an Enumeration, you are basically getting a list of objects. You can pass through this list of objects, performing an operation on each of them. The beauty of it is that you can use the methods of the Enumeration interface on your list of objects, regardless of their origin.

Let's say that we want to perform the same operation on a Vector, the keys of a Hashtable, or the values of a Hashtable. You could place all of the keys or all of the values of the Hashtable into a Vector and then traverse the Vector. But in many cases, you can use the Enumeration interface instead:

Example 6-11a: Processing an Enumeration.

```
public void printEnumeration(Enumeration e) {
  while (e.hasMoreElements())
    System.out.println(e.nextElement.toString);
    }
```

To use the printEnumeration with Hashtables or Vectors, you need to employ one of the methods in Table 6-16.

Class	Method	Returns
Vector	Enumeration elements()	An Enumeration of all elements in the Vector.
Hashtable	Enumeration keys()	An Enumeration of all the keys of the Hashtable.
Hashtable	Enumeration elements()	An Enumeration of all the elements of the Hashtable.

Table 6-16: *Enumeration returning elements.*

To use the printEnumeration method in practice, any of the following statements are sufficient, given a Hashtable H and a Vector V:

Example 6-11b: Using Enumeration.

```
Hashtable H=giveMeHashtable();
Vector V=giveMeVector();
printEnumeration(V.elements());
printEnumeration(H.keys());
printEnumeration(H.elements());
```

In our simple printEnumeration example, we used all of the methods of the Enumeration interface! So we can't rely on the Enumeration interface too heavily. Though its methods are a convenient way to deal with Hashtables and Vectors, we can only proceed through the list once.

java.lang.Cloneable & java.lang.Runnable

These two interfaces play primarily a structural role, but a less obtuse role than those of java.applet and java.awt.peer. When we see that a class implements Cloneable, that tells us that we can use the clone method to create a copy of that class. Let's create a copy of an instance of the Vector class, which implements Cloneable.

We will assume that V1 is an existing instance before we try to make the copy.

Example 6-12: Using the clone method.

```
Vector V1=new Vector();
String V1Element="First element in V1";
V1.addElement(V1);

Vector V2=(Vector)V1.clone();
String V2Element="Second element in V2";

System.out.println("Vector V1");
EnumerationPrinter.printEnumeration(V1.elements());
System.out.println("-----");
System.out.println("Vector V2");
EnumerationPrinter.printEnumeration(V2.elements());
System.out.println("-----");
```

Here we use the printEnumeration method to display the contents of the Vector. The output of this code fragment is as follows:

```
Vector V1
First Element in V1
------
Vector V2
First Element in V1
Second Element in V2
------
```

If we replaced the clone statement with a simple assignment, V1 would be identical to V2. Our output would be as follows:

```
Vector V1
First Element in V1
First Element in V2
----
Vector V2
First Element in V1
First Element in V2
```

Although the Cloneable interface is important, it's not as important as the clone method. When we see that a class implements the Cloneable interface, we know that the writer of that class provides for the class to be cloned. The same is true for the Runnable interface—its importance is that a class that implements Runnable can be threaded. We already saw an anecdotal example of this in Chapter 5, "How Applets Work," when we made our Applet capable of running an animation. We'll fully explore the Runnable interface and issues involved in having multithreaded programs in Chapter 10, "Advanced Program Design."

Event Handling With java.util.Observer

The java.util.Observer interface is designed to help our program manage objects. When it is combined with the java.util.Observable class, we can create a family of classes that keep track of each other. An instance of the Observable class or subclass keeps track of instantiations of classes that implement the Observer interface, as shown in Figure 6-11.

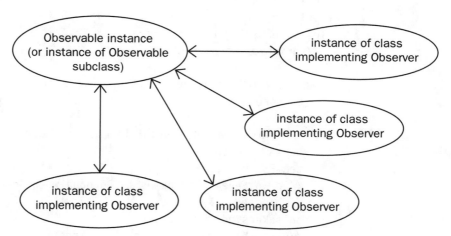

Figure 6-11: *Relationship of Observer and Observable.*

By using this interface, we can implement our own system of event handling, similar to the system we utilized in the Applet class. Let's say that we have a program in which the actions of one object are of concern to many other objects. To use a pertinent real-world example, let's say we have an object that represents a UNC-Duke basketball game. In the world of college basketball, especially in certain parts of North Carolina, this event is of concern to a wide variety of entities—the fans, the press, other NCAA basketball teams, the United Nations, and orbiting spacecraft. If we write classes representing each of these different entities, we should implement the Observer interface so that each object in our system can be easily informed of the game's progress. Then we write our game class, which tells an Observable object to inform all of the other objects when something happens.

Example 6-13a: Using the Observable class.

```
class bigGame {

    private Observable onlookers;
    private int teamAScore;
    private int teamBScore;
    private String teamWinning;
    //variables, constructors

    public void setObservable(Observable o) {
        onlookers=o;}

    public void updateScore(int teamA, int teamB) {
        teamAScore=teamA;
        teamBScore=teamB;
        //Do whatever else needs to be done when score
        //changes
        onlookers.notifyObservers(this);
        //pass the game to all the onlookers.
        }
```

By defining the update method, the various classes that implement Observer define what they should do when they are notified that the state of the game has changed:

Example 6-13b: Using the Observer interface.

```
class UNCFan implements Observer{
  //variables, constructors

  public void update(Observable o, Object Game) {
    BigGame BG=(BigGame)Game;
    String winningTeam=BG.getWinningTeam();
    if (winningTeam.equals("UNC"))
      System.out.println("yeaaaa!!!");
    else
      System.out.println("booo!!!!!");
    }
    }

class DukeFan implements Observer {

  //variables, constructors
  public void update(Observable o, Object Game) {
    BigGame BG=(BigGame)Game;
    String winningTeam=BG.getWinningTeam();
    if (winningTeam.equals("Duke"))
      System.out.println("yeaaa!!!!");
    else
      {System.out.println("booo!!!");
    }
    }
```

At the start of the game, we would create the Observable class and use the addObserver method to incorporate the onlookers into the game:

Example 6-13c: Adding Observer implementing objects.

```
Observable onlookers=new Observable();
onlookers.addObserver(UNCFanInstance);
onlookers.addObserver(DukeFanInstance);
onlookers.addObserver(Press);
onlookers.addObserver(UnitedNations);
//etc, etc.
```

Besides the addObserver method, we have several other methods to help us manage our observing objects. They are outlined in Table 6-17.

Method	Description
void addObserver(Observer o)	Adds an observer for the Observable instance to keep track of.
void deleteObserver(Observer o)	Deletes the observer.
void notifyObservers(Object arg)	Notifies observers that something has happened; they can examine arg to figure out what happened.
int countObservers()	Returns a count of the number of observers.
boolean hasChanged()	Returns true if something has changed; setChanged and clearChanged must be used to set and unset the flag.
void setChanged()	Causes hasChanged to return true.
void clearChanged()	Causes hasChanged to return false.

Table 6-17: *Methods of the Observable class.*

Math & the API

We covered the basic operators in Chapter 2, "Java Programming Basics," but sooner or later you are going to need to do more complex operations. The Math class of the java.lang package contains 30 methods to do arithmetic, such as finding the maximum or minimum of a pair of numbers or deriving the natural log. It also holds the values for e and pi as static variables.

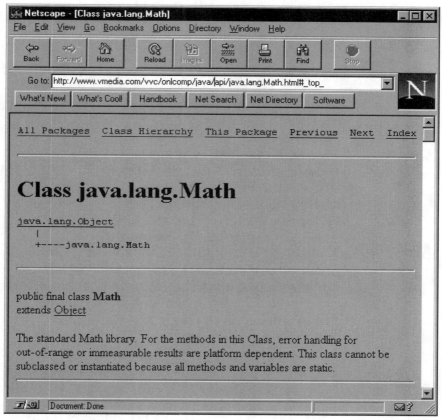

Figure 6-12: *The Math home page.*

Figure 6-12 shows the home page of the Math class in the Java online documentation. Instead of attempting to describe the methods in more detail, we'll focus on how to use them in practice.

Example 6-14: Using the Math class.

```
class doSomeMath {

//Other declarations

public void useMathMethods(int i1,int i2, double d, float
f,long l) {

int intAbsValue=Math.abs(i1);
double doubAbsValue=Math.abs(d);
float floatAbsValue=Math.abs(f);
long longAbsValue=Math.abs(l);
//These will return the Absolute
//value. method abs is overloaded

int minInt=Math.min(i1,i2);
double maxDoub=Math.max(i1,d);

//The min and max methods are overloaded
//for each numeric type.
//In second line, i1 is cast to double.

}
```

As we said, we can also get the values of e and pi from the Math class. The wrapper classes also have some values of interest to us. For instance, have you ever had to calculate the maximum value for an integer by hand? Each of the primitive wrappers provides us with static variables for the maximum value for a given primitive type, as well as other useful values. All of these are described in Table 6-18.

Variable	Meaning	Class(es) Contained In
E	Natural logarithmic base.	Math
PI	Value for pi.	Math
MIN_VALUE	Minimum value for a given type.	Integer, Float, Long, Double
MAX_VALUE	Maximum value for a given type.	Integer, Float, Long, Double
NEGATIVE_INFINITY	Represents negative infinity.	Float, Double
POSITIVE_INFINITY	Represents positive infinity.	Float, Double
NaN	"Not-a-Number"; can be used to represent unassigned values.	Float, Double

Table 6-18: *Useful static variables.*

Moving On

We have just begun to explore the API. Now that you have mastered the basics of the API, we can move on to the Abstract Windowing Toolkit packages. We'll cover these in Chapters 7, "Basic User Interface," Chapter 8, "Advanced User Interface," and Chapter 9, "Graphics & Images." The entire networking section (Section IV, "Java & the Network") will cover the java.io and java.net packages extensively.

7

Basic User Interface

I n this chapter, we begin our exploration of the *Advanced Windowing Toolkit* (AWT). We focus on the basic screen elements contained in the java.awt package and how to use them to create a great user interface. And we create sample applets using the following AWT tools and techniques:

- ❧ Keyboard input
- ❧ Text fields and text areas
- ❧ Buttons
- ❧ Checkboxes
- ❧ Lists
- ❧ Choices, or pop-up menus
- ❧ Scrollbars
- ❧ Labels

Java offers far greater flexibility with these common user input elements than does HTML. The ability to simulate user input is an important and effective tool available to the Java developer. The movement of the mouse, as well as mouse focus, can be used to make these simple input elements interactive. For example, we can make a text area display sample "input" when the user moves the mouse over it.

Chapter 8, "Advanced User Interface," will build on what you learn here and show you how to make your user interfaces really stand out. Then, when you get to the networking section (Section IV, "Java & the Network"), you will have powerful front ends that can connect to remote servers of any type, including HTTP.

This chapter prototypes different versions of the same applet to demonstrate usage of the basic screen elements. The example we use is a currency converter—a program that takes a number, multiplies it with a conversion ratio, and returns the result.

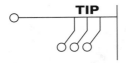

TIP

This chapter's code example files can be found on the Companion CD-ROM (for Windows 95/NT and Macintosh users) and on the Online Companion (for UNIX users). Visit the Online Companion at http://www.vmedia.com/java.html.

JAVA USER INTERFACE VS. HTML FORMS

If you have ever worked with HTML forms and Common Gateway Interface (CGI) programming, be prepared to be blown away. Java provides you with more tools, more functionality, and the interoperability of object orientation. Moreover, your existing CGI applications can be interfaced directly by the Java applet on your HTML page. This means that you can begin developing Java applets to replace your HTML forms without having to significantly change the CGI program used to process the user's input. For example, the tutorial in Chapter 17 uses a URL connection and an HTTP POST to pass data back to a specialized CGI program after a user has made a selection.

You are also no longer restricted to running CGI programs to process form data. You can now process the form data in the Java applet running in the Web browser. Doing so can save you considerable Web server load because the CGI programs don't need to be run for every HTML form a user wishes to submit.

➡

Moreover, your Java applet can directly access other servers on the Web server. A CGI gateway for databases is a common example: a user fills out a form, and upon submission, a CGI program is run on the Web server, which then connects to the database server. With a Java applet, you can bypass the Web server altogether! It is very possible to connect directly to the database server and make queries, and several Java packages already exist for doing so.

Our Currency Converter

Suppose we are managing a travel agency that wishes to allow its visitors to browse ticket prices and package offerings (via the World Wide Web, of course!). To attract more visitors to its Web site, the agency advertises a Web page where visitors can get the latest foreign currency values and convert from one currency to another. This service is particularly useful for foreign visitors, who can quickly calculate the price of the travel agency's services in their own currency. As the webmaster for this company, you have been given the task of setting up this service. You begin by thinking of HTML forms and CGIs you can run to do this, but decide that you can make a far greater (and faster!) impression by using Java applets. We'll be using the Currency Converter example throughout this chapter, learning the AWT classes in the process.

In the next section, we demonstrate how to capture a user's keystrokes, and we provide a quick, bird's-eye view of the Currency Converter.

Getting Keyboard Input

Chapter 5, "How Applets Work," covered the handling of some events in a general sense. Events are tied directly to the component classes and, in general, are tied directly to any object. We can handle events (such as mouse movement over a component) that occur within an object (component) as well as events that occur between components. Events can also be used at a higher level to enhance the user interface. You can use them to catch user interaction with several objects and even interaction with specific objects in a specific order.

In our first example, pictured in Figure 7-1, we show an initial prototype of our Currency Converter Applet so that you can quickly get acquainted with it. In this version of the converter, the user types a number into the input field and then presses Enter or Return to display the converted number. We use the keyDown event handler to catch the event of a keystroke, and inside the keyDown method, we look for an "\n" or Return key. (For a detailed explanation of the TextField and TextArea classes, see the next section.) Example 7-1 shows the code for our Currency Converter Applet.

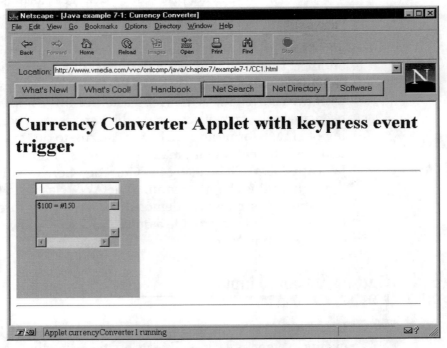

Figure 7-1: *The Currency Converter with keypress event trigger.*

Example 7-1: Currency Converter Applet with keypress event trigger.

```
import java.awt.*;
import java.applet.Applet;

public class currencyConverter1 extends java.applet.Applet {
    float conversion_ratio = 1.50f;
    TextField field1 = new TextField(20);
    TextArea field2 = new TextArea(4,20);
    //screen elements for text input/output
    //see next section

public void init() {
    field1.setEditable(true);
    field2.setEditable(false);
    field1.resize(field1.preferredSize());
    field2.resize(field2.preferredSize());
    add(field1);
    add(field2);

show();
    } //init

public void convert() {
    float currency1, currency2;
    String InputString = field1.getText();
    field1.setText("");
    currency1 = Float.valueOf(InputString).floatValue();
    currency2 = conversion_ratio * currency1;
    String OutputString =
    "$" + InputString + " = " + "#" + Float.toString(currency2)
+ "\n";
    field2.appendText(OutputString);
} //convert

public boolean keyDown(Event evt, int key)
    //This is the event handler for keystrokes

{char c=(char)key;
    //Caste key to a char for comparison.
```

```
if (c == '\n')
//Does the key == ENTER?
//if so, run convert()!
{ convert();
return true;
}
else { return false; }
} //end KeyDown()
}   //end applet currencyConverter1
```

Notice that, here, we use the keyDown event handler, the event handler for keystrokes. Later, under "Creating Checkboxes," we'll again use the Enter key to initiate the conversion, but we'll use the handleEvent method instead. The handleEvent method is a "generic" event handler in that it overrides all other event handlers and lets you define which events you want to watch for. (Refer to the checkbox example to see how it catches the event of the Enter key, as well as the event of either of the two checkboxes being clicked by the mouse.) The point is, there are several ways to catch the same event, and often times they are equally functional and fast. For applets that you know will have many events you wish to trap, a generic event handler like handleEvent or action is the best choice. They each allow you to consolidate the event handling into one piece of code, which makes it possible to improve the speed and structure of your code by using switch and similar techniques to handle multiple user input possibilities.

Also, using the handleEvent method, we can accommodate sequences of events and the specific location of events inside the applet. We do this in the Checkbox example applet; the event handler is coded to see if the mouse was clicked over a specific checkbox. We will have more examples of handling complex events in Chapter 8, "Advanced User Interface," and throughout the rest of the book, especially in the tutorial chapters.

Creating TextFields & TextAreas

A TextArea can be used to display text in an applet, as well as to allow text *input*. TextAreas accommodate multiple lines of text, and they have scrollbars. TextFields are TextAreas without scrollbars and are limited to only one row. TextAreas and TextFields both inherit from TextComponent and, aside from the two mentioned differences, are alike. A TextField was used in the example applet:

```
TextField field1 = new TextField(20);
field1.setEditable(true);
```

The first line creates a TextField with a column width of 20. The second line sets the TextField we just created to be editable. We can also set this value to "false," which prohibits the user from changing the contents of the TextField.

We also create a TextArea with a width of 20 and a height of 4:

```
TextArea field2 = new TextArea(4,20)
```

Nothing needs to be done to enable the TextArea's scrollbars; they are automatically handled within the TextArea class.

Showing text in the TextField or TextArea is straightforward. We can use either of the methods shown below:

```
field1.setText("");
field2.appendText(OutputString);
```

We use setText to specify the text to place in a field (here, we've used empty quotes in order to clear field1). We use appendText to add new text to existing text, as in field2 above. Note that we must manually insert new lines because appendText does not do this for us.

We also wish to set the displayed size of the two components. This is a way to ensure that the proper size is set for the components, and that they take up the space we expect them to. We use the resize method to set the size and use the preferredSize method to get the size the components "want" to be:

```
field1.resize(field1.preferredSize());
field2.resize(field2.preferredSize());
```

We have to add the created and initialized TextField and
TextArea to the applet. This is done with the add method. We
want to show the components we have added as well, so we'll use
the show method to do so. We add field1 and field2 to the applet
with:

```
add(field1);
add(field2);
show();
```

There are many methods you can use to create TextFields and
TextAreas. Table 7-1 describes the methods shared by both via the
parent TextComponent class.

Method	Description
getSelectedText()	Returns the selected text contained in the TextComponent.
getSelectionEnd()	Returns the selected text's end position.
getSelectionStart()	Returns the selected text's start position.
getText()	Returns the text contained in the TextComponent.
isEditable()	Returns the boolean indicating whether the TextComponent is editable or not.
paramString()	Returns the String of parameters for the TextComponent.
select(int, int)	Selects the text found between the specified start and end locations.
selectAll()	Selects all the text in the TextComponent.
setEditable(boolean)	Sets the specified boolean to indicate whether or not the TextComponent should be editable.
setText(String)	Sets the text of the TextComponent to the specified text.

Table 7-1: *TextComponent class methods.*

The TextField class has fewer specific methods than the TextArea class. This is due mainly to the row limit of one on the TextField. The methods available for the TextField are shown in Table 7-2.

Method	Description
echoCharIsSet()	Returns true if this TextField has a character set for echoing.
getColumns()	Returns the number of columns in this TextField.
getEchoChar()	Returns the character to be used for echoing.
minimumSize(int)	Returns the minimum size Dimensions needed for the TextField with the specified amount of columns.
minimumSize()	Returns the minimum size Dimensions needed for the TextField.
paramString()	Returns the String of parameters for the TextField.
preferredSize(int)	Returns the preferred size Dimensions needed for the TextField with the specified amount of columns.
preferredSize()	Returns the preferred size Dimensions needed for the TextField.
setEchoCharacter(char)	Sets the echo character for the TextField.

Table 7-2: *TextField class methods.*

The TextArea class has several forms of its constructor. We have shown one above in the example code. Table 7-3 contains the complete list of TextArea constructors, and Table 7-4 explains the TextArea class methods.

Constructor	Description
TextArea()	Constructs a new TextArea.
TextArea(int, int)	Constructs a new TextArea with the specified number of rows and columns.
TextArea(String)	Constructs a new TextArea with the specified text displayed.
TextArea(String, int, int)	Constructs a new TextArea with the specified text and the specified number of rows and columns.

Table 7-3: *TextArea constructors.*

Method	Description
appendText(String)	Appends the given text to the end.
getColumns()	Returns the number of columns.
getRows()	Returns the number of rows in the TextArea.
insertText(String, int)	Inserts the specified text at the specified position.
minimumSize(int, int)	Returns the specified minimum size Dimensions.
minimumSize()	Returns the minimum size Dimensions.
paramString()	Returns the String of parameters for the TextArea.
preferredSize(int, int)	Returns the specified row and column Dimensions.
preferredSize()	Returns the preferred size Dimensions.
replaceText(String, int, int)	Replaces text from the indicated start to end position with the specified new text.

Table 7-4: *TextArea class methods.*

Creating Buttons

We just looked at a version of the Currency Converter that used the Enter key to activate the conversion. Now let's use a button, instead, which the user can click to perform the conversion after entering the input value in field1. Here's the instantiation, which creates a new Button with the label "Convert":

```
Button ConvertButton = new Button("Convert");
```

In Example 7-2 below, we work this into our Currency Converter Applet. We no longer need to look for the keystroke of newline, since we want to trigger the calculation and display of the conversion using the newly added button. Figure 7-2 shows our applet with a button added.

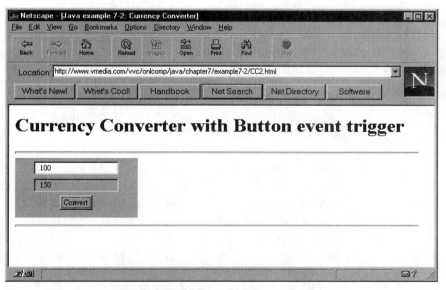

Figure 7-2: *Convert Button in the Currency Converter.*

Example 7-2a: Currency Converter Applet with a Button added.

```java
import java.awt.*;
import java.applet.Applet;

public class currencyConverter2 extends java.applet.Applet {
 float conversion_ratio = 1.50f;
 TextField field1 = new TextField(20);
 TextArea field2 = new TextArea(4,20);
Button ConvertButton = new Button("Convert");

 public void init() {
  field1.setEditable(true);
  field2.setEditable(false);

  field1.resize(field1.preferredSize());
  field2.resize(field2.preferredSize());
  add(field1);
  add(field2);
  add(ConvertButton);
  show(); // This shows the added elements
 } // end init method
```

The section of code shown above creates a clickable button labeled "Convert", which is used to signify when the entered number should be converted and displayed. The init method is used to set up the applet. We set field1 to allow user input and to prevent field2 from being changed. The add method adds the screen elements to the applet. Elements *must* be added to a container (here the default container is the applet window) if they are to be displayed. The resize method changes the appearance of the text fields based on their defined size (we have set it to 20) and the Web browser.

The conversion happens here:

Example 7-2b: The conversion.

```java
public void convert() {
 float currency1, currency2;
 String InputString = field1.getText();
```

```
currency1 =
Float.valueOf(InputString).floatValue();
currency2 = conversion_ratio * currency1;
String OutputString =
Float.toString(currency2);
field2.setText(OutputString);
} // end convert()
```

A string variable is created and set equal to whatever is in the input field1. The InputString is converted to a float number and assigned to currency1. This is the processing part of the applet. A variable named OutputString is assigned the value of currency2, but currency2 must be converted to a String type first. Finally, we set the output field2 to the converted value for display to the user. This is the method that we'll call when the event handler (below) finds that the Convert button has been clicked:

Example 7-2c: Catching the button-click.

```
public boolean action( Event evt, Object obj)
  {
  if ("Convert".equals(obj))
  {
  convert();
     return true;
  }
  else { return false; }
  } //end action()

} //end currencyConverter Applet
```

This event handler method is used to catch the event of the Convert button being clicked. To handle this event, we override the action event handler. The code looks to see if the Convert button has been clicked. It compares the label of the object in which the action event happened to the label "Convert," to which we set the button in our applet. This comparison is not really necessary, since we don't need to look for more than one event, but it will be needed if we add more features, such as buttons and mouse functionality. Table 7-5 lists the Button class methods.

Method	Description
getLabel()	Gets the label of the button.
paramString()	Returns the parameter String of this button.
setLabel(String)	Sets the button with the specified label.

Table 7-5: *Button class methods.*

Of course, you will need an HTML page on which to place the Currency Converter Applet. Simply start a new page and include the following code. Put the HTML page in the same directory as the applet's compiled currencyConverter2.class file. You can load the HTML page directly by using the Open File menu item in Netscape Navigator 2.0.

```
<applet code="currencyConverter2.class" height=200 width=200>
</applet>
```

Creating Checkboxes

If our travel agency really wants to attract visitors to the site, we ought to provide more than a few conversion ratios. We can use checkboxes to give the user the option of selecting a currency to convert to U.S. dollars. Checkboxes are similar to checkboxes and radio buttons in HTML: they allow the user to pick from pre-defined selections by clicking on them. Checkboxes exist as part of a group of Checkboxes. Creating a checkbox is easy:

```
Checkbox Check1 = new Checkbox("UK Pound");
```

This line creates a checkbox named Check1 with the label "UK Pound," and by default initializes it to false. To construct a Checkbox with a specified label, a Checkbox group, and boolean state, use the constructor:

```
Checkbox UKCheck = new Checkbox("UK Pound",
CurrencyCheckGroup, false);
```

Here, we create a checkbox labeled "UK Pound," belonging in the CurrencyCheckGroup, with the state set to "false." Each checkbox needs to belong in a CheckboxGroup. You can only have one checkbox selected within a CheckboxGroup. In Java, all checkboxes should belong to a CheckboxGroup instance. You will need to create the CurrencyCheckGroup, as follows:

```
CheckboxGroup CurrencyCheckGroup = new CheckboxGroup();
```

Remember that you must add the checkbox to the applet! In the example below, you see that we use the add method to add two checkboxes, just like any other component. You also probably want to add another Checkbox to the CheckboxGroup:

```
Checkbox FrancCheck = new Checkbox("Franc",
CurrencyCheckGroup, true)
```

Now you can see which Checkbox (Pound or Franc) is picked:

```
if (UKCheck == CurrencyCheckGroup.getCurrent()){
    System.out.println("UK Pound is checked");
    } else {
        System.out.println("Franc is checked");
        }
```

We can further modify our example Currency Converter Applet to use checkboxes to switch between currencies or conversion ratios. The code that incorporates this follows in Example 7-3. We have also used the code for catching the Enter key so that the Convert button is no longer needed. We look for the event of the Enter key being pressed and then do the conversion (for a discussion of capturing this keystroke, refer to "Getting Keyboard Input" earlier in this chapter). Figure 7-3 shows the Currency Converter with Checkboxes added.

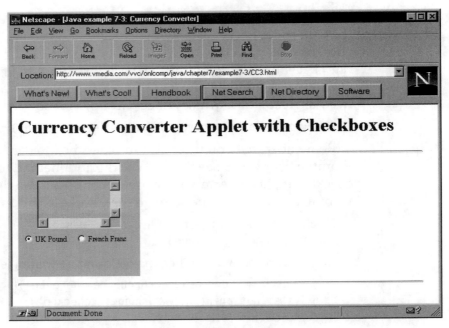

Figure 7-3: *Checkboxes in Currency Converter.*

Example 7-3: Currency Converter Applet with Checkbox.

```java
import java.awt.*;
import java.applet.Applet;
public class currencyConverter3 extends java.applet.Applet {

  final float UKratio = 1.50f;
  final float FRANCratio = 6.00f;
  float conversion_ratio = UKratio;
  TextField field1 = new TextField(20);
  TextArea field2 = new TextArea(4,20);
  CheckboxGroup CurrencyGroup = new CheckboxGroup();
  Checkbox UK_Pound = new Checkbox("UK Pound", CurrencyGroup,
  true);
  Checkbox French_Franc = new Checkbox("French Franc",
  CurrencyGroup, false);
```

```
public void init() {
 field1.setEditable(true);
 field2.setEditable(false);
 add(field1);
 add(field2);
 add(UK_Pound);
 add(French_Franc);

resize(field1.preferredSize());
 resize(field2.preferredSize());
 show();
   }
public void convert() {
//convert() does not change
     float currency1, currency2;
   String InputString = field1.getText();
   field1.setText("");
   currency1 = Float.valueOf(InputString).floatValue();
   currency2 = conversion_ratio * currency1;
   String OutputString =
   "$" + InputString + " = " + "#" +
Float.toString(currency2) + "\n";
   field2.appendText(OutputString);
   } //convert

public boolean handleEvent(Event evt) {
//We look for the Checkbox to be clicked

 if (evt.target == CurrencyGroupList)
  {if ( "UK Pound" == CurrencyGroupList.getSelectedItem() )
    { conversion_ratio=UKratio; }

   if ( "French Franc" ==
(CurrencyGroupList.getSelectedItem()) )
    { conversion_ratio=FRANCratio; }
 }
//See which one was clicked, and
//set the corresponding ratio!
```

```
    if (evt.target == field1)
     { char c=(char)evt.key;
      if (c == '\n')
       {convert();
        return true;}
      else { return false; }
     }
     return false;
    }
   } // Applet
```

SETTING UP CHECKBOX GROUPS

When you're setting up checkboxes, you must assign them to a CheckboxGroup, as shown above. But you *don't* have to use the add method to add the group itself to the applet. The group functions only as an identifier. Later in this chapter, you'll see that you *do* have to add a List box or Choice pop-up menu to an applet. For these two components, you add items directly to the List or Choice, and not the applet.

Table 7-6 contains the methods in the CheckboxGroup class, and Table 7-7 lists the methods in the Checkbox class.

Method	Description
getCurrent()	Gets the current choice.
setCurrent (CheckboxInstance)	Sets the current choice to the specified CheckboxInstance.
toString()	Returns the String representation of this CheckboxGroup's values.

Table 7-6: *Methods in the CheckboxGroup class.*

Method	Description
getCheckboxGroup()	Returns the checkbox group.
getLabel()	Gets the label of the button.
getState()	Returns the boolean state of the Checkbox.
paramString()	Returns the parameter String of this Checkbox.
setCheckboxGroup (CheckboxGroupInstance)	Sets the CheckboxGroupInstance to the specified group.
setLabel(String)	Sets the button with the specified label.
setState(boolean)	Sets the Checkbox to the specifed boolean state.

Table 7-7: *Methods in the Checkbox class.*

Creating a List Box

A *List* is a scrolling, selectable list box. It allows the user to select one or more of the items contained in the List. In the preceding section, we let the users choose a currency conversion by clicking a checkbox. But what if we wanted to include more currencies than two or three? Perhaps a List like the one shown in Figure 7-4 would be better. An advantage of List is that many selectable items can be presented in a more organized fashion than in a checkbox arrangement.

We use a List in the Currency Converter example below to allow the users to select which conversion they wish to perform. The List constructor in the AWT creates a scrolling list box in which the number of visible list items can be specified. We can also use the scrolling list box to specify whether multiple list items can be picked. An example constructor for a List is:

```
List CurrencyList = new List( 3, false );
```

This specifies that a new list named CurrencyList shows three items all the time, but not more than one item can be selected. If "true" were used instead of "false," multiple selections would be allowed. Putting a label on a List is not as straightforward as it is with the Checkboxes or Buttons. A label class must be used and positioned with the List. We again modify our example applet to use a List to select between different currency conversions. Example 7-4 shows the code to add a list to our applet.

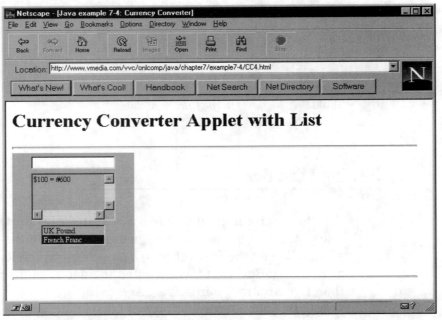

Figure 7-4: *A List in the Currency Converter.*

Example 7-4a: Currency Converter Applet with a List box.

```java
import java.awt.*;
import java.applet.Applet;

public class currencyConverter4 extends java.applet.Applet {

    final float UKratio = 1.50f;
    final float FRANCratio = 6.00f;
    float conversion_ratio = UKratio;
    TextField field1 = new TextField(20);
    TextArea field2 = new TextArea(4,20);
    List CurrencyGroupList = new List(2, false);

public void init() {
    field1.setEditable(true);
    field2.setEditable(false);
    CurrencyGroupList.addItem("UK Pound");
    CurrencyGroupList.addItem("French Franc");
    CurrencyGroupList.select(0);
    add(field1);
    add(field2);
    add(CurrencyGroupList);
    field1.resize(field1.preferredSize());
    field2.resize(field2.preferredSize());
    show();
} //init
```

The code above makes a new list with two visible items, only one of which may be selected at a time. We have to add items to the List instance we created above. Adding items to a List is different than adding them to the Checkboxes: we add items directly to the List instance, instead of creating multiple instances for each item and then grouping them together. We only have to declare the List instance once and can add as many items to the list as we want. We make the first item in the list the default selected by using the select(0) method. Then we just need to add the List Group to the applet.

Example 7-4b: Adding the List Group to the applet.

```java
public void convert() {
//convert() does not change
    float currency1, currency2;
    String InputString = field1.getText();
    field1.setText("");
    currency1 = Float.valueOf(InputString).floatValue();
    currency2 = conversion_ratio * currency1;
    String OutputString =
    "$" + InputString + " = " + "#" +
Float.toString(currency2) + "\n";
    field2.appendText(OutputString);
  } //convert

public boolean handleEvent(Event evt) {
//We look for the List to be changed here.
 if (evt.target == CurrencyGroupList)
  {if ( "UK Pound" == CurrencyGroupList.getSelectedItem() )
    { conversion_ratio=UKratio; }

    if ( "French Franc" ==
(CurrencyGroupList.getSelectedItem()) )
    { conversion_ratio=FRANCratio; }
 }

 if (evt.target == field1)
  { char c=(char)evt.key;
   if (c == '\n')
    {convert();
     return true;}
   else { return false; }
  }
  return false;
 }
} // Applet
```

Table 7-8 contains descriptions of useful methods in the List class.

Method	Description
addItem(String)	Adds the String item to the end of the list.
addItem(String, int)	Adds the specified item to the end of the scrolling list.
allowsMultipleSelections()	Returns true if this list allows multiple selections.
clear()	Clears the list.
countItems()	Returns the number of items in the list.
delItem(int)	Deletes an item from the list.
delItems(int, int)	Deletes multiple items from the list.
deselect(int)	Deselects the item at the specified index.
getItem(int)	Gets the item associated with the specified index.
getRows()	Returns the number of visible lines in this list.
getSelectedIndex()	Gets the selected item on the list or −1 if no item is selected.
getSelectedIndexes()	Returns the selected indexes on the list.
getSelectedItem()	Returns the selected item on the list or null if no item is selected.
getSelectedItems()	Returns the selected items on the list.
getVisibleIndex()	Gets the index of the item that was last made visible by the method makeVisible.
isSelected(int)	Returns true if the item at the specified index has been selected; false otherwise.
makeVisible(int)	Forces the item at the specified index to be visible.

Method	Description
minimumSize(int)	Returns the minimum dimensions needed for the number of rows in the list.
minimumSize()	Returns the minimum dimensions needed for the list.
paramString()	Returns the parameter String of this list.
preferredSize(int)	Returns the preferred dimensions needed for the list with the specified amount of rows.
preferredSize()	Returns the preferred dimensions needed for the list.
replaceItem(String, int)	Replaces the item at the given index.
select(int)	Selects the item at the specified index.
setMultipleSelections (boolean)	Sets whether this list should allow multiple selections or not.

Table 7-8: *Useful methods in the List class.*

Creating a Pop-Up Choice Menu

We've already seen how to use checkboxes and lists to present the user with choices. An alternative that is more compact is the Choice, or pop-up menu. A Choice lets you present a menu of choices that appears only when the user clicks on it, as shown in Figure 7-5. As you saw with List in the last section, you create one instance of Choice and then add choices to it.

A Choice is created exactly the way we created the List. We only need to modify the above List example applet by changing all of the identifiers "CurrencyGroupList" to "CurrencyGroupChoice". We would declare a new Choice as shown in Example 7-5.

Example 7-5: Adding a Choice to the List example applet.

```
Choice CurrencyGroupChoice = new Choice();
CurrencyGroupList.addItem("UK Pound");
CurrencyGroupList.addItem("French Franc");
```

The code shown in Example 7-5 takes the place of the CurrencyGroupList declaration at the beginning of the List example applet, Example 7-4. Table 7-9 shows the useful methods in the Choice class.

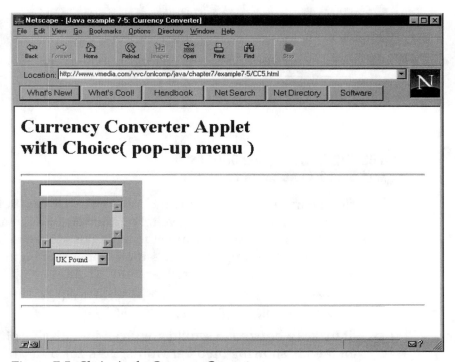

Figure 7-5: *Choice in the Currency Converter.*

Method	Description
addItem(String)	Adds an item to this Choice.
countItems()	Returns the number of items in this Choice.
getItem(int)	Returns the String at the specified index in the Choice.
getSelectedIndex()	Returns the index of the currently selected item.
getSelectedItem()	Returns a String representation of the current choice.
paramString()	Returns the parameter String of this Choice.
select(int)	Selects the item with the specified position.
select(String)	Selects the item with the specified String.

Table 7-9: *Useful methods in the Choice class.*

Creating & Using Scrollbars

Scrollbars are automatically included in TextAreas, but you can use them in other ways as well. For example, we can add a scrollbar to the example applet to let the user change the conversion ratio of the applet to a specific number (see Figure 7-6). Here is the constructor for a Scrollbar:

```
Scrollbar ratioScrollBar = new Scrollbar(
Scrollbar.HORIZONTAL, 150, 25, 50, 250 );
```

It makes a horizontal scrollbar with an initial value of 150, with 25 of the 150 showing (in other words, the size), 50 as the minimum value of the bar, and 250 as the maximum value of the bar. (*Note:* The scrollbar is limited to an integer value.)

Let's add a scrollbar to our Currency Converter Applet. We specified the conversion ratio to be 1.5 in the example applet, but we can attach a scrollbar to the conversion ratio so that it changes by +0.1 when the bar is scrolled right or −0.1 when the bar is scrolled left. We will also display the conversion ratio so the user knows its value when it is changed via the scrollbar:

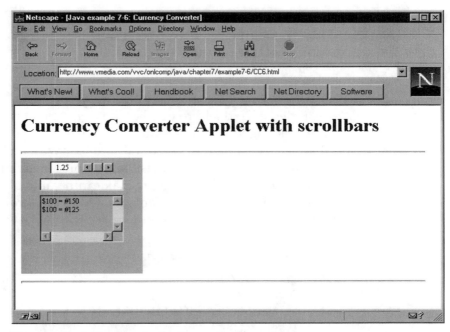

Figure 7-6: *A Scrollbar in the Currency Converter.*

Example 7-6a: Currency Converter Applet with Scrollbar.

```
import java.awt.*;
import java.applet.Applet;
public class currencyConverter5 extends java.applet.Applet {
    float conversion_ratio = 1.5f;
    TextField field1 = new TextField(20);
    TextArea field2 = new TextArea(4,20);
    TextField ratioField = new TextField(5);
Scrollbar ratioScrollBar = new Scrollbar(
Scrollbar.HORIZONTAL, 150, 25, 50, 250 );

public void init() {
    field1.setEditable(true);
    field2.setEditable(false);
    add(ratioField);
    add(ratioScrollBar);
    add(field1);
    add(field2);
```

```
        ratioField.setText("1.50");
        resize(field1.preferredSize());
        resize(field2.preferredSize());
        show();
    } //init
```

We've added a TextField to display the Conversion ratio, so that when it is changed by the scrollbar, we can see its value. Above the TextField, we make a horizontal scrollbar with an initial value of 150 units and with 25 units visible, 50 units as the minimum value of the bar, and 250 units the maximum value of the bar.

Now we must handle the events related to the scrollbar in our code:

Example 7-6b: Handling scrollbar events.

```
public void convert() {
 float currency1, currency2;
 String InputString = field1.getText();
 field1.setText("");
 currency1 = Float.valueOf(InputString).floatValue();
 currency2 = conversion_ratio * currency1;
 String OutputString =
 "$" + InputString + " = " + "#" + Float.toString(currency2)
+ "\n";
 field2.appendText(OutputString);
} //convert

public boolean handleEvent(Event evt) {
 if (evt.target == ratioScrollBar)
   { int in;
    in = ratioScrollBar.getValue();
     conversion_ratio = in/100f;
ratioField.setText(Float.toString(conversion_ratio));
    }
 if (evt.target == field1)
  {char c=(char)evt.key;
   if (c == '\n')
    { convert();
     return true;
    }
   else { return false; }
```

```
    }
    return false;
  } // handleEvent()
} // Applet()
```

We can look for any events occurring in the ratioScrollBar object and get the current value of the scrollbar, since it has probably been changed. Since we were limited to using integer values for the scrollbar, we must divide by 100 to get the range and precision we desire. We have to set the conversion ratio field every time it is changed, as well. Look at Table 7-10 for useful methods of the Scrollbar class.

Method	Description
getLineIncrement()	Gets the line increment for the Scrollbar.
getMaximum()	Returns the maximum value of this Scrollbar.
getMinimum()	Returns the minimum value of this Scrollbar.
getOrientation()	Returns the orientation for the Scrollbar.
getPageIncrement()	Gets the page increment for the Scrollbar.
getValue()	Returns the current value of this Scrollbar.
getVisible()	Returns the visible amount of the Scrollbar.
paramString()	Returns the String parameters for the Scrollbar.
setLineIncrement(int)	Sets the line increment for the Scrollbar.
setPageIncrement(int)	Sets the page increment for the Scrollbar.
setValue(int)	Sets the value of this Scrollbar to the specified value.
setValues(int, int, int, int)	Sets the values for the Scrollbar.

Table 7-10: *Useful methods in the Scrollbar class.*

Labels

Labels are exactly what their name implies—a way to print text to the applet window. We use them in our example applet to show the user the function of the various components. Table 7-11 contains a list of useful methods in the Label class. Figure 7-7 shows our Currency Converter with a labeled scrollbar. In the code that follows, we use the init method from Example 7-6, adding labels to the user interface.

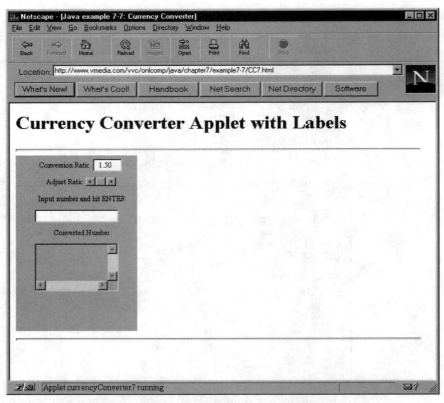

Figure 7-7: *A labeled Scrollbar in Currency Converter.*

Example 7-7: Currency Converter Applet with a Label.

```
public class currencyConverter76 extends
java.applet.Applet {
  float conversion_ratio = 1.5f;
  TextField field1 = new TextField(20);
  TextArea field2 = new TextArea(4,20);
  TextField ratioField = new TextField(5);
Scrollbar ratioScrollBar = new Scrollbar(
Scrollbar.HORIZONTAL, 150, 25,
50, 250 );
public void init() {
  field1.setEditable(true);
  field2.setEditable(false);
  add( new Label("Conversion Ratio"));
  add(ratioField);
  add( new Label("Adjust Ratio"));
  add(ratioScrollBar);
  add(new Label("Input number and hit ENTER"));
  add(field1);
  add( new Label("Converted Number"));
  add(field2);

  ratioField.setText("1.50");
  resize(field1.preferredSize());
  resize(field2.preferredSize());
  show();
    } //init
```

Method	Description
getAlignment()	Gets the current alignment of this Label.
getText()	Gets the text of this Label.
paramString()	Returns the parameter String of this Label.
setAlignment(int)	Sets the alignment for the Label to the specified alignment.
setText(String)	Sets the text for the Label to the specified text.

Table 7-11: *Useful methods in the Label class.*

Moving On

You've now seen all the basic components of user interface development. In the next chapter, we'll build on what you've learned by introducing more advanced components and discussing higher-level issues such as design and layout.

SECTION III

Advanced Java Programming

8

Advanced User Interface

Creating a well-designed look for a program can be difficult. The tools provided in the Java Developers Kit make it easy. Java provides you with layout tools to place screen elements easily, without having to diagram exact coordinates and sizes for the elements. This advantage is actually twofold: the developer saves time by passing the low-level details to the layout tools, and the layout tools ensure the developer that the applet has the same "look" regardless of the platform it is running on. The "feel" of your applet will be dependent more on the operating system itself, and specifically the graphical environment, such as Openwin, Windows 95, or Macintosh.

Among the tools in the JDK's bag of user interface tricks is a set of layout managers that are used to organize screen elements. These are an essential part of any applet; in fact, you were already using the default layout manager in the simple applets of Chapter 7, "Basic User Interface."

In this chapter, we discuss each of the layout managers, as well as screen element containers such as panels, dialogs, and frames. We show how to incorporate menus into your applet, how to get available fonts, and how to set fonts for screen elements. We also

continue to build upon the example of the Currency Converter Applet introduced in Chapter 7, but we greatly extend its features and appearance, adding some advanced components and focusing on component layout.

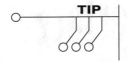

This chapter's code example files can be found on the Companion CD-ROM (for Windows 95/NT and Macintosh users) and the Online Companion (for UNIX users). Visit the Online Companion at http://www.vmedia.com/java.html.

Designing Your Layout

It is a good idea to sketch the intended placement of your screen elements, or at least create a good mental picture, before you begin. This facilitates the coding of the layout and gives you a rough idea of the order in which you'll want to add components. A preliminary sketch also clarifies which components you should group together into *Panels*, which are containers that hold other components.

You have the option of using windows that are separate from the Web browser—using frames or dialogs, you can pop open a free window that can contain all or part of your applet's user interface. Using multiple windows can also help you organize the applet into functional blocks that can be "put away," or iconified, when they are not needed. For example, in the chess client tutorial we present in Chapter 18, we don't want the list of users always showing, so we put it into a frame that is shown when a user clicks a button. The user can then remove the frame by closing it.

Determining the placement of screen elements requires some careful thought, especially if the applet is complex. When you have many user options and a lot of information to present, it's particularly important to consider what kind of layout will make using the applet most intuitive for the user. For example, when you want to present information about the applet, such as its author and its intended use, a help Menu or a help Choice is appropriate—this is where users expect to find such information.

Keep in mind a *typical* user's knowledge of computers and the Internet. Likewise, a typical user will expect to find a help menu on the far right of the screen, so put your help menus there. You needn't feel that this is aesthetically limiting—you still have great flexibility in making your applets original. Remember to keep your applets as user-friendly as possible since it is likely (if you plan on distributing your applet) that you won't be the only user of the applets you create.

Containers

You will often need to group visual objects before placing them on the screen. To group components together, use one of the three *containers* provided in the Java API: Panels, Dialogs, and Frames. Containers inherit from the Component class, but are used as an object to hold other visual elements. In complex user interfaces, especially, containers make it easier to place components with respect to the rest of the applet's components. For example, a group of checkboxes with a related button might be grouped together and placed in a position that is separated from a text input area.

Panels

A Panel is the most generic container in Java. It's the perfect container to use for the checkboxes and button in the example mentioned above. A Panel is an object directly under the Container class. You can use a Panel within another container, such as a frame, or directly within the Web browser's window. When you have numerous elements to place, grouping related elements logically into Panels can simplify your work.

A Panel can also have its own layout manager, independent of the layout manager used for its container. Suppose, for example, you use the simplest layout manager, FlowLayout, to create a frame with components of varying sizes. You now wish to place a group of five buttons that are all the same size. You can do so easily by putting the buttons in a Panel using the GridLayout Manager (which manages the layout of same-sized elements), and then add this Panel to the frame.

Windows

Window is a generic container class, like Panel; but unlike the Panel, Window forms a "window" that is apart from the main Web browser or appletviewer window. You never directly use the Window class; instead, you use one of its three subclasses: Frame, Dialog, and FileDialog. Each subclass provides all the functionality of the parent Window class, with some added features. For instance, the Frame class implements a menu container so that you can add menus to the Frame. All windows have the standard iconify, maximize, and minimize buttons, as well as the control menu. They also provide a title bar, which you must set when you instantiate the window.

Frame

A *Frame* can exist outside of the Web browser's window, so this is the class to use to implement any "free-floating" applet user interface. A Frame is a plain window; there is nothing on it until you add elements. It can contain your entire user interface. For example, in this chapter, we put the Currency Converter Applet entirely within a frame. A Frame can also contain just part of your user interface, such as a list of users in a Frame that pops open by clicking a button in the Web browser (this is done in the chess client tutorial in Chapter 18).

You can tie events to the Frame's iconify, maximize, and destroy buttons, which automatically appear on the title bar of the window. Because frames implement the MenuContainer class, which is used to place Menus in a window, you can add menus to frames. We discuss Menus and MenuContainers later in this chapter.

Dialog

A *Dialog* can be used to direct a user's attention to required input. Dialogs are just like Frames, with two important distinctions: (1) they do not automatically implement MenuContainer, and (2) they can have *modality*—that is, Dialogs can be used to restrict input to other windows, including the Web browser, until the Dialog is disposed of by some predefined user input.

When creating a Dialog, you define whether or not it is modal by setting the appropriate parameter in its constructor. So, your applet can require that users respond to the dialog before proceeding, or it can let them proceed without responding.

A Dialog is perfect for prompting and forcing users to input some data or acknowledge a message. Dialogs can be more compact than Frames because they don't automatically implement menus. Because of their smaller size, they are often a better choice for obtaining quick user input.

There is one important quirk to remember about Dialogs—*every Dialog requires a Frame as its parent*. You can't open a Dialog directly from the base Applet window (the Web browser). You must first create a dummy Frame object, which is the parent of the Dialog you want to create. Of course, if you are already using a Frame in your applet, you can simply use it as the parent for a Dialog. See the example applet under "Dialog Applet: BorderLayout" later in this chapter; there, we use a dummy Frame to pop open a Dialog.

FileDialog

A *FileDialog* cannot be used in an applet, but applications that run directly via the appletviewer or "java" command line interpreter can use the FileDialog to pass file handles for loading and saving via a streams class. For detailed information about FileDialog, see Chapter 12, "Programming Beyond the Applet Model."

SETTING COLORS
You can use setForeground and setBackground to set the color of a specific component. The parameter required for both of these methods is a Color object, as shown here:

```
setForeground( Color.gray);
```

The above line allows you to set the color of the current component to gray. The available color parameters are black, blue, cyan, darkGray, gray, green, lightGray, magenta, orange, pink, red, white, and yellow.

You can also create a custom color by constructing a new Color object and setting the RGB values:

```
Color MyColor = new Color(100, 100, 100);
```

The three number parameters define the amount of red, green, and blue in the color. The base of Java's RGB is 8-bit, so the valid integer values for the above parameters is 0 to 255.

Menus

Menus can add great flexibility to your applets. Using menus, you can give the user quick access to options and functions. And by using them in combination with one of Java's layout managers, CardLayout, you can make your applet's screen dynamic and multifunctional (for an example, see "Adding Menus: CardLayout" later in this chapter). Since Menus in Java generate events that can easily be watched for, they are straightforward to program. Along with the MenuBar class, the Menu class makes it very simple to add a nice-looking menu and incorporate it into the structure of your applet.

Frames implement MenuContainer automatically and are the only place that menus should really appear in an applet. Having another menu bar inside the Web browser doesn't make much sense, and a dialog with a menu is not really a dialog at all, is it? Hence, the Frame is the only Container that automatically implements the MenuContainer class, though theoretically, a menu can be added to any container.

Adding Menus to an Applet

Menus must be added to a MenuBar, and the instance of MenuBar we create needs to be set to the Frame's menu bar. First we instantiate the MenuBar. We then instantiate each Menu and add MenuItems.

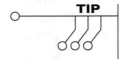

TIP

When you add Menus to the MenuBar, they appear in the order in which they are added, from left to right, so be sure to consider the desired order before you begin.

MenuBar

We begin by declaring a new instance of MenuBar named Bar:

```
MenuBar Bar = new MenuBar();
```

Adding a menu is very simple:

```
Bar.add(m);
```

In this line, *m* is an instance of Menu. The menus are displayed from left to right, in the order they were added to the MenuBar. Likewise, we can remove menus via the remove method. Another interesting option is the ability to add a discrete HelpMenu, as shown here:

```
setHelpMenu(m);
```

The setHelpMenu method distinguishes the Menu *m* by placing it on the far right, set apart from the other menus. Note that we must add the menu to the MenuBar, just like any other Menu. Also note that the setHelpMenu method is contained under the MenuContainer object, which is implemented as a Frame. If we want to call this method outside of a specific Frame's code declaration, we need to do something like this:

```
frameNameInstantiation.setHelpMenu(m)
```

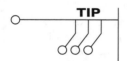

If you use setHelpMenu, you must still add the specified menu to the MenuBar, and you must add it before you execute the setHelpMenu method.

Finally, we have to tell the Frame to use this instance of MenuBar. We do this using the setMenuBar method, which, like setHelpMenu, is in the Frame class:

```
setMenuBar(Bar);
```

This line adds our MenuBar to the Frame. This is generally the last thing you want to do as far as defining your menus: First, create the MenuBar instance; second, create the Menu containers; third, add the MenuItems to the individual Menus. Finish up by adding the Menus to the MenuBar.

Creating MenuItems

We'll create Menu instances for each menu and MenuItem instances for each item in a Menu. The Menu declaration is as follows:

```
Menu m = new Menu("Operation");
```

We label the Menu "Operation" and give it the name *m*. Since we can track things by their labels, it is quite acceptable and efficient to combine the steps of creating a MenuItem and adding it to the menu:

```
m.add(new MenuItem("Adjust Ratio"));
```

This line creates a new MenuItem labeled "Adjust Ratio" and adds it directly to the menu *m*. Similarly, if you need to remove a MenuItem, you can use the remove method. Another interesting option when declaring the Menu is the *tear-off* option. This makes the Menu "sticky," which means that it stays open even after the mouse button has been released. The tear-off option is specified using a boolean like this:

```
new Menu("Operation", true);
```

MenuItems are added in order from top to bottom. If you like, you can insert a separator in the menu using the addSeparator method; this adds a line at the current position in the Menu. You can also create nested menus, since Menu itself is an "extended" MenuItem. Just create a new Menu instance, add it as you would add a MenuItem to a Menu, and see what happens. A nested menu is created in the Java Store tutorial (see Chapter 17); Figure 8-1 shows a screen shot of a nested menu.

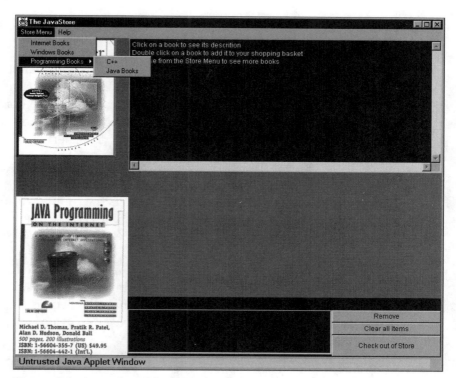

Figure 8-1: *An applet with a nested menu.*

Handling Menu Selections

When the user picks a MenuItem, an event is generated. We look for the event as we look for any other event. In our example applet under "Adding Menus: CardLayout" later in this chapter, we look for the specific menu, then look for the label on the MenuItem picked:

```
if ((evt.id == Event.ACTION_EVENT) && (evt.target==m) )
```

This line looks for an action event *and* finds the target of that action to be Menu *m*. We then get the MenuItem picked via the parameter:

```
(String)evt.arg
```

We look for a MenuItem label matching the (String)evt.arg parameter to see which MenuItem the user actually picked.

Fonts

We'll set the font in many of the examples in this chapter; let's look closely at some of the options available to us. The actual setFont method is in the Component class, not the Font class. This enables us to either set the font individually for each component or allow components to inherit the font properties of their parent. The constructor for fonts is:

```
new Font(String name, int style, int size);
```

where name is the font's name, size is the point size, and style is one of the following: PLAIN, BOLD, or ITALIC. We must create an instance of Font to set the font on a component, thus the instance we create is reusable. To ensure that our users will see the fonts we've chosen, we'll want to get the list of available fonts for the users' Web browsers (see the "Getting a Font List" sidebar). It's important to retrieve the available font list because a particular font may not be available on every user's system.

Font Metrics

We can retrieve a number of metrics for the font we are using, such as the width and height of the characters. Metrics are useful for setting the size of other components and containers properly, so that the font is placed properly in relation to the elements on the screen. For example, the stringWidth method of the FontMetrics constructor class can be used to see how long a string is in a specific font:

```
Font MyFont = new Font("Helvetica",Font.PLAIN, 12));
FontMetrics MyFontMetrics = new FontMetrics( MyFont );
int pixelSizeOfString = MyFontMetrics.stringWidth("Hello");
```

The code shown lets us see how much space the string "Hello" would need if we used MyFont, which is a Helvetica bold 12-point font. The pixelSizeOfString variable contains the number of pixels that the stringWidth method returned.

GETTING A FONT LIST

You can obtain a list of the fonts available on various Web browsers using the AWT Toolkit class:

```
Toolkit Tools = new Toolkit();
FontListString[] = Tools.getFontList();
```

These lines will put the fonts available in an array of Strings; you can then examine them and pick an appropriate font for use from the list.

Layout Managers

Layout managers are indispensable when three or more components are used in an applet; without them, it would be difficult to quickly organize the layout of the screen elements. It would be even more difficult to account for changes in the size of the area of the window in which the applet is running. Absolute positioning of components is not a good solution because it is tedious, and a change in one component's placement will result in the need to reposition the other components. There are several ready-to-use layout managers that are part of the JDK and that will properly manage the needs of most user interfaces.

At the time of this writing, several integrated development environments (IDEs) are in the works that will simplify user interface design with Java. These IDEs are equipped with visual user interface building tools that will do much of the work involved in setting up the Java layout managers. Thus, they will reduce some of the low-level programming you now must do to use the layout managers directly.

The simple layout managers are FlowLayout and GridLayout. BorderLayout, CardLayout, and GridBagLayout are more sophisticated layout managers. The default layout manager for the applet window and Panels is FlowLayout; for Frames and Dialogs, the default is BorderLayout.

We describe each one here, and demonstrate how to use them all in the examples at the end of this chapter.

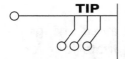

TIP *A useful layout manager that is not included in the JDK is PackerLayout, which was developed by Daeron Meyer. People who have used TCL/TK will recognize PackerLayout. Because of the flexibility PackerLayout offers, we've used it in several of the code examples in this book, and it is available on the Companion CD-ROM and the Online Companion.*

FlowLayout

We have seen several examples of FlowLayout. It was the default layout manager for the Currency Converter applets in the previous chapter. It's really as simple as it seems—add components; if they fit within the row, they will be added; if not, they will be added to the following row. The components will be centered on the row until they run out of space, then a new row is started. If you are careful how you size the applet in the HTML page using the HEIGHT/WIDTH tags, or how you size the Frame or Dialog, you can achieve decent results. For example, you can size the frame so that buttons line up nicely under one another. However, this is a guessing game you may wish to avoid; the layout changes dramatically if you change the width and height of the parent container, and it will produce an undesirable layout. Thus, in the example we just noted, your buttons may no longer line up.

BorderLayout

We will show you how to use BorderLayout later in the example applets. The possible parameters when adding a component to a BorderLayout are "South", "North", "West", "East", and "Center". Components that are added with the parameters South, North, West, and East assume those positions and stay in their assigned areas relative to one another. Center indicates to the layout manager that the item(s) added at the Center position should take up the rest of the space. So, expect elements added at the Center position to stretch and fill in space that is left after other components are placed.

BorderLayout is the most-used layout manager in terms of practicality. It is straightforward and provides a smart way of positioning screen elements. BorderLayout attempts to compensate for components that are not of the same size and tries to use as much of the space available in the container, whether it is a Web browser applet window, Frame, or Dialog.

GridLayout

GridLayout is especially useful for graphics. It provides a way to make a quick, uniform layout of your components. It creates a grid of equal-sized squares, each of which can hold a component. We used GridLayout to set up the chessboard in the tutorial in Chapter 18. Each square contains a Canvas that in turn contains a chess piece. Components are added from left to right, top to bottom.

CardLayout

CardLayout allows you to change onscreen components while the applet is actually running. When used with Panels, it becomes a powerful tool.

CardLayout switches between components based on method calls contained within the class, such as next, previous, or show. You can add as many components as you like and then use these method calls to either cycle through the components or jump directly to a specified component. In the section, "Changing Components Dynamically: CardLayout," later in this chapter, we use CardLayout to switch between two Panels that contain components of our Currency Converter. In one Panel, we include the scrollbar and conversion ratio, so that the user can adjust the ratio. In the other, we include the input and output fields for performing the actual calculations. These Panels are not displayed at the same time.

GridBagLayout

GridBagLayout is the most sophisticated of the layout managers. It reacts well to resizing of the container, and it provides a solution for difficult layout situations in which many components are part of the container, and the components are of varying sizes or must be in precise relation to one another. You must specify the parameters for layout for each component using the setConstraints method. Ideally, you create an instance of gridBagConstraints for each component, so that the component's layout parameters can be configured discretely. These gridBagConstraints are used in a container that is set to use GridBagLayout, but in the example applet later in this chapter (see the section "Precision Layout: GridBagLayout"), we recycle the same gridBagConstraints instance. The following is list of adjustable constraints:

- **gridx, gridy:** Specifies the cell at the upper-most left-hand corner of the component's display area, where the cell has address gridx=0, gridy=0. Use GridBagConstraints.RELATIVE (the default value) to specify that the component be placed just to the right of (for gridx) or just below (for gridy) the component that was added to the container just before this component was added.

- **gridwidth, gridheight:** Specifies the number of cells in a row (for gridwidth) or column (for gridheight) in the component's display area. The default value is 1. Use GridBagConstraints.REMAINDER to specify that the component be the last one in its row (for gridwidth) or column (for gridheight). Use GridBagConstraints.RELATIVE to specify that the component be the next to last one in its row (for gridwidth) or column (for gridheight).

- **fill:** Used when the component's display area is larger than the component's requested size to determine whether (and how) to resize the component. Valid values are GridBagConstraint.NONE (the default), GridBagConstraint.HORIZONTAL (make the component wide enough to fill its display area horizontally, but don't change its height), GridBagConstraint.VERTICAL (make the component tall enough to fill its display area vertically, but don't change its width), and GridBagConstraint.BOTH (make the component fill its display area entirely).

- **ipadx, ipady:** Specifies the internal padding, or how much to add to the minimum size of the component. The width of the component will be at least its minimum width plus ipadx*2 pixels (since the padding applies to both sides of the component). Similarly, the height of the component will be at least the minimum height plus ipady*2 pixels.

- **insets:** Specifies the external padding of the component— the minimum amount of space between the component and the edges of its display area.

- **anchor:** Used when the component is smaller than its display area to determine where (within the area) to place the component. Valid values are

  GridBagConstraints.CENTER (the default)
  GridBagConstraints.NORTH
  GridBagConstraints.NORTHEAST
  GridBagConstraints.EAST
  GridBagConstraints.SOUTHEAST
  GridBagConstraints.SOUTH
  GridBagConstraints.SOUTHWEST
  GridBagConstraints.WEST
  GridBagConstraints.NORTHWEST

◈ **weightx, weighty:** Used to determine how to distribute space; this is important for specifying resizing behavior. Unless you specify a weight for at least one component in a row (weightx) and column (weighty), all the components clump together in the center of their container. This happens when the weight is zero (the default), the GridBagLayout puts any extra space between its grid of cells and the edges of the container.

Choosing a Layout Manager

The next step is to consider which layout manager will work best for you. Table 8-1 provides some general tips to follow, but you will quickly learn what best suits your needs.

Desired Result	Layout Manager to Use
Quick and dirty	FlowLayout
Quick and neat	BorderLayout
All components the same size	GridLayout
Some components the same size	Use GridLayout in a Panel with the same size components, and put components of other sizes in other panel(s).
Components displayed only as needed	CardLayout
Some Components always displayed, and others displayed only as needed	Use CardLayout in one Panel for items to be displayed only as needed, and use separate Panels for components that are always to be displayed.
Precise control over all aspects of the layout; excellent response to resizing	GridBagLayout

Table 8-1: *Choosing a layout manager.*

Remember, you can set a Panel's layout manager to be different than the layout manager used for other Panels and the main panel/window. For example, you can have a CardLayout in a Panel that is in a larger Panel that uses GridBagLayout.

Working With a Layout Manager

A new Container is created with the default layout manager. You can, however, change the layout manager with the following code:

```
setLayout(new BorderLayout());
```

If you are using multiple panels, just remember to specify the panel name:

```
input_panel.setLayout(new BorderLayout());
```

To add components, simply use the same procedures you would use with the default layout manager, with one exception—you may need to pass some parameters. For example, the BorderLayout needs a location parameter:

```
LeftPanel.add("North", ratioField);
```

With GridBagLayout, the parameters are passed as a special class named gridBagConstraints, in which each component is assigned values for layout based on its gridBagConstraints. Components are generally added in order in a row, one after the other, until the vertical or horizontal space is exhausted. Even the BorderLayout loosely adheres to this when more than one component is added to an area, such as "South".

Getting Sizes for Layout

Once you have a great layout designed, how do you know what size its window should be? Use either of the following methods to get and then set the appropriate size for the container:

- **preferredLayoutSize:** public abstract Dimension preferredLayoutSize(Container parent)

  This method calculates the preferred size dimensions for the specified panel given the components in the parent container.

> ❧ **minimumLayoutSize:** public abstract Dimension
> minimumLayoutSize(Container parent)
>
> This method calculates the minimum size dimensions for
> the specified panel given the components in the parent
> container.

Putting It All Together: Examples

We have stepped through the various classes that are used in
producing more advanced user interfaces. We now present code
examples employing the API classes and the techniques discussed.
We build on the Currency Converter example from the previous
chapter, when possible, to show you the variety that is possible
with the look and feel of even a simple applet like the Currency
Converter.

Frame-Based Applet: FlowLayout

Let's look at a simple example of the Currency Converter program
as a frame-based applet. We can maintain the same functionality
without changing around much of the code. We present the
Currency Converter in a Frame, rather than in the Web browser.
We use FlowLayout because we want to do it quickly and aren't
too concerned with precise layout. Figure 8-2 contains a screen
shot of our frame-based applet.

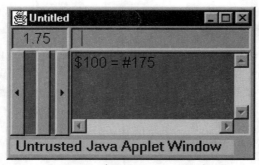

Figure 8-2: *Screen shot of frame-based applet.*

Example 8-1a: Frame-based applet.

```
import java.awt.*;
import java.applet.Applet;

public class Window1 extends Applet {

public void init(){
    new Frame1();
  }
} // Window1
```

First, we have to import the normal libraries for use. Note that Frame falls under the AWT. This is the main declaration of the program. Remember that the applet's filename must match the name of the applet class declaration given above (Window1). Next, we use the init method just as we did in the previous chapter. The above code creates a new instance of Frame1, which is defined below. By "extending" the frame, we can define the features of the specific class, including handling events that occur in the frame. This does a great deal to simplify event handling for a large applet, as the lower-level events can be handled and processed locally, or within a specific panel, frame, or dialog.

Example 8-1b: Frame-based applet.

```
class Frame1 extends Frame {
  float conversion_ratio = 1.5f;
  TextField field1 = new TextField(20);
  TextArea field2 = new TextArea(4,20);
  TextField ratioField = new TextField(5);

  Scrollbar ratioScrollBar = new Scrollbar(
Scrollbar.HORIZONTAL, 150, 25, 50, 250 );
//Declare some variables and AWT components to use in
//Frame1.

public Frame1() {
    setLayout(new FlowLayout());
```

```
            setFont(new Font("Helvetica", Font.PLAIN, 16));
            setBackground(Color.gray);
        field1.setEditable(true);
        field2.setEditable(false);

        add(ratioField);
        add(ratioScrollBar);
        add(field1);
        add(field2);
        ratioField.setText("1.50");
        resize(field1.preferredSize());
        resize(field2.preferredSize());
        resize(300,250);
        pack();
        show();
    } //Frame1()
```

We are *adding* features and functionality to the basic frame implementation, so we use "extends." You may be wondering why we do this when we've already declared Frame1, but if you consider how we begin each applet with "...AppletName extends Applet," you'll see that we are setting up a specialized constructor. In essence, we are creating a specialized, custom component—in this case, a frame. We can then reuse this component as often as we wish, or we can build on it further by extending it in another declared class.

The rest of this example is almost identical to the example in the last chapter. The setLayout method sets the layout manager for the frame, which we'll discuss next. It lets us place the screen elements in specific positions within the window or applet. The setFont method—you guessed it—sets the font for the frame. We can set the font just as easily for individual components. Since we are defining the class Frame1, anything we add within its scope will be added to Frame1, not the applet's window in the Web browser. We are setting the size to 300 X 250, packing the screen contents of the frame, and showing the elements we've added to the frame. The pack method attempts to arrange the components of the Frame as closely as possible within the constraints of the Frame's layout manager.

Example 8-1c: Frame-based applet.

```java
    public void convert() {
      float currency1, currency2;
      String InputString = field1.getText();
      field1.setText("");
      currency1 = Float.valueOf(InputString).floatValue();
      currency2 = conversion_ratio * currency1;
      String OutputString = "$" + InputString + " = " + "#" +
Float.toString(currency2) + "\n";
      field2.appendText(OutputString);
    } //convert
public boolean handleEvent(Event evt) {
    if (evt.target == ratioScrollBar)
      {
        int in;
        in = ratioScrollBar.getValue();
        conversion_ratio = in/100f;
ratioField.setText(Float.toString(conversion_ratio));
      }

    if (evt.target == field1)
      {
        char c=(char)evt.key;
        if (c  == '\n')
          {
            convert();
          }
      }
      return false;
}
} // Applet
```

The above convert method is exactly the same as it was in the previous chapter's Currency Converter example, as is the following handleEvent method. Notice that the handleEvent method has not been changed in any way to accommodate the frame, since we have extended the frame and added this event handling directly to the frame's qualities. We are overriding the handleEvent method for this Frame only, not every handleEvent (such as the base applet class Window1).

By now, you should have a basic feel for how to structure an applet that creates its own window. As we mentioned, panels are an essential part of applets that have many screen elements. When used with the layout managers, they make organizing and laying out the applet much easier. We will demonstrate how to use a panel later in this chapter. But first, we'll discuss the sibling of Frame, which is Dialog.

Dialog Applet: BorderLayout

Let's look at a quick implementation of a Dialog, shown in Figure 8-3. We'll demonstrate how to use dialogs to grab the user's attention and make the user respond. We don't use the Currency Converter in this example, since there's no need to prompt its users specific, required input. We use BorderLayout because we want to place the components at specific locations on the dialog—we want to show a message at the top, give instructions in the center, and put the Continue button at the bottom.

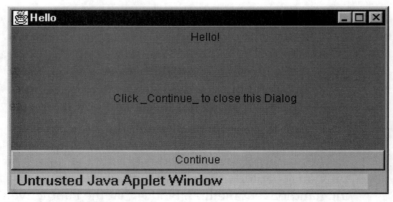

Figure 8-3: *Dialog example*.

Example 8-2a: Dialog applet.

```java
import java.awt.*;
import java.applet.Applet;

public class Show_Dialog extends Applet {
    Frame f;
    Intro_Dialog Hello_Dialog;
public void init(){
        f = new Frame();
        f.resize(50,50);
        f.pack();
Hello_Dialog = new Intro_Dialog(f); add(new Button("Show
Me!"));
}
public boolean action ( Event evt, Object obj)
            {
                if (obj == "Show Me!")

                    Hello_Dialog.show();
                    return true;
                }
                    return false;

            }
} // End applet Show_Dialog
```

Why have we defined a Frame here? It's simple: a Dialog requires a Frame as its parent. Intro_Dialog is a new class defined as an "extension" to Dialog, and we make an instance of it in Hello_Dialog.

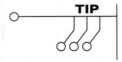

TIP

Remember that a Dialog must have a parent Frame. Hence, a Frame must be declared as a Dialog's parent, even if the Frame is not used.

In the next section of code, we create a new instance of Frame, although we do not even plan to show it. We initialize the size and pack it just to be safe; a NullPointerException may occur if the Frame is not initialized and the Dialog attempts to reference it.

Then, we create the new instance of Intro_Dialog, and pass the Frame we just created as Hello_Dialog's parent. Note that the Button is added to the Applet, not the Frame or Dialog. This is the trigger Button we use to pop open the Dialog window. The above event handling sequence of action is for the applet only. We handle the events that happen in the Dialog in the class declaration below. We are looking for the Button named "Show Me!," and upon its mouse click, we show the Hello_Dialog.

Example 8-2b: Dialog applet with new instance of Frame.

```
class Intro_Dialog extends Dialog {


public Intro_Dialog(Frame parent) {
   super(parent, "Hello", true);
   setLayout(new BorderLayout());
   setFont(new Font("Helvetica", Font.PLAIN, 12));
      setBackground(Color.gray);
      add("North", new Label("Hello!", Label.CENTER));
      add("Center", new Label("Click _Continue_ to close this
Dialog", Label.CENTER));
      add("South", new Button("Continue"));
 resize(250,250);
    }


public boolean handleEvent(Event evt)
   {
    if (evt.id == Event.ACTION_EVENT )
     {
     if("Continue".equals(evt.arg))
       {
            dispose();
            return true;
          }
      }
   return false;
  }
} // Applet
```

Because we use a Dialog, we have several parameters that can be passed during initialization. Since we are in the specific constructor Intro_Dialog of the class Intro_Dialog, we pass the parameters to the super, or the Show_Dialog class. The setLayout(new BorderLayout) line is actually redundant, as BorderLayout is the default layout manager for Frames and Dialogs. We include it as a reminder that, because an add(newComponent) will not work, we need to specify a location—add("Center", newComponent). We add two labels and a Button labeled "Continue" to the Dialog. In the handleEvent method, we look for the clicking of the "Continue" button. When this happens, the Button name is passed in as the evt.arg. We verify that the Button was clicked and dispose of the Dialog. Again, this could have been done with the mouse_click or action event handler instead of handleEvent, but with handleEvent, we can process all events in one method with maximum simplicity.

Panel Applet: BorderLayout

The Panel is the simplest container you can use. The Panel is best used to organize text areas, buttons, and other screen elements within a Web browser applet. It can also be used within a Window, such as a Frame or Dialog. Again, we use BorderLayout for good control over placement of components.

Let's organize our Applet quickly by implementing Panels in it. We won't show the entire code here—just the pertinent part. We begin by creating two panels; one to hold the scrollbar and conversion_ratio text field and the other to hold the output and input text field and text area. We'll add the scrollbar and conversion_ratio text field to the first panel, called LeftPanel, and we'll add the input/output fields to the second Panel, called RightPanel. When we add the panels to the applet, the four basic components become part of the applet's display via the panels. (See Figure 8-4.)

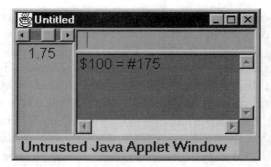

Figure 8-4: *The Panels applet.*

Example 8-3a: Panels applet.

```java
import java.awt.*;
import java.applet.Applet;

public class Panel1 extends Applet {

  public void init() {
   new Frame1();
   }
} // Panel1

class Panel_n_Frame extends Panel_n_Frame {
  float conversion_ratio = 1.5f;
  TextField field1 = new TextField(20);
  TextArea field2 = new TextArea(4,20);
  TextField ratioField = new TextField(5);
  Scrollbar ratioScrollBar = new Scrollbar(
Scrollbar.VERTICAL, 150, 25, 50, 250 );

  public Panel_n_Frame() {
    Panel RightPanel = new Panel();
    Panel LeftPanel = new Panel();
    setLayout(new BorderLayout());
    setFont(new Font("Helvetica", Font.PLAIN, 16));
```

```
setBackground(Color.gray);
    field1.setEditable(true);
    field2.setEditable(false);
    LeftPanel.setLayout(new BorderLayout());
    LeftPanel.add("Center", ratioField);
    LeftPanel.add("North", ratioScrollBar);
    RightPanel.setLayout(new BorderLayout());
    RightPanel.add("North", field1);
    RightPanel.add("South", field2);

    ratioField.setText("1.50");
    field1.resize(field1.preferredSize());
    field2.resize(field2.preferredSize());
    resize(300,250);
    add("East", RightPanel);
    add("West", LeftPanel);
    pack();
    show();
} //init
```

We change the scrollbar to vertical for variety, and we create two new panels for use: RightPanel and LeftPanel. Then we add their components. Note that setLayout and setFont refer to the Panel_n_Frame class, not RightPanel and LeftPanel. If we were working directly inside the Web browser instead of in a Frame, we would be setting the properties of the part of the window in which the browser's applet runs.

We assign layout managers to individual Panels. We also add the screen elements to the respective Panels. The BorderLayout manager accepts values of North, South, East, West, and Center. The Center position is used as a "filler" position; if we add the ratioScrollbar as "Center" instead of "West," the outcome is somewhat surprising. Try it and see! The scrollbar actually stretches until it occupies the rest of the LeftPanel! A text area or Canvas would work well in the Center position in a BorderLayout scheme, as both can be used to fill out the empty spot of the Panel without a noticeable distortion. We then add the Panels to the window instead of directly adding a component to the window.

Example 8-3b: Panels applet.

```java
public void convert() {
    float currency1, currency2;
    String InputString = field1.getText();
    field1.setText("");
    currency1 = Float.valueOf(InputString).floatValue();
    currency2 = conversion_ratio * currency1;
    String OutputString = "$" + InputString + " = " + "#" +
Float.toString(currency2) + "\n";
    field2.appendText(OutputString);
  } //convert

  public boolean handleEvent(Event evt) {

    if (evt.target == ratioScrollBar)
      {
        int in;
        in = ratioScrollBar.getValue();
        conversion_ratio = in/100f;
ratioField.setText(Float.toString(conversion_ratio));
      }

    if (evt.target == field1)
      {
        char c=(char)evt.key;
        if (c  == '\n')
          {
            convert();
          }
      }

    if (evt.id == Event.WINDOW_DESTROY) {
      dispose();
      return true;
    }
    return false;
    }

} // Applet
```

Wait! What's this WINDOW_DESTROY? We always want to handle the user clicking on the close window (or Frame) button. We didn't do this in the first Frame example, but we should have. If you tried closing the Frame in that example, you'd find that it doesn't go away. You can iconify it, but it won't completely go away until you shut down the Web browser completely.

Same-Sized Elements: GridLayout

GridLayout is especially useful for graphics. It creates a grid of equal-sized squares, each of which can hold a component. As we mentioned before, a chessboard is set up using GridLayout in the in the Chess Client tutorial (see Chapter 18), with each square containing a Canvas that in turn contains a chess piece. We demonstrate GridLayout in Example 8-4, building on our Currency Converter example.

Example 8-4: GridLayout applet code.

```
import java.awt.*;
import java.applet.Applet;
public class Grid_Layout1 extends Applet {
  float conversion_ratio = 1.5f;
  TextField field1 = new TextField(20);
  TextArea field2 = new TextArea(4,20);
  TextField ratioField = new TextField(5);
  Scrollbar ratioScrollBar = new Scrollbar(
Scrollbar.HORIZONTAL, 150, 25, 50, 250 );
  public void init() {
    setLayout(new GridLayout(3,3));
setFont(new Font("Helvetica", Font.PLAIN, 12));
    setBackground(Color.gray);
    ratioField.setEditable(false);
    field1.setEditable(true);
    field2.setEditable(false);
    ratioField.setText("1.50");
    field1.resize(field1.preferredSize());
    field2.resize(field2.preferredSize());
    ratioField.resize(15,25);
    ratioScrollBar.resize(ratioScrollBar.minimumSize());
```

```
          add(ratioField);
          add(ratioScrollBar);
          add(field1);
          add(field2);
          show();

     } //init
```

In Figure 8-5, notice how the scrollbar, as well as the other components, have been stretched to fit each square.

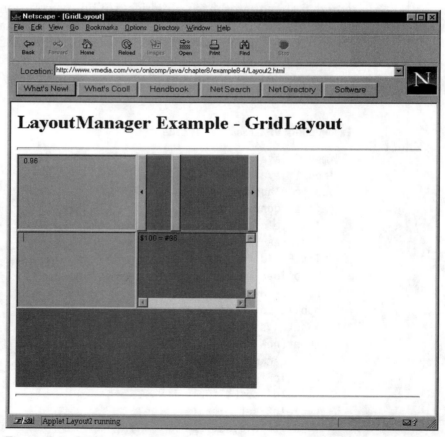

Figure 8-5: *GridLayout example.*

We want a grid with 2 X 2 squares since only four components will be added to the user interface, but let's see what happens when we make the grid too big. Notice in the screen shot (Figure 8-5) how the layout manager compensates for the extra space.

Next, we add the components, just as we did in previous examples. There are no parameters to deal with when adding components using GridLayout; the components are simply added from left to right, top to bottom. The rest of the example is similar to the previous examples; we have a convert method and a handleEvent to handle the processing of the keystroke. We can specify any grid size we want, and we can include "0" as one of the parameters to indicate that we want the grid to grow as big as possible in that parameter's direction.

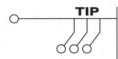

TIP

You can set one of the GridLayout constructor parameters to indicate you want the grid to grow as large as necessary in that direction.

Changing Components Dynamically: CardLayout

CardLayout allows you to dynamically change the components that are shown. When it is used with panels, it becomes a powerful tool. Example 8-5 demonstrates how to implement CardLayout. We group the components involved with the changing of the conversion value into one panel, shown in Figure 8-6, and put the calculation input and output component into another panel, shown in Figure 8-7. We switch between these two panels when the user picks from the Choice we have put on the user interface.

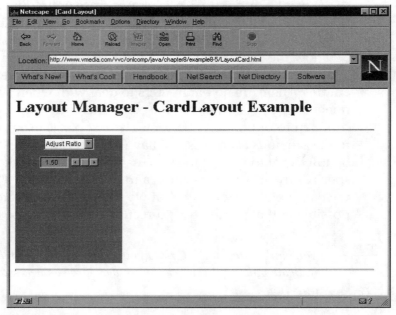

Figure 8-6: *CardLayout option "Adjust."*

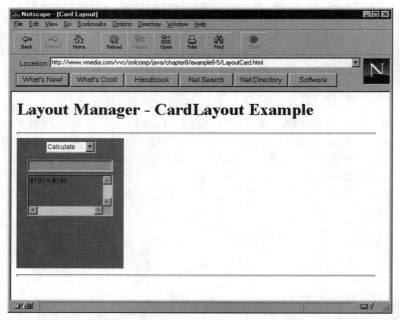

Figure 8-7: *CardLayout option "Calculate."*

Example 8-5a: CardLayout applet code.

```
import java.awt.*;
import java.applet.Applet;

public class LayoutCard extends Applet {

  float conversion_ratio = 1.5f;
  TextField field1 = new TextField(20);
  TextArea field2 = new TextArea(4,20);
  TextField ratioField = new TextField(5);
  Scrollbar ratioScrollBar = new Scrollbar(
Scrollbar.HORIZONTAL, 150, 25, 50, 250 );
  Panel cards_panel;

public void init() {
    setLayout(new BorderLayout());
    setFont(new Font("Helvetica", Font.PLAIN, 12));
    setBackground(Color.gray);
    RatioField.setEditable(false);
    field1.setEditable(true);
    field2.setEditable(false);
    ratioField.setText("1.50");
    field1.resize(field1.preferredSize());
    field2.resize(field2.preferredSize());
ratioField.resize(ratioField.preferredSize());
ratioScrollBar.resize(ratioScrollBar.minimumSize());
```

We'll declare the panel to which CardLayout is assigned global—we can watch for events that we would want to change the screen on. The setLayout(new BorderLayout()) in the previous section of code sets the layout for the applet window:

```
    Panel options_panel = new Panel();
    Choice options = new Choice();
    options.addItem("Adjust Ratio");
    options.addItem("Calculate");
    options_panel.add(options);
    add("North", options_panel);
```

```
        cards_panel = new Panel();
        cards_panel.setLayout(new CardLayout());

        Panel ratio_panel = new Panel();
        Panel calculate_panel = new Panel();
        ratio_panel.add(ratioField);
        ratio_panel.add(ratioScrollBar);
        calculate_panel.add(field1);
        calculate_panel.add(field2);
        cards_panel.add("Adjust Ratio", ratio_panel);
        cards_panel.add("Calculate", calculate_panel);
    add("Center", cards_panel);
    show();
    } //init
```

The code above adds a Choice component to a new panel named options_panel. The Choice contains "Adjust Ratio" and "Calculate" as its two choices. We add the options_panel, which contains the Choice component, to the top of the applet window. Below is the CardLayout specific code. We create a new instance of Panel and give it the CardLayout manager. We create two new discrete panels; we plan on showing only one of these at a time via the CardLayout manager. The two panels are added to the cards_panel. We want to show the ratio field and the ratio scroll bar together, so we add these to the same panel. We add the input and output field into a different panel, since we want to switch to these when the user changes the choice. Next, we add the two panels to the cards_panel, using the labels "Adjust Ratio" and "Calculate."

Then we simply add the cards_panel to the applet window. The applet window contains the cards_panel and the options_panel. The order in which you add items to the cards_panel determines which order they are shown if the next or previous method is used. You can also directly show a specific panel in CardsLayout using the show method in the CardLayout class, which is what we do below in the action event handler:

Example 8-5b: CardLayout appletcode.

```
   public void convert() {
     float currency1, currency2;
     String InputString = field1.getText();
     field1.setText("");
     currency1 = Float.valueOf(InputString).floatValue();
     currency2 = conversion_ratio * currency1;
     String OutputString =
       "$" + InputString + " = " + "#" +
Float.toString(currency2) + "\n";
     field2.appendText(OutputString);
   } //convert

public synchronized boolean handleEvent(Event evt) {
    if (evt.target == ratioScrollBar)
      {
       int in;
       in = ratioScrollBar.getValue();
       conversion_ratio = in/100f;
       ratioField.setText(Float.toString(conversion_ratio));
      }

    if (evt.target == field1)
      {
      char c=(char)evt.key;
      if (c  == '\n')
        {
          convert();
          return true;
        }
      else { return false; }
      }

    return super.handleEvent(evt);
}
```

We need to add *synchronized* to the handleEvent method because we also use the action event handler, and we want to ensure that we do not try to access the two event handlers at the same time. We could move these event handlers into action method, but we leave them here to show you that event handling can be broken into the various event handling methods for simplicity. For example, we can use the mouseDown event handler to handle simple mouse events and use the handleEvent method to process other events:

```
      public boolean action(Event evt, Object arg) {
       if (evt.target instanceof Choice) {
       ((CardLayout)cards_panel.getLayout()).show(cards_panel,
       (String)arg);
 // * See explanation below
         return true;
       }
       return false;
     }
 } // Applet
```

The line marked with an asterisk may seem complicated, but its function is simple: it looks at the Choice component, gets its current selection, and sets the cards_panel directly to the selection using show. The selection is passed in the arg variable. The CardLayout can be "flipped" back and forth as well, using the next and last methods. This can be useful if you have a forward and back button, or if you have a series of components you want to present.

Precision Layout: GridBagLayout

GridBagLayout is the most sophisticated layout manager. When there are numerous components whose placement requires more precision placement than the other layout managers can provide, GridBagLayout is the solution. Suppose we want to put the Currency Converter components in the following order: ratioField and the ratioScrollBar on the same line, the input field (field1) on the next line, and the output field (field2) in rest of the applet's space. We use GridBagLayout to achieve this placement, shown in Figure 8-8. We set constraints on the individual components, then add them to the applet. The GridBagLayout manager interprets these constraints and positions the components accordingly.

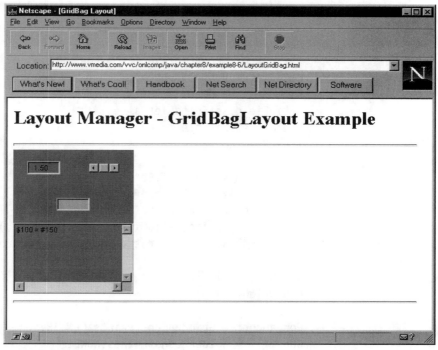

Figure 8-8: *GridBagLayout example.*

Example 8-6: GridBagLayout applet.

```
public class LayoutGridBag extends Applet {

   float conversion_ratio = 1.5f;
   TextField field1 = new TextField(5);
   TextArea field2 = new TextArea(4,20);
   TextField ratioField = new TextField(5);
   Scrollbar ratioScrollBar = new Scrollbar(
Scrollbar.HORIZONTAL, 150, 25, 50, 250 );
   Panel cards_panel;

   GridBagLayout gridbag = new GridBagLayout();
   GridBagConstraints Con = new GridBagConstraints();
```

```
public void init() {

    setLayout(gridbag);
    setFont(new Font("Helvetica", Font.PLAIN, 12));
    setBackground(Color.gray);

    ratioField.setEditable(false);
    field1.setEditable(true);
    field2.setEditable(false);

    ratioField.setText("1.50");
    field1.resize(field1.preferredSize());
    field2.resize(field2.preferredSize());
    ratioField.resize(ratioField.preferredSize());
    ratioScrollBar.resize(ratioScrollBar.preferredSize());

    Con.weightx=1.0;
    Con.weighty=1.0;

    Con.anchor = GridBagConstraints.CENTER;
    Con.fill = GridBagConstraints.NONE;

    Con.gridwidth=GridBagConstraints.RELATIVE;
    gridbag.setConstraints(ratioField, Con);
    add(ratioField);

    Con.gridwidth = GridBagConstraints.REMAINDER;
```

First, we make new instances of GridBagLayout and gridBagConstraints. We set the layout manager to gridbag (an instantiation of GridBagLayout). If the weightx and weighty gridBagConstraints are left to the defaults of 0, everything gravitates towards the center, and this is not the effect we want. The default for the fill is BOTH, which causes the component to stretch. We don't want the scrollbar, ratioField, and input field to stretch, so we set the fill to NONE. We do want the output field to fill, so we change the fill back to BOTH later. We also set the anchor to CENTER, so that all of the components stay in the center of their "assigned" space. We want the ratioField to be the second to the last component on the row, so we set the gridwidth to RELATIVE. We also need to add the constraints to that specific component. We want ratioScrollBar to be the last component on the row, so we set the gridwidth to REMAINDER.

Remember, we are recycling one gridBagConstraints, so we need to set any values back to our desired default. We don't need to change these constraints again if we need to redo a layout, so it's acceptable to use the same gridBagConstraints instance (Con) over again. We would have to set all of the defaults for each instance of gridBagConstraints if we decided to make a separate instance of gridBagConstraints for each component, so it's more economical to just make one and reuse it:

```
gridbag.setConstraints(ratioScrollBar, Con);
add(ratioScrollBar);
Con.gridwidth=GridBagConstraints.REMAINDER;
gridbag.setConstraints(field1, Con);
add(field1);

Con.gridy=GridBagConstraints.RELATIVE;
Con.fill = GridBagConstraints.BOTH;
Con.gridwidth=GridBagConstraints.REMAINDER;
Con.gridheight=GridBagConstraints.REMAINDER;
gridbag.setConstraints(field2, Con);
add(field2);
} //init
```

We want the output text area to take up the rest of the applet's screen area, so we set fill to BOTH and the gridwidth and gridheight to REMAINDER. Then, we set the constraints for field2 and add it. The remainder of the code is the same as the previous example. We now have a neatly organized applet. You can experiment with the various parameters to get a good feel for how to use the GridBagLayout.

Adding Menus: CardLayout

Let's be creative and do a spin-off of our CardLayout example, using a Menu instead of Choice to change the visible components (see Figure 8-9). This example makes the options of changing the conversion value, as well as the actual calculation parts of the applet, into a menu. We use CardLayout to switch between "Calculate" and "Adjust Ratio." There are lots of ways you can experiment with the Menus—a menu event can implement a Choice as its MenuItems, for example.

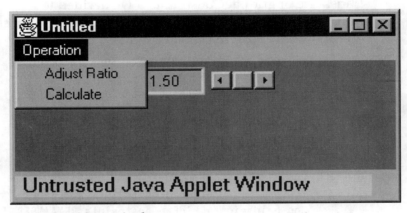

Figure 8-9: *Menus Applet*.

Example 8-7: Menus Applet.

```java
import java.awt.*;
import java.applet.Applet;

public class Menu1 extends Applet {

  public void init(){
   new Menu_Frame();
  }
} // Menu1

// Create a new instance of the Menu_Frame
// class!

class Menu_Frame extends Frame {

  float conversion_ratio = 1.5f;
  TextField field1 = new TextField(15);
  TextArea field2 = new TextArea(4,20);
  TextField ratioField = new TextField(5);
  Scrollbar ratioScrollBar = new Scrollbar(
Scrollbar.HORIZONTAL, 150, 25, 50, 250 );
  Panel cards_panel;

  public Menu_Frame() {
    setLayout(new BorderLayout());
    MenuBar Bar = new MenuBar();
    Menu m = new Menu("Operation");
    m.add(new MenuItem("Adjust Ratio"));
    m.add(new MenuItem("Calculate"));
    Bar.add(m);
    setMenuBar(Bar);
```

In Example 8-7, we create a menu. First, we create a new instance of MenuBar called Bar, and create a new instance of Menu called *m*. We then add newly created MenuItems to the Menu. Next, we add the Menu *m* to the Bar, and finally, setMenuBar to be Bar.

```
      setFont(new Font("Helvetica", Font.PLAIN, 12));
      setBackground(Color.gray);
    ratioField(setEditable(false);
      field1.setEditable(true);
      field2.setEditable(false);
      ratioField.setText("1.50");
      field1.resize(field1.preferredSize());
      field2.resize(field2.preferredSize());
   ratioField.resize(ratioField.preferredSize());
   ratioScrollBar.resize(ratioScrollBar.preferredSize());
```

Below, we use the same steps we used in the CardLayout example. Nothing here has changed; we make sure we use the same labels for the two Panels as we did for the two menu items. They must match exactly for the Panels to change properly in the handleEvent method:

```
      cards_panel = new Panel();
      cards_panel.setLayout(new CardLayout());
      Panel ratio_panel = new Panel();
      Panel calculate_panel = new Panel();
      ratio_panel.add(ratioField);
      ratio_panel.add(ratioScrollBar);
      calculate_panel.add(field1);
      calculate_panel.add(field2);
      cards_panel.add("Adjust Ratio", ratio_panel);
      cards_panel.add("Calculate", calculate_panel);

      add("Center", cards_panel);
      resize(250,300);
      pack();
      show();
    } // Menu_Frame

    public void convert() {
      float currency1, currency2;
      String InputString = field1.getText();
      field1.setText("");
      currency1 = Float.valueOf(InputString).floatValue();
      currency2 = conversion_ratio * currency1;
```

```
        String OutputString ="$" + InputString + " = " + "#" +
Float.toString(currency2) + "\n";
        field2.appendText(OutputString);
    } //convert

  public boolean handleEvent(Event evt) {

      if (evt.target == ratioScrollBar)
        {
         int in;
         in = ratioScrollBar.getValue();
         conversion_ratio = in/100f;
ratioField.setText(Float.toString(conversion_ratio));
         }
      if (evt.target == field1)
        {
        char c=(char)evt.key;

        if (c  == '\n')
          {
            convert();
            return true;
          }
        else { return false; }
        }
      if ((evt.id == Event.ACTION_EVENT) &&
     (evt.target==m) )
         {
        ((CardLayout)cards_panel.getLayout()).show(cards_panel,(String)evt.arg);
            return true;
         }
      if (evt.id == Event.WINDOW_DESTROY) {
        dispose();
        return true;
      }
      return false;
}
  } // Menu_Frame
```

The handleEvent method is where the menu pick is handled. We look for an ACTION_EVENT and the target as the specific menu. Then, we look at what was picked via the evt.arg parameter and set the cards_panel corresponding panel. Just to be neat, we always try to include proper handling of the WINDOW_DESTROY call.

Moving On

We have seen how to create feature-rich user interfaces. The many components that we discussed in Chapter 7, along with the more sophisticated components in this chapter, provide a great toolkit for building the applet's user interface. When used with the layout managers, the Java containers provide a blueprint for designing the applet's user interface. We use these features extensively in the tutorials section of the book, where we show you several production-quality programs disguised as applets.

In the next chapter, we describe the Java classes that are required for using graphics and manipulating images in your applets.

9

Graphics & Images

In the last two chapters, you learned how to easily create power-ful, attractive user interfaces. This chapter will teach you how to draw and manipulate graphical images that can enhance your Java applets and programs.

Java's Graphics class, part of the java.awt hierarchy, gives us a large number of methods with which we can draw geometric shapes and place text on a two-dimensional drawing area. Gener-ally, this drawing area is associated with a visible Component or an Image. The package's functionality closely resembles a simple graphics editor like Microsoft Paintbrush. The java.awt.image package, distinct from the java.awt package and from the java.awt.Image class (although closely related to both) allows you to interact with Images at the byte level, letting you create Images from your own algorithms. The image package also offers power-ful tools for filtering existing Images.

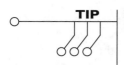

TIP

This chapter's code example files can be found on the Companion CD-ROM (for Windows 95/NT and Macintosh users) and the Online Companion (for UNIX users). Visit the Online Companion at http://www.vmedia.com/java.html.

Drawing Using the Graphics Class

The Graphics class allows you to draw onto a two-dimensional canvas using standard graphics primitives. Note that you cannot create a Graphics object yourself, since the only constructor is designated as private. Normally, either the Graphics object associated with the Component you're working with is passed to you, as is the case when using the Component's paint method, or it can be obtained explicitly with the Component class's getGraphics method.

The Image class also implements a getGraphics method, which returns a runtime reference to a Graphics object associated with the Image. This technique was discussed briefly in Chapter 5, "How Applets Work."

Drawing Outlined Shapes

Because the Graphics class has so many methods, we'll break them up into three sections and discuss each in turn. The first section contains all of the methods concerned with drawing outlined (unfilled) figures in the default color. These methods are listed in Table 9-1.

Method	Description
drawLine(int, int, int, int)	Draws a line from the position indicated by the first two integers (given in X- and Y-coordinate notation) to the position indicated by the second two integers.
drawRect(int, int, int, int)	Draws a rectangle. The first two integers indicate the upper left-hand corner of the rectangle, and the last two integers indicate the width and height.
draw3DRect(int, int, int, int, boolean)	Draws a highlighted 3-D rectangle. The rectangle itself is given by the first four integers, in the same fashion as in the drawRect method, and the boolean indicates whether the rectangle should be raised.

Method	Description
drawRoundRect(int, int, int, int, int, int)	Draws a rectangle with rounded edges inscribed in the normal rectangle given by the first four integers. The last two integers indicate the arc width and height for the corners. The arc width and height specify the horizontal diameter of the arc along either the X- or Y-axis at the four corners. The larger the arc values are, the smoother the corner will look.
drawOval(int, int, int, int)	Draws an oval inscribed in the rectangle specified by the four integers.
drawArc(int, int, int, int, int, int)	Draws an arc inscribed in the rectangle specified by the first four integers. The last two integers indicate the starting and ending angles measured in degrees. Zero degrees indicates the center of the right-hand side of the Graphics area. Positive degree values indicate counter-clockwise rotation, and negative degree values indicate clockwise rotation.
drawPolygon(int[], int[], int)	Draws a polygon. The integer arrays contain the X- and Y-coordinates for the points composing the polygon, and the integer argument indicates the total number of points.
drawPolygon(Polygon)	Draws a polygon. The polygon is given by the Polygon argument.

Table 9-1: *Shape-oriented drawing methods of the Graphics class.*

There are a couple of peculiarities with the Graphics class you should be aware of. Currently, the draw3DRect method draws a rectangle that appears to be identical in every respect to that obtained via the drawRect method, regardless of whether it is raised or not. Presumably, this is a bug and will be fixed in some later release of the Java API—for now, if you want three-dimensional rectangles, you'll have to draw them yourself. The drawArc method is very similar to the drawOval method—in fact, calling drawOval(0,0,X,Y) and drawArc(0,0,X,Y,0,360) will produce the very same picture. Using the drawArc method allows you to request that only a certain portion of the oval be drawn.

Drawing Filled Shapes

You can also paint filled regions of the screen in various geometric shapes. There is a corresponding filled drawing method for each of the outlined drawing methods listed in Table 9-1, except for drawArc and drawLine. Simply substitute the word *fill* for the word *draw* to obtain a new table of methods. Like the draw3DRect method, the fill3DRect method does not appear to draw a rectangle any differently than the normal fillRect method.

In the following simple example, we draw two lines from opposite corners of the screen, a rounded rectangle border of the whole screen, a centered oval, and a centered arc. We fill the very center of the screen with a gray rounded rectangle. This example illustrates the use of the draw and fill methods of the Graphics class. A screen shot of the output appears in Figure 9-1.

Example 9-1: A simple graphics applet.

```
import java.applet.*;
import java.awt.*;

public class GraphicsApplet extends Applet {

    public void init() {
        resize(250,250);
        setBackground(Color.white);
    }

    public void paint(Graphics g) {
        g.setColor(Color.darkGray);
        g.drawLine(0,0,250,250);
        g.drawLine(0,250,250,0);
```

```
        g.drawRoundRect(0,0,250,250,50,50);
        g.drawOval(0,50,250,150);
        g.drawArc(75,75,100,100,0,180);

        g.setColor(Color.gray);
        g.fillRoundRect(100,100,50,50,25,25);
    }


}
```

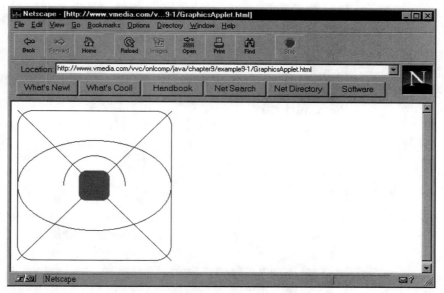

Figure 9-1: *A simple graphics applet.*

Drawing Text & Images

The Graphics class also lets you draw some nongeometrical objects; namely, Images and text in the form of Strings and character and byte arrays. Images, as we saw in Chapter 5, are drawn into rectangles on our Graphics object, but in fact represent a complex picture that would be difficult or impossible to render using the drawing and filling methods supplied by the Graphics class.

The methods for drawing text and Images are listed in Table 9-2. They do not have complementary fill methods.

Method	Description
drawString(String, int, int)	Draws the given String in the current font at the specified location.
drawChars(char[], int, int, int, int)	Converts the character array given as the first argument into a String and draws it in the location specified by the last two integers. The first two integers indicate the starting index value for the array and number of characters to be converted.
drawBytes(byte[], int, int, int, int)	Draws a byte array in the same manner as the drawChars method.
drawImage(Image, int, int, ImageObserver)	Requests that the given Image be drawn at the location specified by the two integers. The ImageObserver argument indicates the class that will watch for the Image data to arrive and draw the Image when the data transfer is complete. This interface will be discussed later in the chapter, under "Importing & Creating Images."
drawImage(Image, int, int, Color, ImageObserver)	Requests that the given Image be drawn at the location specified by the two integers, with a solid background in the given Color.
drawImage(Image, int, int, int, int, ImageObserver)	Requests that the given Image be drawn into the rectangle given by the four integers. The Image will be scaled to fit the rectangle if necessary.

Table 9-2: *Non-shape-oriented drawing methods of the Graphics class.*

Modifying the Graphics Class

There are also a number of methods that let you change the functionality of the Graphics class. You can change the default color and font, as well as copy and clip to regions of the screen. These methods are listed in Table 9-3.

Method	Description
Graphics create()	Creates a new Graphics object that is a copy of this one.
Graphics create(int, int, int, int)	Creates a new Graphics object that is bounded by the rectangle given by the four integers. Any changes made in the Graphics object will be reflected in the specified rectangular region of this one.
Color getColor()	Returns the current drawing color.
setColor(Color)	Sets the current drawing color.
setPaintMode()	Sets the paint mode to always paint with the default color.
setXORMode(Color)	Sets the paint mode to alternate painting with the default color and the specified color. When painting with one color, pixels of that color will be switched to the other color, and, in turn, pixels of that color will be switched to the first color. Other pixels will be changed in an unpredictable yet reliable fashion—if you paint over them twice while XORMode is active, they'll be reset to their original colors. This method can be useful for highlighting or drawing simple animated sprites.
Font getFont()	Returns the current font.

Method	Description
setFont(Font)	Sets the current font.
FontMetrics getFontMetrics()	Returns the FontMetrics object associated with the current font.
FontMetrics getFontMetrics(Font)	Returns the FontMetrics object associated with the specified font.
clipRect(int, int, int, int)	Sets a bounding rectangle, given by the four integers for drawing in this Graphics object. When a bounding rectangle is set, no painting will be done outside of that rectangle.
Rectangle getClipRect()	Returns the bounding rectangle as a Rectangle object.
copyArea(int, int, int, int, int, int)	Copies the rectangle given by the first four integers. The distance to be moved along the X- and Y-axes is given by the last two integers.
dispose()	Renders this Graphics object unusable.

Table 9-3: *Miscellaneous methods of the Graphics class.*

Using the Image Class

While the methods offered by the Graphics class are sufficient for creating simple graphical images like bar graphs or fancy menus, they do not allow you to perform advanced graphics operations by directly manipulating individual pixels. To do that, you must use Images. Images are also useful in that they provide a handy consistent interface for working with pictures imported from a file in one of the popular graphics standards. In this next section, we'll discuss how Images really work and ways of working with Images asynchronously; that is, Images whose pictorial data is not available yet.

The Image class, part of the java.awt package, gives us several methods with which we can request information about the Image, such as its width or height. These methods are listed in Table 9-4.

Method	Description
Graphics getGraphics()	Returns a Graphics object associated with the Image.
int getHeight(ImageObserver)	Returns the height of the Image if known. If the height is unknown, as may be the case if the Image is not yet complete, this method returns −1 and the given ImageObserver is notified when the height is known.
int getWidth(ImageObserver)	Returns the width of the Image if known. If the width is unknown this method will return −1 and the given ImageObserver will be notified when the width becomes known.
Object getProperty(String, ImageObserver)	Requests the value of the property named by the String argument. For instance, the "comment" property name is used to store an optional comment containing a text description of the Image. If the requested property is not defined for this Image, this method will return an UndefinedProperty object. If the requested property is not available yet, as may be the case if the Image is not yet complete, this method will return null and the given ImageObserver will be notified when the property becomes known.
ImageProducer getSource()	Returns the ImageProducer that produced the pixels for this Image.
flush()	Flushed all resources being used by this Image, including all stored pixel data. If this Image is used again, it will have to be recreated or downloaded again.

Table 9-4: *Methods of the Image class.*

The ImageObserver and ImageProducer interfaces mentioned in Table 9-4 are used by the Java API to allow programmers to work with Images whose data is not completely available yet. We discuss these interfaces in the "Interfaces for Asynchronous Images" section later in this chapter. Recall that the Component class implements the ImageObserver interface, so whenever you need to pass an ImageObserver as a parameter, you can pass a reference to your working Component.

Importing Images

We discussed in Chapter 5, "How Applets Work," how to download Images from a network file server using URLs. One of the problems we encountered in downloading Images was that the Image wasn't actually downloaded until we first displayed it using a drawImage method. This behavior was especially noticeable when we created an animation using Images downloaded via URLs. This problem is not unique to pictures downloaded from the network—many pictures are created using complex mathematical formulas that may take a long time to compute. When designing the Java API, Sun decided to allow programmers to start using Images in their programs before the download or calculation process for a given Image was actually completed. This can be very useful, as you don't have to wait for a bunch of pictures to be calculated before drawing them; you can just request that they be drawn when they are ready to be drawn, and your program can continue on its merry way without waiting.

Using the MediaTracker

Although it's usually handy to have Images available for use before the download is complete, there are times when it is desirable to suspend your program's operations until the Image's data is actually complete. As we saw in Chapter 5, an animation consisting of a series of Images will look very jerky and blurry until all of the Images' data is available. In this case, it would probably be best to wait to start the animation until all of the Images are complete.

The MediaTracker class, part of the java.awt hierarchy, gives us an excellent way to accomplish this with a fine degree of control. The basic idea behind the MediaTracker is that when an Image is constructed, it is added to a list of media being tracked by the MediaTracker. Each medium is assigned a priority value, and programmers can at any time opt to suspend operations until all media of a designated priority value are ready to be displayed. The MediaTracker class currently supports only Images, but Sun is planning to extend it to track AudioClips and possibly video clips in the not-too-distant future. The most useful methods offered by the MediaTracker class are listed in Table 9-5.

Method	Description
MediaTracker(Component)	Creates a new MediaTracker that will track media for the given Component.
addImage(Image, int)	Adds an Image to the media being tracked at the specified priority level.
addImage(Image, int, int, int)	Adds an Image to the media being tracked at the priority level specified by the first integer. The target width and height of the Image are indicated by the final value.
boolean checkAll()	Checks to see of all of the media being tracked are complete. If the media are not already being loaded, this method does not start them loading.
boolean checkAll(boolean)	Checks to see if all of the media being tracked are complete. If the media are not already being loaded and the boolean argument is true, this method starts them loading.
waitForAll()	Waits until all media being tracked are complete.

Method	Description
waitForAll(long)	Waits until all media being tracked are complete or the specified number of milliseconds has passed.
waitForID(int)	Waits until all media of the specified priority value are complete.
waitForID(int, long)	Waits until all media of the specified priority value are complete or the specified number of milliseconds has passed.

Table 9-5: *Especially useful methods of the MediaTracker class.*

Here is a simple code fragment that requests an Image via a URL and uses a MediaTracker to track it. Note that we have to watch for an InterruptedException when using the MediaTracker's waitForAll method—any time we suspend the operation of the current thread, directly or indirectly, we have to check for interruptions:

```
MediaTracker tracker;
tracker = new MediaTracker(this);
Image i;
i = getImage(imageURL);
tracker.addImage(i,1);
try {
   tracker.waitForAll();
} catch (InterruptedException e) {}
```

Creating Images

We can now download Images from the network and ensure their timely delivery. Suppose we want to create our own Images? Because the Image class is abstract, we cannot construct Images directly. The Component class gives us some createImage methods that can be used to create empty new instances of the Image class. To draw graphics on these blank images, we can use the getGraphics method to request a Graphics object.

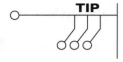

TIP *The Canvas class provides a usable subclass of the generic Component class. Unlike most other usable subclasses of Component, Canvas does not extend Container. The Canvas may not contain other Components, but since the Image class does not descend from the Container class, it can easily be drawn in a Canvas. As a rule, the Canvas class is used almost exclusively to draw Images.*

The Component class also gives us some methods for checking the status of our Images and for preparing them to be displayed, although it is probably easier to use a MediaTracker to keep tabs on them. All of these methods are all listed in Table 9-6.

Method	Description
createImage(int, int)	Creates an empty new Image of the specified width and height.
createImage(ImageProducer)	Requests an Image from the given ImageProducer. This interface is described later in this chapter under "Interfaces for Asynchronous Images."
boolean prepareImage(Image, ImageObserver)	Prepares an Image for display. The ImageObserver argument indicates the object to send the Image's status to; this is generally the Component itself. This method returns a boolean indicating whether or not the Image is ready to be displayed.
boolean prepareImage(Image, int, int, ImageObserver)	Prepares an Image for display at the width and height specified by the integer arguments. The ImageObserver argument works in the same way as the preceding method.

Table 9-6: *Creating Images with the Component class.*

The simplest way to create an Image of your own design is to create a new empty Image and use the getGraphics method of the Image class to draw directly into the Image using the Graphics class's drawing methods (listed in Tables 9-1 and 9-2). As we've seen before, this still doesn't give us the option of dealing with Images at the pixel layer. To work at the pixel layer, we'll need at least a passing familiarity with a few interfaces designed for working with asynchronous Images.

Interfaces for Asynchronous Images

The java.awt.image gives us three interfaces, ImageProducer, ImageConsumer, and ImageObserver, that provide programmers with a consistent framework for producing and handling Image data in real-time. One of the createImage methods provided by the Component class relies on the ImageProducer to give it the initial graphics data for the Image. The ImageProducer's methods for drawing and preparing Images require an ImageConsumer to send an Image's pixel data to. The ImageObservers watch the production process and receive updates from the ImageProducer when new data becomes available.

Some implementations of these interfaces are provided in the Java API. We'll briefly describe the interfaces and then go over the specific implementations in the next section. The average programmer will probably never need to implement these interfaces, but it is important to understand what is actually going on in order to use Images effectively.

The ImageProducer Interface

The ImageProducer interface should be implemented by classes that can produce Image data. An ImageProducer can be used as an argument to the createImage method of the Component class. The given ImageProducer is responsible for giving the data for the Image to the Component. The ImageProducer interface consists of five methods, listed in Table 9-7.

Method	Description
addConsumer(ImageConsumer)	Adds the specified ImageConsumer to the list of consumers interested in receiving the Image data.
boolean isConsumer(ImageConsumer)	Returns a boolean indicating whether the given ImageConsumer is registered for receiving Image data with this ImageObserver.
removeConsumer(ImageConsumer)	Removes the specified ImageConsumer from the list of consumers interested in receiving the Image data.
requestTopDownLeftRightResend(ImageConsumer)	Requests that the Image be resent in top-down-left-right order.
startProduction(ImageConsumer)	Registers the given ImageConsumer as interested in receiving Image data and starts producing the Image.

Table 9-7: *ImageProducer methods.*

The ImageConsumer Interface

The ImageProducer interface is designed to be used hand-in-hand with the ImageConsumer interface. The ImageConsumer interface should be implemented by classes that are interested in receiving Image pixel data from an ImageProducer.

Just as we don't need to implement the ImageProducer interface ourselves, we don't necessarily need to implement an ImageConsumer—that functionality is already built into the Java API. The methods needed by the ImageConsumer interface are listed in Table 9-8. Most of these methods are intended to be called by an ImageProducer when Image data becomes available.

Method	Description
imageComplete(int)	The ImageProducer calls this method when the Image is complete or if an error occurred while loading the Image. The integer argument indicates the status of the Image. The various possible states of the Image are listed in Table 9-10.
setColorModel(ColorModel)	Sets the ColorModel used by the Image. The ColorModel class is described in the "Image Manipulation" section.
setDimensions(int, int)	Sets the width and height of the Image.
setHints(int)	Sets any hints available from the ImageObserver. Hints may include such tidbits as the order in which pixels will be received. The integer argument contains a bit-wise OR of all of the valid hints. The various possible hints are listed in Table 9-9.
setProperties(Hashtable)	Sets the properties associated with the Image. Sometimes comments or a description are included along with the Image data. Uses the keys method to determine what, if anything, is in the Hashtable.
setPixels(int, int, int, int, ColorModel, byte[], int, int)	Sets the pixels in the rectangle given by the first four integers. The ColorModel indicates the ColorModel used by the Image. The byte array contains the actual pixel data, and the last two integers contain the starting index value and the number of pixels in each row (the scan size). The pixel at location (X, Y) within the rectangle lives at the index value in the array given by the following formula: Y*scansize + X (+starting index, if non-zero).

Method	Description
setPixels(int, int, int, int, ColorMode, int[], int, int)	Does the same thing as the previous method, except using an integer array rather than a byte array.

Table 9-8: *ImageConsumer methods.*

There are a number of states an Image can be in during the production process and a number of hints the ImageProducer can give to its registered ImageConsumers about the pixel data it is generating. The status and the hints are each passed to the ImageConsumer, using a single integer, via the imageComplete and setHints methods. The possible hint values and states are defined as static integers on the ImageConsumer interface. They are listed in Tables 9-9 and 9-10. If an ImageProducer wants to indicate that more than one of these states or hints apply to the Image, it will return a bit-wise OR of the applicable states (see the "Bit Manipulation" sidebar for more details).

Hint	Meaning
RANDOMPIXELORDER	Pixels will be delivered in no particular order.
TOPDOWNLEFTRIGHT	Pixels will be delivered in top-down-left-right order.
COMPLETESCANLINES	Pixels will be delivered in complete scanlines (horizontal rows).
SINGLEPASS	Pixels will be delivered in a single pass, and each pixel will be set only once. Some Images, most notably those in the JPEG format, deliver pixels in multiple passes, each a refinement of the previous one.
SINGLEFRAME	Image contains only a single frame of Graphics data and once complete, the Image will not be changed further by the ImageProducer.

Table 9-9: *Hints from the ImageProducer.*

State	Meaning
IMAGEERROR	An error occurred while producing the Image data.
SINGLEFRAMEDONE	One frame of graphics data is complete, but subsequent frames have yet to be produced.
STATICIMAGEDONE	The Image is complete and the ImageProducer will not be delivering any more Image data.
IMAGEABORTED	The Image was intentionally aborted.

Table 9-10: *Status messages from the ImageProducer.*

The ImageObserver Interface

For those classes that aren't necessarily interested in obtaining all of the pixels associated with an Image in production, but do need to be informed of the progress of the production, Sun has provided an ImageObserver interface. This interface consists of a single method, imageUpdate, and a slew of state variables, defined as static integers on the interface. These state variables are very similar in utility and implementation to the state and hints variables of the ImageConsumer class. The ImageObserver method and variables are listed in Table 9-11.

BIT MANIPULATION

Recall that integers are stored in the Java virtual machine's memory as a sequence of 32 bits (we discussed this in Chapter 4, "Syntax & Semantics"). A bit-wise OR of two integers is a new integer that has a bit value of 1 in every position where at least one of the integers has a bit value of 1. For example, the integer 6 is stored as:

    ...0110

in memory (the Java virtual machine is big-endian). The integer 12 is stored as:

    ...1100

The bit-wise OR of these two integers is 14:

    ...1110

For a bit-wise OR of any combination of states or hints, we are guaranteed a unique integer value. This is true because each of the static integers associated with a particular state or hint is a unique power of two, represented in memory as a sequence of 32 bits with only a single bit with a value of 1 (that is, 0100).

A bit-wise AND of two integers gives us a new integer that has a bit value of 1 in every position where both of the integers have a bit value of 1. For example,
0110 & 1100 = 0100

To discover if the status or hints given to the ImageConsumer by the ImageProducer contain a given status or hint, you can use the bit-wise AND operator.

A little later in the chapter, we use the bit-shift operators. The left bit-shift operator is <<. It shifts the left-hand operand to the left by the number of bits specified by the right-hand operand. For instance,

    6<<1 = 12

The right bit-shift operator, >>, works the same way, but shifts to the right instead.

Method & Variables	Description
boolean imageUpdate(Image, int, int, int, int, int)	An ImageProducer calls this method when information previously requested by the ImageObserver becomes available. The Image argument returns a reference to the Image in question and the first integer argument contains a bit-wise OR of all of the states that apply. The last four integers generally are to be interpreted as a bounding rectangle, but this may be overridden by the status integer.
WIDTH	Indicates that the width of the Image is known and can be inferred from the bounding rectangle.
HEIGHT	Indicates that the height of the Image is known and can be inferred from the bounding rectangle.
PROPERTIES	The properties of the Image are known and can be obtained via the getProperty method of the Image class.
SOMEBITS	More pixels, but not all, are now available. The bounding rectangle is guaranteed to be valid.
FRAMEBITS	A complete frame of a multiple-frame Image is now available. The bounding rectangle should be ignored.
ALLBITS	The image is complete and the bounding rectangle should be ignored.
ERROR	An error occurred while the Image was in production.
ABORT	The Image was aborted before Image production was complete. If the ERROR state is not also indicated, then accessing any of the Image data will result in production being restarted.

Table 9-11: *Methods and variables of the ImageObserver interface.*

Like the other interfaces described here, ImageObserver will never need to be implemented by most programmers themselves. The java.awt.Component class implements the ImageObserver interface, allowing it and all of its children to be able to use and display asynchronous Images. Whenever enough new pixels become available to display a complete copy of the Image at or below the desired resolution, the Component class requests a repaint of the Image.

While these interfaces may seem somewhat cumbersome and awkward to work with directly, the ImageConsumer in particular, their full advantage is realized by the classes offered in the Java API that implement them. These classes allow you to decode an Image into an array of integers and to reverse the process—create an Image from an integer array. You can even create filters that allow you to consistently alter Images in some fashion.

Image Manipulation Techniques

In addition to the interfaces for handling asynchronous Image production, the java.awt.image package provides some handy specific implementations of them. These implementations will allow you to perform low-level picture operations. You'll be able to grab pixel data from your Images using the PixelGrabber class, create your own Images from arrays of pixel data using the MemoryImageSource class, and filter existing Images to fit your needs using the ImageFilter classes. All of the classes we describe in this section are part of the Java API's java.awt.image package.

Grabbing Pixels

The PixelGrabber class is an implementation of the ImageConsumer interface that allows you to grab pixel and color data from an Image or an ImageProducer. You can grab all of the pixels in a given Image or just those in a rectangular subsection of the Image. The constructors and other unique methods of the PixelGrabber class are listed in Table 9-12.

Method	Description
PixelGrabber(Image, int, int, int, int, int[], int, int)	Creates a new PixelGrabber that returns pixels from the given Image. The first four integer arguments indicate the bounding rectangle of the region from which we want to receive pixels. The pixel values will be copied into the integer array argument; this array should be at least width*height long. The last two integers indicate the starting index of the pixel data in the array and the number of pixels from each row to put into the array (generally the width of the selected region).
PixelGrabber(ImageProducer, int, int, int, int, int[], int, int)	Creates a new PixelGrabber that returns pixels from the given ImageProducer's Image data. The rest of the arguments are identical to those of the previous constructor.
grabPixels()	Requests that the Image or ImageProducer deliver the pixel data. This method will block until the data has arrived. It will throw an InterruptedException if it's interrupted before the data has arrived.
grabPixels(long)	Requests that the Image or ImageProducer deliver the pixel data. This method will block until the data has arrived or until the number of milliseconds specified by the long argument have passed. It will throw an InterruptedException if it's interrupted before the data has arrived or its timer has expired.
int status()	Returns the status of the Image. The state returned will be a bit-wise OR of all the relevant ImageObserver status variables.

Table 9-12: *Constructors and unique methods of the PixelGrabber class.*

The following code fragment illustrates use of the PixelGrabber class:

```
PixelGrabber grabber;
int width = myImage.getWidth(this);
int height = myImage.getHeight(this);
int ary[] = new ary[width*height];
grabber = new PixelGrabber(myImage,0,0,width,height,
   ary,0,width);
try {
   grabber.grabPixels();
} catch (InterruptedException e) {}
int status = grabber.status();
if ((status & ImageObserver.ABORT) || (status &
ImageObserver.ERROR)) {
   //Problem occurred fetching Image pixels
} else {
   for (int i=0; i<ary.length; i++) {
      //Do something to pixel data in ary
   }
}
```

In this code, a PixelGrabber is constructed on an Image, and we use it to request all of the Image's pixels. After the request is complete, we check the status of the pixels; if the transfer was aborted or erred in some fashion, we handle the problem appropriately. Otherwise, we can read the pixel data from the array we passed to the PixelGrabber.

Color Models

Once we've got an array of pixels, the question remains: what do we do with them? Each pixel is represented in this array by a single integer. It is necessary to extract from that integer all of the data we need to plot or otherwise interpret the pixel. The location of each pixel in the Image can be inferred from its position in the array. We use the ColorModel class to interpret the integer itself as a color.

Almost any color can be represented as a unique combination of shades of red, blue, and green. Combinations based on other sets of colors exist as well, but this is the color combination used almost exclusively in computer graphics. Almost all color monitors paint each pixel as combinations of red, blue, and green pixels. The ColorModel class not only allows us to take apart the integers in the pixel array and decompose each one into its red, blue, and green components, it allows us to specify a transparency component as well. The transparency component controls how opaque a pixel appears—if a pixel is partially transparent, the color of the layer beneath it is calculated into the displayed color of the pixel. Figure 9-2 contains a partially transparent Image overlaid on an opaque Image.

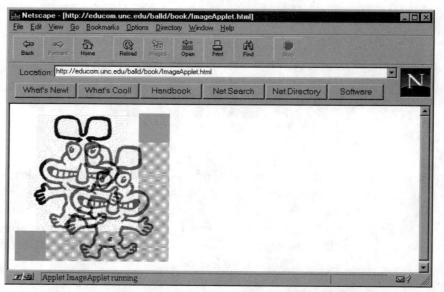

Figure 9-2: *A semitransparent picture superimposed on an opaque one.*

The ColorModel class itself is abstract, although two usable extensions of it are provided in the Java API and are described later in this section. Table 9-13 contains a list of the methods of the ColorModel class. Note that the getRGBdefault method is declared static and thus can be used to return a runtime reference to the nonabstract default RGB ColorModel.

Method	Description
ColorModel(int)	Creates a color model that supports colors of the specified number of bits. The number of bits directly controls the number of unique colors possible in this model. A value of eight bits per pixel allows 256 different colors.
int getAlpha(int)	Returns the transparency component of the pixel specified by the integer argument.
int getBlue(int)	Returns the blue component of the pixel specified by the integer argument.
int getGreen(int)	Returns the green component of the pixel specified by the integer argument.
int getRed(int)	Returns the red component of the pixel specified by the integer argument.
int getPixelSize()	Returns the number of bits per pixel.
int getRGB(int)	Returns the value of the pixel specified by the integer argument in the default RGB color model.
static ColorModel getRGBdefault()	Returns the default RGB ColorModel used by the java.awt.image package. This scheme allocates eight bits for each primary color and transparent component, which gives you 256 gradations of red, blue, green, and transparency, for a total of 16,777,216 colors (not counting shades of transparency).

Table 9-13: *ColorModel methods*.

There are two basic ways of encoding red, blue, green, and transparency components, each an integer number of some number of bits, into a 32-bit integer. The first way treats the pixel's integer value as an array index and looks up the red, blue, green, and transparency components from internal lookup tables. There is no necessary ordering of colors in the tables; that is decided by the creator of the model. The IndexColorModel extends the base ColorModel class so you can create a new ColorModel using your own palette. When constructing the model, you pass to it arrays of color components. When a programmer requests a color component from the model, it uses the pixel value as an array position and returns the value at that position in the appropriate array.

The second way to extract the four color components from a 32-bit integer is to partition the integer into bit arrays, the sizes of which must add up to 32. Figure 9-3 illustrates this idea. Each bit array contains the color information for either the red, blue, green, or transparent components of the overall color. For example, we could allocate 26 bits for red, 2 bits for blue, 3 bits for green, and 1 bit for transparency. Under this scheme, we would have 67,108,864 possible shades of red, 4 shades of blue, 8 shades of green, and 2 shades of transparency (completely opaque or completely transparent). The DirectColorModel class provides an extension of the ColorModel class, which maps pixel values to color components using this technique.

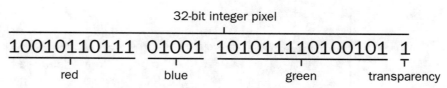

Figure 9-3: *Splitting an integer into color components.*

Now the array of integer pixel values returned by the PixelGrabber class makes sense. The ColorModel used by the PixelGrabber class is the default RGB color model, and we can use the methods listed in Table 9-13 on the default RGB color model to extract color component information from the pixels. We can add the following code to the loop presented in our earlier code fragment to parse out the individual color components from the pixel array:

```
ColorModel cm = ColorModel.getRGBdefault();
int pixel;
for (int i=0; i<ary.length; i++) {
   pixel = ary[i];
   cm.getRed(pixel);
   cm.getBlue(pixel);
   cm.getGreen(pixel);
   cm.getAlpha(pixel);
}
```

We've covered how to convert Images to arrays and how to map the values in those arrays to color components using the ColorModel class. The opposite transformation, turning arrays into Images, is also easily accomplished using the MemoryImageSource class.

Converting Arrays to Images

The MemoryImageSource class gives us a way to convert arrays of integers into pixel data for the Image class. The MemoryImageSource class implements the ImageProducer interface and can be used as an argument to the createImage method of the Component class. The constructors for the MemoryImageSource class are listed in Table 9-14. After we've created a new MemoryImageSource, we can use it to make a new Image with the createImage methods of the Component class.

Constructor	Description
MemoryImageSource(int, int, ColorModel, byte[], int, int)	Creates a new ImageProducer that will create an Image from the pixel values in the byte array argument. The first two integers indicate the desired width and height of the Image, and the ColorModel argument gives the mapping between pixel values and color components to be used in interpreting the byte array. The last two integers indicate the starting index value in the array and the number of bytes each row of pixels occupies in the array (generally, the width of the Image).
MemoryImageSource(int, int, ColorModel, byte[], int, int, Hashtable)	Works the same as the previous constructor. The Hashtable argument sets the properties of the Image.
MemoryImageSource(int, int, ColorModel, int[], int, int)	Creates a new ImageProducer from the given integer array.
MemoryImageSource(int, int, ColorModel, int[], int, int, Hashtable)	Creates a new ImageProducer from the given integer array.
MemoryImageSource(int, int, int[], int, int)	Creates a new ImageProducer from the given integer array using the default RGB color model.
MemoryImageSource(int, int, int[], int, int, Hashtable)	Creates a new ImageProducer from the given integer array using the default RGB color model.

Table 9-14: *MemoryImageSource constructors.*

This class is best illustrated by an example. Here, we give a complete applet that generates and displays an Image from an integer array. We construct the red components of each pixel by adding the sines of the X- and Y-values of each pixel, scaling appropriately. Similarly, we construct the blue components of each pixel by adding the cosines of the X- and Y-values. We construct the final value for each pixel by combining the red and blue color components along with a 100 percent transparency value in a bit-wise OR, shifting the components until they are aligned with their proper positions in the default RGB color scheme. A screen shot of the finished product is in Figure 9-4.

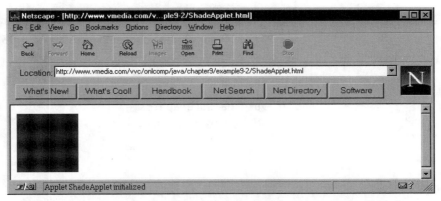

Figure 9-4: *An Image produced by trigonometric functions in the X-Y plane.*

Example 9-2: Using the MemoryImageSource class.

```java
import java.awt.*;
import java.awt.image.*;
import java.applet.*;

public class ShadeApplet extends Applet {

  Image myImage;

  public void init() {
    resize(250,250);
    int ary[] = new int[250*250];
    for (int i=0; i<250; i++) {
      for (int j=0; j<250; j++) {
        double x = (16*Math.PI*j/250);
        double y = (16*Math.PI*i/250);
        double p = (Math.sin(x)+Math.sin(y)+2)/4;
```

```
            int red = (int)Math.round(p*255);
            double q = (Math.cos(x)+Math.cos(y)+2)/4;
            int blue = (int)Math.round(q*255);
            ary[i*250+j] = (255<<24)|((red)<<16)|(blue);
        }
    }
    MemoryImageSource mis;
    mis = new MemoryImageSource(250,250,ary,0,250);
    myImage = createImage(mis);
}


public void paint(Graphics g) {
    g.drawImage(myImage,0,0,this);
}


}
```

Filtering Images

We can now create Images directly at the byte level, bypassing use of the graphics primitives offered by the Graphics class. We can even manipulate Images downloaded from the network; using a PixelGrabber, we can obtain the values of the pixels in an array. After manipulating them in some fashion, we can reverse the process using the MemoryImageSource. As if that wasn't easy enough, the Java API gives us two classes designed specifically for this task: FilteredImageSource and ImageFilter.

The FilteredImageSource class implements the ImageProducer interface. It takes an ImageProducer and an ImageFilter as construction arguments. When it produces an Image, it requests pixel data from the ImageProducer specified in construction. It alters the pixel data in a consistent way dictated by the ImageFilter and sends the modified pixel data on to its ImageConsumers. The ImageFilter class implements the ImageConsumer interface. The base ImageFilter class does not change pixel data in any fashion. The Java API gives us two simple extensions that allow us to insert a color filter or crop a region of an Image to a new Image.

The RGBImageFilter class by default performs no color filtering but does transform pixel values and the ColorModel used by the resulting Image to the default RGB color model. To cause it to filter colors, we need to extend the class's filterRGB method to perform the type of filtering we want. Here is an example that removes all red from an Image:

Example 9-3: Red removing filter.

```
public class NoRedFilter extends RGBImageFilter() {
  public int filterRGB(int x, int y, int rgb) {
    int alpha = (rgb & 0xff000000)>>24;
    int red =   (rgb & 0x00ff0000)>>16;
    int green = (rgb & 0x0000ff00)>>8;
    int blue =  (rgb & 0x000000ff);
    return ((alpha<<24)|(green<<8)|(blue);
  }
}
```

We first split apart the rgb integer variable, indicating the color of the pixel in the default RGB color scheme, and then add the transparency, green, and blue components back into the RGB value, ignoring the red value entirely. Note that since we are passed the X- and Y-values of the pixel here, we could modify the color filtering process based on location, but this is unnecessary for this simple filter. The RGBColorFilter class is a handy filter to extend for your own purposes because it performs the conversion to the default RGB color model if necessary.

The CropImageFilter is much simpler to use; you don't need to extend it to crop your Images. Instead, you simply specify the region to crop to when constructing the filter. The constructor takes four integers as its argument. The integers specify a rectangle in the standard encoding scheme. Here is a short example that crops to the upper-left hand corner:

```
FilteredImageSource fis;
CropImageFilter filter;
filter = new CropImageFilter(0,0,10,10);
fis = new FilteredImageSource(myImage.getSource(),filter);
Image myNewImage = createImage(fis);
```

Moving On

The classes described in this chapter allow you to generate and modify graphical images for use in your Java applets and applications simply and easily. The Graphics class lets you to draw using simple graphics primitives, much like in a simple painting program. The advanced Image production facilities of the Java API also allow you to convert Images to and from integer arrays, giving you precise control over your Images. The picture filtering capabilities afforded to the average Java programmer potentially rival those of commercial products like Adobe Photoshop, although the slowness of the calculations involved will limit the utility of these filters until native compilers become available.

The next chapter takes a turn away from designing pretty user interfaces. Digging deeper into the fundamentals of Java, we show you in detail how exceptions work and explore some of the issues involved in generating your own exceptions in a complete object-oriented design. We also discuss the fundamental objects from which all classes are derived and the implications they have when designing your own class hierarchies.

10

Advanced Program Design

By now, you should have a pretty good feel for how to write some cool applets. Hopefully, you have developed some that explore the Abstract Windowing Toolkit (AWT), some that do animation, and some that handle user input in slick ways. Now it's time to move beyond the simple applets we've been doing so far and really start putting the rest of the Java language to work.

Having animations or games on an HTML page is cool, but it is important to remember that Java is a modern, robust, object-oriented programming language. As your applets become more complicated, you'll need to avoid writing spaghetti code that will be incomprehensible later on and that can't be easily reused. In this chapter, we're going to look at how to create packages of Java classes and interfaces that can be reused for other projects, and how to crash-proof your code with exception handling.

We'll start off by looking at how to describe a large project with an object-oriented mindset, and then we'll discuss how to use the tools of Java to implement your solution. Finally, we will look at how tools we have already learned about—such as inheritance, interfaces, and exception handling—fit into the picture.

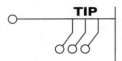

TIP

This chapter's code example files can be found on the CD-ROM (for Windows 95/NT or Macintosh users) and the Online Companion (for UNIX users). Visit the Online Companion at http://www.vmedia.com/java.html.

Building Java Packages

Once applet writers get the basics down, the API gives them enough functionality to go a long way. Of course, you are writing code to make the API do what your program needs. As you grow as an Internet programmer, you'll find that a lot of the same functionality is popping up in all of your programs. So why not "package" it for reuse?

One of the primary benefits of an object-oriented language such as Java is that you only need to write such functionality once—if you create a class correctly the first time. This keeps you from eternally cutting and pasting from old code. Instead, you can reuse objects and interfaces for later projects.

If you work on each project with reusable components in mind, you will build your own personal code library. Eventually, this library could become as important to your projects as the API. Since you don't have to rewrite the same code again and again, with each project you will become a more efficient programmer.

ACHIEVE NET FAME: SHARE A LITTLE CODE

As you begin building your own Java library, consider making some of your code available for others on the Net to use. Not only will you be on the receiving end of many complimentary e-mail messages, but you'll also get feedback on improving your code from those who use it. This sort of collaboration is the true backbone of the Internet, and you can be a part of it! The Online Companion has many links to repositories that you can contribute to or borrow from.

Creating Compatible Classes

When we talked about the Object class in Chapter 6, "Discovering the Application Programming Interface," we showed you that it has several methods that are usually overridden. A couple of them are overridden by every single class in the API and should be overridden by your classes also. For some of the other methods, whether or not to override the default method is an important design decision. Let's look at each of the methods, when they should be overridden, and what the consequences are of not overriding them. We'll start with the ones you should always override.

boolean equals(Object o)

If you ever want to compare two instances of your class, the boolean equals(Object o) method is a must to override. If you don't override it, your instances will only return true if they are exactly the same. How you override the method almost always depends on the variables defined within the class. Let's consider an example class. Assume that the constructors and other methods alter the values of these variables:

```
class exampleClass {
private String S;
private int i;
private int j;
//constructors
//methods
}
```

A reasonable equals method for this class would just compare the instance variables. We could condense this entire method into a very large compound boolean expression, but we chose to do our comparisons individually, as shown below:

```
equals(Object obj) {
if (obj==null) return false;
if (!obj instanceof  exampleClass)
  return false;
```

```
exampleClass ex=(exampleClass)obj;
if (!ex.S.equals(S)) return false;
if (ex.i!=i) return false;
if (ex.j!=j) return false;
return true;}
```

The first thing we do is make sure that we aren't being passed a null reference. Our second statement makes sure that we are being passed an instance of exampleClass. If we aren't being passed an instance of the class containing our equals method, we would usually return false. Once we know that we have an instance of exampleClass, we need to cast obj to an instance of exampleClass. The next three lines return false if they encounter a difference. Notice that we have access to the private members of ex, since we are within the definition of exampleClass.

In this example, all of the instance variables had to be identical for us to consider the two instances of exampleClass to be equal. Of course, this doesn't have to be the case. One of the first design questions you should ask yourself when creating a new class is, "What properties do two instances of this class need to have in common to be considered equal?"

String toString( )

How you override the equals method is a high-level design decision—by comparison, defining the toString method is a no-brainer. Your method should return a String that represents the current state of the object. Its primary use is for debugging with the System.out.println method. In the following example, our class defines a box, and our toString method returns the width and height:

```
class  myBox{
   int width=0;
   int height=0;
   //constructors, methods
String toString() {
   return "width= "+width+", height="+height;}
}
```

int hashcode( )

The int hashcode method, like the two previously mentioned, should always be overridden. If it isn't, you can't use your class in conjunction with the java.util.Hashtable class discussed in Chapter 6. To learn how to define this method and to understand why we need to, you need a little insight into the structure of hashtables.

One of the advantages of hashtables is that they can perform searches very quickly. Hashtables do not examine each and every key when searching. A hashtable with N key–value pairs would require N comparison operations. In Java, this would mean calling the equals method N times. For large N, fetching values out of a hashtable could be quite a time-consuming process.

Instead, hashtables search in a way that usually only requires one comparison operation, which is possible because of the hashtable's structure. Each key–value pair is stored in a bucket. More than one key–value pair can be in a bucket, but optimally, there is only one bucket per key–value pair. When the hashtable is passed a key for which to return a value, it asks itself, "Which bucket would I put the key in?" Then it looks in the appropriate bucket and does a comparison on each key there. The fewer keys in the bucket, the more efficient the search.

How does the hashtable decide which bucket to put a key–value pair into? It decides by performing an algorithm on the key called a *hash function.* The hash function's purpose is to spread the key–value pairs across as many buckets as possible, and thus ensure that each bucket has as few pairs in it as possible. Having more buckets than key–value pairs helps accomplish this.

This is where the hashCode method comes in. The hash function used by java.util.Hashtable takes integers as input. It needs integers, since all different types of keys could exist in the same Hashtable. Keeping in mind the function our hashCode methods play, let's look at the requirements for a good hashCode method. Assume that firstObject and secondObject are two separate instances of the same class:

- If firstObject.equals(secondObject) returns true, then firstObject.hashCode and secondObject.hashCode should return the same integer.

◈ Within the confines of the first constraint, your hashCode method should represent the instance as uniquely as possible. To understand why, consider the simplest hashCode method that fulfills the first constraint:

```
int hashCode() {return 1;}
```

A class that uses this hashCode method will function properly in Java's Hashtable. But every instance of this class that is a key in the Hashtable will reside in the same bucket, and the equals method will have to be called on all of them. If you want your searches to be efficient, you are going to need to work a little harder. Ideally, if you were to list every possible case where two instances of your class are equal, the instances would both return a hashCode that was unique for that particular case.

This is an ideal rarely achieved in practice. We advise you to avoid staying up nights trying to get a hashCode that fulfills the criteria; often, this is impossible. Since the hashCode method returns an int, there are only 4,294,967,296 possible hashCodes. There are more than 9,223,372,936,854,775,897 Strings of length 2, let alone all Strings! Since we know that it's impossible to generate an optimal hash code for the String class, let's look at what the authors of the String class did with their hashCode method in order to return values that are as unique as possible:

```
//hashCode method of java.lang.String
public int hashCode() {
    int h = 0;
    int off = offset;
    char val[] = value;
    int len = count;

    if (len < 16) {
        for (int i = len ; i > 0; i-) {
    h = (h * 37) + val[off++];
        }
    } else {
        // only sample some characters
        int skip = len / 8;
```

```
    for (int i = len ; i > 0; i -= skip, off += skip) {
  h = (h * 39) + val[off];
    }
}
return h;
}
```

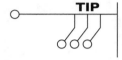

TIP

As is the case with all of the source code in the API, you will find the full source code for the String class in your JDK. It's often a good idea to see how the creators of the API handled writing hashCode methods as well as other Java programming challenges.

Object clone( )

You may remember from Chapter 2, "Java Programming Basics," that the assignment operator = doesn't make copies of instances. Rather, when used with a variable that has already been instantiated, it just assigns another variable to the same object. Suppose we have a simple linked list node class that contains an integer and an object for its data parts. By using the setNext method, we could create a data structure that looks like Figure 10-1.

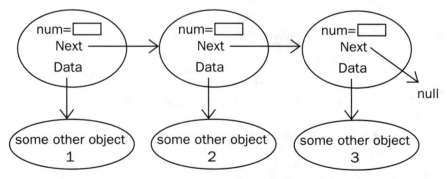

Figure 10-1: *Linked list of nodes containing a primitive variable and two reference variables.*

Notice that we override the methods of the Object class we talked about earlier:

```java
public class Node {
   private Object Data=null;
   private Node Next=null;
   private int num;

   public void setData(Object obj) {
      Data=obj;}

   public void setNum(int someNum) {
      num=someNum;}

   public void setNext(Node node) {
      Next=node;}

   public Object getData() {return Data;}

   public Node getNextNode() {
      return Next;}

   public boolean equals(Object obj) {
    if (!(obj instanceof Node)) return false;
    Node N=(Node)obj;
    return((N.num==num) &&
     Data.equals(N.Data));
    }

   public int hashCode() {
      return Data.hashCode()*num;}

   public String toString() {
      String S="Data= ";
      S=S+Data.toString();
      S=S+", num= "+num;
      return S;}
   }
```

If we do the following:

```
Node A=new Node();
Node B=A;
Integer I=new Integer(32);
B.setNum(16);
B.setData(32);
```

we don't have two distinct linkedListNode instances—just one that is referenced by both *A* and *B*. This means that:

```
System.out.println(A);
```

will output "data=32, num=16". (Remember that System.out.println, when passed an Object, calls toString and outputs the String that is returned.) What if you actually need to make a copy of an instance? This is where the clone method from the Object class comes in. It makes a clone of the instance, including the current state of all of the variables. We can make a subclass of Node that will allow cloning:

```
public class cloneableNode extends Node implements Cloneable
{
public Object clone() {
   try {
     return super.clone();}
   catch (CloneNotSupportedException e) {
     //shouldn't happen, since
     //we implemented Cloneable
     throw new InternalError();}
   }
}
```

All we do is call the clone method from the Object class. Since the clone method throws the CloneNotSupportedException, we need to catch it. Let's say we use our clone method after creating an instance of cloneableNode:

```
cloneableNode A=new cloneableNode();
A.setNum(16);
Integer I=new Integer(32);
A.setData(I);
cloneableNode B=(cloneableNode)A.clone();
```

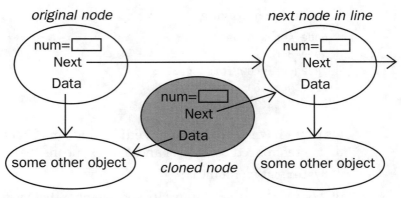

Figure 10-2: *Results of calling clone.*

Now *A* and *B* refer to different instances of cloneableNode, as shown in Figure 10-2. But notice that A.data and B.data are still the same. This is because we made a *shallow copy* of the instance— we didn't make new copies of the reference variables it contained. But let's say we have a linked list of a lot of cloneableNodes, and we want to replicate the list. We would want a definition of clone like this:

```
class List extends cloneableNode implements Cloneable {
public Object clone() {
  try {
    List newList=super.clone();

    cloneableNode oldNode=(cloneableNode)
        this;
    cloneableNode newNode=(cloneableNode)
        newList;
    while (oldNode.getNextNode()!=null) {
        oldNode=oldNode.getNextNode();
        newNode.setNext(oldNode.clone());
        newNode=newNode.getNext();}
    }
  return newList;
 catch(CloneNotSupportedException e) {
  throw new InternalError();}
 }
```

As you can see, we didn't make a copy of the data parts; since clone is a protected method, we can't—unless the class specifically overrides it to be public. This is a design decision the authors of a class must make: Should classes outside of the package be able to make clones? In many cases, it isn't a good idea because it would make no sense to clone an instance of a particular class.

Consider the Graphics class that we covered in the last chapter. The Graphics instance that we draw on is bound to the runtime environment. It's really just a representation of the area of the computer's screen we are allowed to draw in. Cloning the Graphics class wouldn't make any sense; it's not like we can expect to create a new computer screen! Thus, we aren't allowed to clone a Graphics instance. Likewise, you will find yourself developing classes whose instances are closely bound to a larger system that you are developing. In such cases, cloning these internal classes is useless unless someone were to clone the entire program.

This is also where the CloneNotSupportedException comes in. Let's say you write a class that happily clones itself:

```
public class happilyCloning implements Cloneable {

   public Object Clone() {
   try {
     return super.Clone();}
   catch (CloneNotSupportedException e) {
   throw (new InternalError());}
   }


//Other stuff
   }
```

Then, later on you decide that you want to write a subclass, and you don't want anyone to clone it. Since the superclass defines Clone, users of the class are free to clone away unless you override the method. You could simply override the clone method and return null. This would guarantee that someone using your class down the road would curse you because they are getting

NullPointerExceptions that are generated from your code. Instead, you should just toss the CloneNotSupportedException:

```
public class DontCloneMe {

public Object Clone() throws CloneNotSupportedException {
    throw (new CloneNotSupportedException());}

//Other stuff
}
```

void finalize( )

The finalize method is called when we stop using instances of a class. It's the equivalent of a destructor in C++, which are used often to release resources such as large blocks of memory. Unlike C++, Java employs garbage collection to manage memory, as we described in Chapter 2, "Java Programming Basics." If you are experienced with C++, you are probably used to writing destructors for almost every class in order to release memory. In Java, you don't need to worry about releasing memory, so the finalize method is used much less.

Let's consider the linked list class that we built above. If we execute this statement, where curList is a list that already exists:

```
curList=curList.clone();
```

we don't have to worry about releasing all of the memory where curList was originally—the garbage collector will see that it isn't being used anymore and will take care of it for us.

Therefore, we don't need to worry about defining a finalize method to release memory resources that we are using. We may consider defining the finalize method when we are dealing with other resources, such as files and network resources. As of yet, we haven't been using files and the network; in fact, applets can't deal with files anyway. Thus, at this point in the book, we can't give an example of when the finalize method should be used. If you want to see the finalize method in action, look at FileInputStream.java in the java.io package. Remember that the source code is available to you as part of the JDK.

Programming Reusable Components

We have looked at the methods of the Object class and how we should think about overriding them. Now we can look at a more general object-oriented concept: writing reusable components.

Writing reusable components is more of an art than a skill. Thinking through the problem before you start coding is critical to the process. Java has many features to make writing reusable components easy, but a programming language alone can't make you a more efficient programmer. The most important part of good programming takes place before you start coding. To develop programs well, you must think of each code snippet, method, and project in a larger context.

The concept of reusability implies that you need to think of your coding with regard to the big picture—specifically, how it can be used in the future. Your goal is to make it easy to package reusable code, but first, you must figure out what to package and how it should be done.

Many programmers get mired in the syntax of objects and object orientation. It's important to remember that object orientation is meant to be a more intuitive way of programming. But computers, in their very essence, are not intuitive problem solvers. Early programmers learned how to program in assembly language. Could we write a multithreaded user interface in assembly language? Of course! But the language itself doesn't give us the mechanisms to be able to relate the problems of the project into the language with ease.

This is also somewhat true for procedural languages; subroutines are good for defining reusable *actions* of a program, but not reusable *parts*. This is fine if your program is just computing mathematical results, but it doesn't work when you are trying to solve real-world-sized problems. Consider the problem of air traffic control. In a nutshell, we want planes to land and take off without running into each other and without filling all available spaces. To make this happen, we need to think about all the components: planes, flight paths, holding patterns, runways, air traffic control towers, and hangars. In an object-oriented language, we can simply represent the problem as objects, whereas procedural languages force us to deal only with actions within the problem.

Again, we could find a way to solve the problem in a procedural language, but then our focus becomes the language. With object-oriented languages, the most important step is addressing the problem itself, not the nuances of the language. The thinking you do before you start programming is the key to programming efficiently. This shift is often a challenge for programmers who have become accustomed to the hard-learned tricks of a particular language. So before we begin, let's think about how to address our programs so that we can become more efficient.

What is the problem I am trying to solve?

This question seems obvious, but it's alarming how often it is skipped. When it is addressed, the answer is usually very language dependent—how do I program my solution in this particular language? Of course, you do eventually have to write your program in some language, but your first thoughts should just be an exercise in problem solving. Think in terms of how your problem fits into the language at the highest level. For instance, if part of the problem involves working on a variety of platforms, then you need to make certain Java has been ported to all of these platforms. Avoid going into too much detail at this stage. Your description of the problem should make sense to nontechnical people.

What are the parts of the problem, and how do they interact?

This is the critical step of dividing and conquering the problem. Here we think in terms of objects, but not language-specific objects. A sketch is in order at this point, such as the one of our air traffic control problem in Figure 10-3.

The purpose of the sketch is to define, in a very abstract way, how the different parts interact. Now we need to think a little more deeply about what the different parts are. Again, we aren't interested in getting too nerdy at this stage—we don't want to start thinking of them as objects with data members and method members quite yet. A list of attributes is fine. Table 10-1 describes the different attributes well enough at this stage.

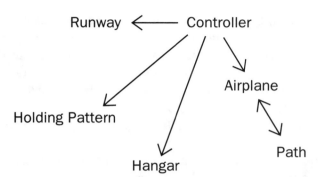

Figure 10-3: *High-level sketch of air traffic control.*

Component	Attributes
Airplane	Has location and trajectory.
	Follows some flight path.
	Has arrival and takeoff time.
Flight Path	Can intersect with other paths.
	Can be affected by weather.
Hangar	Has a fixed capacity and location.
	Can be full or less than full.
Runway	Has a certain length.
	Can be in use or ready for use.
	May not be usable by all planes.
	Usability can be affected by weather.
Holding Pattern	Has some capacity and position.
	Capacity can vary with weather.
Control Tower	Needs to know and be able to manipulate all other components.
	Needs to know about weather.

Table 10-1: *Air traffic control attributes.*

What does my project have in common with other projects?

Before we actually start solving problems, we need to define some areas containing our problems. Basically, we want to think about our project in terms of how most programs are structured. Then, as we address the specific problems of this project, we can solve them so that our solutions can be reused.

This will help to keep us from getting different problems entangled. For instance, most programs have a user interface. If we are going to do something spiffy with our user interface, such as create a new type of dialog box, we will want to be able to reuse it later. Therefore, we should keep it from being too dependent on the particular project that saw its origin. The same is true for low-level networking and data storage code. If you work really hard on some code that understands some exotic protocol, you won't want to have to do that work again.

How can the individual components be generalized?

By answering the preceding question, we isolated user interface and communication concerns from the rest of the project. Now we need to look at each component and think about how it might be reused. For instance, hangars are a lot like parking lots, and both are similar to holding patterns. Along those lines, airplanes are just one type of vehicle. As you think about what is required in your user interface, data storage, and communication routines for the air traffic control program, you should think about other uses for the same types of components in other projects.

The trick at this stage is to identify code that could be made reusable. Then, when you get to the point of actually designing your classes and interfaces, you can design code that can be stashed away in your library. In the above example, we can make an abstract class vehicle, and our class airplane would be a subclass of that.

How do I fit my code into Java's object orientation?

The methodology we just described is one way to arrive at designing reusable components. It's hardly important that you follow it exactly. But you do need to do some thinking about making your code reusable *before* you start coding. Now we are ready to start thinking about how we are actually going to code it. For a fully working system, this involves breaking each of our larger components into several classes and interfaces.

In the next few pages, we are going to discuss the properties of Java that allow us to map our problem's solution into working code. We will see when interfaces should be used instead of subclasses and how to make the best use out of all of those method modifiers. With an understanding of these properties, you will be able to come up with a structure for your library.

DON'T GET LOST IN DIAGRAMS!

As you come up with your classes, you should be asking yourself, "What can go wrong?" and "Am I overdoing it?" Your first question should motivate you to start thinking about developing an exception hierarchy. The second question should be asked to keep you from getting too abstract with your class and interface design. Sometimes, the enticement of reusable code begets a structure so abstract that no one could ever reuse it! As you draw out your class and interface diagrams, keep this in mind.

Turning Your Design Into Working Code

At some point, we need to move on from drawing diagrams to actually working with the language. As you will remember from Chapter 2, "Java Programming Basics," a package is just a container for classes, interfaces, and exceptions. You declare that you want one of these to be in a certain package by giving the package name at the top of your source code file:

```
package somePackage;

public class someClass {
//class definition

}
```

If you want to put your code in a directory structure, then you can use periods to specify what is in each directory:

```
package myPackages.someOtherPackage;
public class someOtherClass {
//class definition
}
```

In either case, your package name should represent a directory that is described by the CLASSPATH environment variable we talked about in Chapter 2. Each period should represent a new subdirectory. But why put stuff in packages? One reason is syntactical: The compiler needs some way to find your code, and you won't always want to keep it in the same directory. Another reason—the most important one—involves the protected modifier. So far, we haven't made much use of this modifier. We have been keeping private the methods and variables that are only used inside of an object, and making everything else public. When we make something protected, it is public to the package.

Why would we want to do this? Sometimes, we want methods to be accessible to *some* other objects, but not all of them. Let's consider the air traffic control example. Our airplane will need to get information about which runway to land on, but that information should only come from the air traffic controller. If we define a method, setRunway, in our airplane class, then we would declare it protected and place it in a package in our air traffic controller class. We would not place certain other classes, such as the runway class, in this package. To do so would keep the runway class from telling the airplane to land directly on the runway, which could have tragic consequences!

You may be thinking, "These classes don't have a life of their own. I programmed them and can just not write the code that would cause the runway class to call the setRunway method on an airplane class." This may be true for simple projects. But in large projects, the different modules do, in a sense, have a life of their own. After you finish up the initial implementation, someone else may come along and decide that it is easier for them to do something that violates the fundamental design of the system. No matter how well you document your design, no documentation can be better than the compiler simply not allowing a method to be called from a class that it shouldn't be called from. Even for simple projects that only you would be working on, the protected keyword can be valuable. Since programmers forget about how their projects are designed over time, you are effectively another programmer after a couple of months and could make chaos of your well-designed system just as easily as someone else could.

This same logic applies to the *final* modifier. Though it isn't dependent on packages, we can use it to force our design on our code's maintainers. As discussed in Chapter 4, "Syntax & Semantics," the final modifier declares that a class, method, or variable cannot be subclassed. Consequently, once we start describing a class with the final modifier, we lose a lot of reusability. But sometimes, we don't want people to be tempted to change a method, variable, or entire class through subclassing. Let's consider our runway example, as follows:

```
class Runway {

   private static final physicalLocation;
   private static final physicalLength;
   private static final physicalWidth;

//other variables

Runway(int i, int j, int k) {
   physicalLocation=i;
   physicalLength=j;
   physicalWidth=k;}

//other constructors

public final int getPhysicalLocation() {
   return physicalLocation;}

public final int getPhysicalLength() {
   return physicalLength;}
```

```
public final int getPhysicalWidth() {
  return physicalWidth;}

//other methods

}
```

As we discussed earlier, the usable distance of a runway may change due to weather. However, the physical dimensions of the runway are not going to change during the life of the runway. Therefore, we declare these methods and variables final, because we don't want subclasses to change their meanings.

As with the protected modifier, we use the final modifier to imprint our design of a system on the code itself. This makes the code more maintainable, and by doing so, it also makes it more reusable.

Using Object Casting

One way to reuse a class is to subclass it into another class. This way, you only have to write a couple of new methods, and you can use the other ones that are already defined. But when you are designing a large system, you'll want to take advantage of Java's object casting.

Let's look at our airplane class again. When we thought about generalizing the modules in our system, we proposed that our airplane class should be a subclass of an abstract vehicle class. The vehicle class would describe characteristics that all vehicles have, as shown below:

```
abstract class Vehicle {
  String vehicleType();
  Vector getLocation();
  Vector getTrajectory();
  Path getPath();

  float currentFuelAmount();
    //returns a value between 0 and 1
  }
```

Our getPath method returns a Path object, which is also defined abstractly:

```java
abstract class Path {
    String pathType();
    Vector startingPoint();
    Vector endingPoint();
    int Length();
    }
```

So far, this has just been an academic exercise. Though others may admire our object-oriented style, we have yet to do anything really useful. The advantage comes when we subclass these for different types of vehicles and paths. Then, we can manage instances of these subclasses through the methods we have defined here. The same is true for interfaces, which can also be subclassed.

Crash-Proofing Your Java Code

Running programs always need to be prepared to deal with the unexpected. For instance, users may not give input appropriately, or your program may not be able to acquire the appropriate resources. In older programming languages, crash-proofing your program meant making complicated if-then-else blocks. The Java language uses exception handling to help you crash-proof your code. Exception handling isn't magical—you still have to identify where your program might crash and write code that allows your program to recover. Rather, exception handling allows us to write cleaner, more understandable code.

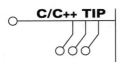

C/C++ TIP

Java's exception handling is equivalent to the exception handling of C++, with the addition of a finally block that is run after any catch blocks.

We've been using exception handling for some time. We have had to *catch* the exceptions that many of the methods and constructors in the Application Programming Interface (API) *throw*. An exception is thrown when something occurs in a method that the method wasn't expecting, while the catch block determines what should be done with the unexpected. Since we have already been catching exceptions, we will start here by discussing how to catch exceptions most effectively. Once we understand how to use methods and constructors that throw exceptions, we will examine how to write such methods and constructors ourselves. We will wrap up by writing our own exception subclasses, which will allow us to highly customize our error handling.

Exception Catching Examined

We first put exception handling to work in Chapter 5, "How Applets Work," when we were downloading image files. As you may remember, the URL constructor throws an exception if it can't turn the String we give it into a URL. Let's review what we had to do:

```
public class someApplet extends Applet {

Image I;
//other declarations

public void init() {

String imageName=getParam("image");
try {
    URL imageURL=new URL(imageName);
    //may throw MalformedURLException
    I=getImage(imageURL);
    //initialize rest of applet
    }
catch (MalformedURLException e) {
    String err=e.getMessage();
    showStatus("Couldn't get " +imageName+":"+e.getMessage);
```

```
    stop();
    }
}
//other methods
}
```

This is a simple example of using exceptions. The try block defines what we want to do if all goes well, while the catch block defines what the program should do if a MalformedURLException is generated in the try block.

Dealing with exceptions is an important part of using a method or constructor appropriately. But what is the appropriate way of catching an exception? Our example only shows the most simplistic use of the syntax; now we need to explore the capabilities of exception handling more fully. Specifically, we need to deal with the following issues:

- Exceptions are classes in their own right. As such, we can call methods of the instance to gain more information about what actually happened.

- Some exceptions must be explicitly caught, while others don't have to be. The latter are called RuntimeExceptions, and we need to look at when we should catch them anyway.

- We are not limited to only one *catch* block per *try* block. Thus, we can put more than one exception-throwing statement in each try block. For each unique exception that may be thrown, we can have our own catch block.

- We can make use of *finally* blocks in conjunction with try and catch blocks.

As we examine the finer points of exception handling, we'll continue to build on our simple example. By the end of this discussion, we will have a clean model for gaining resources based on information on the HTML page itself. Also, you will understand the conceptual tools necessary to effectively use methods and constructors that throw exceptions.

Exceptions as Objects

Our catch block had the following statement:

```
showStatus(e.getMessage());
```

This implies that *e* is an object, and one of its members is a method, getMessage, that returns a String. Indeed, all of these assumptions are correct. Anything that can be caught is a subclass of Throwable, which is contained in the java.lang package. Since the Throwable class is always a superclass of anything we catch, we can always use its public members to analyze the situation. The public members of the Throwable class are given in Table 10-2.

Method	Purpose
String getMessage()	Gets a detailed message. If the Throwable was constructed with a String, the String is displayed.
void printStackTrace()	Prints the stack trace, which lists all of the methods that were interrupted by the exception.
String toString()	Returns a description.
Throwable fillInStackTrace()	Fills in the execution stack trace. Useful when you catch an exception and throw it again.

Table 10-2: *Public members of the Throwable class.*

The methods of the Throwable class can be overridden in the Exception subclass, and of course, methods can be added. If we are dealing with exception classes in the API, we can go to the exception's home page, shown in Figure 10-4.

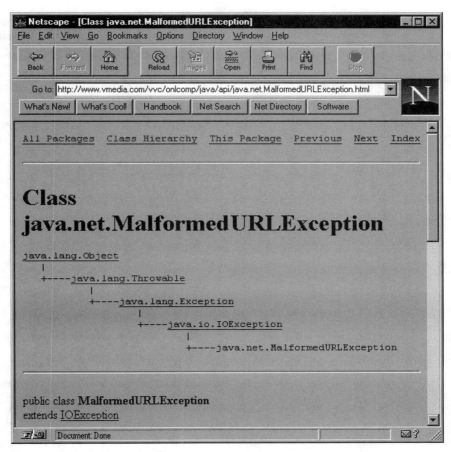

Figure 10-4: *An exception home page.*

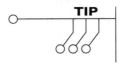

TIP

In case you are wondering, you never have to worry about being thrown just any type of object. It is illegal for a method or constructor to throw a String, for instance, because the String class is not a subclass of Throwable. The only type of object that can ever be thrown or caught is an instance of a subclass of Throwable.

Different Types of Exceptions

So far, we have been thinking about exceptions as entities that can be caught with the catch statement. Now we know that exceptions are just part of the hierarchy that descends from the class Throwable. Besides the Exception subclass, the Throwable class has two other descendants that have special meaning: the Error class and the RuntimeException class. The three classes and their relationships with Throwable are outlined in Figure 10-5.

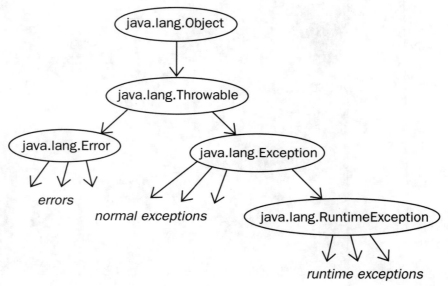

Figure 10-5: *Throwable hierarchy.*

The three groupings in Figure 10-6 are differentiated both functionally and stylistically. As programmers, we are only affected by one functional difference. The second grouping, whose members are known simply as Exceptions, must be explicitly caught if they might be thrown. This means that the following code fragment won't compile because MalformedURLException, an Exception, has not been caught:

```
URL U=new URL("http://www.vmedia.com/?.?");
Image I=getImage(U);
//Won't compile! no try-catch
```

Unlike Exceptions, Errors and Runtime Exceptions do not have to be explicitly caught. If we had to catch them in every case, our code would be unreadable. For example, if we were forced to catch the OutOfMemoryError, we would have to catch it every time we instantiated any kind of data type! The same is true for NullPointerException, which is generated when we attempt to access an object's nonstatic members without first instantiating it. The following code fragment will generate a NullPointerException:

```
String S;
S.toLowerCase();
//generates NullPointerException
```

If we were forced to always catch NullPointerException, we would have to catch it every time we deal with an object. This would be as painful as always catching OutOfMemoryError.

The main difference between Runtime Exceptions and Errors lies in the type of failures they represent. Errors represent conditions that you can do little about, like running out of memory. We hardly ever need to catch Errors, and when we do, we usually can do no more than politely exit.

Runtime Exceptions are easier to recover from, and sometimes we *do* want to catch them. Remember in Chapter 6, "Discovering the Application Programming Interface," when we were converting Strings to ints? In that case, we set up a try-catch block like this:

```
String S="20";
try {
int i=Integer.parseInt(S);
} catch (NumberFormatException e) {
  System.out.println("Couldn't convert "+S);}
```

NumberFormatException is a runtime exception; we don't have to catch it. But if we are getting the String as input from the user, we certainly *want* to catch it. If the String given to us isn't valid, then the NumberFormatException will be thrown and will crash our program.

CATCHING THE SUPERCLASS OF AN EXCEPTION

So far, we have always caught the same exception that may be thrown. But since exceptions follow the assignment rules of all of Java's classes, we can catch the exception as an instance of the superclasses—besides the Object class—of the exception that is actually thrown. For instance, we could always catch an instance of Throwable, and that would catch anything that could possibly be thrown. That's going a bit too far—we'd never know what actually happened! But sometimes when there are extensive hierarchies of exceptions, you may find it more convenient to catch a superclass of several exceptions rather than catch one individually.

Using Multiple Catch & Finally Blocks

So, exception handling forces us to deal with the possibility of unexpected behavior. But Example 10-1 doesn't show how exception handling is cleaner than if-then-else blocks. Here, we have one catch statement associated with the try statement. In fact, we can have multiple catch statements associated with one try statement. This means that the code in the try block will be executed in order if everything goes all right. Someone reading our code will have no problem figuring out what we are trying to do. As programmers, it is easy for us to separate out how we are going to deal with varying errors.

Let's switch to an example that demonstrates this advantage. Previously, we were just pulling one image into our applet. Now, let's say we are doing an animation in which the Web designer specifies how long a particular image is going to stay on the screen. If the image specified isn't available, we will just slip a standard dead image in its place. This can act as feedback to the Web designer in the same way that the broken icon acts as feedback in standard Web page authoring. If a pause isn't specified, we will just give the image a standard pause. The following code will implement this:

```
class animApplet extends Applet {

Image imgs[];
Integer pauses[];
//other declarations

public void init() {
Vector imgVec=new Vector();
Vector pauseVec=new Vector();
Image deadImage=createDeadImage();
Integer defaultPause=new Integer(100);

int indx=1;
String imgName=getParam("image"+indx);

while (imgName!=null) {
  try {
      URL imgURL=new URL
        (getDocumentBase,imgName);
        //may generate malformedURLException
        imgVec.add(getImage(imgURL));
      String pauseParam=getParam
        ("pause"+indx);
        Integer thisPause(pauseParam);
        //may generate NumberFormatException
        pauseVec.add(thisPause);}

      catch (malformedURLException e) {
         showStatus(e.getMessage());
         System.out.println(e.getMessage());
         imgVec.add(deadImage);}
      catch (NumberFormatException e) {
          pauseVec.add(defaultPause);}
     finally {indx=indx+1;}
     }

 imgs = new Image[imgVec.size()];
 imgVec.copyInto(imgs);
 pauseVec.copyInto(pauses);
 }
```

As long as everything goes all right, the try block will run completely and then the finally block will run. Someone looking at our code can easily figure out what we want to happen, and can look at each catch block to see how we plan to handle various errors.

Let's consider how this code is cleaner than it would be if Java didn't have exception handling. Think of the following as very Java-like pseudocode; because some of the exceptions need to be caught, this code wouldn't actually compile. For the purpose of this example, we're going to imagine a couple of methods that don't actually exist, but would need to exist in the absence of exception handling. The first, boolean validURL, returns true if the URL is valid. The other is validIntString, which returns true if the String represents an integer:

```java
//Java-like pseudocode
//won't actually compile!

public void init() {

Vector imgVec=new Vector();
Vector pauseVec=new Vector();
Image deadImage=createDeadImage();
Integer defaultPause=new Integer(100);

int indx=1;
String imgName=getParam("image"+indx);

while (imgName!=null) {
  if (validURL(imgName)) {
    URL imgURL=new URL(imgName);
    imgVec.add(getImage(imgURL));
    String pauseParam("pause"+indx);
    if (validIntString(pauseParam)) {
        Integer thisPause(pauseParam);
      pauseVec.add(thisPause));}
    else pauseVec.add(defaultPause);
  else {showStatus(imgName+" invalid");
      System.out.println(imgName+" invalid");}
  indx++;}
}
```

Notice that it is harder to figure out what happens when everything goes right. You just can't look at what is contained in the try block. Also, our code fragment has grown in size.

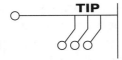

TIP

We mentioned before that you can catch the superclass of an exception. If you try to catch both the superclass and the actual exception, the compiler will complain that the second catch block is unreachable—unless the second catch block is able to catch exceptions that are thrown by the runtime environment.

Throwing Exceptions

We know how to use methods that throw exceptions. Now we can take the next step and write our own methods that throw exceptions. The syntax for throwing exceptions is pretty straightforward. Let's consider the following method:

```
class sampleConvert {

public static byte intToByte(int I) throws Exception {

if (I>127 || I< -128) throw Exception();
//don't need else - control will shift
//to catch block upon throw
return (byte)I;}

//other methods

}
```

When we are throwing an exception other than Errors and Runtime Exceptions, we must declare them as part of a method's declaration. As you will soon see, our method can throw more than one exception if we want it to. If we find that we need to throw the exception, we use the *throw* keyword. What if a method that calls our method can't handle the exception itself? It can catch it and throw it again to the method that called it. The throw statement can only be followed by an instantiation of a Throwable subclass. Of course, we are allowed to use any constructor available to us.

We're going to develop a class that will give a lot of exercise to exception handling. As you will recall from Chapter 4, "Syntax & Semantics," the numeric primitives can always be cast between each other. Even if we are converting an int to a byte and the int is out of range, the conversion won't cause an error—the value of the byte will just be meaningless. But what if you need to know if the conversion from one primitive type to another is going to lose information? The best way to check for this would be to create a Convert class that contains methods that will check for you. If the conversion can't be safely performed, the method will throw an exception. We are going to develop a method for each conversion where information may be lost. Below, we'll write one method that would belong in such a class:

```
public static byte toByte(int I) throws Exception {
String mesg="toByte: ";

if (I>127) {
   mesg=mesg+I+" is greater than byte range";
   throw new Exception(mesg);}
if (I<-128) {
   mesg=mesg+I+" is less than byte range";
   throw new Exception(mesg);}
return (byte)I;}
```

In one aspect, our method makes good use of exception handling. If we couldn't throw exceptions, we would have no way to communicate that the integer is out of range. The best we could do is write a separate method that would return false when some integer is out of range.

However, our simple example fails completely in usability. When things go wrong, we want our programs to know why. Otherwise, people who study our code later will have trouble figuring out what kind of error we are dealing with. Also, remember that you can only have one catch statement for each type of exception. This means that someone using your method might not be able to differentiate the instance of Exception that your method might throw with another method's instantiation.

The problems that our method has are semantic, because the Exception instantiation has little meaning. Instead, we need to write our own exception subclasses that have meaningful names that communicate information about the failure. Since each method in our convert class is going to need to throw its own unique exception, we would develop an exception hierarchy as shown in Figure 10-6.

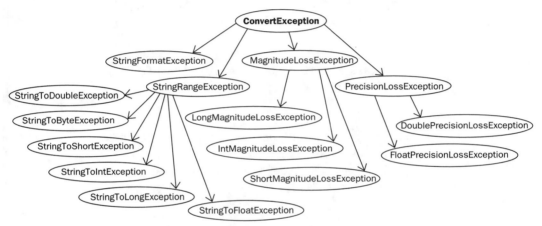

Figure 10-6: *Hierarchy of convert exceptions.*

Coding our exception hierarchy is pretty simple. The only work we do is to add a constructor for the various types in the exceptions in the MagnitudeLoss and PrecisionLoss part of the hiearchy. Remember that, as with all classes, we will need to put each exception in its own file:

Example 10-1a: Conversion exceptions.

```
public class ConvertException extends Exception {
  public ConvertException(String S) {
    super("Couldn't convert: "+S);}
  }
```

```java
public class StringFormatException extends
ConvertException {
  public StringFormatException(String S) {
    super("Bad String format: "+S);}
}

public class MagnitudeLossException extends
ConvertException {
    public MagnitudeLossException(String S) {
      super("magnitude loss: "+S);}
    }

public class MagnitudeLossException (double d) {
  this(""+d);}
  }

public class LongMagnitudeLossException extends
MagnitudeLossException {
    public LongMagnitudeLossException(long l){
    super("long "+l);}
    }

public class IntMagnitudeLossException extends
  MagnitudeLossException {
    public IntMagnitudeLossException(int i) {
    super("int "+i);}
    }

public class ShortMagnitudeLossException extends
MagnitudeLossException {
  public ShortMagnitudeLossException(short s){
    super("short "+s);}
    }

public class PrecisionLossException extends
ConvertException {
 public PrecisionLossException(String S) {
    super("Precision loss: "+S);}
  }
```

```
public class DoublePrecisionLossException extends
PrecisionLossException
 public DoublePrecisionLossException(double d){super
("double "+d);}
   }

public class FloatPrecisionLossException extends
PrecisionLossException
 public FloatPrecisionLossException(float f){
   super("float "+f);}
   }
```

When developing an exception hierarchy, the issues are quite different than when developing the usual object-oriented hierarchies. For one thing, our Exception subclasses do very little except communicate information about the failure. Most exceptions defined in the API don't define additional methods and constructors beyond those in Throwable.

The single most important thing about an Exception subclass is its name. When people look at catch statements, they should be able to decipher what kind of error has occurred. The MalformedURLException is an example of a good name; we don't need to look at the documentation to figure out what kind of problem our catch block is dealing with.

Also, you should group your exceptions intelligibly. Remember when you ran javadoc on your code in Chapter 2? Since exceptions are just classes, you can also run javadoc on them. Your Exception subclass will have its own home page, and there will be a link from your class's home page to the Exception's home page. Those using your code will have a hyperlinked reference of your exception hierarchy, and that hierarchy should give them a good feeling of how those exceptions are related.

Now that we have our exception hierarchy developed, we can develop our Convert class. The complete Convert class is on the Companion CD-ROM and the Online Companion. Here are the methods that convert to bytes, as well as one other method that toByte(String S) uses:

Example 10-1b: Convert class.

```
public class Convert {

public static byte toByte(short s) throws
ShortMagnitudeLossException {
  byte b=(byte)s;
  if (b==s) return b;
  else throw(new ShortMagnitudeLossException(s));}

public static byte toByte(int i) throws
IntMagnitudeLossException{
        byte b=(byte)i;
        if(i==b) return b;
        else throw (new IntMagnitudeLossException(i));}

public static byte toByte(long l) throws
   LongMagnitudeLossException{
        byte b=(byte)l;
        if(l==b) return b;
        else throw (new LongMagnitudeLossException(l));}


public static byte toByte(String S) throws
        StringFormatException,StringToByteException {

        try {
        double d=toDouble(S);
        byte b=(byte)d;
        if (b==i) return b;
        else throw (new StringToByteException(d));}
        catch (StringFormatException e) {
          throw (e);}
        }

public static byte toByte(float f) throws
   MagnitudeLossException, FloatPrecisionLossException {
```

```
    if(f>127 || f< -128)
        throw (new MagnitudeLossException(f));
    byte b=(byte)f;
    if (b==f) return b;
    else throw (new FloatPrecisionLossException(f));}

public static byte toByte(double d) throws
  MagnitudeLossException, FloatPrecisionLossException {
    if(d>127 || d< -128)
        throw (new MagnitudeLossException(d));
    byte b=(byte)d;
    if (b==d) return b;
    else throw (new DoublePrecisionLossException(d));}

//*** toDouble

public static double toDouble(String S) throws
    StringFormatException {
    S=S.trim();
    try {
    double d=Double.valueOf(S).doubleValue();
    return d;}
    catch (NumberFormatException e) {
        throw (new StringFormatException(S));}
}
```

Runtime Information About Objects

Since Java is a dynamic language, we are able to access information about objects on the fly. We do this through the Class class—java.lang.Class (see Figure 10-7). With it, we can figure out what type of object we are dealing with and what interfaces it implements, as well as other characteristics.

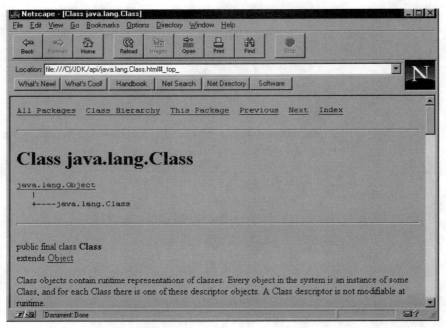

Figure 10-7: *The Class class.*

This class has little use in simple systems when we know what all of our instantiations are going to be. In larger, more complex systems, we can use this class to allow us to deal with various instantiations appropriately. Table 10-3 outlines the methods defined in the Class class. When these methods return Class, that instance describes specifically a certain Java class or interface.

Method	Purpose & Exceptions Thrown
static Class forName (String className)	Given a className, this method returns a Class instance specific to that class. Exception thrown: ClassNotFoundException.
String getName()	Returns the name of this class associated with this instantiation. No exception thrown.
String toString()	As above, except interface is prepended if it is an interface, class is prepending if it is a class. No exception thrown.
boolean isInterface()	Returns true if the object is an interface. No exception thrown.
Class[] getInterfaces()	Returns Class instantiations corresponding to the interfaces that the corresponding class implements, or a 0 length array if none are implemented. No exception thrown.
Class getSuperclass()	Returns a Class instantiation of the superclass. No exception thrown.
Object newInstance()	Creates a new instance of the associated class. Exceptions thrown: InstantiationException, IllegalAccessException.
ClassLoader getClassLoader()	Returns the class loader. No exception thrown.

Table 10-3: *Methods of the Class class.*

The first six methods in our table are useful in using objects that may be any of several subclasses and that may or may not implement certain interfaces. The method newInstance is used to instantiate classes on the fly. With only a String describing the class name, we can create an instance of it with the following code (*S* is the name of a valid subclass of Path):

```
try {
   Path p=Class.forName(S).newInstance();
catch (InstantiationException e) {
    System.out.println(S+" is not a valid subclass of "
+Path);}
catch (IllegalAccessException e) {
    System.out.println(S+" is not allowed to be accessed.");
catch (ClassNotFoundException e) {
    System.out.println(S+" wasn't found");}
```

Moving On

We have given you a quick introduction to advanced program design. We've covered the advanced thinking that goes into both making your programs reusable and taking advantage of all the power Java's object orientation has to offer. And, to make your code even stronger, we've shown you how to crash-proof it in ways that let others easily identify problems when they occur. In the next chapter, "Advanced Threading," we look at how to make your code really powerful through the use of threads.

11

Advanced Threading

Until now, we have looked only briefly at the use of threads in Java. We have been able to do this because Java handles threads in a very elegant fashion: it is the first popular language to incorporate multiple threads in the definition of the language. For Java to succeed as a network language, it must perform multiple operations at once. The inclusion of threads makes Java uniquely suited for Internet development.

Why are threads a good thing? Imagine you are writing a spreadsheet program and want the spreadsheet to be recalculated in the background. In a normal, single-threaded program, you would have to perform some intricate tricks to get this to work. For example, you might decide to write a loop that checks for keyboard input and, if there is none, does some calculations. It's not an elegant solution, but it might work.

But your solution becomes even less elegant when, later in the project, someone requests a background printing routine and someone else asks for autosaving. Now you have to go back and hack in these additional chores to be performed between keystrokes. Your keyboard input loop is quickly becoming a tangled mess, all because you have only one thread of execution.

Of course, it's possible to use a third-party library that provides threading support. Although this certainly is an option, it's not optimal. Every time you change jobs, you might encounter a new threading library and have to learn a whole new API. The designers of Java realized this and chose to implement threads in the specification for the language. Using Java's standard threads, we can solve our spreadsheet program problems much easier. Each new task is implemented as its own thread. We needn't hack in each new feature. Having the language support threads also makes the implementation cleaner.

This chapter focuses on how Java implements threads and on the issues surrounding programs that consist of multiple threads. If your experience with multiple threads is limited, this chapter just may change the way you think about programming. The shift from one megaprogram to a program composed of small threads can be radical. There are pitfalls to avoid and concepts to learn. So, let's dive in and discover how Java creates and runs multiple threads.

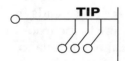

TIP

This chapter's code example files can be found on the Companion CD-ROM (for Windows 95/NT and Macintosh users) and the Online Companion (for UNIX users). Visit the Online Companion at http://www.vmedia.com/java.html.

Creating Threads With the Thread Class

Creating a new thread in Java is a simple operation. All you have to do is extend the java.lang.Thread class and override its run method. Each instance of your new class will be run as a separate thread. With a few lines of Java code, you can create a program with multiple threads of execution. If you've ever had to fake threads, you will appreciate the simplicity of Java's implementation.

As a warm-up exercise, let's create a thread, outputThread, to output some text. This thread displays three numbers and then ends:

Example 11-1: Simple thread.

```
class outputThread extends Thread {
   outputThread(String name) {
      super(name);
   }

   public void run() {
      for(int i=0; i < 3; i++) {
         System.out.println(getName());
         Thread.yield();
      }
   }
}

class runThreads {
   public static void main(String argv[]) {
      outputThread t1 = new outputThread("Thread 1");
      outputThread t2 = new outputThread("Thread 2");

      t1.start();
      t2.start();
   }
}
```

When the code is executed, it generates the following output:

```
Thread 1
Thread 2
Thread 1
Thread 2
Thread 1
Thread 2
```

Notice that we create two threads in this program. We do this by creating two instances of the class outputThread. Next, we call each thread's start method. The start method creates a new thread and then calls our overridden run method. You have now created a program with multiple threads. It's not a scary or complicated process—in fact, you've been using multiple threads throughout the book.

Remember how we created applets for our Web pages? We extended java.applet.Applet. Well, this is just a thread. Each applet on a page is made up of one or more threads, and the Java runtime system creates a few threads for itself. You are already familiar with the garbage collection thread, which cleans up after programs and frees unused memory. As you can see, threads are an integral part of the Java system.

OUTPUT DIFFERENCES
Some readers may be surprised that their example output differs from ours. You might have seen all of Thread 1's output followed by all of Thread 2's output. If so, you have a multitasking system, which does not perform time slicing. We will discuss how this affects your programs in "Scheduling Threads" later in this chapter.

Creating Threads With the Runnable Interface

What if we didn't want to extend the Thread class in the example above? Maybe we have a class that has the functionality we want, and we just want it to run as a separate thread. The answer is simple: use the Runnable interface. In Chapter 3, "Object Orientation in Java," we discussed Java's interfaces. Interfaces provide a good way to define a standard set of functionality for a class to implement. The Runnable interface specifies one method, the run method, to be implemented. This is very similar to how the thread class works.

Imagine that we have a class, called outputClass, that we want to make into a thread. All we have to do is implement the Runnable interface by creating a public method run:

Example 11-2 : Using the Runnable interface.

```java
class outputClass implements Runnable {
   String name;

   outputClass(String s) {
      name = s;
   }

   public void run() {
      for(int i=0; i < 3; i++) {
         System.out.println(name);
         Thread.yield();
      }
   }
}

class runThreads {
   public static void main(String argv[]) {
      outputClass out1 = new outputClass("Thread 1");
      outputClass out2 = new outputClass("Thread 2");
      Thread t1 = new Thread(out1);
      Thread t2 = new Thread(out2);

      t1.start();
      t2.start();
   }
}
```

Example 11-2 is functionally equivalent to Example 11-1, but it is set up differently. Here, we create two instances of outputClass. This could be any class, but it must implement the Runnable interface. Next, we create two new threads and pass references to our newly created outputClass instances. Then we just start the threads as usual.

The difference between the two examples is in our constructor calls to the Thread class. In the first example, we called the Thread(String) constructor. In Example 11-2, we call the Thread(Runnable) constructor. We could have also called the Thread(Runnable,String) constructor to name it. The Thread class has the following constructors:

- Thread()
- Thread(String)
- Thread(Runnable)
- Thread(String,Runnable)
- Thread(ThreadGroup, String)
- Thread(ThreadGroup, Runnable)
- Thread(ThreadGroup, Runnable, String)

We'll discuss ThreadGroups a little later. Right now, let's explore how to control these threads. Creating the threads is only part of the story—the rest is how to control these critters after they're spawned!

Managing Threads

Until now, we have run only threads that end on their own. They perform a task and then exit. But when does a Java program end? How do you stop a thread? These are important questions, and we will need some background to answer them.

Think back to the days of single-threaded programs. We had some main execution body which ran some code. When the program was finished executing, it just exited and the program ended. In Java, we get the same response, but with a slight twist. The program doesn't end until *all* threads exit. So, if we have a thread that runs forever, our program will never exit.

Each thread can be in one of four states: new, running, waiting, or done. When a thread is first created, it is placed in the *new* state. In the new state, threads are not running—they are waiting to be started. A thread can then either be started with the start method, or it can be stopped, in which case it will be sent to the *done* state. Threads in the done state have finished executing. This is the final resting place for threads. Once a thread reaches this state, it cannot be resurrected. And once all the threads in the Java virtual machine are in the done state, the program halts.

All threads that currently are executing are in the *running* state. The processor is time-sliced between the threads in some manner. (We'll discuss how Java partitions the processor soon.)

Each thread in the running state is available to be run, but at any given time, only one program can be running per system processor. Unlike threads in the running state, those in the *waiting* state have been removed from the set of executable threads for some reason.

The *waiting* state is where threads go if their execution is interrupted. A thread can be interrupted in several ways. It can be suspended, waiting on some system resource, or told to go to sleep. From this state, a thread can either be returned to the running state or sent to the done state by the stop method. Table 11-1 summarizes the methods that control a thread's execution.

Method	Description	Valid States	Dest State
start()	Start a thread's execution.	New	Running
stop()	End a thread's execution.	New, running	Done
sleep(long)	Pause for some number of milliseconds.	Running	Waiting
sleep(long,int)	Pause, allow nanosecond detail.	Running	Waiting
suspend()	Suspend execution.	Running	Waiting
resume()	Resume execution.	Waiting	Running
yield()	Explicity give up control.	Running	Running

Table 11-1: *Thread control methods.*

The commands in Table 11-1 are not valid at all times; most work when the thread is currently running. If you use a command in an inappropriate state—for example, if you try to suspend a dead thread—an IllegalThreadStateException will be generated. Generally, you should know what state the thread is in during development. If you need a program to determine a thread's state, use the isAlive method: A result of true means that the thread is running or waiting. Otherwise it is new or dead. There is no way to determine the difference between running and waiting.

You're well on your way to using threads. You can now create threads and control their execution. What we haven't told you is how multiple threads act in relation to each other—that's up next.

Scheduling Threads

The order in which threads are run and the amount of time they receive from the processor are major concerns for the developer. Each thread should get its share of processor time. We don't want one thread to hog the whole system. How threads are scheduled is closely related to two concepts: preemption and time slicing. Let's examine each concept closely.

A system that deals with multiple threads can be either preemptive or non-preemptive. A *preemptive* system promises that, at any given time, the thread with the highest priority will be running. All threads in the system have a priority. The class variable Thread.NORM_Priority is the default for a thread. The Thread class provides the setPriority and getPriority methods to set and get a priority. By using the setPriority method, we can change a thread's importance to the Java virtual machine. The setPriority method takes an integer. It has a valid range determined by two class variables, Thread.MIN_PRIORITY and Thread.MAX_PRIORITY.

The Java machine is preemptive, which means that it guarantees that the thread with the highest priority will always be running. Let's say we change a thread's priority to the highest in the Java machine. The currently running thread's position will be usurped by the newly exalted thread. It will get all the processor time until it either ends or is placed in the waiting state, possibly by a sleep command. That's acceptable, but what happens to threads with the same priority? Let's look at an example to see Java's behavior:

Example 11-3: Scheduling.

```
class outputThread extends Thread {
outputThread(String name) {
   super(name);
}

public void run() {
   for(int i=0; i < 3; i++) {
      System.out.println(getName());
   }
}
}

class runThreads {
   public static void main(String argv[]) {
      outputThread t1 = new outputThread("Thread 1");
      outputThread t2 = new outputThread("Thread 2");
      outputThread t3 = new outputThread("Thread 3");

      t1.start();
      t2.start();
      t3.start();
   }
}
```

When we write this code, we generally expect that threads of the same priority should run for some time and then allow another thread to run. Here's the output from Example 11-3, run on a Windows 95 machine. As you can see, we get what we expected:

```
Thread 1
Thread 2
Thread 3
Thread 1
Thread 2
Thread 3
Thread 1
Thread 2
Thread 3
```

But notice what we get when we run the same code on a Sun box:

```
Thread 1
Thread 1
Thread 1
Thread 2
Thread 2
Thread 2
Thread 3
Thread 3
Thread 3
```

The outputs are different! What happened to portability? Welcome to the dark side of multithreading. Not all machines are created alike, and the underlying operating system affects the order in which threads are executed. The difference lies in a concept called *time slicing*.

How threads of the same priority run is not addressed in the Java specification. It would seem that each thread should share the processor, but that's not always the case. Their execution order is determined by the underlying operating system and hardware. Obviously, on systems with one processor, we can't expect more than one thread to be running at a time. The operating system generally handles this by having a scheduler that determines the execution order.

Let's look more closely at what happened when we ran our program on the Sun box. Thread 1 ran until completion, as did thread 2, and lastly thread 3. But if thread 1 had never ended, threads 2 and 3 would never have run. As you can imagine, this could cause some major problems. The highest-priority thread will be running at all times, while threads of a lower priority may not be run, depending on the operating system. If we want a specific ordering, or even a sane ordering, we will need to do some work.

The *yield* method offers a simple way around the problem of time slicing. If the yield method is used, a thread will voluntarily give up the processor. This gives other threads a chance on the processor. Yielding is especially important in tight loops. Let's rewrite the previous program to use the yield command:

Example 11-4: The yield method.

```
class outputThread extends Thread {
    outputThread(String name) {
        super(name);
    }

    public void run() {
        for(int i=0; i < 3; i++) {
            System.out.println(getName());
            Thread.yield();
        }
    }
}
```

This rewrite required only one change. We added a yield command inside the main loop for the thread. Although this gives us what we want, it has a few drawbacks. The yield command requires the system to do work. If there is only one thread, using yield is a waste of time. Remember also that some systems already handle this for us. Another drawback is that we have to explicitly give up control, which raises some difficult questions. How do we know where to do it and how often? Let's tackle these issues one at a time.

Since some systems perform time slicing and others don't, we might develop a simple test to determine a system's abilities. The following code determines if a system is "fair," meaning that it has time slicing:

Example 11-5a: Fairness testThread.

```
class testThread extends Thread {
    protected int val=0;

    public void run() {
        while(true) {
            val++;
        }
    }

    public int getVal() {
        return val;
    }
}
```

This first class is just a test thread. It increases some variable forever. In a system with time slicing, all running threads should generally have equal values. Systems without time slicing will probably end up with one thread getting considerably more time than another. This code determines whether or not a system performs time slicing:

Example 11-5b: Fairness time slicing determination.

```java
class isFair extends Thread {
    boolean fair=false;
    boolean determined=false;

    public boolean isFair() {
        if (determined) return fair;
        start();

        while(!determined) {
            // Wait till value is determined
            try {
                sleep(1500);
            }
            catch (InterruptedException e) {
            }
        }

        return fair;
    }

    public void run() {
        testThread t1 = new testThread();
        testThread t2 = new testThread();

        setPriority(MAX_PRIORITY);

        t1.start();
        t2.start();

        try {
            sleep(500);
```

```
        }
        catch (InterruptedException e) {
        }

        t1.stop();
        t2.stop();

        if (t1.getVal() > 2 * t2.getVal()) {
            fair = false;
        }
        else {
            fair = true;
        }

        determined = true;
    }
}
```

The isFair class is the meat of this example. It has a method, isFair, which can be called to determine if a system has time slicing capabilities. It works by running two testThreads for a few milliseconds. Then it stops the threads and tallies the result. If one thread got more than twice another thread's time, we will call it unfair. Generally it's an all-or-nothing deal; one thread, usually thread1, gets all the processor time. This will be dubbed as unfair:

Example 11-5c: Fairness test.

```
class test {
    public static void main(String argv[]) {
        isFair tThread = new isFair();

        if (tThread.isFair()) {
            System.out.println("System has time slicing");
        }
        else {
            System.out.println("System does not time slice");
        }
    }
}
```

The final component is a test program. You might use something similar in your programs to probe a system's capabilities. On a time-slicing system, you can go blissfully on with your programming and not worry about the problem of fairness. On other systems, you're on your own—it's up to you to ensure that your threads get appropriate time.

Placing yields in your code is not hard, but it's easy to forget to do it. Here's another method, which uses the Java definition to our advantage, although it will cost us. The highest-priority thread in the system is always running unless it's waiting. We can use this knowledge to mimic time slicing. Example 11-6 creates a thread called slicerThread whose priority is set to the MAX_PRIORITY. Its only task in life is to sleep. When it is sleeping, it is no longer eligible for scheduling. This means that our normal priority threads will get a chance to run. Each time the slicerThread is put to sleep, the scheduler will pick a new thread to run. It picks them in round-robin fashion, so each normal priority thread will get a chance to run, as shown in the following example:

Example 11-6: Time-slicing hack.

```
class outputThread extends Thread {
    outputThread(String name) {
        super(name);
    }

    public void run() {
        for(int i=0; i < 3; i++) {
            System.out.println(getName());
            Thread.yield();
        }
    }
}

class slicerThread extends Thread {
    slicerThread() {
        setPriority(Thread.MAX_PRIORITY);
    }
```

```
        public void run() {
           while(true) {
              try {
                 Thread.sleep(10);
              }
              catch (InterruptedException ignore) {
              }
           }
        }
     }

     class runThreads {
        public static void main(String argv[]) {
           slicerThread ts = new slicerThread();
           outputThread t1 = new outputThread("Thread 1");
           outputThread t2 = new outputThread("Thread 2");
           outputThread t3 = new outputThread("Thread 3");

           t1.start();
           t2.start();
           t3.start();
           ts.start();
        }
     }
```

We need to make a few comments on this example: First, it's ugly. It does the job, but it wastes system resources. You can make it use fewer resources by making it sleep longer. Just remember, though, the longer it sleeps the longer each thread will run before giving up the processor. You need to keep the sleep periods fairly low, or your output won't be fluid. Imagine one thread spitting out characters one at a time. You will have some burst of characters, followed by a pause, and then another burst—not exactly ideal.

In terms of efficiency, you're better off putting yield statements in your code. Neither method is pretty, but something is required to make threads time slice. Don't assume that just because your system performs time slicing, everyone else's will. Java is one of the most portable languages around, but you can make it less so by ignoring scheduling issues.

You may be asking why the designers of Java did this. The best answer is that they had to. Scheduling is best left up to the operating system. If the Java runtime were to schedule threads, it would be wasteful and terribly inefficient. Most modern processors have support for multitasking in the hardware. No matter how good their code is, it can't compare to a hardware implementation. Under Solaris, Sun provides fully preemptive kernel threads, and Java will some day be able to take advantage of this capability of the underlying OS.

Grouping Threads

Managing a few threads is no real problem, but suppose you have hundreds of threads to keep track of. Having to cycle through each thread would be tedious. You might encounter this situation when writing an Internet server—some server machines handle thousands of concurrent sessions. Let's say you need to do some maintenance on the system, so you need to end all of the sessions. You have two choices—cycle through each thread and stop it explicitly or use thread groups.

A thread group is a hierarchy grouping of threads. Each group can contain an unlimited number of threads. You can name each thread and perform operations such as suspend and stop on whole thread groups. Let's create a few thread groups:

```
ThreadGroup parent = new ThreadGroup("parent");
ThreadGroup child = new ThreadGroup(parent, "child");
```

This snippet of code shows the two ways a ThreadGroup can be created. The first method creates a ThreadGroup with some name. The second method creates a TheadGroup with a parent group and some name. A thread's parent group will affect which threads it can command.

Once we have created some ThreadGroup objects, we can add Threads to them. Remember those Thread constructors dealing with ThreadGroup? We can use them to add threads to a thread group. In fact, this is the only mechanism we can use—a thread group cannot be changed after it's been created.

```
Thread t1 = new Thread(parent);
Thread t2 = new Thread(child, "t2");
```

Now that we have some threads in different groups, what can we do with them? The most useful methods to use with thread groups are stop, suspend, and resume. Each thread in the ThreadGroup will have its appropriate method called. The children of the ThreadGroup are also affected. By using these methods, we can easily perform operations on large numbers of threads.

Thread groups have other functions that are primarily used by the Java runtime and deal with interthread security. Basically, the Java machine needs to keep our threads from tampering with its own threads. A child thread in a ThreadGroup can not command a thread in a parent group. You will probably not need this type of behavior. The documentation on this is currently sparse, so your best bet will be to look at the source code. This is normally used by Java machine implementations to protect its threads from user threads.

One last piece will complete the threading puzzle. Until now, our threads have all been generally unaware of other threads in the system. We had to worry about sharing time, but we haven't shared data between threads. This is academic material, typically taught in college computer science courses. We can give you an overview, but the nature of this book prevents us from exploring these topics in great detail. We suggest you do some research on your own. Check out a book on transaction processing or maybe one on operating systems. Some topics that may be of interest to you are synchronization, semaphores, spin locks, and race conditions. Have fun!

Synchronizing Threads

Let's assume for a moment that you have a doctorate in computer science. You spent many years learning the intricacies of computer programming. You probably took at least one class on transaction processing, or concurrent programming. You learned about multitasking and spent a great deal of time learning the latest algorithms for handling its associated problems.

Now let's return to the real world. Maybe you do have a doctorate in computer programming, or you're a wizard in the area of concurrent programming. If so, this section will be review. If not, we'll teach you the basics and hopefully answer most of your questions.

Having multiple threads running in your program can cause some headaches. If they just leave each other alone, it's not a problem, but that's not always the case. Multithreading sometimes requires that one thread communicate with another, usually in the form of a shared resource. Through the shared resource, two or more threads can communicate with each other. That's where the fun—and trouble—begins.

Monitors: Protecting a Shared Variable

We'll use a simple example to illustrate some of the problems we can have when dealing with multiple threads. Imagine a train station with several tracks serving the main line, but only one track serving the loading area. Somewhere along the main line, the trains have to switch to the line serving the loading area in order to get into the station. Suppose we have two rail lines coming into the train station that eventually merge into one line. At the point where they merge, we are faced with a problem—if two trains try to enter at the same time, they will collide. In the case of our train station, a collision could cost lives; in our programs, a collision involving multiple threads probably just means bugs. But bugs are annoying and even they can cost lives.

We've written a simple train simulator to illustrate this point. We have two trains entering a station at the same time. If nothing is done to intervene, a disaster is in the works. Here is the first implementation, in which intervention does not occur:

Example 11-7a: Train station: No intervention.

```
class Display {
    int switch1Loc=15;
    int switch2Loc=10;
    int begin1, begin2;
    int end1, end2;
```

```
public void showLoc(String train, int seq, int len) {
    if (train.compareTo("train1") == 0) {
        begin1=seq;
        end1=seq + len - 1;
        if (seq > switch1Loc) {
            System.out.println("train1 near switch @ "+seq);
        }
        else if (seq + len > switch2Loc) {
            System.out.println("train1 @ " + begin1);
        }
    }
    if (train.compareTo("train2") == 0) {
        begin2=seq;
        end2=seq + len - 1;
        if (seq > switch1Loc) {
            System.out.println("train2 near switch @ "+seq);
        }
        else if (seq + len > switch2Loc) {
            System.out.println("train2 @ " + begin2);
        }
    }

    // Check for collision

    if ((begin1 <= switch1Loc && end1 >= switch2Loc) &&
        (begin2 <= switch1Loc && end2 >= switch2Loc) &&
        (begin1 <= end2) && (begin1 >= begin2)) {

        System.out.println("CRASH @ " + seq);
        System.exit(-1);
    }
}
}

class train1 extends Thread {
    int seq=15;
    int switch1Loc=10;
    int switch2Loc=5;
    int trainLen=3;
```

```
Display display;

train1(String name, Display display) {
    super(name);
    this.display = display;
}

public void step() {
    seq--;
}

public void run() {
    while(seq > 0) {
        step();
        display.showLoc(getName(),seq,trainLen);
        yield();
    }

    System.out.println(getName() + " finished");
    }
}
```

The train1 class is our first attempt at a train object. Each train will run in its own thread. The run method will call two supporting methods, step and showLoc. The step method is used to move some finite distance forward. In our example we have made the train station five steps in length. On either side, we will monitor a train's actions for five steps.

The Display class is used to display our trains as they move. It also has the task of detecting when trains collide. It does this by checking to see if the trains overlap. This is only checked while the trains are in the train station. We've included the code for the Display class for your convenience:

Example 11-7b: Train station test code.

```
class testTrains1 {
    public static void main(String argv[]) {
        Display display = new Display();
```

```
        train1 t1 = new train1("train1",display);
        train1 t2 = new train1("train2",display);

        t1.start();
        t2.start();
    }
}
```

The test code is simple. It just creates two new trains and starts them on their way. Here's the output of our first attempt:

```
train1 near switch @ 14
train2 near switch @ 14
train1 near switch @ 13
train2 near switch @ 13
train1 near switch @ 12
train2 near switch @ 12
train1 near switch @ 11
train2 near switch @ 11
train1 @ 10
train2 @ 10
CRASH @ 10
```

The derailment makes headlines, and the programmer is fired for incompetence. Lawyers are threatening liability suits. The company needs to fix the programs immediately.

Someone finally remembers—in that operating system class they took, the professor mentioned something about monitors. A monitor is simply a thread that looks after a variable. In this case, the variable is a switch. Only one train at a time should be in that switch. We need some way to make a train pause while another is passing through.

Java provides a mechanism to protect variables in our program. The problem boils down to two threads trying to do some operation at the same time. We need one thread to wait for the other to finish. The operation might involve several instructions. These instructions are called the *critical section*. The critical section is that piece of code that must be protected or the system will fail. In our train case, the critical section is in the step method. A train should not be allowed to enter the switch while it is in use.

We can create a class called trainSwitch that will protect our switch. It will have two methods, lock and unlock. For a train to enter the switch, it must have the lock. Once it leaves the switch, it will call unlock. All other trains must wait until the trains is safely out of the switch before entering.

Java marks critical sections of code with the keyword *synchronized*. You can mark any block of code as synchronized, but ordinarily you mark methods. Marking a section of a method as synchronized is generally bad programming. Programmers should be able to look to class definitions for multithreading issues; if you don't mark a method as synchronized, people will need the code to figure out what's going on. For this reason we will only use the synchronized keyword on the method level.

So, what does marking a method as synchronized do? Each class has one monitor associated with it. When a synchronized method is called, it checks the monitor. If the class is already locked, then the calling routine must wait. This means that only one thread will be in a critical section at a time. Let's see how this is implemented:

Example 11-7c: TrainSwitch class.

```java
class trainSwitch extends Thread {
    protected boolean inUse=false;

    public synchronized void lock() {
        while (inUse) {
            try wait();
            catch (InterruptedException e);
        }
        inUse = true;
    }

    public synchronized void unlock() {
        inUse = false;
        notify();
    }
}
```

The trainSwitch class has two synchronized methods, lock and unlock, that are protecting the class variable inUse. We want to make sure that only one thread is using the switch at a time. So we have a boolean variable for the switch's state. When a train is using the switch, we will set inUse to true. Any other trains that have to use the switch must wait until the boolean variable is set to false.

Example 11-7b has also used two new methods, *wait* and *notify*. They have two purposes. The first is to resolve a tricky situation. What would happen if the wait statement was missing from the example above? The lock routine would be sitting in a loop and would have the monitor for the class. How would someone call the unlock method, which also needs the monitor?

The wait and notify methods are used to solve this problem. The wait method causes the thread to wait for a notify event. In the meantime, the monitor is freed. This allows other routines needing the classes' monitor to run. When control is returned from the wait method, the monitor is also regained. The rest of the critical section is still protected.

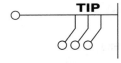

TIP

The methods wait and notify are not part of the Thread class. They are actually part of the java.lang.Object class. The wait method is overloaded with three methods: wait() waits an indefinite amount of time, wait(long) waits for some number of milliseconds and wait(long,int) waits for some milliseconds plus some nanoseconds.

Let's look at the rest of the code for this example:

Example 11-7d: Train station corrected.

```
class train2 extends Thread {
    int seq=15;
    int switch1Loc=10;
    int switch2Loc=5;
    int trainLen=3;
    Display display;
    trainSwitch ts;
```

```java
train2(String name, Display display, trainSwitch ts) {
    super(name);
    this.display = display;
    this.ts = ts;
}

public void step() {
    if (seq == switch1Loc + 1) {
        // Coming to switch
        System.out.println("Locking Switch: " + getName());
        ts.lock();
    }
    else if (seq + trainLen == switch1Loc) {
        // Passed Switch
        System.out.println("Unlocking Switch: "+getName());
        ts.unlock();
    }
    seq--;
}

public void run() {
    while(seq > 0) {
        step();
        display.showLoc(getName(),seq,trainLen);
        yield();
    }

    System.out.println(getName() + " safe");
}
}
```

In this last section of the code, we have changed the step method to use the trainSwitch class we developed. When we come to the switch, we request a lock on it. After we get the lock, we are clear to go through it. When the end of the train has passed the switch, we can release the switch. These operations ensure that only one train is in the switch at a time. Here's the output for the corrected program. Notice that both trains make it through the switch without crashing:

```
train1 near switch @ 14
train2 near switch @ 14
train1 near switch @ 13
train2 near switch @ 13
train1 near switch @ 12
train2 near switch @ 12
train1 near switch @ 11
train2 near switch @ 11
Locking Switch: train1
train1 @ 10
Locking Switch: train2
train1 @ 9
train1 @ 8
train1 @ 7
Unlocking Switch: train1
train1 @ 6
train2 @ 10
train1 @ 5
train2 @ 9
train1 @ 4
train2 @ 8
train1 @ 3
train2 @ 7
Unlocking Switch: train2
train2 @ 6
train2 @ 5
train2 @ 4
train2 @ 3
train1 safe
train2 safe
```

By now, you should have a basic understanding of monitors. In the next section, we'll look at another type of problem.

Semaphores: Protecting Other Shared Resources

In the preceding example, we showed you how to use monitors to protect a variable. Let's expand this concept to any general resource. We would like to protect any system resource that might be shared by multiple threads. One common shared resource is a

file. Two threads writing to a file at once will generate garbage. Having one thread reading a file while another thread is writing to it is also dangerous. We need some way to protect the integrity of our file.

To protect a file, we can apply concepts similar to those we used to protect the train switch in our last example. This type of protection is called an exclusive lock. Only one thread can read or modify the value at a time. When dealing with files, especially information databases, we generally do more reading than writing. We can use this fact to streamline our code.

Suppose we have an employee database. It contains information such as the employees' addresses and phone numbers. These items are occasionally changed, but more often, they are read. We want to protect the data from corruption, but we want to be as efficient as possible. Instead of just allowing exclusive locks, we'll allow a read lock and a write lock. We can have as many readers as we like, but when someone wants to write, they must have an exclusive lock. This is the concept behind a semaphore.

How might we go about creating this semaphore? We want to allow threads to read freely, but we stipulate that when some thread is writing, it must be the only one accessing the database.

Our semaphore has four states. In the first, *empty*, no thread is reading or writing. We can accept both read and write requests, and they can be serviced immediately. The second state is the *reading* state. Here, we have some number of threads reading from the database. We track the number of readers, and if this number goes to zero, we return to the empty state. A write request will result in the thread being made to wait.

We can only get to the *writing* state from the empty state. All readers must be done, and no other threads may be writing to the file. Any requests for reading or writing must wait for this thread to be done writing. Any process in the *waiting* state must be waiting for a write to finish. When a write finishes, we return to the empty state. When a notify message is sent, a waiting thread can be serviced. Here is the code to implement this semaphore:

Example 11-8a: Semaphore.

```
class Semaphore {
    final static int EMPTY = 0;
    final static int READING = 1;
    final static int WRITING = 2;

    protected int state=EMPTY;
    protected int readCnt=0;

    public synchronized void readLock() {
        if (state == EMPTY) {
            state = READING;
        }
        else if (state == READING) {
        }
        else if (state == WRITING) {
            while(state == WRITING) {
                try wait();
                catch (InterruptedException e);
            }
            state = READING;
        }
        readCnt++;
        return;
    }

    public synchronized void writeLock() {
        if (state == EMPTY) {
            state = WRITING;
        }
        else {
            while(state != EMPTY) {
                try wait();
                catch (InterruptedException e);
            }
        }
    }
}
```

```
public synchronized void readUnlock() {
    readCnt--;
    if (readCnt == 0) {
        state = EMPTY;
        notify();
    }
}

public synchronized void writeUnlock() {
    state = EMPTY;
    notify();
}
}
```

The semaphore class implements the semaphore we described. It makes use of *synchronized* methods and wait/notify methods. This class can be used to protect a shared resource. We can now use this class to protect our file access. Our test code will create some reader and writer processes:

Example 11-8b: Semaphore test code.

```
class process extends Thread {
    String op;
    Semaphore sem;

    process(String name, String op, Semaphore sem) {
        super(name);
        this.op = op;
        this.sem = sem;
        start();
    }

    public void run() {
        if (op.compareTo("read") == 0) {
            System.out.println("Trying to get ReadLock: " +
getName());
            sem.readLock();

            System.out.println("Read op: " + getName());
```

```
            try sleep((int)Math.random() * 50);
            catch (InterruptedException e);

            System.out.println("Unlocking readLock: " +
getName());
            sem.readUnlock();
        }
        else if (op.compareTo("write") == 0) {
            System.out.println("Trying to get writeLock: " +
getName());
            sem.writeLock();

            System.out.println("Write op: " + getName());
            try sleep((int)Math.random() * 50);
            catch (InterruptedException e);

            System.out.println("Unlocking writeLock: " +
getName());
            sem.writeUnlock();
        }
    }
}

class testSem {
    public static void main(String argv[]) {
        Semaphore lock = new Semaphore();

        new process("1", "read", lock);
        new process("2", "read", lock);
        new process("3", "write", lock);
        new process("4", "read", lock);
    }
}
```

The testSem class starts four instances of the process class. This class is just a thread that wants to either read or write to the shared file. The semaphore class insures that this access will not corrupt the file. Here is the program output:

```
Trying to get readLock: 1
Read op: 1
Trying to get readLock: 2
Read op: 2
Trying to get writeLock: 3
Trying to get readLock: 4
Read op: 4
Unlocking readLock: 1
Unlocking readLock: 2
Unlocking readLock: 4
Write op: 3
Unlocking writeLock: 3
```

In Example 11-8, we have three reader threads and one writer thread. The readers get there before the writer, so the writer must wait until the readers are done before it can write to the file. Notice that multiple readers can be accessing the database, but when someone wants to write, he or she must have exclusive access to the file. Our example illustrates an efficient way to implement a semaphore.

If you're curious about semaphores or need to implement file locking, you will want to do some further reading on transaction processing. Our semaphore works, but it has certain problems. For example, it gives preference to reading threads. A writing thread must wait until all readers leave before it gets control. If more readers arrive while the writing thread is waiting, they will get access before the writer. A better implementation would stop any new read requests when a writer is waiting.

Semaphores and resource control are complicated topics. Most programmers will not have to deal with them. But, as your use of multiple threads increases, you may be confronted with these issues.

Avoiding Deadlock

You can now synchronize the efforts of multiple threads and make sure they respect shared resources. You've begun to experiment with multiple threads and suddenly the system hangs. There is no response—it just sits there. You rerun the code and it works fine. Two weeks later, it happens again. You may be the victim of a deadlock problem.

Deadlock is a concept that is easy to explain and difficult to avoid. Imagine that you are walking down the sidewalk. Someone is in your way, so you swerve to your left. To avoid you, they swerve to their right. You are now face to face. So this time, you swerve to your right. They go left. This goes on forever. This is deadlock.

The solution to this predicament is pretty simple for humans—someone finally figures it out. You go left, they go left, and off you go. If we could bottle the human brain and have it mediate computer deadlock situations, we would have some solutions. Our current state of the art has not reached that caliber of design yet.

So how does this affect your Java programming? Replace the humans on the sidewalk with threads. Let's say we have two protected resources, file1 and file2. Suppose a thread needs both resources to complete its task. Thread1 grabs file1 for itself. At the same time, thread2 grabs file2. Thread1 now goes for file2, but can't get it, so it sits and waits. Thread2 tries to get file1, and it waits, too. Now we have two threads waiting for resources they will never get. Since neither thread can get both files, they will wait indefinitely—classic case of deadlock.

We can handle deadlock in two ways. The quote "an ounce of prevention is worth a pound of cure" applies here. Anything we can do to avoid the situation is best. We need to design our threads to be smart about how they grab multiple resources. Let's have each thread try for file1 first. Thread1 would get file1, and thread2 would then wait for it. Thread1 can then get file2, do its operation, and free both resources. In this case, the solution is simple.

Some cases of deadlock can not be avoided so simply. In fact, some cases of deadlock are so difficult to avoid that it is sometimes better to deal with deadlock in a different manner—by trying to detect it. We might have a thread that watches other threads; if it seems that no progress is being made, it tries to fix the problem. Fixing the problem generally involves forcing one or more threads to give up protected resources. The newly freed resources may allow a thread to finish its operation and give up its resources. This may unstick the system and cure the deadlock.

If all of this sounds complicated, it's because it is. If you're going to experiment with multiple resources, be prepared to read some textbooks. Let us offer one piece of advice: avoid having to lock multiple resources. This is where the problem starts. The more resources each thread needs, the harder the problem becomes.

Volatile Variables

Our final topic in this chapter is the variable modifier *volatile*, which most programmers will not encounter. Let's look at the official definition in the *Java Language Specification* and then try to make sense of it: "A variable declared volatile is known to be modified asynchronously. The compiler arranges to use such variables carefully." To understand the use of the adverb "carefully" in this definition, you need to have a good understanding of the Java virtual machine. What it basically means is that the variable will be reloaded for every reference. Java does some fancy variable caching for multiple threads, and the volatile modifier tells the Java machine to stop that.

What is a volatile variable? Imagine you have a variable that is not really a memory location, but actually a changing value. A common example would be the carrier detect signal from your modem. This signal is on when you are connected. Since this variable is changed by an external source, it is considered volatile. This value might change in between two operations, which could cause bugs in some situations, so we want the compiler to reload the value every time we access it.

Unless you are using native methods and accessing hardware registers or other changing data values,you will probably never need to specify a variable as volatile. Java code can not directly access a memory location, so this particular need for the volatile variable will occur infrequently.

Moving On

You should now be comfortable dealing with threads in Java. At this point in the book, we've covered some of the most complex issues surrounding Java coding. In the next chapter, we discuss how to create Java programs that overcome some of the limitations of applets. Though the programs we'll develop aren't as portable as applets, you will be able to access the file system and integrate C code into your programs.

12

Programming Beyond the Applet Model

So far, our focus has been on writing applets. Since they must run safely on the host machine, they have certain limitations. In this chapter, we look at ways to move beyond the applet model.

There are two good ways to do this. The simplest way is to write stand-alone Java applications. They're like other programs on your desktop and are allowed to access the file system. A more advanced way is through the use of native methods. Native methods let us integrate Dynamic Linked Libraries (DLLs), which are platform specific. With DLLs, we can use preexisting C libraries to enhance our Java programs. Since Netscape Navigator 2.0 allows us to link to DLLs at runtime, we can also use them to enhance our applets. Of course, we need to get the DLLs to the host *before* the applet downloads. But in many cases, we can expect that people would trouble themselves to acquire our DLLs just as they do traditional software.

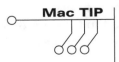

Mac TIP

Note that, at the time of this printing, the JDK for Macintosh allows the creation of applets, but not stand-alone applications. If you develop on a Macintosh, this chapter is currently irrelevant to you. As the development environment becomes more robust, we will keep you up-to-date via the Online Companion.

From Applets to Stand-alone Applications

Now that we know the ins and outs of building Java packages, we can reuse code for different applets. We can also use our packages with Java applications that don't need a Web browser to run. You have already developed Graphical User Interfaces (GUIs) for your applets as described in Chapter 7, "Basic User Interface." Now let's see how to create the same GUIs in stand-alone applications and how to use your existing applets in your new stand-alone applications.

The applications we develop here are more traditional programs. We escape the restrictions of the applet model, but we also forego its advantages. Our users have to download or otherwise acquire our applications, and the worries about harm to their computer come back into play.

Security issues have to be considered when deciding whether to develop an applet or an application. But before we start making these transitions, we will talk about how to make your GUIs work without the help of a Web browser's runtime environment.

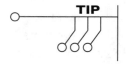

TIP

This chapter's code example files can be found on the Companion CD-ROM (for Windows 95/NT and Macintosh users) and the Online Companion (for UNIX users). Visit the Online Companion at http://www.vmedia.com/java.html.

The Basics of Graphical Java Applications

To create a stand-alone application, all you need to do is have a main method defined in a class. Then, when you run the Java interpreter on that class, it will call the main method. This is what we did for our simple Hello World example in Chapter 2, "Java Programming Basics." Of course, that example wasn't very pretty—we didn't use any of the widgets discussed in Chapter 8, "Advanced User Interface," nor were we able to use the mouse.

It isn't hard to make our stand-alone applications as user-friendly and graphical as the applets we discussed in Chapter 8. All we have to do is create a frame, either directly in our main method or in one of the methods that is called by the main method. The program below uses the Frame2 developed in Chapter 8. Instead of being shown by the applet, the Frame2 is shown as part of our stand-alone application, sampleStand:

```
import java.awt.*;
import Frame2;

class standAlone {

    public static void main(String S[]) {
        Frame2 f2=new Frame2();
        f2.show();}
}
```

We discussed the Abstract Windowing Toolkit (AWT) in Chapters 7 and 8. What you've already learned about the AWT is almost sufficient to write graphical stand-alone applications. By subclassing the Applet class, we are able to get images and audio data from the Internet. Unfortunately, there isn't any way to get and play audio data for our stand-alone applications without implementing native methods ourselves. We can get image data across the Internet using the Toolkit class.

The Toolkit class is an abstract class that, by and large, is the glue between the AWT and the local windowing system. Most of the methods defined in it are of little use to us because they are only used in binding the AWT to our particular platform. However, it is valuable to us in that it defines a getImage method that works just like the one we are used to. In order to get images from within our stand-alone application, we can use the following code within any frame subclass where U is a valid URL:

```
Toolkit T=getToolkit();
Image I=T.getImage(U);
```

With the exception of playing audio, we can now do everything with our stand-alone applications that we can do with our applets. Since our Java application isn't some applet of questionable repute, we can also access the local file system. For instance, we can use the overloaded getImage method to fetch our image data directly from the file system by passing it a String describing the path to the file:

```
String S="myImage.gif";
Toolkit T=getToolkit();
Image I=T.getImage(S);
```

As with our previous experience with the getToolkit method, we need to use this within a component subclass. Our getImage method will look for the myImage.gif file in the current directory on the local file system.

The FileDialog class in the java.awt package instantiates into a dialog box that allows the user to browse the file system. This class is off-limits to applets, which have no business accessing the host file system onto which they were downloaded. But since our stand-alone applications are trustworthy enough to be installed on the host computer, we can program with the FileDialog class now. Its methods and constructors are outlined in Table 12-1.

Member	Description
final static int LOAD	The mode variable that sets this file dialog to read files.
final static int SAVE	The mode variable that sets this file dialog to save files.
FileDialog(Frame parent, String title)	Creates an instance with the default mode.
FileDialog(Frame parent, String title, int mode)	Same as FileDialog(Frame parent, String title), but with the specified mode.
int getMode()	Gets the mode of this dialog.
void setDirectory(String dir)	Sets the directory of the dialog.
void setFile(String file)	Sets default file for dialog if called before dialog is shown.

Member	Description
String getFile()	Gets the name of the file specified.
String getDirectory()	Gets the name of the directory of the dialog.
String paramString()	Overrides paramString inDialog.
FilenameFilter setFilenameFilter()	Sets the filename filter.
FilenameFilter getFilenameFilter()	Gets the filename filter.

Table 12-1: *FileDialog class.*

Using the FileDialog class is pretty simple—all it does is present the user with the standard dialog box for browsing files for a particular platform, as shown in Figure 12-1. When that task is completed, we use the getFile method to get the name of the file and the getDirectory method to get the path to the file. The file dialog does not actually manipulate the file system directly; it only makes available the choices that the user made.

We can affect the appearance and functionality of the dialog box in a few ways. We are required to set some sort of title for our file dialog when we construct it. We can also choose whether or not to have a Save button or an Open button for the dialog box; this is done by setting the mode in the FileDialog(Frame parent, String title, int mode) constructor. Notice that this is mainly cosmetic, since the FileDialog class does nothing to actually change files. Of course, it would be rather user-unfriendly to set the mode to FileDialog.LOAD and then overwrite the file later on! Since this is the default, we want to explicitly set the mode to FileDialog.SAVE when we do intend to use the user's choice in creating a file or a directory. Setting the mode to FileDialog.SAVE will also protect the user from overwriting existing files. The dialog box itself will spawn an alert dialog box if the user chooses a file that already exists—our application doesn't have to worry about it. The following two methods show how to use the FileDialog class in either of the two modes. Since we pass these methods their parent Frame, they can be in any class we want:

```
public String fileToWrite(Frame parent, String title) {
  FileDialog fD=new FileDialog(parent,title,FileDialog.SAVE);
  if (!parent.isVisible()) parent.show();
  fd.show();
  //execution will stop here until user
  //makes a selection
  String path=fD.getDirectory()+fd.getFile();
  return path;}

public String fileToOpen(Frame parent, String title) {
  FileDialog fD=new FileDialog(parent,title);
  //since SAVE is the default mode, don't
  //need to set it
  if (!parent.isVisible()) parent.show();
  fd.show();
  //execution will stop here until user
  //makes a selection
  String path=fd.getDirectory()+fd.getFile();
  return path;}
```

Notice that we check to see if the parent Frame is visible — as with all dialog boxes, the parent Frame needs to be active before we attempt to show it. Since the FileDialog is a modal dialog box, execution will stop after the dialog is shown and will continue after the user makes a choice.

Besides setting the mode, we can also alter the behavior of our dialog box by setting the FilenameFilter before our FileDialog is shown. By implementing the interface in some class and then passing the class to the FileDialog with setFilenameFilter, we can limit the choice of Files that the FileDialog displays to the user. A common use for the FilenameFilter would be to only display certain types of files, such as HTML files, or to only display files after a certain date. To implement FilenameFilter, we only have to override one method, as shown below:

```
class FilenameFilterWrapper implements FilenameFilter {
//variables, constructors
  public boolean accept(File dir, String name) {
  //decide whether to accept or not.}
}
```

As you can see, we are passed a File object in that one method, and we don't know what the File class is yet. After you learn about the File class, you'll understand how to use the FilenameFilter to filter files according to substrings of the filename, readability and writablity, and the date last modified.

Accessing the File System

We just saw that the FileDialog box can be used to let our users browse the file system. But it doesn't help us to actually access the file they choose. To access the file system, we can use two classes in the java.io package, File and RandomAccessFile.

FILE STREAMS & THE FILE SYSTEM

If you have been browsing the online documentation on the Online Companion, you may have noticed the FileInputStream and FileOutputStream classes. To use them, you will need to understand the basics of their superclasses—InputStream and OutputStream respectively. These will be covered in Chapter 13, "Networking With Sockets & Streams."

The first step in understanding these classes is to avoid being misled by their names. The File class is an abstraction of both files and directories. It is the class we use for file management tasks, such as making sure a given file exists, deleting files, creating new directories, and navigating up and down the directory structure. The RandomAccessFile class, on the other hand, is the class we use to actually read and write files. Think of the File class as the Navy and the RandomAccessFile class as the Marines—one provides the transportation while the other is used to get the job done.

The File Class

Let's first look at the File class and its very important static variables. The static variables are useful in resolving a very superficial variant of different file systems—different file and path separators. The methods and constructors of this class assume that they are passed Strings that adhere to the conventions of the host file system, so it is important that you use these variables when you create file names. Table 12-2 lists the file and path separators with their UNIX and Windows 95/NT values.

Variable	Meaning	UNIX Value	Windows 95/ NT Value
String separator	File separator for the host system.	/	\
String pathSeparator	Path separator for the host system.	:	;
char separatorChar	File separator as a character.	/	\
char pathSeparatorChar	Path separator as a character.	:	;

Table 12-2: *File and path separators.*

Though character representations are available, it is safer to use the String representations listed first. The FileDialog class mentioned previously is guaranteed to return a correct representation for the system. With these variables in mind, we can instantiate a File object with the constructors listed in Table 12-3. As we said before, the File object we create can refer to either a directory or a regular old file.

Constructor	Description
File(String path)	Creates a file object based on path; can be either a directory or a file.
File(String dir, String fileName)	Creates a file object representing the file fileName in dir.
File(File dir, String fileName)	Creates a file object representing the file fileName in dir.

Table 12-3: *File constructors.*

You may be wondering why there is a single class to deal with both directories and files. On the operating system level, a directory is often just a special file that contains information about what we think of as "normal" files. Beyond this implementation detail, they have many practical similarities, as the methods in Table 12-4 show. These methods are equally applicable to directories or files.

Method	Description
boolean exists()	Returns true if file or directory exists.
String getPath()	Returns path the file object was constructed with.
boolean isAbsolute()	Returns true if creation path is absolute.
String getAbsolutePath()	Returns absolute path.
String getParent()	Returns absolute path of Parent directory; returns null if at top of hierarchy or if Parent isn't accessible.
public boolean delete()	Tries to remove the file or directory, and returns true if successful.
public boolean renameTo(File dest)	Tries to rename the file or directory to dest, and returns true if successful.
public boolean equals(Object o)	Compares for equality with other Java objects.
public int hashCode()	Allows files to be stored in java.util.Hashtable.

Table 12-4: *General file methods.*

Although throwing files and directories into the same basket affords some elegance, there are differences between the two. Tables 12-5 and 12-6 outline the remaining methods that apply more specifically to directories and files, respectively.

Method	Description
public boolean mkdir()	Tries to create a directory, returning true if successful.
public String[] list()	Lists the files in the directory, other than the current and containing directory.
public String[] list(FilenameFilter filter)	Lists the files in the directory applying the input filter.

Table 12-5: *Directory-specific file methods.*

Method	Description
boolean canWrite()	Returns true if a writable file exists.
boolean canRead()	Returns true if a readable file exists.
long lastModified()	Returns the system assigned modification time.
long length()	Returns length of the file.

Table 12-6: *File-specific file methods.*

Usually, we use the FileDialog class to ask the user what file or directory in the file system they would like to deal with. If our program lets the user manipulate the file system—for instance, to make directories, delete directories or files, or move directories or files—then we would create a File class and use the appropriate methods to manipulate the file system. If we are concerned with the data inside the chosen file, we will use the File class to make sure the file is valid and then create a RandomAccessFile class to manipulate the data. Such checks should include making sure the file is readable and/or writable. In some cases, we may also be concerned with the last modification date of the file.

RandomAccessFile Class

Although we can get basic information about a file, such as when it was modified or how big it is, we still aren't able to read it or write to it. To do that, we need the RandomAccessFile class. This class allows us to read from the file directly into Java arrays, Strings, and primitive types. We are able to write data out to the file in the reverse manner.

We can construct the RandomAccessFile with either a File object or a String describing the path to the file. When we construct it, we need to say whether we want it to be read only or read/write. The file is opened for reading and/or writing upon instantiation of the RandomAccessFile object. Once opened, the most straight-forward way to read or write data is either byte by byte or line by line. The basic methods and constructors for file handling are described in Table 12-7. Like all of the methods in the File class, each throws the IOException.

Method	Description
RandomAccessFile(String path, String mode)	Constructs based on path with specified mode; "r" for read only, "rw" for read/write.
RandomAccessFile(File f, String mode)	Constructs based on File object with specified mode.
void close()	Closes the file.
public long getFilePointer()	Returns the location of the file pointer; distance in bytes from the start of the file.
public int read()	Reads a byte of data, or -1 if at the end of the file.
public String readLine()	Returns a String starting at the current location of the file pointer and ending at '\n' or the end of the file.
public int read(byte b[])	Reads file into the array of bytes, returning number of bytes read.
public int read(byte b[], int shift, int len)	Shifts the file pointer and reads len bytes.

Method	Description
public int skipBytes(int n)	Shifts the file pointer *n* bytes forward in the file, or to the end of file.
public void seek(long pos)	Sets the file pointer to pos bytes after the start of the file.
public void write(int b)	Writes the int to the file, first casting to a byte.
public void write(byte b[])	Writes the array of bytes.

Table 12-7: *Simple File Input/Output methods.*

Native Methods

Right up front, we need to be clear about what integrated C libraries cannot be used for. We cannot integrate just any C library into an applet, send it across the Internet, and have it use functionality contained in that library on the client side. If that option were available to us, we would have covered it much, much earlier in the book!

The C library must reside where ever the code is actually run. We actually wrap our C code into a Java class and then call the C functions through the Java class. The C functions make up a Dynamic Linked Library(DLL) and are accessed with native methods.

WATCH FOR CHANGING STANDARDS!
The following pages describe the native method interface for the JDK 1.0. However, the native method interface for Java is going to be changed in a future release of Java. Don't expect that native libraries you create today will work with future versions of Java. For information about the current state of the native method interface, consult the Online Companion.

When to Use Native Libraries

Using a DLL is preferable when writing stand-alone applications. Since C is an enormously popular language, you can often find C libraries that can accomplish whatever it is you want to do. This eliminates your need to completely rewrite everything in Java— you can access the DLL instead.

Applet writers can still benefit from DLLs, but not as profoundly as those writing stand-alone applications. Since the C programming language isn't platform independent, DLLs can't be sent across the Internet; if they could, sooner or later they would land on a platform that they couldn't run on. Using DLLs would also raise questions about the safety of applets, since C wasn't designed to be a safe language for distributed computing.

However, some Java-capable Web browsers allow an Applet to use any libraries that have been installed beforehand on the client side. What does this mean to the Applet writer? If you are running an intranet at your organization, you can see to it that a simple C library can be installed on the client side, and you can ensure that it doesn't have a virus and that it can't be misused. You can then allow your applets to do some of the things you don't want just any applet doing, such as accessing the local file system.

If shrink-wrapped software is your game, you can distribute CDs that contain DLLs or give out a code to download the software from the Internet. After your DLL is checked for viruses, it can be installed so that the Java-capable Web browser can find it. Your library can overcome the limitations of the basic Applet model while still benefiting from the connectivity of a Java-capable Web browser. For example, you can use a DLL to connect your spreadsheet program directly to an Applet connected to a stock price server. Or, you can make your Internet games faster by providing graphics on the client side that can be accessed via your DLL. Then, you can use the networking features of Java purely for communication and not for downloading weighty resources.

TO LINK OR NOT TO LINK: YOUR WEB BROWSER'S DECISION

Our discussion of native libraries assumes that your Java-capable Web browser allows DLLs to be linked into the runtime environment. Netscape Communications Corporation has decided to allow this in its Java-capable Web browsers—unfortunately, Netscape has not announced how developers can link DLLs at the time of this writing. For current information, please point your browser to http://www.vmedia.com/olc/java/updates/native.html

So, DLLs can be useful to Internet application development. Before we get down to the nitty-gritty of building DLLs, we need to examine the importance of DLLs to the runtime environment of Java. Java is platform independent, but there still has to be some kind of link to the underlying operating system. That link is provided by DLLs that are linked into the API. They play a significant role regarding what the runtime environment will allow some bit of Java code to do. Since DLLs are not platform independent, they are the crucial player when Java as a whole is ported to new platforms. When we examine building Java packages later in this chapter, we look at how the API is structured to ease porting and allow differently shaped runtime environments.

Native Methods Explained

Java is a platform-independent language, but Java code has to actually deal with the platform it is running on during the program execution. The same Java code can draw images on many different platforms, though each platform is fundamentally different in how it deals with graphics. For all low level input-output activities, including keyboard and mouse input, graphical display, audio output, and networking, Java must make platform-*dependent* calls to the operating system. The implementation of these platform-dependent calls are made through Dynamic Linked Libraries, which are part of the runtime environment.

The Java language isolates its platform-dependent calls cleanly with the *native* keyword. Whenever you see the native keyword, it means that the functionality of the associated method is written in another language and a DLL must be loaded at runtime for that method to be called. Currently, the only "other language" that DLLs can be written in is C. Since C++ is a complete superset of C, it is technically feasible to use C++ to write DLLs. Unfortunately, you will have to use straight C to glue your C++ code to your Java code. The problems will be apparent when we actually get down to creating DLLs.

In most ways, native methods are exactly like other methods. Surprisingly, this includes taking Java objects as parameters, returning Java objects, and throwing exceptions. There are two very notable differences. First, native methods contain no body, and they are forbidden by the compiler from having one:

```
public native String getUserName();
```

Native methods gain their functionality from one particular
DLL loaded at runtime, and this is our second difference. The DLL
must be loaded when the class that contains a native method is
instantiated. Here, we have defined a native wrapper class that
loads a DLL named profile. The purpose of this class is to allow
Applets to read a file on the client's machine that contains information about the user. We have created two exception classes,
NoProfileException and ProfileWriteUnallowedException, which
are written in Java. These classes are defined on the CD-ROM.

Example 12-1: LocalProfile class.

```java
import java.awt.Color;

class LocalProfile {

   private int CfilePointer=0;

   public LocalProfile() throws UnsatisfiedLinkError,
   NoProfileException {

      try {System.loadLibrary("profile");
         }
      catch (UnsatisfiedLinkError e) {
         throw(e);}

      //openProfile should throw the exception
      //directly, but this will makes for an
      //easier example when we write the DLL

      CfilePointer=openProfile();

      if (CfilePointer==0)
         throw new NoProfileException();
      }

   private native int openProfile();

   public native void setPublicKey(byte pubKey[]);
```

```
public native String getAttrib(String key);
//reads a String from the Profile file on the host

public native Color getFavoriteColor();
//by looking at the Profile file, creates an
//instance of the user's favorite color

public synchronized native void setAttrib(String key,
String value) throws ProfileWriteUnAllowedException;

//writes to the Profile file on the host, if allowed

}
```

When this class is instantiated, the profile DLL is loaded. Any DLL is only accessible through the native methods declared in its wrapper class, and it must be loaded before those methods are called. Each native method corresponds to a C function contained in the DLL. When a native method is called, that C function is called instead. Of course, the DLL can have as many functions as we want it to have, but they can only be called indirectly. However, any function in the DLL can both construct new Java objects and manipulate current ones—including calling public methods! As it is implied in our code example, this capability also extends to throwing exceptions.

The intent of native methods is to act like any other Java method. The same is basically true for classes containing Java methods, but some nuances do come into play. Most stem from having to make sure the library gets loaded. For our example, this is especially important. If we write an applet that includes our class and it lands at a client that doesn't have a DLL, we would want our applet to recover. We guarantee this by loading it in the constructor and rethrowing the UnsatisfiedLinkError.

The requirement to load the library also causes problems with static methods. In any other case, all of our methods would be declared static. But if we declared all of them static, the constructor wouldn't be called and the library wouldn't be loaded. We can circumvent this by loading the library in a static block:

```
class LocalProfile {

//variable declarations

    static {
        try {System.loadLibrary("profile");}
            catch (UnsatisfiedLinkError e) {
            //deal with error}
            }
    //static methods
}
```

However, loading the library in a static block makes it difficult to recover from the UnsatisfiedLinkError. In many cases, it won't matter. If the purpose of your Applet or Application is to do high speed graphics rendering and it uses native code to do this, you're pretty much dead in the water if you can't load the library. In such a case, a polite exit is probably the best you can do.

Preparing the C Library

Once we define the methods that we want to use in a native wrapper class, we're free to compile the Java code. Since the library is loaded at runtime, the compiler doesn't need to know anything about the library itself. Of course, before we use the DLL, we need to write and compile it in such a way that it can be loaded.

Before we get into this, be forewarned: creating a DLL that interfaces with Java code is quite like playing Twister. If you're among those who find the C preprocessor to be intricate and beautiful, this section will whet your appetite for the mysteries of the java/include/*.h files. Otherwise, you should just think of this section as a recipe. The key ingredient is a program called *javah*. Javah is a tool that creates a couple of special files that provide definitions of our native methods and Java data types. Before javah can do its magic, the class containing the native methods needs to be compiled—this is our first step. We use javac to compile it just like any other class.

Our second step is to use javah to make a header file for our class. For our LocalProfile class, we would type the following at the command prompt:

javah LocalProfile

Javah looks at the file LocalProfile.class and produces C declarations for the native methods *and* other members of our LocalProfile class. It dumps these into a .h file; in this case, LocalProfile.h. This step actually produced something that we'll need to look at when we write our DLL. Our next step does not, and it is the most magical step in our process. Now that we have a header file, we need to create a .c file that will be incorporated into our library. This file represents the runtime glue between the DLL and the Java code. We create this file with the following command:

javah -stubs LocalProfile

This command creates a file called LocalProfile.c.—a file that is either very ugly or fascinating, depending on what breed of hacker you are. Either way, we never have to look at this file again. Unlike LocalProfile.h, it contains no information that we are going to need later.

This concludes the first part of our game of Twister; we can now start actually writing the DLL. Here is a summary of the magical incantations we need to chant before we begin coding in C:

- Use javac to compile the .java file containing native methods.

- Use javah to create a .h file that provides declarations for the native wrapper class.

- Use javah -stubs to make a .c file that provides the runtime glue.

Before we move on, let's examine javah a little more closely. First, you can give it multiple arguments. If you have written several classes that intend to load the same DLL, compile all of them and then list them all after javah and javah -stubs. Also, you can give it several command line options to help you out. Any combination of the options described in Table 12-8 should be given before the Java class names.

Option	Description
-o *outputfile*	Pushes output to *outputfile* instead of the default.
-d *directory*	Saves files to *directory* instead of the current directory.
-td *tempdirectory*	Saves temporary files to *tempdirectory* instead of the default, /temp.
-classpath *classpath*	Looks for the API's .class files in the directory *classpath* instead of /usr/local/java or the environment variable CLASSPATH if set.
-verbose	Causes javah to print to the screen details about its actions.

Table 12-8: *Javah options.*

Now we're ready to actually write our Dynamic Linked Library. But before we start writing functionality, we need to get some formalities out of the way. First, we have to name our .c file. We can't name it LocalProfile.c, because javah -stubs generated a file of that name. The name is arbitrary, but just to be sane about it, we will name it profile.c. The next step is to do our preprocessor declarations, as shown below:

```
#include <StubPreamble.h>
#include <javaString.h>

#include "LocalProfile.h"
```

These header files are needed to translate C data structures to Java types. The header, javaString.h, gives us some special functionality for dealing with Java Strings. Next, we need to include whichever C header files our DLL needs for this particular system. This will vary from DLL to DLL and from platform to platform. Here are the ones we need for our profile library:

```
#include <sys/types.h>
#include <sys/param.h>
#include <stdio.h>
#include <fcntl.h>
#include <errno.h>
```

The following list is a summary of the steps we have just gone through:

1. Write and compile the Java class.
2. Run javah on the compiled class.
3. Run javah -stubs on the compiled class.
4. Implement the native methods in C, which we explain in the next section.

Implementing Native Methods in C

Now that we have the formalities out of the way, we can start implementing the native functionality. Since native methods are supposed to act just like other methods, our main difficulty is making C functions act as member methods of our native wrapper class. Many of the mysteries of doing this are revealed by looking at the LocalProfile.h file:

Example 12-2: LocalProfile.h.

```
/* DO NOT EDIT THIS FILE - it is machine generated */
#include <native.h>
/* Header for class LocalProfile */

#ifndef _Included_LocalProfile
#define _Included_LocalProfile

typedef struct ClassLocalProfile {
    long CfilePointer;
} ClassLocalProfile;
HandleTo(LocalProfile);

extern long LocalProfile_openProfile(struct HLocalProfile *);

extern void LocalProfile_setPublicKey(struct HLocalProfile
*,HArrayOfByte *);

struct Hjava_lang_String;
```

```
extern struct Hjava_lang_String
*LocalProfile_getAttrib(struct HLocalProfile *,struct
Hjava_lang_String *);

extern struct Hjava_lang_Color
*LocalProfile_favoriteColor(struct HLocalProfile *);

extern struct Hjava_lang_String
*LocalProfile_setAttrib(struct HLocalProfile *,struct
Hjava_lang_String *,struct Hjava_lang_String *);
#endif
```

The first struct is a C representation of the Java class. Remember that native methods behave like other methods and therefore can access private members of the class containing them. The struct, "ClassLocalProfile", makes this possible. Notice that this struct is passed to all of our functions, in addition to the parameters the equivalent Java native method takes. This ensures proper data hiding while still allowing our C functions to be true members of our class.

Following the struct are the C function declarations for our native methods. Simply stated, writing our DLL is just defining these functions. But to do this, the differences between Java and C must be resolved:

- Our Java types have to be converted to valid C types.

- We need to be able to access other members of the class from the DLL.

- We need mechanisms to make Java arrays in C.

- We must be able to create Java objects from the DLL and access public member methods and variables of existing Java objects.

- We need to throw exceptions from the DLL.

Our example covers all of these cases. We start with the simplest functions and move toward the ones that are most complicated to implement in C. Our two private native methods, validProfile and openProfile, are the easiest to implement because they require only that we know how to translate Java primitive types to C types. Table 12-9 outlines how to do these translations.

Java Primitive Type	C Equivalent
boolean	long
char	unicode
byte	char
short	short
int	long
long	int64_t
float	float
double	double

Table 12-9: *Translating Java primitive types to C types.*

With the translations from Java primitive types to C revealed, we can make short work of LocalProfile_openProfile. This method simply opens the file described by the environment variable, APPLETPROFILE:

```
long LocalProfile_openProfile(struct HLocalProfile *this) {
char profileName[1024];
strcpy(profileName,getenv("APPLETPROFILE"));
return (long) fopen(profileName,"r");}
```

You'll remember that this private method will be used to assign value to the private variable CFilePointer. Since our other native methods will use this file, it makes sense to store it as part of the object. When we need to access it, we do so through the struct HLocalProfile pointer that is passed to each native method implementation. Whenever we compile a native wrapper class, a struct is generated. The name begins with an H, followed by the name of the class.

Don't worry, we don't have to go through this struct to access members of the native wrapper instance. To access method members, we can use the execute_dynamic_method function. This function can be used both for the native wrapper instance and other instances—we'll discuss this shortly. What concerns us now is accessing the data members of the native wrapper instance. To access the CFilePointer variable in LocalProfile, we use the un-hand macro, as shown below:

Example 12-3: Simple native method implementations.

```
long LocalProfile_getAttrib(struct HLocalProfile *this,
HJava_lang_String *key) {
FILE *profile=(FILE *)unhand(this)->CFilePointer;
/*Rest of function */
}
```

To actually implement the rest of these functions, we need to understand how to deal with Java arrays and Strings in C. We cover these in the next section.

Java Arrays & Strings in C

Since we often need to represent arrays and Strings within our DLLs, the java/include/*.h files give us lots of tools for dealing with them. Let's start with Strings and our LocalProfile_getAttrib function. This function is going to look at our profile file as if it were a hashtable. It will look for a line of the form key=value, where key is the String that has been passed to us. If it can't find the key, it will return null. Otherwise, it will return the string starting just past the = character and ending at the first white space encountered.

To accomplish this, we first need to establish an array of characters that represents our Java string. If we find our value, we need to translate it from our array of characters to a Hjava_lang_String struct, which the runtime environment will convert to a String. The functions that do this are described in Table 12-10, along with several others that are available to us.

Function	Description
void javaString2CString(Hjava_lang_String *jString,char *buf,int size)	Converts jString to character array buf, with last parameter specifying length.
char *makeCString(Hjava_lang_String *jString)	Returns a character array based on jString that will be garbage collected by the runtime system.
char *allocCString(Hjava_lang_String *jString)	Like makeCString, except malloc is used and you are responsible for de-allocating the memory.
int javaStringLength(Hjava_lang_String *jString)	Returns length of jString.
Hjava_lang_String *makeJavaString(char *s, int size)	Makes a C representation of a Java String based on the array s, with last parameter specifing length.
void javaString2unicode(Hjava_lang_String *jString,unicode *buf,int size)	Converts jString to unicode array buf, with last parameter specifing size.

Table 12-10: *Java string-manipulation functions.*

Now we can write our LocalProfile_getAttrib function.

Example 12-4: Using Java Strings in C.

```
struct Hjava_lang_String * LocalProfile_getAttrib(struct
HLocalProfile *this, Hjava_lang_String *key) {
char Ckey[1024];
char Cvalue[1024];

Hjava_lang_String *JValue;
FILE *profile=(FILE *)unhand(this)->CfilePointer;
int keyLength=javaStringLength(key);

javaString2CString(key,Ckey,keyLength);
strcat(Ckey,"=%s");

rewind(profile);
```

```
if (fscanf(profile,Ckey,Cvalue)!=EOF) {

return makeJavaString(Cvalue,strlen(Cvalue));
}
else {
  return NULL;}
}
```

In Example 12-4, we were able to resolve the differences between Java Strings and C strings. Now let's move on and look at the functions that make Java Arrays and C arrays compatible. While the members of C arrays are simply an ordered set of pointers, Java Arrays are ordered sets of a specified data type. We can't simply create a C array and expect that our Java code will know what to do with it. We need to specify what kind of Java Array we are trying to declare within our library. Table 12-11 describes this information for primitive types. We'll cover objects when we understand how to create them. The second column represents a predefined struct that represents the array type. As before, we can use the unhand macro to access the data portion of the array. The third column gives a constant that describes that type. We pass that constant to the ArrayAlloc macro so that space is properly allocated.

Java Array	C Representation	Type Signature
boolean[]	HArrayOfInt *	T_BOOLEAN
byte[]	HArrayOfByte *	T_BYTE
char[]	HArrayOfChar *	T_CHAR
short[]	HArrayOfShort *	T_SHORT
int[]	HArrayOfInt *	T_INT
long[]	HArrayOfLong *	T_LONG
float[]	HArrayOfFloat *	T_FLOAT
double[]	HArrayOfDouble *	T_DOUBLE
Object[]	HArrayOfObject *	T_CLASS

Table 12-11: *Primitive Java arrays in C.*

When we want to create a Java array, we use the ArrayAlloc function, which is passed two parameters. The first parameter describes the type of array, which is described in our second column. The second parameter is the size of the array we want. Then, we use the unhand macro once again to actually access the data portion of the array. The following code fragment creates an array of bytes of size 10 and assigns it the values 0 through 9. Remember that a Java byte is a C char, and thus we must cast to char when assigning:

```
HArrayOfByte *bytes=ArrayAlloc(T_BYTE,10);
for (int i=0;i<10;i++) {
unhand(bytes)->data[i]=(char)i;}
```

Now we can proceed to write our LocalProfile_getPubKey() function. We use an environment variable, APPLETPUBKEY, to tell us where the file is, and the stat library function to give us the size. If the file can't be found, we return null:

Example 12-5: Java Arrays in C.

```
HArrayOfByte *LocalProfile_getPubKey(struct HLocalProfile
*this) {
    int i;
    FILE *pubKeyFile=NULL;
    char pubKeyFileName[1024];
    char *buf=NULL;
    HArrayOfByte *pubKey=NULL;
    int counter=0;
    strcpy(pubKeyFileName,getenv("APPLETPUBKEY"));
    pubKeyFile=fopen(pubKeyFileName,"r");

    if (pubKeyFile==NULL) return NULL;

    pubKey=(HArrayOfByte *)ArrayAlloc(T_BYTE,256);
        buf=unhand(pubKey)->body;
    while (!feof(pubKeyFile) && counter<256) {
    buf[counter] = (char)fgetc(pubKeyFile);
    counter++;}
  return pubKey;}
```

Creating & Manipulating Java Objects

Now that we have a feeling for dealing with primitive types, we can start creating Java objects from within our DLLs. This is the trickiest part of writing DLLs because it is where the differences between Java and C are exposed the most. Our problems are solved by the data structures and functions in Tables 12-12 and 12-13, respectively.

Structure	Description
ExecEnv	An execution environment. NULL represents the current environment, which is generally what we want.
ClassClass	A data structure that holds information about a Java class.
Signature	A C string that describes the parameters a constructor/method takes.

Table 12-12: *Utility data structures.*

Function	Description
Hobject *execute_java_constructor(ExecEnv *E, char *className,ClassClass *cb, char *signature,...)	Constructs an instance of className with parameter set described by signature.
ClassClass *FindClass(ExecEnv, char *className, bool_t resolve)	Returns a C representation of the Java class className.
long execute_java_static_method(ExecEnv *E, ClassClass *cb,char *methodName, char *signature,...)	Executes the static method methodName of the Java class described by cb.
long execute_java_dynamic_method(ExecEnv *E, HObject *obj,char *methodName,char *signature)	Executes a dynamic method of Java object represented by obj.

Table 12-13: *Utility functions.*

As you can see, it takes a lot of work to do in C what is very simple in Java. Table 12-13 shows us that we have to call different functions for constructors, static methods, and dynamic methods.

Of course, Java forces us to differentiate between the types of functionality also, but in Java it is much more elegant. Likewise, the Java runtime environment has to look at what the class definition actually consists of before creating it. It also has to make sure that the programmer isn't trying any trickery. When we are working in the DLL, we have to do this manually with the FindClass and the execute_java_constructor functions.

We also have to hack a bit to get our parameters to pass correctly. Since methods can be overloaded, we need to explicitly describe the parameter set that we wish to pass. Additionally, we need to describe the parameter types and return values so that the appropriate C representations will be built. This is where our signature string comes into play. Our utility functions look at the signature and figure out what to expect as parameters and what it should return. The signature consists of the keys defined in Table 12-14 and inner and outer parentheses that contain the parameters.

Key	Java Type
Z	boolean
B	byte
C	char
F	float
S	short
V	void
[	*array of any type*
L*;	*any Java object — * is replaced by classname*

Table 12-14: *Keys for Java signatures.*

The syntax of the signature is as follows:

```
(Parameter Keys) Return Key
```

A method that takes no parameters and returns nothing will have the signature ()V, for instance. Table 12-15 gives a few examples of how to use the signatures. Notice that you don't need to specify a return type for constructors. Assume that the class someClass is located in our working directory.

Constructor/Method	Signature
Hashtable	()
Integer(int j)	(I)
Integer(String S)	(Ljava/lang/String;)
String(char c[])	([C)
boolean S.beginsWith(String S1, int len)	(Ljava/lang/String;I)Z
someClass(Hashtable H)	(Ljava/util/Hashtable;)
someClass sC.reverse(someClass s)	(LsomeClass;)LsomeClass;

Table 12-15: *Example signatures.*

Now that we have an idea of how the signatures work, let's try using a dynamic method of the String class. The following function will compare to Strings using compareTo from within the DLL. Assume that "sample" is the name of our native wrapper class.

```
long sample_CbeginsWith(sample *this,Hjava_lang_String
*S1,Hjava_lang_String *S2,long len) {

char sig[]="(Ljava/lang/String;I)Z";
return execute_java_dynamic_method((ExecEnv
 *)NULL,(HObject *) S1,
 "beginsWith",sig,S2,len);}
```

We need to notice a couple of things about our parameters to execute_java_dynamic_method. First, we pass NULL as the first parameter. By passing NULL, execute_java_dynamic_method will use the current thread as the execution environment—almost always what we want. Our next parameter is the object that we want to use. By using S1, this native method is equivalent to S1.compareTo(S2). The next parameter is the name of the method. If the method doesn't exist or is static, this function will throw an exception. Next is the signature that we figure out from Table 12-15. Our next argument is the parameter that we want to pass, in this case, S2. Those of you who are advanced C programmers will have noticed from Table 12-13 that execute_java_dynamic_method is an elliptical function. This means that you can give it a variable number of arguments at the end. Since we are passing S2 and len, we just tack those on last. Of course, they should appear in the same order as the corresponding keys in the signature.

ExecEnv & the Execution Environment

If you really wanted to, you could pass a different Execution Environment, and your method would be run on other than the current thread. Before you start doing this, remember that you can access a given Java Thread as an object. In the long run, this will make your life easier. Simply access the Thread by passing it to your native method as a parameter.

We pass parameters to constructors, dynamic methods, and static methods in the same way—we provide a signature and tack the actual parameters to the end. Of course, with constructors and static methods, we can't provide a representation of the object since no object has been instantiated. Instead, the execute_java_constructor and the execute_java_static_method need information about the class.

The ClassClass data structure contains the information about what members a given class has and their attributes. The FindClass function will fetch this data into a ClassClass struct for us. We use it as follows for the java.awt.Color class:

```
ClassClass *cb;
cb=FindClass((ExecEnv *)NULL,"java/awt/Color",TRUE);
```

Again, we set the ExecEnv to null. Our last parameter tells the FindClass function to resolve the class with any superclasses that it might have. There is little reason not to do this. If we set it to false, we may not get all of our members!

Once we have a ClassClass pointer for some class, we can use the execute_java_static_method and execute_java_constructor functions. Using the execute_java_static_method function is pretty much the same as the execute_java_dynamic_method function. Here, we use it to turn a String into an int:

```
long sample_strToInt(Hsample *this, Hjava_lang_String *S) {

    ClassClass *cb;
    char sig[]="(Ljava/lang/String;)I";
    cb=FindClass((ExecEnv *)NULL,"java/lang/String",TRUE);
    return (long)
        execute_java_static_method((ExecEnv *)NULL,
        "parseInt",sig,S);}
```

Now we can return to the DLL that we have been building and implement the favoriteColor native method. This method returns a Color object, which means we have to create it in LocalProfile_favoriteColor. The constructor we are going to use is:

```
Color(int red, int green, int blue)
```

The red, green, and blue values are contained in our profile file. We are going to use a couple of functions within our DLL to help us out getting the values. Here is our native implementation:

Example 12-6: Java object construction in C.

```
struct Hjava_awt_Color *
LocalProfile_favoriteColor(HLocalProfile *this) {

    Hjava_lang_String *RedColorParam;
    Hjava_lang_String *BlueColorParam;
    Hjava_lang_String *GreenColorParam;
    long red; long green; long blue;

    char sig[]="(III)LHjava_awt_Color";
    char intSig[]="(LHjava_lang_String)I";
    ClassClass *Colorcb;
    ClassClass *Integercb;
```

```
Colorcb=FindClass((ExecEnv *)NULL,"java/lang/Color",TRUE);
Integercb=FindClass((ExecEnv *)NULL,"java/lang/
Integer",TRUE);

RedColorParam=LocalProfile_getAttrib(this,makeJavaString("red",3));
BlueColorParam=LocalProfile_getAttrib(this,makeJavaString("blue",4));
GreenColorParam=LocalProfile_getAttrib(this,makeJavaString("green",5));

red=(long) execute_java_static_method(
   (ExecEnv*)NULL, Integercb, "parseInt", intSig,
RedColorParam);
blue=(long)execute_java_static_method(
   (ExecEnv *)NULL, Integercb, "parseInt", intSig,
BlueColorParam);
green=(long) execute_java_static_method((ExecEnv  *) NULL,
Integercb, "parseInt", intSig, GreenColorParam);

return (struct Hjava_awt_Color*)
execute_java_constructor((ExecEnv *) NULL,
"Color",Colorcb, sig, red, green,blue);
}
```

Here, we just return our object as soon as we construct it. If we wanted, we could call its dynamic methods by assigning it to a struct Hjava_lang_Color pointer and then passing it to execute_java_dynamic_method.

CONSTRUCTION & GARBAGE COLLECTION
Garbage collection is done inside of a DLL. When you instanti-ate with execute_java_constructor, you need to cast and assign it to the appropriate struct pointer. This requirement also ap-plies to arrays. If you don't use ArrayAlloc, but use C arrays instead, the garbage collector doesn't know to hold on to the allocated memory.

Exception Throwing

We've just about covered everything that will allow native methods to behave just like other methods. With an understanding of how to throw exceptions, you will be able to seamlessly integrate your native methods with the rest of Java.

We use the SignalError function to throw exceptions from within the DLL. It takes the following arguments:

```
void SignalError(ExecEnv *e, char *ExceptionName,char
*description);
```

Now we can write the last function of our LocalProfile class, setAttrib. This method is going to read the attribute "write" from the profile file to see if writing is allowed. If it isn't, it will throw the exception:

Example 12-7: Exception throwing from the DLL.

```
void LocalProfile_setAttrib(struct HLocalProfile *this,
Hjava_lang_String * key, Hjava_lang_String * value) {

Hjava_lang_String *writeAllowed;

writeAllowed=LocalProfile_getAttrib(this,
   makeJavaString("write",5));
if (strcmp("yes",makeCString(writeAllowed))!=0) {
SignalError(0,      "profileWriteUnAllowedException", NULL);}
else {writeToProfile(this,key,value);}
   }
```

Compiling & Using the DLL

Now that we have written all of our code for our native methods, it's time to compile it. First, we cover how to do it for Windows 95/NT. You'll need Visual C++, Version 2.0 or higher, to compile the DLL. Simply go to the DOS prompt and type the following:

C:> cl LocalProfile.c profile.c -Feprofile.dll -MD -LD javai.lib

Then, add the placement of profile.dll to the LIB environment variable.

Solaris users should type the following, assuming that java resides in /usr/local/java:

cc -G -I/usr/local/java/include -I/usr/local/java/include/solaris LocalProfile.c profile.c -o libprofile.so

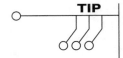

TIP

The third argument should be adjusted for different flavors of UNIX. Check the documentation for your JDK distribution for details.

Once you have the DLL compiled, you are ready to use the LocalProfile class in your programs. If you wish to use it with applets, the class and the DLL will have to be within the CLASSPATH on the local machine. Remember that the ability to link to a DLL will depend on whether or not the Java-capable Web browser will allow it.

Moving On

In this chapter, we've seen how to use Java to access the local file system and how to use native code. By moving away from the applet model, we can reduce our dependence on the Web as we develop Internet and intranet applications. In Section IV, "Java & the Network," we'll see how we can use the Internet to its fullest extent.

Java & the Network

13

Networking With Sockets & Streams

So far in the book, we've covered the essentials of working with the Java language itself, the many nifty packages included in the Java API, working with graphics and windows, and the underlying subtleties of Java's threads. It's now time to expand our scope somewhat and discuss the java.net package, which will allow you to extend your Java applets and programs to interact with other computers over networks.

Much of the current interest in Java can be attributed to the fact that two freely available Web browsers, Netscape and Hotjava, can load and execute Java applets over the Internet. Applets have a very close relationship to the Internet and to networks in general. Thus, it should come as no surprise that the Java API includes a rich package of network classes. Indeed, since applets are unable to load data from files on the local computer, they must turn to the network for storage and retrieval of data. The network classes provided by the API can be divided into two basic groups: classes dealing with sockets and classes dealing with URLs. We will discuss using sockets in this chapter and URLs in Chapter 14, "Networking With URLs."

Sockets don't implement a method for data transfer—instead, they create instances of more generic input/output classes, called *streams,* to handle that job. Sockets can be thought of as telephone connections. Extending that analogy, you can compare output streams to your voice and input streams to your listener's ears. The socket carries the data (your voice) across the network; the streams are responsible for putting the data into and pulling it out of the socket. Streams are useful in their own right, although you are unlikely to use a stream when programming applets except in association with a socket or in interapplet communication.

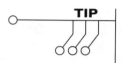

TIP

This chapter's code example files can be found on the Companion CD-ROM (for Windows 95/NT and Macintosh users) and on the Online Companion (for UNIX users). Visit the Online Companion at http://www.vmedia.com/java.html.

Sockets

The idea of a socket is integral to TCP/IP, the protocol suite used by the Internet. A socket is essentially a seamless data connection between two hosts in a network. It is identified by the network address of the computers at its endpoints and a port on each host. Networked computers route incoming streams of data from the network to specific receiving programs by associating each program to a different number, the program's port. Similarly, when outgoing traffic is generated, the originating program is assigned a port number for the transaction. Otherwise, the remote computer could not respond to the input. Certain port numbers are reserved in TCP/IP for specific protocols—for example, 25 for SMTP and 80 for HTTP. All port numbers below 1024 are reserved for the superuser of each host.

The Java API implements a class for handling socket communication, java.net.Socket. The constructors for the Socket class are listed in Table 13-1. The following code fragment uses the simplest constructor:

```
try {
  //Creates a socket connection
  Socket s = new Socket("www.vmedia.com",25)
  /*
     Code here interacts with the socket
  */
  //Closes the socket connection
  s.close();
} catch (UnknownHostException e) {
  //The host is unknown
} catch (IOException e) {
  //An I/O error occurred while connecting
}
```

Constructor	Description
Socket(String, int)	The hostname and port to connect to.
Socket(String, int, boolean)	The hostname, port, and a boolean indicating whether the socket is for streams (true) or datagrams (false).
Socket(InetAddress, int)	The Internet address and port to connect to.
Socket(InetAddress, int, boolean)	The Internet address, port, and a boolean indicating whether the socket is for streams (true) or datagrams (false).

Table 13-1: *Socket constructors.*

When constructing a socket, you can specify which host to connect to either by a String containing its host name or a special class, java.net.InetAddress. What is the difference between the two? You'll need a bit of background about TCP/IP to understand fully.

Each host on a TCP/IP network, including the Internet, has a unique numeric identifier, called an IP address, assigned to it. An IP address currently consists of four bytes and is generally represented in dotted octet notation—for example, 127.0.0.1. Although IP addresses are particularly easy for computers to use to talk to each other, they are very difficult for humans to remember and use regularly. The Internet uses the Domain Name System (DNS) to make it easier for people to use networked resources. Someone can specify a host by name, and his or her computer can determine the IP address for a given hostname by querying its local DNS server. The Socket class allows you to specify either a hostname, in the form of a String, or an IP address, in the form of an Inet Address.

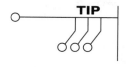

TIP

The InetAddress for a given Socket can be determined by using the getInetAddress method defined on the Socket class. If you want to open another connection to the same machine, it may be somewhat faster to use the InetAddress instead of the hostname to avoid the extra DNS lookup.

You might be wondering why the java.net package uses a class, InetAddress, instead of a 4-byte array containing the IP address. The InetAddress class also provides you with methods that act on the IP address; the getHostName method, for instance, performs a reverse DNS lookup on the InetAddress and returns the hostname. The InetAddress has no public constructors. But it does give you two static functions, getByName and getAllByName, which take a hostname and return the InetAddress or InetAddresses that correspond to that host.

SOCKETS & APPLET SECURITY

Netscape Navigator 2.0 does not allow untrusted applets downloaded from remote servers to open sockets to any machine on the Internet. It will open only sockets to the host from which the code came. This feature prevents applets from generating unwanted or unnoticed network traffic from every machine they are run on. Trusted applets, which are verified by digital authentication, will have fewer restrictions than untrusted applets. They will be given the ability to communicate with any host on the Internet. At the time of this writing, Sun has not designed or implemented the mechanism by which an applet can be designated as trusted, so all remote applets are considered untrusted for now. ➡

The socket security restriction does not apply to applets loaded from the user's local class directory. One way around the restriction is to have users install the applet code in their local class directories. Another way is to write a server that runs on the applet code's host and redirects the traffic coming into a certain port to a destination specified by the traffic. A third method is to have multiple applets on a single Web page, each residing on a different host with which the applet wants to communicate. Because applets sharing a Web page are allowed to communicate with each other, each applet could then communicate with all the other applets' hosts. However, many operating systems limit the number of sustainable network connections, so the last method cannot be guaranteed to work.

Table 13-2 lists the methods for the Socket. The getInputStream and getOutputStream are particularly important, because you will use them to actually communicate with the remote host. Streams in general are used to handle data transfer; in Example 13-1, we use them to transfer data between hosts on a network.

Method	Description
close()	Closes the socket.
InetAddress getInetAddress()	Returns the InetAddress of the computer at the other end of the socket.
int getLocalPort()	Returns the local port number this socket is bound to.
InputStream getInputStream()	Returns an InputStream attached to this socket.
OutputStream getOutputStream()	Returns an OutputStream attached to this socket.
setSocketImplFactory(SocketImplFactory)	Sets the socket implementation factory for the system.

Table 13-2: *Socket methods.*

TIP

If you're running a non-UNIX operating system and are loading the Time Client Applet from your local hard drive or the Companion CD-ROM, Example 13-1 will not work (nor will the other examples in this chapter) unless you happen to be running a time server. To see this applet in action, go to http://www.vmedia.com/ vvc/onlcomp/java/chapter13/example1/TimeApplet.html.

The following example implements a simple time client. It connects to the time server running on the host the applet was downloaded from. The time server waits for a connection, sends the current time, and closes the connection. All our client has to do is open a connection and read the data:

Example 13-1: Time client.

```
import java.applet.*;
import java.awt.*;
import java.net.*;
import java.io.*;

public class TimeApplet extends Applet {
  private Exception error;
  private String output;
```

In the code below, we attempt a connection to the remote host on port 13, the time server's port. If the connection is successful, we then attempt to bind an InputStream to the Socket. We return early if we catch any exceptions (UnknownHost or IO). Once the InputStream is connected, we read a String from it and close the connection:

```
  public void start() {
    Socket TimeSocket;
    InputStream TimeInput;
    try {
      TimeSocket = new Socket(getCodeBase().getHost(),13,
true);
      TimeInput = TimeSocket.getInputStream();
    } catch (Exception e) {
      error = e;
      return:
```

```
    }
    output = readString(TimeInput);
    try {
      TimeInput.close();
      TimeSocket.close();
    } catch (IOException e) {}
  }
```

Now we're ready to read the output from the time server. We initialize a byte array to hold the data and read from the InputStream one byte at a time. The InputStream's read method will return –1 when the stream is complete (after the socket is closed on the remote host). To keep it simple, we'll assume that the input will be less than 50 bytes, although we will show you better ways to get an unknown amount of data from a server later.

```
    private String readString(InputStream in) {
      byte ary[] = new byte[50];
      byte buf;
      int count = 0;
      try {
        buf = (byte)in.read();
        while (buf!=-1) {
          ary[count] = buf;
          count++;
          buf = (byte)in.read();
        }
      } catch (IOException e) {
        error = e;
        return null;
      }
      return new String(ary,0).trim();
    }
```

The paint method will display the output from the time server if all went well, or display the error information if something went awry:

```
    public void paint(Graphics g) {
      g.setColor(Color.white);
      g.fillRect(0,0,499,249);
```

```
            g.setColor(Color.black);
            g.drawRect(0,0,499,249);
            if (error!=null) {
               g.drawString(error.toString(),25,25);
               g.drawString(error.getMessage(),25,25);
            } else {
               g.drawString(output,25,25);
            }
         }
      }
```

Sockets are particularly easy to work with in Java; the real work in using them is handling the input and output. The time server is one of the simplest servers to interact with because it requires no input. We'll have to explore the stream classes in greater depth to show you how to interact with more functional servers. Before we go on to streams, we'll briefly describe the API classes that enable you to use datagrams for network communication.

Socket Implementations

There is one method of the Socket class we haven't used yet: the setSocketImplFactory method. The Socket class itself does little more than provide a consistent interface for communicating with remote hosts. Each socket has a private SocketImpl—another class in the java.net package—which actually does the work of connecting and passing data to and from a remote host. The default SocketImpl is designed to handle normal TCP/IP traffic, but you might want to communicate using another protocol, such as AppleTalk or IPX.

You can write a class that implements SocketImplFactory, an interface that allows Sockets to request a SocketImpl. The new SocketImplFactory will create SockImpls that can speak IPX or AppleTalk but can be used by the standard Socket class without requiring users to learn a whole new set of methods. This technique of using layered levels of abstraction is very common in networking computers.

Connectionless Datagrams

The TCP/IP protocol suite also supports connectionless datagram delivery and retrieval via *User Datagram Packet* (UDP). UDP datagrams, like TCP sockets, allow you to communicate with a remote host over a TCP/IP network. While TCP sockets are connection-oriented, UDP datagrams are connectionless. If a TCP socket is comparable to a telephone call, a UDP datagram is comparable to a telegram. UDP datagrams are not guaranteed to be delivered, and even if they *are* delivered, they're not guaranteed to be delivered in any particular order. If you choose to program with datagrams, you must handle packets that are lost or out of order yourself.

Because UDP is unreliable, most programmers choose to work with TCP sockets when programming networked applications. You might, however, wish to use datagrams if you want to write a Java client for an existing UDP server, like NFS Version 2, for instance. Datagrams also have less overhead than TCP sockets, because no handshaking or flow control mechanisms are necessary when sending or receiving a UDP datagram. UDP datagrams can also be used in a Java server that sends periodic updates to a set of clients. The server would have to do less work, and consequently would be faster, if it could simply send out UDP datagrams instead of having to initiate a TCP connection to each client.

There are two classes in the Java API associated with UDP datagrams: DatagramPacket and DatagramSocket. The DatagramPacket class is used when sending or receiving UDP datagrams. The constructors and methods for the DatagramPacket class are listed in Table 13-3.

Constructors & Methods	Description
DatagramPacket(byte[], int)	Constructs a packet to be used for receiving a datagram. The contents of the datagram will be copied into the byte array when the datagram is received. The integer specifies the number of bytes to be copied into the array. ➡

Constructors & Methods	Description
DatagramPacket(byte[], int, InetAddress, int)	Constructs a packet to be used for sending a datagram. The contents of the byte array will be sent to the port remote host specified by the second integer and the InetAddress. The first integer specifies the number of bytes to be sent.
InetAddress getAddress()	Returns the packet's InetAddress.
int getPort()	Returns the packet's port.
byte[] getData()	Returns the packet's data.
int getLength()	Returns the packet's length.

Table 13-3: *DatagramPacket constructors and methods.*

Once you've constructed your DatagramPacket, you need a DatagramSocket in order to send or receive with it. These sockets are bound to a specific port on your local computer, just like TCP sockets. Port numbers below 1024 are reserved for the root user on UNIX computers. The constructors and methods for the DatagramSocket class are listed in Table 13-4.

Constructor or Method	Description
DatagramSocket()	Creates a UDP socket on an unspeci- fied free port.
DatagramSocket(int)	Creates a UDP socket on the specified port.
receive(DatagramPacket)	Waits to receive a datagram and copies the data into the specified DatagramPacket.
send(DatagramPacket)	Sends a DatagramPacket.
getLocalPort()	Returns the local port the socket is bound to.
close()	Closes the socket.

Table 13-4: *DatagramSocket constructors and methods.*

We'll use these classes to implement a simple UDP client. We connect to the UDP echo server, which resides on port 7 on most UNIX machines. The echo server takes any UDP datagram it receives and returns a copy of it in another UDP datagram to the sender of the first datagram. Here is the code for our echo client:

Example 13-2: A datagram applet.

```java
import java.applet.*;
import java.awt.*;
import java.net.*;

public class DatagramApplet extends Applet {

  private InetAddress addr;
  private String message;
  private TextArea output;

  public void init() {
    try {
      String me = getCodeBase().getHost();
      addr = InetAddress.getByName(me);
    } catch (Exception e) {
      handleException(e);
    }
    message = "abcde";
    output = new TextArea(5,60);
    output.setEditable(false);
    add(output);
    show();
  }

  public void start() {
    byte b[] = new byte[message.length()];
    message.getBytes(0,message.length(),b,0);
    try {
      DatagramSocket ds;
      ds = new DatagramSocket();
      DatagramPacket outPacket;
      outPacket = new DatagramPacket(b,b.length,addr,7);
```

```
                b = new byte[message.length()];
                DatagramPacket inPacket;
                inPacket = new DatagramPacket(b,b.length);
                ds.send(outPacket);
                output.appendText("Sent: "
                   +message+"\n");
                ds.receive(inPacket);
                b = inPacket.getData();
                output.appendText("Rec'd: "
                   +new String(b,0)+"\n");
                ds.close();
            } catch (Exception e) {
              handleException(e);
            }
        }

        public void stop() {
           output.setText("");
        }

        public void handleException(Exception e) {
           System.out.println(e.toString());
           e.printStackTrace();
        }

    }
```

Datagrams, while sometimes useful because of their lack of overhead, are no substitute for a network transport mechanism that supports reliable connections, like TCP sockets. As we saw before, however, sockets as implemented in Java are closely tied to streams. To learn how to use sockets effectively, it's necessary for you to learn how to use streams.

Streams

The Java API uses the stream paradigm to handle input and output from programs. A stream is essentially a method for transferring data from programs to some external device, such as a file or a network connection. You put something in one end, and it comes out the other end (Figure 13-1). The basic stream classes are InputStream and OutputStream, part of the java.io package. In this section, we'll also be covering the rich package of extended stream types that make parsing data much easier than dealing directly with bytes.

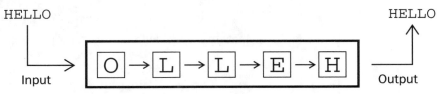

Figure 13-1: *Stream diagram.*

Input Streams

There are some difficulties associated with taking input from remote devices. Most input streams are actually being transferred over a device that may be significantly slower than the program that is trying to use them. It is easy, but generally not good programming style, to get caught waiting for slow or nonexistent data. Network connections, especially, tend to vary widely in speed and oftentimes hang for several seconds or minutes while data is incoming. The InputStream class is structured in a way that makes it relatively easy to compensate for these delays.

The InputStream class defines an available method that returns the number of bytes that can be read from the stream without blocking; that is, waiting idly for new data to arrive. The stream's read methods will block until at least some of the requested data is available. This means if you try to read data that isn't there yet, the thread running the stream will wait until at least part of the data has arrived before continuing. If the data never arrives, the thread won't continue until the socket times out. The read methods return –1 when they reach the end of the stream. All of the methods throw an IOException if they encounter an error. The methods of the InputStream class are listed in Table 13-5.

Methods	Description
int available()	Returns the number of bytes that can be read from the stream without blocking.
int read()	Returns the next byte from the stream.
int read(byte[])	Fills as much as possible of the byte array from the stream and returns the number of bytes actually read.
int read(byte[],int,int)	Fills as much as possible of the byte array from the stream. The first integer indicates an offset to start reading from, and the second indicates the maximum number of bytes to read.
long skip(long n)	Skips *n* bytes of input and returns the number of bytes actually skipped.
close()	Closes the stream.
mark(int)	Marks the current position in the stream. The integer argument specifies the minimum number of bytes that must be read before the mark is lost.
reset()	Returns the stream to the last marked position.
boolean markSupported()	Tells you if this particular stream supports the mark and reset methods.

Table 13-5: *InputStream methods.*

Output Streams

Writing data to a stream is much simpler than receiving input. The class consists of three write methods, a flush method, which writes all buffered outgoing data to the stream, and a close method, which closes the stream. The write methods will block until the data is actually written. The methods are all listed in Table 13-6. All of the methods throw an IOException when they encounter an error.

Method	Description
close()	Closes the stream.
flush()	Flushes the outgoing buffer of any data.
write(int)	Writes a byte to the stream.
write(byte[])	Writes an array of bytes to the stream.
write(byte[],int,int)	Writes a subarray of the given array to the stream. The first integer indicates the offset and the second indicates the length of the subarray.

Table 13-6: *OutputStream methods.*

Using an OutputStream, we can now connect to a server that requires input. This could be, for example, the finger server, which runs on most UNIX computers. Upon connection, the client provides a user name, and the server responds with information about that user. Here is code for a simple applet finger client:

Example 13-3: Finger Client Applet.

```
import java.applet.*;
import java.awt.*;
import java.net.*;
import java.io.*;
```

We'll use a TextArea instead of drawString because the finger server often returns multiple lines of output. For simplicity, we get the user name we're requesting information about as a parameter from the Web page. Because we're using a standard output stream, we must convert the String to a byte array before sending, although later in the chapter we'll discuss subclasses of OutputStream that can write Strings directly. The EOL byte is used when parsing the output from the finger server to check for the end of a line:

```
public class FingerApplet extends Applet {
   private TextArea output;
   private byte user[];
   private byte EOL;
```

```
public void init() {
    String userStr;
    userStr = getParameter("USER")+"\n";
    user = new byte[userStr.length()];
    userStr.getBytes(0,userStr.length(),user,0);
    output = new TextArea(10,80);
    output.setEditable(false);
    add(output);
    show();
    String eolStr = new String("\n");
    byte eolAry[] = new byte[1];
    eolStr.getBytes(0,1,eolAry,0);
    EOL = eolAry[0];
}
```

The section of code shown below is almost identical to the TimeClientApplet—the finger server resides on port 79 and we'll need an OutputStream as well as an InputStream. Once we have connected, we send the user we are searching for as a byte array. We have a new method, readText (shown below), which copies the contents of an InputStream to a TextArea:

```
public void start() {
    Socket FingerSocket;
    InputStream FingerInput;
    OutputStream FingerOutput;
    try {
        FingerSocket = new Socket(getCodeBase().getHost(),79);
        FingerInput = FingerSocket.getInputStream();
        FingerOutput = FingerSocket.getOutputStream();
        FingerOutput.write(user);
    } catch (Exception e) {
        output.appendText(e.toString()+"\n");
        output.appendText(e.getMessage()+"\n");
        return;
    }
    readText(FingerInput,output);
}
```

We are now ready to accept data from the finger server. We use the byte array to hold each line of data. When we reach an EOL character or exceed the array's length (given by the number of columns in the TextArea), we copy the byte array to the TextArea and create a clean new byte array. This is a more sophisticated way of handling unknown amounts of data than was shown in our first example, where we simply assumed an upper bound and created a single array:

```
private void readText(InputStream in, TextArea text) {
    int bufsize = text.getColumns();
    byte ary[] = new byte[bufsize];
    byte buf;
    int count = 0;
    try {
      buf = (byte)in.read();
      while (buf!=-1) {
        ary[count] = buf;
        count++;
        if (buf==EOL || count==bufsize) {
            String aryStr;
            aryStr=new String(ary,0);
            text.appendText(aryStr);
            ary = new byte[80];
            count = 0;
        }
        buf = (byte)in.read();
      }
    } catch (IOException e) {
        text.appendText(e.toString()+"\n");
        text.appendText(e.getMessage()+"\n");
        return;
    }
    text.appendText(new String(ary,0));
  }
```

When the applet stops, we simply clean the TextArea so it will be ready for next time:

```
public void stop() {
    output.setText("");
  }
}
```

Stream Varieties

The java.io package provides much more than the simple InputStream and OutputStream classes. They both have several subclasses in the API that enable programmers to interact with streams at a much higher level and that make parsing and sending data easier. We briefly describe these subclasses in Table 13-7. Unless otherwise specified, each input stream also has a corresponding output stream.

Subclass	Description
FilteredInputStream	A filtered input stream of bytes.
BufferedInputStream	An input stream of bytes with a buffer. Using a buffer may speed up stream access, since bytes are written in chunks. This class is descended from FilteredInputStream.
DataInputStream	Allows you to read primitive data types from the stream. This class is descended from FilteredInputStream.
FileInputStream	Allows streams to connect to files.
PipedInputStream	This stream, paired with a PipedOutputStream, allows a one-way stream between threads.
LineNumberInputStream	An input stream that keeps track of its line numbers. This class is descended from FilterInputStream and has no corresponding OutputStream.
PushbackInputStream	An input stream that allows you to rewind. This class is descended from FilterInputStream and has no corresponding OutputStream.
SequenceInputStream	Allows you to bundle together several InputStreams and read from them in round-robin fashion. This class has no corresponding OutputStream.

Subclass	Description
StringBufferInputStream	Allows you to treat a String as an InputStream. This class has no corresponding OutputStream.
ByteArrayInputStream	Allows you to treat a byte array as an InputStream.
PrintStream	Allows you to print out primitive data types as text. This class has no corresponding InputStream.

Table 13-7: *Specialized InputStreams.*

Most of the specialized streams described in Table 13-7 can be constructed on top of normal Streams. For instance, to create a BufferOutputStream from a normal OutputStream, all you have to do is something like this:

```
OutputStream out = mySocket.getOutputStream();
BufferedOutputStream bufferOut;
bufferOut = new BufferedOutputStream(out);
```

Now anything you write using the bufferOut stream will be written to the original OutputStream and have the added advantage of being buffered.

Data Streams

Two of the most useful streams of the extended stream varieties are the DataInputStream and the DataOutputStream, which can be constructed on top of ordinary Input and OutputStreams. In addition to allowing you to pull Java primitives (ints, Strings, and so on) straight from the stream without bothering with a byte array, they let you write variables straight to the stream. Using a DataInputStream, we can shorten our TimeApplet's readString method. Instead of reading from the stream into a byte array and then casting that to a String, we can read a String directly from the stream using the readLine method:

Example 13-4: Time client Applet using DataInputStream.

```java
private String readString(InputStream in) {
  DataInputStream dataIn;
  dataIn = new DataInputStream(in);
  try {
    return dataIn.readLine();
  } catch (IOException e) {
    error = e;
    return null;
  }
}
```

Table 13-8 lists the new methods added by a DataInputStream. All of these methods throw an IOException if they encounter an error. The readFully methods throw a java.io.EOFException if they encounter an EOF before the byte array is full. They are distinct from the read(byte[]) and read(byte[], int, int) methods of the original InputStream in that they will block until *all* of the requested data is available or they reach an EOF. Likewise, the skipBytes method will block until all of the requested bytes have been skipped.

Method	Description
boolean readBoolean()	Reads a boolean.
int readByte()	Reads a byte (8 bits).
readUnignedByte()	Reads an unsigned byte (8 bits).
readShort()	Reads a short integer (16 bits).
readUnsignedShort()	Reads an unsigned short (16 bits).
readChar()	Reads a character (16 bits).
readInt()	Reads an integer (32 bits).
readLong()	Reads a long integer (64 bits).
readFloat()	Reads a floating point number (32 bits).
readDouble()	Reads a double precision floating point number (64 bits).
readLine()	Reads a String terminated by \r, \n, \r\n, or EOF.
readUTF()	Reads a UTF format String.

Method	Description
readFully(byte[])	Reads bytes into the specified byte array, blocking until the array is full.
readFully(byte[], int, int)	Reads bytes into the specified byte subarray, blocking until the subarray is full.
skipBytes(int n)	Skips *n* bytes, blocking until all bytes have been skipped.

Table 13-8: *DataInputStream methods.*

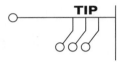

TIP

When using readByte and its partner, writeByte, you don't need to worry about converting to and from network byte order. The bytes are written out and read in strictly as they are represented in the Java Virtual Machine's memory.

DataOutputStreams work in much the same way as DataInputStreams, except in reverse. You can write variables, including Strings, directly to the stream without converting to byte arrays first. Table 13-9 lists the new methods added by the DataOutputStream class.

Method	Description
writeBoolean(boolean)	Writes a boolean.
writeByte(int)	Writes a byte (8 bits).
writeChar(int)	Writes a character (16 bits).
writeShort(short)	Writes a short integer (16 bits).
writeInt(int)	Writes an integer (32 bits).
writeLong(long)	Writes a long integer (64 bits).
writeFloat(float)	Writes a floating point number (32 bits).
writeDouble(double)	Writes a double precision floating point number (64 bits).
writeBytes(String)	Writes a String in bytes.
writeChars(String)	Writes a String in characters.
writeUTF(String)	Writes a String in UTF format.

Table 13-9: *DataOutputStream methods.*

Bear in mind that the DataInputStream methods do not parse incoming text data for things that look like primitive Java data types, nor do the DataOutputStream methods write out text representations of the variables passed to them. These methods read and write variables to the stream exactly as they are represented in the Java Virtual Machine's memory.

For instance, when you call readInt, it reads 32 bits from the stream and returns the integer that corresponds to those 32 bits. It does not parse a string of text data for something that looks like an integer. Similarly, the DataOutputStream method, writeInt, will not write "10" to the stream if you pass it an integer whose value is 10. It will write a sequence of 32 bits indicating a value of 10 when interpreted as an integer. If you want to parse textual data for numbers, you can either read the text data into a String and use the StringTokenizer, or you can use the StreamTokenizer class, which we discuss in the next section.

Parsing Data From a Text Stream

The StreamTokenizer class, much like the DataInputStream class, is constructed on top of an ordinary InputStream. It is distinct from the other extended InputStream types in that it is not directly descended from the InputStream class—if you use a StreamTokenizer class, you will be unable to use the ordinary InputStream methods on the StreamTokenizer. But the StreamTokenizer *does* allow you to read some primitive Java data types, namely Strings and double precision floating point numbers, from a textual stream of data. You'll want to use this feature when communicating with a server that transmits data in text, such as a MUD.

The StreamTokenizer class separates items in an InputStream into chunks called tokens. It recognizes five kinds of things as tokens: words, numbers, the EOL character, the EOF character, and ordinary characters. Let's say, for example, the stream contained the data:

```
You are user 9 of 100:
```

The StreamTokenizer would return seven tokens from this stream. "You," "are," "user," and "of" would be recognized as Strings, "9" and "100" would be recognized as numbers, and ":" would be returned as an ordinary character.

The workhorse of the StreamTokenizer class is the nextToken method. It reads the next token from the stream and returns an integer indicating what kind of token it found. The integer will be a TT_WORD, TT_NUMBER, TT_EOL, or TT_EOF if the token is a word, number, EOL, or EOF, respectively. These TT_* variables are defined as static integers on the StreamTokenizer class. If the token is an ordinary character, it returns the value of that character. If the token type is TT_WORD, the actual String is placed in the StreamTokenizer's sval variable. If the token type is TT_NUMBER, the actual double is placed in the StreamTokenizer's nval variable, which is a double.

By default, the StreamTokenizer class understands numbers as a sequence of numerics, possibly separated by a decimal point, that are terminated on either side by white space or ordinary characters. It understands words two ways—as a sequence of alphabetics, terminated on either side by white space or ordinary characters, or as anything contained inside single or double quotes.

There are many ways to customize the StreamTokenizer class to fit your needs. You can define new sets of characters to be recognized as word characters, as whitespace characters, or as ordinary characters. The StreamTokenizer class can be configured to ignore comments as well. You can define a single character as a comment character, and whenever the StreamTokenizer reads that character, it will ignore it and everything after it until the next EOL character. It can also understand /*...*/ and //... style comments. You can even define new characters to delimit Strings. Let's look at a short example. Suppose your input looks like this:

```
#This is a comment
This is a bunch of words?
:This is an entire string!!!:
```

By default, the StreamTokenizer will recognize '#', '?', ':', and '!' as ordinary characters and everything else as words. Suppose we create a StreamTokenizer and make the following modifications to it:

```
InputStream in = mySocket.getInputStream();
StreamTokenizer st = new StreamTokenizer(in);
st.commentChar('#');
st.wordChars('?','?');
st.quoteChar(':');
```

The StreamTokenizer will now ignore the first line entirely, return 'words?' as a whole word, and consider everything between the colons on the third line to be a String. See Table 13-10 for a comprehensive listing of the methods of the StreamTokenizer class.

Method	Description
int nextToken()	Reads the next token from the input stream and returns an integer indicating the kind of token it found.
commentChar(int)	Allows the specified character to start a one-line comment.
quoteChar(int)	Allows the specified character to delimit Strings. When nextToken reaches a String delimited by this character, it will return the character itself (not TT_WORD) and set sval to be the body of the String.
whitespaceChars(int, int)	Allows the characters in the range specified to be skipped as white space.
wordChars(int, int)	Allows the characters in the range specified to be accepted as words.
ordinaryChar(int)	Allows the specified character to be recognized as ordinary; when nextToken reaches this character, it will return the value of the character. ➡

Method	Description
ordinaryChars(int, int)	Same as ordinaryChar(int), except a range is specified.
resetSyntax()	Resets all characters to be special.
parseNumbers()	Requests that numbers be parsed.eolIsSignificant(boolean) If true, requests that nextToken return TT_EOL when it reaches an EOL. If false, EOLs will be ignored as whitespace.
slashStarComments(boolean)	If true, nextToken recognizes comments of the form /*...*/ and ignores them.
slashSlashComments(boolean)	If true, nextToken recognizes comments of the form //... and ignores them.
lowerCaseMode(boolean)	If true, forces words into lower case before putting them in the sval variable.
pushBack()	Pushes the last token back onto the stream.
int lineno()	Returns the current line number.
String toString()	Returns the current token in String format.

Table 13-10: *StreamTokenizer methods.*

The StreamTokenizer class is a very powerful and flexible class. But don't be intimidated by the wide range of options it offers. The standard configuration works well for most InputStreams. Using a StreamTokenizer, we can revise the TimeApplet to parse its input into variables. Recall that the time server returns a string of the form:

```
Sun Jan 21 19:15:01 1996
```

We can have the StreamTokenizer parse this into two Strings, containing the day and the month, and five doubles, containing the date, hour, minute, second, and year. Because we use the Vector class in the new code, we need to add "import java.util.*" to the top of the applet code. Here is the revised start method and a new readTokens method:

Example 13-5: Parsing data from the time server.

```java
public void start() {
    Socket TimeSocket;
    StreamTokenizer st;
    try {
        TimeSocket = new Socket(getCodeBase().getHost(),13,true);
        st = new StreamTokenizer(TimeSocket.getInputStream());
    } catch (Exception e) {
        error = e;
        return;
    }
```

We want to ignore the colons in the time server's output, so we declare them to be white space for the purpose of tokenizing. To make parsing easier, we have written a readTokens method which, given a StringTokenizer and a Vector of Strings and Doubles, attempts to parse the stream for Strings and Doubles. The tokens in the stream must occur in the same order they occur in the Vector, and they must be separated only by white space. Otherwise, a new Exception is thrown. Here we initialize the Vector to contain two Strings followed by five Doubles:

```java
st.whitespaceChars(':',':');
Vector tokens = new Vector(7);
tokens.addElement(new String());
tokens.addElement(new String());
tokens.addElement(new Double(0));
tokens.addElement(new Double(0));
tokens.addElement(new Double(0));
tokens.addElement(new Double(0));
tokens.addElement(new Double(0));
```

```
  try {
    readTokens(st,tokens);
  } catch (Exception e) {
    error = e;
    return;
  }
  output="The date is "+tokens.elementAt(0)+", ";
  output = output+tokens.elementAt(1)+
  " "+tokens.elementAt(2);
  output = output+", "+tokens.elementAt(6);
  try {
    TimeSocket.close();
  } catch (Exception e) {}
}
```

The method below is the new method for reading tokens. It steps through the Vector element by element, reading tokens from the Stream and setting the elements of the Vector appropriately. If the token type read from the Stream does not correspond to the type of Object specified in the Vector, or if the Vector contains an Object type we can't parse for, we throw an Exception:

```
private void readTokens(StreamTokenizer st, Vector v) throws
Exception {
  int token;
  int i = 0;
  Enumeration en = v.elements();
  while (en.hasMoreElements()) {
    //This is the object type we want
    Object o = en.nextElement();
    //This is the next token from the stream
    token = st.nextToken();
    //If our target type is String
    if (o instanceof String) {
      //If the token isn't a word
      if (token!=st.TT_WORD) {
        Exception e;
        e = new Exception("Unexpected token type:"+token);
        throw e;
```

```
        //We're okay, fill in the Vector
        } else {
          v.setElementAt(st.sval,i);
        }
      }
      //If our target type is Double
      else if (o instanceof Double) {
        //If the token isn't a number
        if (token!=st.TT_NUMBER) {
          Exception e;
          e = new Exception("Unexpected token type: "+token);
          throw e;
        //We're okay, fill in the Vector
        } else {
          Double d = new Double(st.nval);
          v.setElementAt(d,i);
        }
      }
      //If our target type is invalid
      else {
        Exception e;
        String type = o.getClass().getName();
        e = new Exception("Cannot parse for"
          +type);
        throw e;
      }
      i++;
    }
  }
```

InterApplet Communication With Pipes

The Java API implements a way to connect streams between different threads. You can use this feature to allow your threads to communicate without having to design a rigid, complicated system of methods for doing so. You can create a pair of piped streams, a PipedInputStream and a PipedOutputStream. Anything that is written to the PipedOutputStream will be received on its connected PipedInputStream. One thread can construct a pair of piped streams and give one of them to another thread. The threads can now communicate in one direction via a stream. If two-way communication is desired, another pair of pipes can be created and the opposite type given to each thread.

This technique is not only useful for interthread communication in a single applet, it allows applets sharing an applet context (on a Web page, for example) to talk to one another. The AppletContext provides a method, getApplets, that enumerates the applets it's providing resources to, and a getApplet method that takes the name of an applet and returns a reference to the named applet if it exists. You specify names for your applets in the HTML code:

```
<APPLET CODE="..." WIDTH=### HEIGHT=### NAME="...">
```

Once you have a reference to the applet you want to talk to, you can create a pair of piped streams and pass one to the applet via some predefined method. There are many ways to accomplish this—for simplicity's sake, we chose to create a subclass of the Applet class, ListenApplet, which acts as a passive listener. Another applet can request an OutputStream from it, write to the OutputStream, and tell it to read from the stream. The ListenApplet takes the data from the stream, interprets it as text, and prints it to a TextArea. Here is the code for ListenApplet:

Example 13-6a: The Listening Applet.

```java
import java.applet.*;
import java.io.*;
import java.awt.*;
import java.util.*;

public class ListenApplet extends Applet {
   //This is our output window
   private TextArea output;
   //Contains InputStreams keyed by Applet
   private Hashtable inpipes;

   public void init() {
      inpipes = new Hashtable(1);
      output = new TextArea(10,60);
```

```
output.setEditable(false);
output.appendText
    ("This Applet listens for master applets.\n");
add(output);
}
```

An applet can use this method to request that an OutputStream be piped to it. The ListenApplet keeps track of its InputStreams by keeping a Hashtable of the streams keyed by their respective Applets. The Hashtable makes it possible to handle connections between multiple applets. An applet that wants to talk to this one initiates a conversation by calling the ListenApplet's call method. The call method creates a pair of piped streams and passes the PipedOutputStream back to the talking applet:

```
public PipedOutputStream call(Applet a) throws IOException
{
    //Just in case a is already connected
    inpipes.remove(a);
    PipedInputStream in;
    in = new PipedInputStream();
    PipedOutputStream out;
    out = new PipedOutputStream();
    //We connect the pipes to each other
    in.connect(out);
    out.connect(in);
    //Keep the InputStream for later use
    inpipes.put(a,in);
    //Return the paired OutputStream
    return out;
}
```

Other applets use the hangup method to close their pipe with this applet. Once the connection is severed, we remove the stream from our Hashtable:

```
public void hangup(Applet a) throws IOException {
    PipedInputStream in;
    in = (PipedInputStream)inpipes.get(a);
    in.close();
    inpipes.remove(a);
}
```

Once the other applet has written to the stream, our applet reads from the stream until it is complete, coverts it to String format, and prints it to our TextArea. If you were to want to handle multi-applet communication synchronously, it would be better to put this method into a separate Thread. We read into a buffer of length 8 initially. As we reach the bounds of the array, we create a new array with double the length of the previous array. This is an even more sophisticated way of handling unknown amounts of data using arrays. Instead of simply copying data into a series of arrays as in our previous example, we use a single array, but we double its size whenever it becomes full:

```
public void listen(Applet a) throws IOException {
  PipedInputStream in;
  in = (PipedInputStream)inpipes.get(a);
  if (in==null) {
    return;
  }
  int count = 0;
  int arysize = 8;
  byte ary[] = new byte[arysize];
  byte b;
  b = (byte)in.read();
  //While the stream is incomplete
  while (b!=-1) {
    //If we've filled our array
    if (count==arysize) {
      arysize = arysize*2;
      byte temp[];
      temp = new byte[arysize];
      //This is a fast system call
      //for copying arrays
      System.arraycopy(ary,0,temp,0,count);
      ary = temp;
    }
    ary[count] = b;
    count++;
    b = (byte)in.read();
  }
```

```
        String buffer = new String(ary,0);
        output.appendText("Received: "+buffer);
    }
}
```

By itself, the Listening Applet will sit on a Web page with nothing to do. It is necessary to bring in a second applet to talk to it. Here is the code for our talking applet. Note that since we make use of the extended features of the ListenApplet, we must import it:

Example 13-6b: The Talking Applet.

```
import ListenApplet;
import java.awt.*;
import java.io.*;
import java.applet.*;

public class MasterApplet extends Applet {

    //This is our user input window
    private TextArea output;
    //This signals to send the input
    private Button send;

    public void init() {
        output = new TextArea(10,60);
        output.setEditable(true);
        send = new Button("Send");
        add(send);
        add(output);
    }
```

The action method is run whenever the user presses the send button. We find the applet we want to talk to and send the contents of our TextArea to it:

```
public boolean action(Event evt, Object o) {
    if (evt.target!=send) {
        return false;
    }
```

```
    ListenApplet slave;
    slave =
(ListenApplet)getAppletContext().getApplet("listener");
    if (slave==null) {
      output.appendText("Found no listening applet.\n");
    } else try {
      sendMessage(output.getText(),slave);
      output.setText("");
    } catch (IOException e) {
      output.appendText(e.toString()+"\n");
    }
    return true;
  }
```

In the code below, we actually attempt to send a String to the target applet. First we call the applet to get an OutputStream. Then we convert the String to a byte array and write that to the stream, followed by a new line and an EOF character. We ask the other applet to read the contents of the stream and then close the connection:

```
public void sendMessage(String s, ListenApplet a) throws
IOException {
    PipedOutputStream out;
    out = a.call(this);
    byte b[] = new byte[s.length()];
    s.getBytes(0,s.length(),b,0);
    out.write(b);
    byte NL = '\n';
    out.write(NL);
    byte EOF = -1;
    out.write(EOF);
    a.listen(this);
    a.hangup(this);
    out.close();
  }
}
```

The HTML code for a Web page that includes both of these applets looks like this:

```
<APPLET CODE="ListenApplet.class" WIDTH=500 HEIGHT=250
NAME="Listener"></APPLET>
<APPLET CODE="MasterApplet.class" WIDTH=500 HEIGHT=250></
APPLET>
```

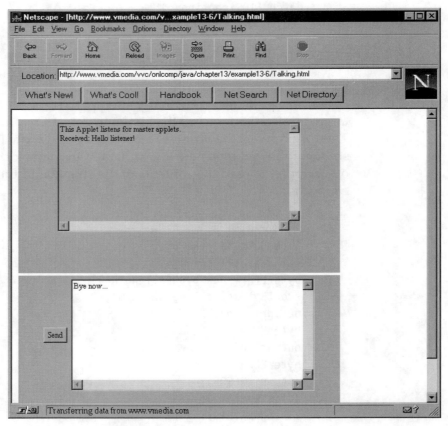

Figure 13-2: *Two applets talking.*

Moving On

The sockets and streams method of handling network communication has existed for many years now; it is by far the simplest and fastest way of talking across the network. URLs are a relatively recent addition to the ever-evolving standards for network communication. They provide a consistent way to encode all of the information needed to identify and retrieve an object over the Internet using a variety of protocols. Typically, the protocol type, the hostname, and a path and file name are bound together in a single, easily parsed string.

Your Web browser is able to support at least the HyperText Transfer Protocol (HTTP). Most popular browsers support the HTTP and File Transfer Protocols for object transfer, and some support the Network News Transfer Protocol for browsing newsgroups. All of these protocols can be encoded into URLs. The Java API handles some protocols by default—it also provides a mechanism for developing your own URL handlers that can understand other protocols. Additionally, the Java URL classes make it possible to easily retrieve objects from the network as Java Objects, not just primitive data types. We've already seen one instance of this, name getImage(URL). In the next chapter, we'll show you how to retrieve Objects of your own design.

14

Networking With URLs

Uniform Resource Locators (URLs), are used to locate resources on the Internet. Web page designers can create links in their documents with URLs that point to other Web pages or resources on the Internet. URLs provide consistency for encoding the locations of networked resources. The Java API includes a complete suite of classes designed for programmers to use URLs to access network resources.

We can improve the reusability of our code by using URLs instead of programming with sockets directly. As we shall see, Java's URL classes let us separate the process of connecting to a networked resource from the process of interpreting its data. URLs are primarily used for data retrieval, although some, such as the Telnet URL, are used to access interactive network resources. In Table 14-1, we've listed URLs that meet the specifications for the most common protocols. The URL classes provided by the Java API are geared toward using URLs for data retrieval, although it is very simple to work with interactive URLs as well.

Protocol	URL
HTTP (HyperText Transfer Protocol)	http://www.vmedia.com/
FTP (File Transfer Protocol)	ftp://ftp.vmedia.com/pub
SMTP (Simple Mail Transfer Protocol)	mailto:user@host
News (Usenet)	news:comp.lang.java
WAIS (Wide Area Index and Search)	wais://sunsite.unc.edu/ linux-faq
Telnet	telnet://www.vmedia.com/

Table 14-1: *Common URLs.*

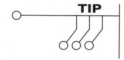

TIP   *The official specification for the format and structure of URLs is RFC 1738, available at http://www.cis.ohio-state.edu/htbin/rfc/ rfc1738.*

Netscape Navigator 2.0 has imposed some fairly severe security restrictions on using URLs in applets. While these restrictions make untrusted applets more secure, they also incidentally make it impossible, using the URL classes, to create handlers for protocols and content types that aren't provided by Netscape. Although this limits the utility of the URL classes somewhat, Netscape Navigator 2.0 does provide support for the most commonly used protocols. Although Netscape Navigator 2.0 does not provide support directly in the URL classes for any content types, we will show you how to get around the restriction for content handlers in the "MIME Types & ContentHandlers" section of this chapter. For retrieving Images and AudioClips, you can, of course, still use the getImage and getAudioClip methods of the Applet class.

Using the URL Class

Java provides a class, java.net.URL, that allows us to deal with URLs natively in Java. Java also provides built-in support for the most common protocol types and gives programmers the capability to add support for new protocols. We discussed the absolute and relative URL constructors in Chapter 5, "How Applets Work." All four URL constructors are listed in Table 14-2.

Constructor	Description
URL (String, String, int, String)	Creates an absolute URL from the specified protocol type, hostname, port number, and directory location.
URL (String, String, String)	Creates an absolute URL from the specified protocol type, hostname, and directory location. The port number is assumed to be the default for the specified protocol type.
URL (String)	Creates an absolute URL from an unparsed string.
URL (URL, String)	Creates a relative URL from an unparsed string containing a directory relative to the given URL.

Table 14-2: *URL constructors.*

Sun has provided URL support for a very limited number of protocols—doc, file, and http. In "Working With Other Protocols," later in this chapter, we discuss how to add support for more protocols to the URL class. All of the public methods of the URL class are listed in Table 14-3.

Method	Description
boolean equals(URL)	Compares two URLs to see if they are equivalent.
String getFile()	Returns the absolute path to the resource on the given host.
String getHost()	Returns the hostname.
int getPort()	Returns the port number.
String getProtocol()	Returns the protocol type. ➡

Method	Description
String getRef()	Returns the reference to a specific location within the file. For example, http://www.vmedia.com/index.html#middle contains a reference, "middle," to a marked location inside the index.html file.
sameFile(URL)	Compares two URLs to see if they are equivalent, ignoring any references.
String toExternalForm()	Prints the fully qualified URL.
Object getContent()	Retrieves the contents of this URL.
InputStream openStream()	Returns an InputStream from the resource.
openConnection()	Returns a URLConnection for this URL.
setURLStreamHandlerFactory (URLStreamHandlerFactory)	Sets the URLStreamHandlerFactory.

Table 14-3: *Public URL methods.*

Once we have an instantiation of the URL class, we'll want to access the resource it points to. There are three main methods provided by the URL class to help us with this. The simplest method is to read directly from an InputStream supplied by the URL. The openStream method accomplishes this:

```
InputStream is;
try {
  is = myURL.openStream();
  //Read data from is
} catch (IOException e) {}
```

Using a URL in this manner is not much different than using a socket. The main difference is that when you program with URLs, the socket connections are opened automatically to the proper port, and any protocol handshaking and file request procedures are done for you. For instance, when you request a stream from a standard HTTP URL, the URL opens a socket to port 80 on the specified machine and issues a GET command for the specified directory location. The InputStream returned by the openStream method is positioned at the beginning of the resource's byte stream. Here is a short example of reading directly from a URL's InputStream:

```
URL myURL;
try {
   myURL = new URL(getCodeBase(),
      "/index.html");
} catch (MalformedURLException e) {}
try {
   InputStream is = myURL.openStream();
   int i = is.read();
   while (i!=-1) {
      //Read data from the stream
   }
} catch (IOException e) {}
```

In this example, we create a URL to the home page of our applet's Web server, open an InputStream connected to the home page, and read the HTML file from the InputStream.

Getting Content

The getContent method is a nice feature of the URL class that currently is somewhat underused. This method opens a stream to the resource just like the openStream method does, but then attempts to determine the MIME type of the stream and convert the stream into a Java Object. Knowing the MIME type of a data stream allows the URL to pass the data stream to a method designed to handle that particular type of data. The method should give us the data encapsulated in an appropriate type of Java object. For instance, if we created a URL that pointed to a picture in GIF format, the getContent method would (or should) recognize the stream to be of type "image/gif" and return an instance of the Image class. The Image would contain a copy of the GIF picture. The exact mechanism used by the getContent method is explained

later in this chapter under "MIME Types & ContentHandlers."
Here is an example of how to use the getContent method. In this
example, we create a URL to the applet's Web server's main index.
We call the getContent method to retrieve the resource into a Java
Object and then use the instanceof operator to determine what
kind of Object was returned:

```java
URL myURL;
try {
  myURL = new URL(getCodeBase(),
    "/index.html");
} catch (MalformedURLException e) {}
try {
  Object o = myURL.getContent();
} catch (IOException e) {}
if (o instanceof Image) {
  //Code here runs if o is an Image
} else if (o instanceof String) {
  //Code here runs if o is a String
} else {
  //Default
}
```

MIME

The MIME (Multipurpose Internet Mail Extensions) type specification was originally proposed in RFC 1341 as a way to make it
easier to send binary data via e-mail. Instead of simply sending
binary data in the middle of an ordinary e-mail message and
hoping that the recipient can interpret it properly, MIME allows
you to specify a variety of information about binary data, such
as the method used to encode the data and the type of program
the mail client should use to view the decoded data. ➡

MIME has proven useful in areas other than e-mail; most notably, in transferring files via HTTP. When an HTTP client requests a file, it can opt to receive MIME information about the file and act on the data in a manner appropriate to its content type. For instance, if an HTTP client received a file with MIME type "image/gif," it would probably pass the data along to an image viewing subroutine or utility.

For a good collection of links to Web pages and RFCs about MIME, point your Web browser to: http://www.worldtalk.com/web/text/email.html.

Connecting With URLConnections

If you are using a URL that needs some additional input, like a URL to a CGI script, or if you need more information about a resource, you can use the openConnection method. This method returns a URLConnection object bound to the URL. The URLConnection class, included in the Java API, gives us an abstraction for the actual connection between the applet's computer and the computer that contains the resource.

You might want to use a CGI script as a simple server-side back end to your Java applets. Applets can't easily write files on either their client or their server, but you can easily write a secure CGI script that allows read/write access to files that reside on the server. Your Java applets can then establish a URLConnection to your CGI script. The URLConnection gives you the ability to send data to a network resource, so your applet can pass its file requests to the script via CGI variables. The script would in turn perform the requested file operations and report the status of the operations in its output. This technique is used in Chapter 17, "Interfacing With CGI: The Java Store."

Some protocols, in addition to simply allowing access to network resources, can provide information about the resource, such as its MIME type or the date the resource was last modified. The URLConnection class provides you with a consistent set of methods for accessing that data.

You can create URLConnections by using the openConnection method of the URL class or by constructing them with the desired URL as the argument. The URLConnection class provides programmers with more information about and finer control over the resource specified by a URL. The class as described in the Java API is abstract; subclasses that provide implementations for certain protocols are included in JDK, specifically the HTTP, FILE, and DOC protocols (the FILE URL is used for local files and the DOC URL was used in the HotJava Web browser). Netscape Navigator 2.0 only allows applets to use the HTTP protocol when working with URLs.

There are many public methods defined on the URLConnection class that provide easy access to information about the resource available at the given URL. These methods are listed in Table 14-4. Some of these methods are applicable only when using HTTP URLs and return null or zero otherwise.

Method	Description
String getContentEncoding()	Returns the encoding of the resource's output or null if not known (i.e., base64, 7bit).
String getContentLength()	Returns the size of the resource in bytes.
String getContentType()	Returns the MIME type of the resource (i.e., image/gif).
String getDate()	Returns the sending date of the resource.
String getExpiration()	Returns the expiration date of the resource.
String getHeaderField(String)	Returns the header field named by the given String.
String getHeaderField(int)	Returns the header field indexed by the given integer.
String getHeaderFieldKey(int)	Returns the name of the header field indexed by the given integer.

Method	Description
long getHeaderFieldDate(String, long)	Returns the header field named by the given String, parsed as a date. The long integer argument serves as a default if the header field can not be parsed or found.
int getHeaderFieldInt(String, int)	Returns the header field named by the given String, parsed as an integer. The integer argument serves as a default if the header field can not be parsed or found.
long getIfModifiedSince()	Returns the if modified since field.

Table 14-4: *Informational URLConnection methods.*

HTTP & the URLConnection Class

To see how the URLConnection class works with a simple HTTP URL, let's take a quick look at the inner workings of the HTTP protocol. Here is a transcript of a typical HTTP session; the first line is the request from the client, and the rest is the server's response:

```
GET /index.html HTTP/1.0

HTTP/1.0 200 Document follows
Date: Sun, 10 Mar 1996 03:52:15 GMT
Server: NCSA/1.4
Content-type: text/html
Last-modified: Fri, 08 Mar 1996 20:24:18 GMT
Content-length: 4611

<html>
. . .
</html>
```

If we create a URLConnection to the index.html page indicated by this example, the getContentType method will return "text/html" and the getContentLength method will return 4611. Note that determining these values is particularly easy with HTTP—the server returns them in the HTTP header. Many other protocols do not provide this information.

Now, we come back to the real workhorse of the URLConnection class's method, the getContent method. This is the method that is actually run when we call the getContent method on a URL. First, the getContent method attempts to determine the content type of the resource in question, either by examining the HTTP header, the stream itself, or the filename extension. Once it has decided which MIME type to use, the getContent method requests a ContentHandler class for that MIME type and passes itself to the ContentHandler.

MIME Types & ContentHandlers

Each MIME type can have a ContentHandler class devoted to it. The ContentHandler class is what ultimately processes a resource's data when we call getContent on a URL or a URLConnection. It consists of one method, getContent, which takes a URLConnection as an argument and returns an Object, hopefully one that has some relation to the resource. For instance, a resource of MIME type image/gif would probably be returned as an Image, or some subclass of Image, from the getContent method. The ContentHandler class as described in the Java API is abstract; subclasses of the ContentHandler class provide implementations for various MIME types. Here is a (not very complex) ContentHandler for any of the "text/*" types:

```java
import java.net.*;
import java.io.*;

public class TextContentHandler extends ContentHandler {

    public Object getContent(URLConnection urlc) {
```

```
try {
  InputStream is;
  is = urlc.getInputStream();
  DataInputStream ds;
  ds = new DataInputStream(is);
  int length;
  length = urlc.getContentLength();
  if (length!=-1) {
    byte b[] = new byte[length];
    ds.readFully(b);
    String s = new String(b,0);
  } else {
    //The length is unknown
    String s = "";
    int i = is.read();
    while (i!=-1) {
      s = s+(char)i;
      i = is.read();
    }
  }
    return s;
  } catch (Exception e) {
    e.printStackTrace();
    return null;
  }
}

}
```

How does the URLConnection fetch the appropriate ContentHandler when getContent is called? It first determines the MIME type of the stream and requests the ContentHandler for that MIME type from its ContentHandlerFactory. The ContentHandlerFactory as described in the Java API is an interface. It consists of one method, createContentHandler, which takes a String as an argument and returns a ContentHandler. The String indicates which MIME type the ContentHandler should be able to handle. Here is some code for a simple ContentHandlerFactory to be used with our TextContentHandler:

```
import java.net.*;
import java.io.*;

public class MyContentHandlerFactory
   extends Object
   implements ContentHandlerFactory {

   public ContentHandler
   createContentHandler(String type) {
     if (type.startsWith("text")) {
       return new TextContentHandler();
     }
     else {
       return null;
     }
   }
}
```

Setting the ContentHandlerFactory

We can set the ContentHandlerFactory for our URLConnections with the setContentHandlerFactory method. Unfortunately, applets are not allowed to set any factories related to networking under Netscape Navigator 2.0 and are thus forbidden to use this method. It is difficult to understand why applets are forbidden to set a ContentHandlerFactory, because all ContentHandlers do is transform streams of data into Java Objects. Fortunately, we can read and write to and from the streams associated with the URLConnection, so we can bypass this hindrance. Furthermore, we can still use the ContentHandler and ContentHandlerFactory classes in a slightly roundabout way when working with URLs. Consider the following applet:

Example 14-1: An applet using a ContentHandler.

```
import java.applet.*;
import java.net.*;
import java.awt.*;
import java.io.*;
```

```
import TextContentHandler;

public class URLApplet extends Applet {

  private TextArea output;
  private ContentHandler handler;

  public void init() {
    handler = new TextContentHandler();
    output = new TextArea(12,80);
    output.setEditable(false);
    add(output);
    show();
    resize(500,250);
  }

  public void start() {
    try {
      URL myURL = new URL(getCodeBase(),
        "/index.html");
      URLConnection myUC =
    myURL.openConnection();
      myUC.connect();
      Object o = handler.getContent(myUC);
      output.setText((String)o);
    } catch (Exception e) {
      handleException(e);
    }
  }

  public void stop() {
    output.setText("");
  }

  public void handleException(Throwable t) {
    System.out.println(t.toString());
    t.printStackTrace();
    stop();
  }
}
```

A screen shot of this applet appears in Figure 14-1. Our applet reads in the site's home page and displays the raw HTML code in a TextArea. We ignore the getContent methods of the URL and URLConnection classes and call the ContentHandler's getContent method directly. This bypasses the use of the default ContentHandlerFactory and allows us to use our own ContentHandlers. Notice that we don't have to deal directly with streams or sockets in this applet. All of the hard work is accomplished in the URLConnection and TextContentHandler classes. We can extend this applet to use a ContentHandlerFactory as well:

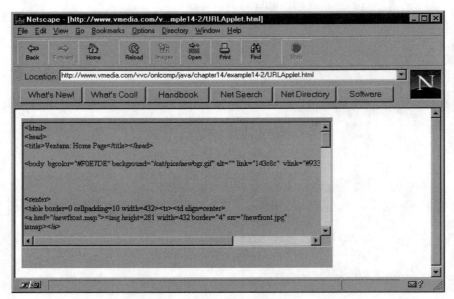

Figure 14-1: *The URLApplet in Netscape Navigator 2.0.*

Example 14-2: An applet using a ContentHandlerFactory.

```
import java.applet.*;
import java.net.*;
import java.awt.*;
import java.io.*;
import myContentHandlerFactory;
```

```java
public class URLApplet extends Applet {

  private TextArea output;
  private ContentHandlerFactory factory;

  public void init() {
    factory = new MyContentHandlerFactory();
    output = new TextArea(12,80);
    output.setEditable(false);
    add(output);
    show();
    resize(500,250);
  }

  public void start() {
    try {
      URL myURL = new URL(getCodeBase(),
        "/index.html");
      URLConnection myUC =
    myURL.openConnection();
      myUC.connect();
      String type = myUC.getContentType();
      ContentHandler handler =
  factory.createContentHandler(type);
      Object o = handler.getContent(myUC);
      output.setText((String)o);
    } catch (Exception e) {
      handleException(e);
    }
  }

  public void stop() {
    output.setText("");
  }

  public void handleException(Throwable t) {
    System.out.println("CAUGHT: "+t.toString());
    t.printStackTrace();
    stop();
  }
}
```

This applet does more or less the same thing as the applet in Example 14-1, except this one demonstrates use of the ContentHandlerFactory. We first determine the MIME type of the URL's resource and then request the proper ContentHandler for that type. Currently, our ContentHandlerFactory only supports MIME type "text/*", but we can later create new ContentHandlers and add them to the factory.

The default ContentHandlerFactory used by URLConnections under Netscape Navigator 2.0 currently doesn't support any MIME types. When we call the getContent method on a URL or URLConnection, we will most likely receive an InputStream; this signifies that the ContentHandlerFactory couldn't figure out what to do with the resource. The InputStream returned by the getContent method is connected to the resource; it is left to the programmer to interpret the bytes. Other implementations of the ContentHandlerFactory interface are sure to arrive and provide functionality for this aspect of the Java API.

Do it Yourself With Streams

For the time being, given the current restrictions on setting the ContentHandlerFactory for URLConnections in applets, you'll probably want to read directly from the streams associated with the URLConnection to retrieve data from a network resource. The URLConnection class provides two methods for this purpose: getInputStream and getOutputStream. Should you attempt to call either of these methods on a URL type that doesn't support them, you'll get an UnknownServiceException. Here is a quick example:

```
InputStream is;
OutputStream os;
try {
  is = myURLConnection.getInputStream();
  os = myURLConnection.getOutputStream();
  //Read from and write to is and os
} catch (Exception e) {
  //Deal with IO- or UnknownServiceException
}
```

THE URLENCODER CLASS

When you write data to an OutputStream connected to a re-source via the HTTP protocol, you must make sure your output is URL safe— there are certain characters that are considered special by the HTTP protocol and must be encoded to be trans-mitted. The Java API provides a class, URLEncoder, that accom-plishes this for you. It consists of a single method, *encode*, which takes a String and returns it with all special characters encoded.

Setting Options

There are a number of options you can configure on the URLConnection class. Some of them have default values that you can set, and setting them causes any new URLConnections to have the new default value chosen as the initial setting for that option. The methods for setting these options are described in Table 14-5.

Method	Description
boolean getAllowUserInteraction()	Returns the user interaction flag (indicating whether or not this URL type allows user interaction).
setAllowUserInteraction(boolean)	Sets the user interaction flag.
boolean getDefaultAllowUserInteraction()	Returns the default for the user interaction flag.
setDefaultAllowUserInteraction(boolean)	Sets the default for the user interaction flag.
boolean getUseCaches()	Some protocols allow resources to be cached locally. This returns a boolean indicating the status of this behavior.
setUseCaches(boolean)	Sets the cache option for this URLConnection.
boolean getDefaultUseCaches()	Returns the default value of the cache option. ➡

Method	Description
setDefaultUseCaches(boolean)	Sets the default value of the cache option.
String getRequestProperty(String)	Returns the property indexed by the given String.
setRequestProperty(String, String)	Sets the property indexed by the first String to the second String.
String getDefaultRequestProperty(String)	Returns the default value for the property indexed by the given String.
setDefaultRequestProperty(String, String)	Sets the default value for the property indexed by the first String to the second String.
boolean getDoInput()	Returns a boolean indicating whether this URLConnection supports input.
setDoInput(boolean)	Sets the doInput flag.
boolean getDoOutput()	Returns a boolean indicating whether this URLConnection supports output.
setDoOutput(boolean)	Sets the doOutput flag.

Table 14-5: *Miscellaneous options for the URLConnection class.*

Working With Other Protocols

We can extend the functionality of the URL class to work with more protocols than those supplied by Sun and Netscape. The URLStreamHandler class, described in the Java API, is used by the URL class when opening a URLConnection. The URLStreamHandler is responsible for initiating the necessary sockets to the computer containing the resource and performing any handshaking required by the protocol. Like the ContentHandler class, each protocol has or could have a URLStreamHandler class devoted to it. The methods of the URLStreamHandler class are listed in Table 14-6.

Method	Description
URLConnection openConnection(URL)	Creates a URLConnection connected to the specified URL.
void parseURL(URL, String, int, int)	Parses the given String into the given URL. The integers refer to starting and ending indices of the URL within the String. By default, this method parses URLs in standard Internet form (//hostname/directory).
String toExternalForm(URL)	Returns the given URL in standard String notation.
setURL(URL, String, String, int, String, String)	Sets the protocol type, hostname, port number, directory location, and reference for the given URL.

Table 14-6: *Methods of the URLStreamHandler class.*

We can change the default URLStreamHandler for a given URL by using the setURLStreamHandlerFactory method on the URL. This method is static, so it can be called before our URL is constructed. It sets the default URLStreamHandlerFactory for all subsequently created URLs. We will want to change the URLStreamHandlerFactory if we create a new implementation of it and want our URLs to use it to handle their connections. Like the ContentHandlerFactory interface, the URLStreamHandlerFactory interface consists of a single method, createURLStreamHandler, which takes a String as an argument and returns a URLStreamHandler. The String indicates which protocol the URLStreamHandler is expected to handle.

Currently, you're not permitted to set the URLStreamHandlerFactory for your URLs in applets running under Netscape Navigator 2.0. Again, the reasoning behind this restriction is obscure, as this limits the ability of programmers to extend Java applets to communicate via other protocols, like FTP or HTTP-NG. It's still possible to create an applet that communicates via other protocols by programming with sockets directly, but you can't use the URL framework described in the Java API.

If you are interested in extending the URL classes to work with a new protocol, you'll need to implement a URLConnection and a URLStreamHandler that are specific to the protocol, and either create or extend a URLStreamHandlerFactory to include your new classes. Until Netscape relaxes the security on setting factories in applets, you will not be able to use your own URLStreamHandlerFactory classes in applets unless you chose to rewrite the URL classes entirely.

What URLs Are Good For

You might be wondering why we bothered to write this chapter, given that much of the functionality of the URL classes is not allowed or supported in Java applets running under Netscape Navigator 2.0, currently the most popular Web browser. URLs are great because they provide a consistent way to store all of the information necessary to communicate with a particular resource in a single class. They perform all of the socket creation, protocol handshaking, and header interpretation necessary for retrieving resources via HTTP. With the advent of new ContentHandlers that can translate more complex resources into Java Objects such as video or database files, the ease of using URLs to retrieve resources will make using URLs far more efficient than decoding byte streams yourself. Netscape will probably eventually allow applets to set their own stream and content-handling handlers. If not, new ContentHandlers will probably be added to their default ContentHandlerFactory as Netscape Navigator's Java support matures.

Moving On

In this chapter, we've described how and why to use URLs when you are programming using resources from the network. One of the most prevalent uses for URLs in Java is connecting to programs via CGI.

The next chapter diverges momentarily from applets; in addition to discussing how to program servers in Java, we discuss some of the issues that arise when doing so. Using CGI programs as server back ends for Java applets has some merits—backward compatibility with existing forms interfaces, for instance, and speed and ease of development. However, CGI has many limitations; most notable is its stateless nature. We'll show you how to write servers in Java that provide you with far more functionality than even a very complex CGI program could offer.

15

Writing Java Servers

The focus of this section thus far has been on writing network clients in the applet paradigm. We now step back a bit to address broader issues involving client/server computing in the context of the World Wide Web.

When a service needs to be centralized, for reasons such as tracking and data sharing, you'll need to write an independent server. A server can also be used to strictly control data security. For example, in the chat program we present in this chapter, the server could be used to limit access to only authorized users and to allow private chat sessions between users.

In this chapter, we will:

※ Implement a protocol.

※ Chart the flow of data in a dynamic client-server system.

※ Build a server written in Java that implements our protocol.

※ Build a client based on our protocol.

We have chosen to design a protocol specifically for asynchronous character-based conferencing between two or more people. In other words, we want to design a *chat* protocol. We'll call our chat protocol Internet Turbo Chat, or ITC.

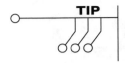

This chapter's code example files can be found on the Companion CD-ROM (for Windows 95/NT and Macintosh users) and the Online Companion (for UNIX users). Visit the Online Companion at http://www.vmedia.com/java.html.

Designing Your Server & Protocol

We begin by laying out our "blueprint" for the protocol. We want to be flexible in our design of the protocol so that we can add extra functionality; at the same time, we want to be specific and rigid enough to ensure robustness. We want to implement these high-level features initially:

* Usernames
* Asynchronous network operation
* Notification of new connections
* Notification of terminated connections
* A server window that lists the connected users

It seems apparent that we will need a "login" procedure so that users can enter a username before accessing the chat system. We can then pass messages typed by the user to the server without having to alter them by encoding them. We'll use a simplistic approach by limiting the data passed over the network to strings. The readln and println methods in the DataInputStream and PrintStream classes provide a nice way to transmit data without encoding/decoding the data.

The protocol we use is not very complex. It consists of an initial username transaction on both the client and the server and then an echoing of the client's messages to all of the other clients connected to the server. The server only processes the client's initial input, which is the username. This is used by the server to maintain the list of connections. We preformat the messages sent by the clients to the server so that the server need not parse the inputs. This cuts down on lag and improves server efficiency. However, if we choose to implement more features, such as a "private" chat, we'll need the server to parse a client's input so it can be properly routed.

Defining the Server's Tasks

As we noted above, the need for a specialized server often comes into play when specialized functions need to be performed. In our case, we need to do a few specialized tasks: echo the inputs over all the connections and keep track of the connections to the server. We could add a twist to the chat program by having each chat client also act as a simple server to enable communication between two chat programs. But since we want to be able to communicate between more than just two chat clients at once, this is not desirable.

We also want to keep the chat client applet as small as possible, since it must be downloaded along with the Web page for each user every time the user visits the Web page. To accomplish this, we can put more demand on the chat server for functions, like parsing input and output data, that can either be handled by the server or the client. We also have to consider the amount of load a server puts on the machine it is running on—if the machine is slow, the services provided by the server will run slow.

Defining Client/Server Interaction

Coordinating a server with multiple clients is an important issue when features require synchronous updating. For instance, if you wish to update all of your clients connected to a server with some specific data or command, you must build some robustness into your server so that it does not "hang" while trying to pass data to a connection.

In our chat program, we would like for all of the chat clients to receive data from the server at the same time, so that multiple lines sent by the same user will be kept together when the other users see it. We'll deal with this issue by making only one independent thread that handles the data output to the clients. This way, the independent thread can freely send data to all the client connections without getting stuck on a particular connection's data input. Since we only do one thing in this thread, write data to clients, this ensures us that the clients will receive data at the same time. To coordinate this interaction well, we have to consider issues of timing, complexity, and speed.

Timing

We addressed the need to write data simultaneously to client ports. Although this is not entirely possible, we do want to reduce the time it takes to write data to all the clients so it appears that the data is being delivered simultaneously. The free-running thread we use to write this data to client connections can be given a high priority over the threads that read data from each client. We can afford to wait until the writer thread has finished to start reading data from the client connections. The other timing issue we need to address is associated with a client sending data to the server. If two clients send data to the server at once, the thread that writes the outgoing data may be busy; we use a synchronized block of code to avoid this race condition. This is discussed in the section below.

Complexity

The fact that we have multiple connections adds a level of complexity to our chat server that is not highly visible at first. There are several things we must track, the first of which is the condition of each connection. If a user terminates the chat client without informing the chat server, we'll get a lingering connection that is not functioning properly. The writer thread may attempt to write to the defunct connection, and we may still be trying to read data from the connection on the server. The solution to this is twofold: when an operation is performed on a connection that is no longer active, catch an exception and terminate the connection; then do routine clean-up of the connections by checking them occasionally. By checking and terminating connections, we free up valuable system resources. The routine checking of the connections is done via the ConnectionWatcher class in the example. It runs in its own thread as well, so it can perform its duties without holding up the other functions.

We must be able to read from a client connection without losing the ability to read from the other connections. If we use a loop that simply does a sequential readln on each client connection, we may end up waiting for a user who is no longer using the chat client but has left it running while he has gone to lunch. We deal with the problem by making the entire server asynchronous—we create a reader thread for every connection. This way, an individual thread can wait as long as necessary for a user to enter a message without suspending the operation of the server. When a user does enter a message, we simply pass it off to the writer (which is on its own thread), which will write the message to every client. The reader thread can then immediately resume reading another message sent by the user. By having a reader thread for every connection, we avoid having to wait for any single connection to finish reading data, and it makes the server truly asynchronous. We must be careful, however, not to try to access the shared writer and ConnectionWatcher thread when another thread is attempting to use it. This is done via a synchronized declaration around the block of code that may have attempted multiple accesses.

The ServerWriter thread, as we have mentioned, writes output data to all of the connections. We use a notify call to "wake up" the ServerWriter. When it resumes execution, it looks in a pre-defined variable for the data it needs to send over the connections to the clients. We use a First In First Out (FIFO) data structure to hold this output data to avoid the race condition resulting from two reader threads calling notify. The FIFO class is discussed in detail in Chapter 17, "Interfacing With CGI: The Java Store."

If we did parsing of input and output data, we would need an additional thread whose job would be to handle requests from other threads to parse their data and dispatch it. This raises the level of complexity further, as we may need one of these threads for each connection. We do no parsing of data in our chat server.

Speed
The number of threads that the server has spawned can be quite large, since we must create a thread for each connection. This raises the issue of how fast the server performs when many threads are competing for the two ever-present ServerWriter and ConnectionWatcher threads. This is something that must be accounted for if we expect a large number of connections. We have to streamline these two classes as much as possible to account for their heavy usage. Additionally, if a large number of chat client connections is anticipated, we may want to duplicate the server itself to divide the load. We must then deal with the problems of running multiple servers and passing data between them, which is beyond the scope of the discussion in this chapter.

Building a Java Server

In this section, we implement the protocol described in the previous section. We'll begin by discussing the chat server in detail and end with a brief discourse on the corresponding chat client.

The chat server, shown in Figure 15-1, runs as a Java application as opposed to an applet. The applet paradigm is not very useful for this server example, as we want the server to have a static location, as well as a minimum amount of restriction from where the server can accept connections. Note that the entire chat server is contained in one class—chatserver. The only exception is the FIFO class, which we import.

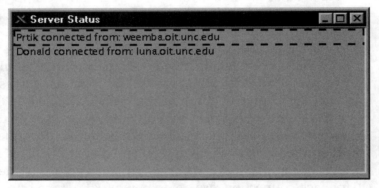

Figure 15-1: *Screen shot of chat server window.*

We make extensive use of multithreading to improve the structure and operation of the server. We make a new thread for each client connection and run three other threads constantly: a ServerWriter thread, which writes data to every connected client; a chatserver base thread, which listens for new clients attempting to create a connection with the server; and a ConnectionWatcher thread, which removes connections that have terminated. As we discussed in the "Complexity" section, additional threads may be necessary, so don't be afraid to use them! Threads offer a very nice way of organizing the control flow and complex interaction that you'll see when we go over the code. Threads do add some overhead to the entire system, but are generally worth the resource expense as long as the number of connections is not very large.

You'll notice that the chat server code has many, many try and catch statements. It's important to take full advantage of the chance to catch exceptions to make our code more robust. For example, we use an exception to trigger the process of checking connections. In a more complex server, exceptions play a critical role in stabilizing the overall functionality. They should be used whenever an error is even remotely likely to occur. They can also be used to call cleanup methods, to free system resources, to debug, and to tightly control the execution flow of the server.

The base class is chatserver, which extends Thread. The reason for implementing the base class as a thread is to be able to run the socket listening segment without having to stop to do other processing. This thread creates a new thread for each connection, and passes the newly created client socket to it.

Example 15-1a: Chat server code.

```java
import java.awt.*;
import java.net.*;
import java.io.*;
import java.util.*;
import FIFO;

public class chatserver extends Thread
    {
    public final static int DEFAULT_PORT = 6001;
    protected int port;
    protected ServerSocket server_port;
    protected ThreadGroup CurrentConnections;
    protected List connection_list;
    protected Vector connections;
    protected ConnectionWatcher watcher;
    protected ServerWriter writer;

    // Exit with an error message, when an exception occurs.
    public static void fail(Exception e, String msg) {
        System.err.println(msg + ": " +  e);
        System.exit(1);
    }
```

```java
    // Create a ServerSocket to listen for connections on;
    // start the thread.
    public chatserver(int port) {
        // Create our server thread with a name.
        super("Server");
        if (port == 0) port = DEFAULT_PORT;
        this.port = port;
        try { server_port = new ServerSocket(port); }
        catch (IOException e) fail(e, "Exception creating
server socket");
        // Create a threadgroup for our connections
        CurrentConnections = new ThreadGroup("Server Connec-
tions");

        // Create a window to display our connections in
        Frame f = new Frame("Server Status");
        connection_list = new List();
        f.add("Center", connection_list);
        f.resize(400, 200);
        f.show();

        // Initialize a vector to store our connections in
        connections = new Vector();
        // Create a ConnectionWatcher thread to wait for
        // other threads to die.
        // It starts itself automatically.
        writer = new ServerWriter(this);
        watcher = new ConnectionWatcher(this, writer);
        // Start the server listening for connections
        this.start();
    }

    public void run() {
        try {
            while(true) {
                Socket client_socket = server_port.accept();
                Connection c = new Connection(client_socket,
CurrentConnections, 3, watcher, writer);
                // prevent simultaneous access.
                synchronized (connections) {
                    connections.addElement(c);
```

```
                            connection_list.addItem(c.getInfo());
                    }
                }
            }
        catch (IOException e) fail(e, "Exception while lis-
tening for connections");
    }

    // Start the server up, listening on an optionally
    // specified port
    public static void main(String[] args) {
        int port = 0;
        if (args.length == 1) {
            try port = Integer.parseInt(args[0]);
            catch (NumberFormatException e) port = 0;
        }
        new chatserver(port);
    }
}
```

We have started our server at this point, and it is listening on port 6001 for new incoming connections. Again, for each new connection, it creates a new thread, called Connection, and passes it the appropriate parameters. We add the new thread to a vector containing all the active connection threads. The vector is used later for checking the state of the connection. The ServerWriter uses it as well, to write to the connections. We also add the connection to the list displayed in the frame.

Communicating Via Sockets & Handling I/O Streams

The Connection class is the thread that handles all incoming communication with a client. It passes the outgoing stream handler to the ServerWriter, since we have designated that thread for writing data for the connections. It initializes the input and output streams by attaching the respective input and output component of the socket. We also get the initial username in this method, since this is the first thread to start specifically for the connection. We pass the username to the chatserver class using the getInfo method.

Example 15-1b: Chat server code.

```java
class Connection extends Thread {
    static int numberOfConnections = 0;
    protected Socket client;
    protected ConnectionWatcher watcher;
    protected DataInputStream in;
    protected PrintStream out;
    protected ServerWriter writer;

    public Connection(Socket client_socket, ThreadGroup
CurrentConnections,
int priority, ConnectionWatcher watcher, ServerWriter writer)
    {
//Give the thread a group and name
super(CurrentConnections, "Connection number" +
numberOfConnections++);

        this.setPriority(priority);
//set the thread's priority
        //localize the parameters
        client = client_socket;
        this.watcher = watcher;
        this.writer = writer;

        try {
            in = new
DataInputStream(client.getInputStream());
            out = new PrintStream(client.getOutputStream());
            writer.OutputStreams.addElement(out);
        }
//Attach the streams to the client socket's
//input and output streams and add this
//outputstream to the vector containing all
//of the output streams, used by writer

        catch (IOException e) {
            try client.close(); catch (IOException e2) ;
            System.err.println("Exception while getting
socket streams: " + e);
```

```
            return;
        }
        //Fire up the thread!
        this.start();
    }


    //The run method loops reading lines until
    //it is falls out due to a broken
    //connection.
    public void run() {
        String inline;
out.println("Welcome to Internet Turbo Chat");
//Send a welcome message to the client

        try {
//Loop until the connection is broken!
            while(true) {
                // read in a line
                inline = in.readLine();
                if (inline == null) break;
//We have a broken connection if null
                writer.outdata.push(inline);
//save the line for the writer

synchronized(writer)writer.notify();
//and call the writer! Note that this is
//synchronized() to prevent two Connection
//threads from calling it at the same time.
//It is a form of "locking".
            }
        }
        catch (IOException e);

//When we have a broken connection,
//clean up and call the watcher to
//remove it from the active connections
//vector and remove it from the list.
```

```
//The watcher also removes the outputstream
//from the writer's vector of outputstreams.
        finally {
            try client.close();
        catch (IOException e2) ;
synchronized (watcher) watcher.notify();
            }
    }

//This method gets the username name on
//initial connect, prints it to all currently
//connected clients, and passes back
//some info to use in the list of
//current connections.

    public String getInfo() {
       String inline="";
       try { inline = in.readLine(); }
       catch (IOException e) System.out.println("Caught an
Exception:" +e);

       writer.outdata.push(inline+" has joined chat\n");
       synchronized(writer)writer.notify();
//Again, call the writer to display the
//new user message. Do it in a synchronized
//form so you don't have multiple access.

return (inline+ " connected from: " +
client.getInetAddress().getHostName());
//return the name and the client computer
//name to be added to the connection list
    }
}
```

We now have an input reader defined and running for each client connection. Whenever we read a new message from the chat client, we call the writer to write the message to every chat client. We also nicely handle exits from a chat client by immediately invoking the watcher to remove the terminated client connection from all of the storage vectors.

Handling Multiple Connections & Multiple Applet Clients

We have been referring to the two workhorse threads, ServerWriter and ConnectionWatcher, that manage the connections and generate the output of the incoming messages to all of the clients. ServerWriter's sole purpose is to wait until it has been "called" via its notify, take the message to be sent to the clients, and send it. The ConnectionWatcher is spurred into action by its own notify, but it also wakes up and runs every 10 seconds. Its purpose is to check every connection's integrity and remove connections that are defunct.

Example 15-1c: Chat server code.

```
class ServerWriter extends Thread {
    protected chatserver server;
    public Vector OutputStreams;
    public FIFO outdata;
    private String outputline;
//We make the OutputStreams and outdata
//public for convenience; this allows
//direct
//access to add and remove a outputstream or
//message data, respectively.

    public ServerWriter(chatserver s) {
        super(s.CurrentConnections, "Server Writer");
//Put this thread into the parent ThreadGroup
//and name this thread
        server = s;
        OutputStreams = new Vector();
        outdata = new FIFO();
        this.start();
//Start this thread right away.
    }

    public synchronized void run() {
        while(true) {
```

```
//The thread loops forever, but is really
//only run when the wait condition has been
//reset by a notify. Again, we do this in a
//synchronized block to lock the thread to
//prevent multiple access.

        try this.wait(); catch (InterruptedException e)
                System.out.println
                ("Caught an Interrupted Exception");

    outputline = outdata.pop();
//Get the message at the top of the FIFO
//outdata, which the notifying method should
//have added the message to.

        synchronized(server.connections) {
//We must also lock the watcher thread so
//that it doesn't try to do something before
//this code finishes.

            for(int i = 0; i < OutputStreams.size(); i++) {
                PrintStream out;
                out =
(PrintStream)OutputStreams.elementAt(i);
                out.println(outputline);

//We iterate through the outputstreams,
//and print the message to each one.
                }
            }
        }
    }
}
```

The above class does a fair bit of work, as it is run every time a new message arrives from any of the clients. It also locks the ConnectionWatcher thread, which is a necessary procedure to ensure that an output stream is not removed from the

ServerWriter's OutputStreams vector before it can finish. The
ConnectionWatcher thread modifies the ServerWriter's
OutputStreams vector when a connection is found terminated.

Example 15-1d: Chat server code.

```
class ConnectionWatcher extends Thread {
    protected chatserver server;
    protected ServerWriter writer;
    protected ConnectionWatcher(chatserver s, ServerWriter
writer) {
        super(s.CurrentConnections, "ConnectionWatcher");

//Put the thread in the parent's ThreadGroup,
//and give it a name
        server = s;
        this.writer = writer;
        this.start();
    }


    //This is the method that waits for notification of
    //exiting threads and cleans up the lists.  It is a
    //synchronized method, so it acquires a lock on the
    //'this' object before running.  This is necessary so
    //that it can call wait() on this.  Even if the
    //Connection objects never call notify(), this method
    //wakes up every five seconds and checks all the
    //connections, just in case. Note also that all access to
    //the Vector of connections and to the GUI List component
    //are within a synchronized block as well. This prevents
    //the Server class from adding a new connection while
    //we're removing an old one.
public synchronized void run() {

//We lock this thread when it is running so
//we do not create a situation where multiple
//access is allowed.
```

```
            while(true) {
//The thread loops forever.
                try this.wait(10000);
//The thread "runs" every 10 seconds to
//remove any zombie connections that may be
//present.
                catch (InterruptedException e){
                    System.out.println("Caught an Interrupted
Exception");
                }

                synchronized(server.connections) {
//Go through each connection
                    for(int i = 0; i < server.connections.size();
i++) {
                        Connection c;
                        c =
(Connection)server.connections.elementAt(i);

                        if (!c.isAlive()) {
//if the connection isn't alive anymore,
//remove it from the Vector.
server.connections.removeElementAt(i);
                        writer.outdata.push(server.connection_list.getItem(i)+"
has left chat\n");
synchronized(writer)writer.notify();
//Tell the other clients that the user has
//left!
 server.connection_list.delItem(i);
//Finally, remove it from the server's
//connection list.
                            i=i-1;
//We have to decrement the counter since we
//just made the connection's vector smaller by one!
                        }
                    }
                }
            }
        }
```

That completes the code for the server. Using the many classes provided in the Java API, we have created a fairly robust, multithreaded server. The server can be seen in action using the chat client at http://www.vmedia.com/onlcomp/java/chapter 15/ ChatClient.html. We'll now move on to the chat client. We use multiple threading in the client, as well, to achieve complete asynchronous communication.

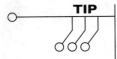

TIP

For another example of implementing servers in Java, see the tutorial in Chapter 19, "Writing Your Own Servers: A Meeting Scheduler."

Building the Chat Client

The chat client Applet is contained within the Web browser window (see Figure 15-2). It automatically connects to port 6001 on the host from which the Web page was loaded. We pop open a Frame so the user can enter a name for other users to identify them with. We create two independent threads—one to read from the network and one to write to the network. This makes the client truly asynchronous as the user can be typing a message while new messages from other users are displayed.

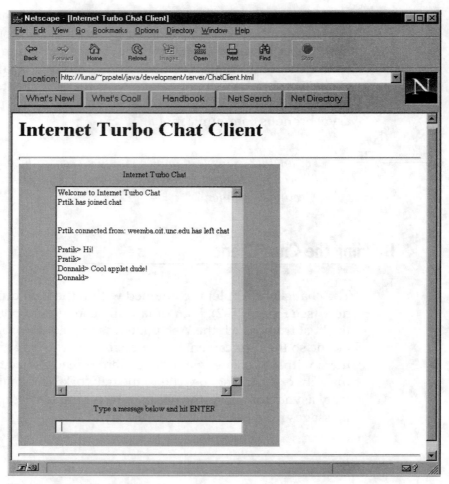

Figure 15-2: *The chat client.*

Example 15-2: Chat client.

```
import java.io.*;
import java.net.*;
import java.awt.*;
import java.applet.*;
```

```java
public class chatclient extends Applet {

public static final int DEFAULT_PORT = 6001;
public  Socket socket;
private  Thread reader, writer;
public TextArea OutputArea;
public TextField InputArea;
public PrintStream out;
public String Name;
public UserInfoFrame NameFrame;

    //Create the reader and writer threads
    //and start them.
    public void init () {
      OutputArea = new TextArea(20, 45);
      InputArea = new TextField(45);
      NameFrame = new UserInfoFrame(this);
      add( new Label("Internet Turbo Chat"));
      add(OutputArea);
      add( new Label("Type a message below and hit ENTER"));
      add(InputArea);
      resize(400,400);

        try {
            socket = new Socket(getDocumentBase().getHost(),
DEFAULT_PORT);
            reader = new Reader(this, OutputArea);
          out = new PrintStream(socket.getOutputStream());
//Set unequal priorities so that the
//console is shared effectively.
            reader.setPriority(3);
            reader.start();
        }
        catch (IOException e) System.err.println(e);
    }
```

```java
public boolean handleEvent(Event evt) {
  if (evt.target == InputArea)
    {
       char c=(char)evt.key;
       if (c  == '\n')
//Watch for the user to hit the ENTER key.
//This lets us know that the message is ready
//to be sent!

         {
            String InLine = InputArea.getText();
            out.println(Name + "> " + InLine);
            InputArea.setText("");
//Send the message, but add the user's name
//to it so that the other clients know who
//has sent it.
            return true;
         }
    }
  else if ( evt.target == NameFrame) {
//The initial entering of the username is
//passed to this base Applet. We must send it
//to the server, so it can set the user list!

    Name = (String)evt.arg;
    out.println(Name);
//Send the username to the chat server.
    return true;
  }
  return false;
}
}
/
//The Reader method reads input from the
//socket and updates the OutputArea with
//the new messages.

class  Reader extends Thread {
  protected chatclient client;
  private TextArea OutputArea;
```

```java
    public Reader(chatclient c, TextArea OutputArea) {
        super("chatclient Reader");
        this.client = c;
        this.OutputArea = OutputArea;
    }
    public void run() {
        DataInputStream in = null;
        String line;
        try {
            in = new
DataInputStream(client.socket.getInputStream());
            while(true) {
//Loop forever
                line = in.readLine();
                if (line == null) {
                OutputArea.setText("Server closed
                connection.");
                    break;
//But break when the connection has died.
                }
                OutputArea.appendText(line+"\n");
//Add the new message to the OutputArea
            }
        }
        catch (IOException e) System.out.println("Reader: " +
e);
        finally try if (in != null) in.close(); catch
(IOException e) ;
        System.exit(0);
    }
}

//This is the frame class which is used to
//get the user's name.
class UserInfoFrame extends Frame {
public TextField UserNameField;
public Applet parent;
```

```java
public UserInfoFrame(Applet parent) {
  UserNameField = new TextField(10);
  this.parent=parent;
  add("North", new Label("Please enter your name and hit
ENTER"));
  add("South", UserNameField);
  resize(300, 100);
  show();
}

//We pass the entered name in the form of a
//posted event to the parent Applet.
public boolean keyDown( Event evt, int key)
  {
    char c=(char)key;
    if (c  == '\n')
      {
        Event NewEvent = new Event(this, Event.ACTION_EVENT,
UserNameField.getText());
        parent.postEvent(NewEvent);
//generate the event on the parent Applet
        dispose();
//destroy the frame now.
    return true;
      }
    else { return false; }
  } //action
}
```

Moving On

You have had a full plate for the main course, now prepare for dessert! We have outlined and discussed the topics essential to developing toy applets, building full-featured client-server systems, and almost everything in between. In Section V, we present four tutorial applets that use the design principles, techniques, and tools we have covered during the course of this book. Enjoy!

SECTION V

Internet Applications by Example

In the following tutorials, we create a highly configurable, interactive animation applet; an online store; a client to the popular Internet Chess Server; and a client-server meeting scheduler. In each tutorial, we create a scenario in which an imaginary client comes to us with an idea for an Internet application. We then walk you through the steps necessary to meet the client's needs. All files for the tutorials are provided on the Companion CD-ROM and the Online Companion.

16

Interactive Animation: An Advertising Applet

What You'll Learn

In this tutorial, we are going to create a highly configurable interactive animation applet. Designing animations and interactions is fairly simple in and of itself, but we want to write an applet that will be very easy for Web designers who have no Java programming background to work with. This will involve developing several skills we have looked at previously:

- Using the URL class to access a configuration file.
- Dynamically loading remote classes using the Class class.
- Creating an interface to enhance configurability.
- Tracking images with the MediaTracker.
- Employing double buffering to eliminate flicker.
- Distributing mouse events.

The Contract

An online advertising agency has seen how effectively applets can spice up a Web page. They are especially interested in the interactive animation that Java has made possible and have asked us to create an applet that can animate a series of images as well as interact with the user. For instance, they would like the user to be able to click or move the mouse over one part of an image to load a new page or change the animation. However, since they aren't ready to do programming in-house, they need an applet that is highly configurable. They want to be able to change the images that make up the animation and configure how the applet will respond to the user.

Our applet is thus going to have two audiences—the Web public, who will see it, and the Web designers, who will use it to fit their needs. But before we start hacking away, let's look at how to use what we already know to achieve the desired results. Then we'll do a high-level design and implement it.

Features

We know that our applet has two audiences—the Web public and the Web designers of the online advertising agency. Let's look at the features that will be needed to satisfy the first audience.

The purpose of our applet will be to jazz up the Web page and allow the online advertising service to communicate their message to the Web surfer. Our applet is the medium for their message, and our job is to make sure it functions well as a medium. The first difficulty we face is getting the applet downloaded and started. Since it will just be one element in the Web page, people may not wait around for it to appear. In fact, if it takes too long, they might leave the page before they even know an applet exists. This is a problem that is especially difficult to solve for animated applets such as ours because they must load a lot of images, and transferring image data across the Internet takes time. The trick will be to get the applet started immediately, well before all images are loaded.

We also need to make sure that our applet will animate images smoothly. We'll accomplish this by employing the double-buffering techniques we learned in Chapter 5, "How Applets Work."

By planning how to handle quick loading, smooth animation, and an easy-to-use interface, we've dealt with the technical aspects of how our applet will function as a medium for the message. Now we need to consider how to make it easy for the Web designer to express that message. We can't influence the Web designer's choices regarding snazzy graphics for the applet, but we can make the images easy to fit into the applet.

As discussed in Chapter 5, a Web designer can use the PARAM and VALUE tags to change the way an applet works, which would be fine if we were just describing a series of images to be animated. In our applet, though, the Web designer will not only need to describe areas inside each of those images, but also how the user can interact with them. This is a lot of information to be contained within the applet tag. And if the Web designer wants to use the same configuration on a different Web page, cutting and pasting from one Web page to another will be required.

All that cutting and pasting would be tedious, so we'll keep the configuration information in a separate file. The param-value tag will be used solely to point at the configuration file. The configuration file will be written in a very simple programming language that we will develop for this applet. Of course, it would be easy for us to get carried away, resulting in the Web designer having to learn lots of made-up syntax. We need to be wary of this, since our client wants the applet to be configurable so they don't have to deal with complication.

We've considered the two primary audiences of our applet—Web surfers and Web designers. Now we need to consider how we as programmers can benefit from the exercise of creating an applet. We'll use the techniques we learned in Chapter 10, "Advanced Program Design," to make sure we gain some reusable components, and we'll structure our applet in such a way that it will be simple for us to add features later on.

Design

Now that we have some parameters for the problems we'll face, we can start thinking of solutions. Let's think of our applet as having a front end and a back end. The front end is the part that the Web surfer sees, and the back end is what the Web designer uses to configure the applet. The front end is the logical place to start, since it's hard to think about configuring something we haven't designed yet.

Structuring the Display

We already know how to handle a lot of the basics of our display . We know how to animate images, and we know how to interact with the mouse. Essentially, all we are doing is combining the two. When the mouse moves or clicks, we will look at the areas described for the current image, and perform the appropriate action if the mouse is inside one of them.

Let's ignore the animation for now and focus on how to pull off the interactive part of our applet. Our first problem is detecting when the mouse is inside an area described by the Web designer. A quick glance at the online documentation for the Abstract Windowing Toolkit shows that we have the Polygon class at our disposal. The AWT also defines the methods to use to see if a particular point is inside the shape. So we don't have to worry about writing complicated algorithms to detect when the mouse is inside a particular area; we can just instantiate the Polygon classes and let them figure it out for us.

Now we need to address the problem of generating the right action when the mouse clicks or moves over one of our areas. One solution is to have a long series of if-then-else statements within our mouseMove and mouseDown methods. We can load each of our areas and their actions into a Hashtable when we configure the applet and look up in the table each time a mouse action occurs. Let's assume we just use Polygons to describe the areas, and we put all of them in a hashtable called areasTable. Then, the mouseDown method can take care of the clickable areas like this:

```java
public boolean mouseDown(Event evt, int x, int y) {

    Enumeration e=areasTable.keys();
    while (e.hasMoreElements()) {
      Polygon p=e.getNextElement();
      if (p.inside(x,y)) {
      String S=(String)areasTable((Polygon)p);
      if (S.equals("sound action"))
        //make sound
      if (s.equals("link action"))
        //link to page
```

```
    if (s.equals("redirect action"))
      //change the animation
    //.... and so on, for all of our types
    // of areas


      }
    return true;
  }
```

Our example has a few efficiency problems that we could clean up. However, making this code more efficient won't make it more extensible. With our table look-up method, we have to add code every time we come up with a new type of action. Instead, let's create a base class for our action areas. Then, our applet can just tell the action area to do whatever it is supposed to do. Our mouseDown method will be much simpler. Since we don't need a Hashtable any more, we store our actionAreas in a Vector called aAreas:

```
public boolean mouseDown(Event evt, int x,int y) {
  Enumeration e=aAreas.elements();
  while(e.hasMoreElements()) {
    actionArea A=e.nextElement();
    if (A.inside(x,y))
      A.doAction();
    }
```

Now we don't have to worry about rewriting our applet every time we create a new action area. Also, our mouseDown method is much cleaner. But what if we want to have two simultaneous animations, or we want to add additional functionality to the applet? Our problem is that we are tying all of our functionality directly into the applet's central methods.

It would be better to develop a component that then could be contained by the applet. Since the Applet class is a subclass of Container, it will automatically transmit events to components contained by it. Actually doing our work inside a component will make it easier to swap the interactive animation into any applet. We can use it just like we use a Scrollbar or any other subclass of Component. But what should we subclass? We could subclass

Component directly, but instead let's subclass Canvas. The Canvas class will make it easier to position the image, which will be important if we want the image to be able to move around. We'll name this Canvas subclass actionImageCanvas.

So far, we have created the need for several classes. We will definitely have an Applet subclass, but from here on out it will play a fairly minor role—it just contains actionImageCanvas. We also have the actionArea subclasses. Should we hook the actionArea subclasses directly to the actionImageCanvas? This will require relating the images directly to the drawing surface, which will be restrictive if we ever want to create or extensively manipulate the images on the client side.

Instead, let's create a class, actionImage, that is responsible for displaying itself and for keeping track of the actionAreas. This creates the hierarchy for our front end shown in Figure 16-1. Note that this isn't a hierarchy in terms of inheritance, just in terms of how we are structuring the display. It's more of a hierarchy of containment.

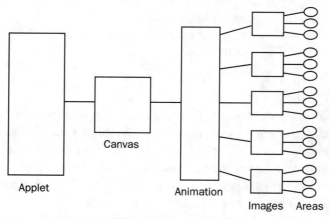

Figure 16-1: *Front end hierarchy.*

Now let's figure out how animation fits into our scheme. The concept is the same as it is for any animation, except instead of simply displaying an image, we need to activate the appropriate actionImage object. The only question is, which class in our hierarchy should start and maintain the thread? We can safely eliminate the Applet subclass—the whole point of actionImageCanvas is to isolate the project from the applet. Running the thread from actionImageCanvas will also be problematic if we ever want to run more than one animation inside a given canvas. Thus, we will leave responsibility for running the animation to the actionImage class. Table 16-1 outlines the responsibilities we have delegated to each of the classes in our system.

Class	Responsibilities
Applet subclass	Pass events to actionImageCanvas(es).
actionImageCanvas	Provide drawing surface for actionImage(s).
	Do bounds/collision checking for multiple animations.
	Pass events to actionImage(s).
actionImage	Run animation.
	Swap in correct actionAreas.
	Pass events to actionAreas.
actionArea	Create action.

Table 16-1: *Class responsibilities.*

Yes, we do indeed pass events through every single one of our classes, and we could have handled everything within an applet. But by creating the hierarchy as we do, we allow plug-and-play extensibility at each level.

Configuring the Display Structure

Now that we have a flexible structure for our display, we need to consider how it is going to be configured. As we have already observed, it would be less than ideal to read all of the necessary parameters from the Web page. Instead, we will open a URL connection and read a text file of parameters from there. In keeping with our object-oriented style, we will create a class to handle the configuration. Let's call it actionAnimConfigure.

As we do this, we need to be careful to make the flexibility of our structure accessible to the Web designer. If we want to plug in a new type of actionArea, it would be nice to not have to rewrite actionAnimConfigure. Our secret weapon here is Java's dynamic loading and binding, which we discussed in Chapter 10, "Advanced Program Design." Given some base class, we can create an instance of a subclass given the subclass's name. For instance, let's say we have a subclass of actionArea, called linkArea, whose action is to load a given page. Given the String "linkArea", we can create an instance as follows. As can be expected, a few exceptions may be thrown in the process of loading a class over the network based solely on its name!

```
try {
String S="linkArea";
actionArea baseArea=
(actionArea)Class.forName(S).newInstance();
}catch (ClassNotFoundException e) {
    System.out.println("Couldn't find"+S);
    System.out.println(e.getMessage());}
catch (InstantiationException e) {
    System.out.println("Couldn't create"+S);
    System.out.println(e.getMessage());}
catch (IllegalAccessException e) {
    System.out.println("Couldn't access"+S);
    System.out.println(e.getMessage());}
```

We create an instance of linkArea, but it is cast to actionArea. This means that we can only call one of the methods defined in our base class, actionArea. But when that method is called, the method in linkArea is actually invoked.

The trick is to read in a string that the Web designer supplies in the configuration file and use it to create subclasses of our base classes. We would like to do this in a way that ensures the highest degree of configurability. If we subclass ActionImageCanvas later on and add functionality, we would like for the Web designer to be able to use the functionality by just learning a couple of new parameters to set in the configuration file. At the same time, we need to isolate the Web designer from the underlying complexity as much as possible. This is after all, a large part of our responsibility as programmers!

As we mentioned before, our system will come with its own very simple programming language. Let's first consider the demands our system places on the language. We will need a way to figure out which class the Web designer wants, but remember that simply creating an instance of the class doesn't get it ready to function. We also need a way to feed additional information to the instance. For example, our actionAreas need to know where their location is on the image. Additionally, each subclass of actionArea will need information relating to its particular action. The linkArea needs to know which page to link to, for instance. Therefore, the language needs a way to relay an indefinite amount of configuration information to the object.

Also, we need to make sure that it is relaying that information to the correct object. A single frame of animation can have several linkAreas, and we need to make sure we don't get the linkAreas of one frame mixed up with those of another. Thus, we need a way to differentiate the configuration information so that it goes to the right place.

At the same time, we have to keep the language simple. We know that our Web designer knows HTML and has had to keep up with the seemingly endless introduction of extensions. This can be our benchmark—can our language be similar in complexity to HTML? We can also use HTML as something of a model.

Let's try to create an HTML-like configuration language. We want to describe an interactive animation with two images. The first image will have two ShowDocAreas, and the second will have a ShowDocArea and a soundArea:

```
<ActionImage=ActionImage>
image=someImage.gif
next=1
<ShowDocArea=ShowDocArea>
doc=http://www.vmedia.com
area=0,0;10,0;10,10;0,10
</ShowDocArea>
<ShowDocArea=ShowDocArea>
doc=http://www.vmedia.com/java
```

```
area=10,10;10,20;20,20;20,10
</ShowDocArea>
</ActionImage>

<ActionImage=ActionImage>
image=someOtherImage.gif
next=0
<ShowDocArea=ShowDocArea>
doc=http://www.vmedia.com/java
area=0,0;10,0;10,10;0,10
</ShowDocArea>
<SoundArea=SoundArea>
sound=someSound.au
area=10,10;10,20;20,20;20,10
</SoundArea>
</ActionImage>
```

By borrowing from HTML's style, we can create a small language that meets our needs, but is still familiar to anyone with Web authoring experience. We still have a few problems to solve. First, we haven't allowed for multiple animations within the same ActionImageCanvas. We can solve this by adding a higher-level tag, animation:

```
<ActionImageAnimation=ActionImageAnimation>
ActionImage tags...
</ActionImageAnimation>

<ActionImageAnimation=ActionImageAnimation>
ActionImage tags...
</ActionImageAnimation>
```

Now we know the enclosed tags refer to different animations. We can use the same strategy to both solve the problem of specifying the size of the canvas and allow for the possibility that we may subclass ActionImageCanvas with additional functionality. We can also allow defaults for some of the type declarations in the frame and canvas tags. When we implement the Configure class, we will fully formulate the language. For now, we can describe the language loosely as follows. Remember that each tag lower than animation can have multiple occurrences:

```
<ActionImageCanvas=subclass name>
parameters=values
<ActionImageAnimation=subclass name>
parameters=values
<ActionImage=subclass name>
parameters=values
<ActionArea=subclass name>
</ActionArea>
</ActionImage>
</ActionImageAnimation>
</ActionImageCanvas>
```

Now that we have the language built for the Web designers, we need to decide how the Configure class will use it to start the applet. Interfaces come in handy in this type of situation. We can have an Interface called Configurable. Our Configure class will be able to pass information by calling the methods defined in the Configurable interface, as shown in Figure 16-2.

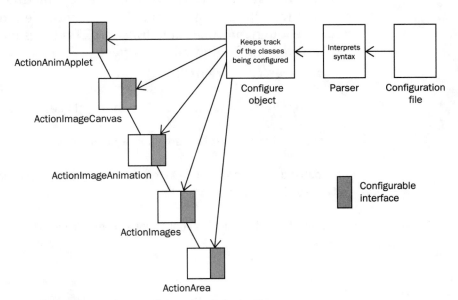

Figure 16-2: *Passing configuration information.*

Implementation

Now that we have planned our high-level design, we can start writing code. But where should we start? We could write an applet, get the animation working, and retrofit our design ideas later. Considering how many different parts must interact for our system to work, it would be best to flesh out each module first. This means it will be longer until we actually have some running program, but when we do, it will be closer to what we want.

Making Our Applet Configurable

Let's start by laying out the Configurable interface, which we need to set up the system. We know that we'll have to attach the modules in our hierarchy to the next higher module. We also know that once the module is attached, it will need to be passed configuration information. It would be nice to tell the module when we are done with the configuration. Then, the module can look to see if it has enough information to function. This gives us three methods for our Configurable interface:

```
Interface Configurable {

    public void attachObject(Object o) throws Exception;

    public boolean setParent(Configurable parent);

    public void configureObject(String param, String value)
throws Exception;

    public void completeConfiguration() throws Exception;

}
```

Notice that the attachObject method is passed an Object instance; this implies that Configure is going to instantiate the class and then pass it to one of the modules in our system. Also, note that the last two methods will be invoked from the object that is to be configured, not the one it was attached to.

We have designated the last two methods to throw exceptions, but as we learned in Chapter 10, "Advanced Program Design," it's bad practice not to give them more descriptive names. So let's set up an exception hierarchy to go along with the Configurable interface. The top exception can be ConfigurableException so that we know where the exceptions are coming from. Now we need to consider what can go wrong in the last two methods:

- configureObject may not recognize the parameter.
- configureObject may not be able to evaluate the value.
- completeConfiguration may not be able to take the information and complete the configuration.

This yields the exception hierarchy for Configurable shown in Figure 16-3.

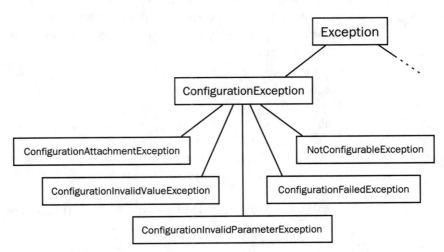

Figure 16-3: *Configurable exception hierarchy.*

We can now finish coding the Configurable interface and complete the first actual code of our project. We will put it in the package ventana.util, since it isn't specific:

```java
package ventana.util;

public interface Configurable {

  public void attachObject(Object o) throws
    ConfigurationAttachmentException;

   public void setParent(Object o);

   public void configureObject(String param, String value)
throws ConfigurationInvalidParameterException,
ConfigurationInvalidValueException;

   public void completeConfiguration() throws
ConfigurationFailedException;
```

The next step is to develop the Configure base class. We may want to use it later, so we will write a general class to go along with the Configurable interface and put it in ventana.util. To keep it general, we will parse our language in a separate class called ConfFileParser:

```java
package ventana.util;
import java.util.*;

public class Configure {
   private ConfFileParser parser;
   private Stack Configurables;
   private Configurable original;

public Configure(ConfFileParser cFP, Configurable
startObject) {
   parser=cFP;
   parser.setConfigure(this);
   Configurables=new Stack();
   Configurables.push(startObject);}
```

```
public boolean startConfiguration() {
   return parser.start();}

protected Configurable currentConfigurable() {
   return (Configurable)Configurables.peek();}

//the following methods are called by the parser

public void attach(String className) throws
   NotConfigurableException,
   ConfigurationAttachmentException,
   ClassNotFoundException,
   InstantiationException,
   IllegalAccessException{
   //let the parser figure out what went wrong

   Class thisClass=Class.forName(className);

   //Check to see if it's Configurable
   Class interfaces[]=thisClass.getInterfaces();
   boolean isConfigurable=false;
   for (int i=0;i<interfaces.length;i++)
      if(interfaces[i].equals(Class.forName
      ("ventana.util.Configurable")))
      isConfigurable=true;
   if(!isConfigurable)
   throw (new NotConfigurableException(className));

   Object instance=thisClass.newInstance();
   currentConfigurable().attachObject(instance);
   Configurables.push((Configurable)instance);}

public void passToCurrent(String parameter, String value)
throws ConfigurationInvalidParameterException,
ConfigurationInvalidValueException{
   currentConfigurable().configureObject(parameter,value);}
//Could be called directly from the parser,
//but this preserves integerity -
//it's preferable that the parser doesn't
//have access to the stack
```

```
public void configureCurrent() throws
ConfigurationFailedException{

currentConfigurable().completeConfiguration();

if (!Configurables.empty())
  Configurables.pop();
else throw
  (new ConfigurationFailedException("empty stack"));}
}
```

Base Classes for the Display

Now that we have the Configurable interface written, we can
write the base classes for our display. The most important part of
this step is implementing the methods of Configurable as we
move down our display hierarchy. As we go, we will also define
other methods that our classes will need.

We'll start with a base applet class for our system. Although
any class that implements Configurable will be able to parse files
and configure themselves, applets that want to run
ActionImageAnimations will need to subclass this class. The
ActionImage class needs the mediaTrackerHandle method so that
its instances can load images:

```
package ventana.aia;
import java.awt.*;
import java.applet.*;
import java.util.*;
import java.net.*;
import java.io.*;
import ventana.util.*;

public class ActionAnimApplet extends Applet implements
Configurable{

    private boolean configOk=false;
```

```java
Vector canvases=new Vector();
MediaTracker imageLoader;

public void init() {
   imageLoader=new MediaTracker(this);
   URL docURL=getDocumentBase();
   String confName=getParameter("conf");
   try {
   URL confURL=new URL(docURL,confName);
      AIAnimParser p=new AIAnimParser(confURL);
   Configure Conf=new Configure(p,this);
      configOk=Conf.startConfiguration();
      if (!configOk) return;
    }

    catch (MalformedURLException e) {
       showStatus(confName+" invalid URL");
       System.out.println(confName);
       System.out.println(e.getMessage());
          stop();}

    catch (IOException e) {
       showStatus(confName+" not accessible");
       System.out.println(e.getMessage());
       stop();}
    System.out.println("init complete");

  }

  public void paint(Graphics g) {
     paintComponents(g);}

private ActionImageCanvas getCanvas(int i) {
  return
  (ActionImageCanvas)canvases.elementAt(i);}

  public void start() {
       if (configOk) {
```

```
        for (int i=0;i<canvases.size();i++) {
           getCanvas(i).show();
           getCanvas(i).beginAction();}
              }


   }

public void stop() {
   for (int i=0;i<canvases.size();i++)
      getCanvas(i).stopAction();}

protected MediaTracker mediaTrackerHandle() {
   return imageLoader;}

protected ActionAnimApplet actionAnimAppletHandle() {
   return this;}

//implementation of Configurable

public void attachObject(Object o) throws
   ConfigurationAttachmentException {
   if (!(o instanceof ActionImageCanvas))
   throw(new ConfigurationAttachmentException(
   "not ActionImageCanvas"));
   //check to make sure we are getting
   //the right type of object
   ActionImageCanvas cur=
      (ActionImageCanvas)o;
   canvases.addElement(cur);
      cur.setParent(this);
   add(cur);}

public void configureObject(String param, String value)
   throws ConfigurationInvalidParameterException,
   ConfigurationInvalidValueException {

   throw (new ConfigurationInvalidParameterException
      ("No Configuration parameters"));
   }
```

```
public String toString() {
   String S="ActionAnimApplet: \n";
   for (int i=0;i<canvases.size();i++) {
      S=getCanvas(i).toString();}
   return S;}

public void completeConfiguration() throws
   ConfigurationFailedException {
   for (int i=0;i<canvases.size();i++)
      getCanvas(i).setParent(this);


   }

public void setParent(Object o) {
 System.out.println("no parent can be set for
ActionAnimApplet");}


}
```

This Applet subclass just gets everything started. Notice that our paint method simply tells the components to paint themselves. This lets us easily incorporate other functionality into the applet. Now we can start down our hierarchy with the ActionImageCanvas base class:

```
package ventana.aia;

import java.util.*;
import java.awt.*;
import java.awt.image.*;
import java.applet.*;
import ventana.util.*;
import ventana.awt.*;

public class ActionImageCanvas extends Canvas implements
Configurable{

   private int  canvasWidth=200;
   private int canvasHeight=200;
   private Vector Anims=new Vector();
   private Color backGroundColor=Color.lightGray;
```

```java
      private Vector curActionImages=new Vector();
      private ActionAnimApplet motherApplet;
      private BufferedImageGraphics buffer;
      private Event curEvent;

   public void paint(Graphics g) {
      if (buffer.needBuffer()) {
         Image bI=createBackground();
         buffer.setBuffer(bI);}
      buffer.paintBuffer(g);}

   public synchronized Image createBackground() {
    //Should be subclassed if you want the background
    //to be an image,etc.

      return createImage(size().width,size().height);}

   // allow the ActionImageAnimation thread
   // to keep the canvas up to date

   public ActionImage getCurActionImage(int i) {
      return (ActionImage) curActionImages.elementAt(i);}

   public synchronized void addToCanvas(ActionImage AI) {

      curActionImages.addElement(AI);
      buffer.addImage(translateActionImage(AI));
   }

   private PositionedImage translateActionImage(ActionImage AI)
   {
      Image I=AI.getImage();
      int x=AI.XPos();
      int y=AI.YPos();
      int iWidth=I.getWidth(motherApplet);
      int iHeight=I.getHeight(motherApplet);
      Rectangle r=new Rectangle(x,y,iWidth,iHeight);
```

```
    return new PositionedImage(I,r);}

public synchronized boolean removeImageFromCanvas(ActionImage
AI) {

    return buffer.removeImage(translateActionImage(AI));
        }

public synchronized void removeAreaFromCanvas(ActionImage AI)
{
    curActionImages.removeElement(AI);}

public boolean handleEvent(Event evt) {
    curEvent=evt;
    return super.handleEvent(evt);}

public void updateCanvas() {
    if (curEvent!=null)
    handleEvent(curEvent);
    refreshCanvas();}

public void refreshCanvas() {
    repaint();}

//deliver events to current ActionImages

private boolean insideActionImage(int x, int y, ActionImage
AI) {

    if(x<AI.XPos() || y<AI.YPos())

    return false;
    int imgWidth=AI.getImage().getWidth(motherApplet);
    int imgHeight=AI.getImage().getHeight(motherApplet);
    if(x>AI.XPos()+imgWidth)
       return false;
    if(x>AI.YPos()+imgHeight)
       return false;

    return true;}
```

```java
private Rectangle AIrect(ActionImage AI) {
   int x=AI.XPos();
   int y=AI.YPos();
   int width=AI.getImage().getWidth(motherApplet);
   int height=AI.getImage().getHeight(motherApplet);
   return new Rectangle(x,y,width,height);}

public boolean mouseMove(Event evt, int x, int y) {

   boolean shouldRefresh=false;
   for (int i=0;i<curActionImages.size();i++)    {
      ActionImage someAI=getCurActionImage(i);

   if(insideActionImage(x,y,someAI)) {
      int relativeX=x-someAI.XPos();
      int relativeY=y-someAI.YPos();
        Graphics gC=buffer.graphicsContext(AIrect(someAI));
   shouldRefresh=someAI.mouseMove(relativeX,relativeY,gC);

   }
   }
if (shouldRefresh) refreshCanvas();
return true;
}

public boolean mouseDown(Event evt, int x, int y) {
   boolean shouldRefresh=false;

   for (int i=0;i<curActionImages.size();i++)    {
      ActionImage someAI=getCurActionImage(i);

   if(insideActionImage(x,y,someAI)) {
      int relativeX=x-someAI.XPos();
      int relativeY=y-someAI.YPos();
      Graphics gC=buffer.graphicsContext(AIrect(someAI));
      shouldRefresh=someAI.mouseDown(relativeX,relativeY,gC);

   }
}
```

```
    if (shouldRefresh) refreshCanvas();
    return true;

}

public boolean mouseDrag(Event evt, int x, int y) {
    boolean shouldRefresh=false;

    for (int i=0;i<curActionImages.size();i++)    {
        ActionImage someAI=getCurActionImage(i);

    if(insideActionImage(x,y,someAI)) {
        int relativeX=x-someAI.XPos();
        int relativeY=y-someAI.YPos();
        Graphics gC=buffer.graphicsContext(AIrect(someAI));
        shouldRefresh=someAI.mouseDrag(relativeX,relativeY,gC);
    }
}
    if (shouldRefresh) refreshCanvas();
    return true;
}

public boolean mouseUp(Event evt, int x, int y) {
    boolean shouldRefresh=false;
    for (int i=0;i<curActionImages.size();i++)    {
        ActionImage someAI=getCurActionImage(i);

    if(insideActionImage(x,y,someAI)) {
        int relativeX=x-someAI.XPos();
        int relativeY=y-someAI.YPos();
        Graphics gC=buffer.graphicsContext(AIrect(someAI));
        someAI.mouseUp(relativeX,relativeY,gC);}
    }

if (shouldRefresh) refreshCanvas();

return true;
    }
```

```java
//implementation of Configurable

public void setParent(Object o) {
   motherApplet=(ActionAnimApplet)o;
   setBackground(motherApplet.getBackground());}

public ActionAnimApplet getApplet() {
   return motherApplet;}

public void attachObject(Object o) throws
   ConfigurationAttachmentException {
   if (!(o instanceof ActionImageAnimation))
     throw (new ConfigurationAttachmentException(
     "not ActionImageAnimation"));
   ActionImageAnimation cur=(ActionImageAnimation)o;
   Anims.addElement(cur);
   cur.setParent(this);
}

public void configureObject(String param, String value)
throws ConfigurationInvalidParameterException,
ConfigurationInvalidValueException {
   param=param.toLowerCase();
   value=value.toLowerCase();
   try {
   if (param.equals("width")) {
     canvasWidth=Integer.parseInt(value);
     return;        }
   if (param.equals("height")) {
     canvasWidth=Integer.parseInt(value);
     return;        }
   } catch (NumberFormatException e) {
   throw new ConfigurationInvalidValueException
   ("Not a number");}

   throw
   (new ConfigurationInvalidParameterException
       ("Unrecognized: "+param));}
```

```
public void completeConfiguration() throws
   ConfigurationFailedException {

      buffer=new
BufferedImageGraphics(motherApplet,getBackground());
   for (int i=0;i<Anims.size();i++) {
      getAnim(i).setParent(this);
      getAnim(i).setApplet(motherApplet);}
   }

public String toString() {
   String S="ActionImageCanvas\n";
   S=S+"bgColor"+backGroundColor.toString()+"\n";
   for (int i=0;i<Anims.size();i++)
      S=S+getAnim(i).toString();
      return S;}

//this method starts the animation threads in the canvas -
called by the applet

protected void beginAction() {
   for (int i=0;i<Anims.size();i++)
      getAnim(i).startAnimation();}

protected void stopAction() {
   for (int i=0;i<Anims.size();i++)
      getAnim(i).stopAnimation();}

private ActionImageAnimation getAnim(int i) {
   return
(ActionImageAnimation)Anims.elementAt(i);}

public Dimension minimumSize() {
   return new Dimension(canvasWidth,canvasHeight);
}

public Dimension preferredSize() {
   return minimumSize();
}
```

Again, we allow for multiple instances of the next member of the hierarchy, ActionImageAnimation. This class actually handles the painting of the frames. We use a seperate class, BufferedImageGraphics, to handle the double buffering:

```java
package ventana.awt;
import java.awt.*;
import java.awt.image.*;
import java.util.*;

public class BufferedImageGraphics {

    private Graphics graphicsBuf;
    private Image imageBuf;
    //Used to perform double buffering

    private ImageObserver imageObsv;
    private Vector curImages=new Vector();

    private int originalWidth;
    private int originalHeight;

    private Rectangle cropRect=new Rectangle();
    //cropping area
    private boolean waitToTouchImages=false;
    //keeps the buffer from being drawn if we're in the
    //process of adding or subtracting images
    Color backgroundColor;

    public BufferedImageGraphics(ImageObserver observer,
    Color c) {
        imageObsv=observer;
        backgroundColor=c;
    }

public boolean needBuffer() {
    return (graphicsBuf==null && imageBuf==null);}

public void setBuffer(Image i) {
    imageBuf=i;
```

```
        originalWidth=i.getWidth(imageObsv);
        originalHeight=i.getHeight(imageObsv);
        graphicsBuf=imageBuf.getGraphics();
        graphicsBuf.setColor(backgroundColor);
        graphicsBuf.fillRect(0,0,originalWidth,originalHeight);}

public synchronized void addImage(PositionedImage pI) {
    while (waitToTouchImages);
    waitToTouchImages=true;
    //since we have to draw an image and reset the cropping,
    //it would be possible to be asked to dump the buffer
    //before we finished. Chaos would ensue.
    Rectangle r=pI.getRect();
    //figure out how this affects our cropping area
    if (cropRect==null || cropRect.isEmpty()) cropRect=r;
    else
        cropRect=cropRect.union(r);
    curImages.addElement(pI);
    if (graphicsBuf!=null)
        graphicsBuf.drawImage(pI.getImage(),r.x,r.y,
        backgroundColor,imageObsv);
    waitToTouchImages=false;}

private PositionedImage getCurPosImage(int i) {
    return (PositionedImage)curImages.elementAt(i);}

public synchronized boolean removeImage(PositionedImage I)
{
    while (waitToTouchImages);
    waitToTouchImages=true;
    int imgIndx=curImages.indexOf(I);
    if (imgIndx==-1) {
    waitToTouchImages=false;
    return false;}
    Rectangle clearReg=getCurPosImage(imgIndx).getRect();
    //region to clear
    curImages.removeElementAt(imgIndx);
    graphicsBuf.fillRect(clearReg.x,clearReg.y,clearReg.width,
    clearReg.height);
    //clear the area
```

```
        cropRect=new Rectangle();
        //prepare to reset the cropping region

        for (int i=0;i<curImages.size();i++) {
            PositionedImage somePI=getCurPosImage(i);
            Image img=somePI.getImage();
            Rectangle someRect=somePI.getRect();
            cropRect.add(someRect);
            int x=someRect.x;
            int y=someRect.y;

            graphicsBuf.drawImage(img,x,y,imageObsv);

        }

        waitToTouchImages=false;

        return true;}

    public Graphics graphicsContext(Rectangle r) {
        cropRect.add(r);
        return graphicsBuf.create(r.x,r.y,r.width,r.height);}

    public synchronized void paintBuffer(Graphics g) {
        while (waitToTouchImages);
        waitToTouchImages=true;
        Rectangle curCR=g.getClipRect();
        if (curCR==null) curCR=new
        Rectangle(0,0,originalWidth,originalHeight);
        g.clipRect(cropRect.x,cropRect.y,cropRect.width,
        cropRect.height);
        g.drawImage(imageBuf,0,0,backgroundColor,imageObsv);
        g.clipRect(0,0,originalWidth,originalHeight);
        cropRect=new Rectangle();
        //reset the cropping area
        waitToTouchImages=false;
    }

}
```

Let's look at how events will be transmitted. We pass the events directly to all the ActionImages that are currently being displayed. Since our ActionImageCanvas is a component contained by the applet, we don't have to manually transmit events out of the applet—this is done automatically for us. And since ActionImage isn't a Component subclass and ActionImageCanvas isn't a Container subclass, the ActionImageCanvas has to handle the transmission. We make sure that the event is transmitted to the correct ActionImage and that the coordinates are relative.

WHY NOT SUBCLASS COMPONENT?

We could have resolved the transmission of events by making ActionImageCanvas a Container subclass and ActionImage a Component subclass. However, the Container is really meant to contain screen elements that aren't going to be moving. Instead of hacking through the difficulties of creating a layout manager that can respond to moving images, we write a new class that knows how to handle mouse events.

Now we create the ActionImageAnimation base class. The base class doesn't try to move images around, but it can be subclassed to allow patterns of movement. For instance, we can create an EllipticalActionImageAnimation class that moves images around in an elliptical pattern. As mentioned before, a subclass can also respond to collision with other images on the canvas. Additionally, this class can create effects such as morphing two images together. As it merges two images, it can simply call the updateImage method of the ActionImageCanvas class:

```
package ventana.aia;

import java.util.*;
import java.net.*;
import java.awt.*;
import java.applet.*;
import ventana.util.*;
```

```
public class ActionImageAnimation implements Configurable,
Runnable {

    private ActionImage ActionImages[];
    private Thread animator;
    private ActionAnimApplet motherApplet;
    private ActionImageCanvas parentCanvas;
    private boolean checkSequence=false;

    private Vector loadingActionImages=new Vector();
    private int curPause=100;
    private ActionImage curActionImage;

    public void attachObject(Object o) throws
        ConfigurationAttachmentException {
        if (!(o instanceof ActionImage))
            throw (new ConfigurationAttachmentException
                ("not an ActionImage"));
        ActionImage cur=(ActionImage)o;
        loadingActionImages.addElement(cur);
        cur.setParent(this);}

    public void setParent(Object o) {
        if (o instanceof ActionImageCanvas) {
            parentCanvas=(ActionImageCanvas)o;
            motherApplet=parentCanvas.getApplet();
        }
    }

    public ActionAnimApplet getApplet() {
        return motherApplet;}

    public void checkSequence() {
        checkSequence=true;}

    public void configureObject(String param, String value)
    throws
```

```java
ConfigurationInvalidParameterException,
ConfigurationInvalidValueException { }

public String toString() {
   String S="ActionImageAnimation\n";
   for (int i=0;i<ActionImages.length;i++)
     S=S+ActionImages[i].toString();
     return S;
}

public void completeConfiguration() throws
   ConfigurationFailedException {
   ActionImages=new ActionImage[loadingActionImages.size()];
   loadingActionImages.copyInto(ActionImages);
   if (checkSequence) orderActionImages();
 }

public void orderActionImages() {
   ActionImages[ActionImages.length-1].setNext(0);
   for (int i=0;i<ActionImages.length-1;i++)
     ActionImages[i].setNext(i+1);
}

public void startAnimation() {
   if (curActionImage==null)
     curActionImage=ActionImages[0];
   animator=new Thread(this);
   animator.start();}

public void stopAnimation() {
   animator.stop();}

public void run() {
   while(animator==Thread.currentThread()) {
   MediaTracker tracker=motherApplet.mediaTrackerHandle();
   if ((tracker.statusAll(true) & MediaTracker.ERRORED) !=0) {
     System.out.println("One or more images failed to load");
     return;}
```

```java
//if ((tracker.statusAll(true) & MediaTracker.COMPLETE)!=0)
//{
parentCanvas.removeImageFromCanvas(curActionImage);
parentCanvas.removeAreaFromCanvas(curActionImage);
//first pass through, we don't have to worry about these
//bombing on us.
int indx=curActionImage.next();

curActionImage=ActionImages[indx];
if(!(tracker.checkAll())) {
   if (!(tracker.checkID(curActionImage.priority(),true))) {
      try {
      animator.sleep(10);}
   catch (InterruptedException e) {break;}
      continue;}
   }
else {
   curActionImage.updateValues();
   parentCanvas.addToCanvas(curActionImage);
   parentCanvas.updateCanvas();
try {
   animator.sleep(curActionImage.pause());
      }catch (InterruptedException e) {
   break;}
   }

}
}

private protected ActionImage getNextActionImage(int i) {

   MediaTracker tracker=motherApplet.mediaTrackerHandle();
   int nextAI=curActionImage.next();
   if((tracker.statusAll(true) & MediaTracker.COMPLETE) !=0)
      return ActionImages[nextAI];
   else return curActionImage;}

   public void setApplet(ActionAnimApplet ap) {
   motherApplet=ap;}
}
```

We have only two base classes left to write! The first is the ActionImage class. In its simplest form, it draws its image on demand and transmits events to the ActionImageAreas. As we mentioned before, it could be subclassed to create images on the client side and thus avoid the problems associated with network speed:

```
package ventana.aia;

import java.util.*;
import java.net.*;
import java.awt.*;
import java.applet.*;
import ventana.util.*;

public class ActionImage implements Configurable{

    private Image thisImage;
    private URL imageURL;
    private int width=0;
    private int height=0;
    private int x=0;
    private int y=0;
    private int next=-1;
    private int imagePriority=0;
    private int pause=100;

    private ActionImageAnimation animParent;
    private ActionAnimApplet motherApplet;

    private ActionArea actionAreas[];
    private Vector loadingAreas=new Vector();

    public int XPos() {return x;}
    public int YPos() {return y;}
    public Rectangle getBoundingRect() {
        return new Rectangle(x,y,width,height);}

    public int pause() {return pause;}
```

```java
public void attachObject(Object o) throws
   ConfigurationAttachmentException {
   if(!(o instanceof ActionArea))
      throw (new ConfigurationAttachmentException
         ("not action area"));
   ActionArea curActionArea=(ActionArea)o;
   loadingAreas.addElement(curActionArea);
   curActionArea.setParent(this);
}

public void configureObject(String param, String value)
throws ConfigurationInvalidParameterException,
ConfigurationInvalidValueException {
   boolean paramHandled=false;
   param=param.toLowerCase();
   value=value.toLowerCase();
if (param.equals("image")) {
try {
   URL docBase=motherApplet.getDocumentBase();
imageURL=new URL(docBase,value);
paramHandled=true;

catch(MalformedURLException e) {
   throw (new ConfigurationInvalidValueException("not a URL:"
   +value));}

}

   try {
      if (param.equals("priority")) {
         imagePriority=Integer.parseInt(value);
         paramHandled=true;}
      if (param.equals("width")) {
         width=Integer.parseInt(value);
         paramHandled=true;}
      if (param.equals("height")) {
         height=Integer.parseInt(value);
         paramHandled=true;}
```

```
        if (param.equals("x")) {
          x=Integer.parseInt(value);
          paramHandled=true;}
        if (param.equals("y")) {
          y=Integer.parseInt(value);
          paramHandled=true;}
        if (param.equals("next")) {
          next=Integer.parseInt(value);
          paramHandled=true;}
        if (param.equals("pause")) {
          pause=Integer.parseInt(value);
          paramHandled=true;}
        } catch (NumberFormatException e) {
        throw (new ConfigurationInvalidValueException
        (e.getMessage()));}
      if (!paramHandled) {
        throw (new ConfigurationInvalidParameterException
        (param));}


    }

    public String toString() {
      String S="ActionImage\n";
      S=S+"width="+width+"\n";
      S=S+"height="+height+"\n";
      S=S+"next="+next+"\n";
      for (int i=0;i<actionAreas.length;i++)
        S=S+actionAreas[i].toString();
        return S;}

    public void completeConfiguration() throws
      ConfigurationFailedException {
      MediaTracker mT=motherApplet.mediaTrackerHandle();

      actionAreas=new ActionArea[loadingAreas.size()];
      loadingAreas.copyInto(actionAreas);
```

```
    if (imageURL==null) throw (new
        ConfigurationFailedException("no image URL"));
    else
        thisImage=motherApplet.getImage(imageURL);

    if (next==-1) animParent.checkSequence();

    if (width>0 && height>0)
        mT.addImage(thisImage,imagePriority,width,height);
    else {
    if (width>0 && height<=0) throw(new
        ConfigurationFailedException
        ("width specified, but not height"));
    if (height>0 && width<=0) throw(new
        ConfigurationFailedException
        ("height specified, but not width"));
    }

mT.addImage(thisImage,imagePriority);
mT.checkID(imagePriority,true);
//makes sure the media tracker goes and gets this one

}
```

Now we're left with the ActionArea class. The ActionImage class has already figured out what kind of event it is and calls the right event handling method directly:

```
package ventana.aia;
import java.applet.*;
import java.awt.*;
import java.util.*;
import ventana.util.*;

public class ActionArea implements Configurable {

    private Polygon thisArea;
    private protected ActionAnimApplet motherApplet;
    private ActionImage parentActionImage;
```

```
    public void setParent(Object o) {
    parentActionImage=(ActionImage)o;
       motherApplet=parentActionImage.getApplet();}

    public void attachObject(Object o) throws
       ConfigurationAttachmentException
    {throw (new ConfigurationAttachmentException("Can't
    attach"));}

public void configureObject(String param, String value)
throws ConfigurationInvalidParameterException,
ConfigurationInvalidValueException {

    param=param.toLowerCase();
    if(param.equals("area"))
       parseArea(value);
    else throw (new
       ConfigurationInvalidParameterException (param));
    }

public String toString() {
    String S="ActionArea\n";
    S=S+thisArea.toString();
    return S;}

public void completeConfiguration() throws
    ConfigurationFailedException {
    if (thisArea==null)
       throw (new ConfigurationFailedException
          ("no area described",false));}

private void parseArea(String value) throws
    ConfigurationInvalidValueException {
    StringTokenizer sT=new
    StringTokenizer(value,";");
    Vector pairs=new Vector();
    while (sT.hasMoreTokens())
       pairs.addElement(sT.nextToken());
```

```
        if (pairs.size()==0) throw (new
           ConfigurationInvalidValueException
              ("no pairs found"));

        for (int i=0;i<pairs.size();i++) {
           String thisPair=(String)pairs.elementAt(i);
           StringTokenizer st2=new
           StringTokenizer(thisPair,",");
           if (st2.countTokens()!=2) throw (new
              ConfigurationInvalidValueException
              ("invalid pair: "+thisPair));
           String xAsString=st2.nextToken();
           String yAsString=st2.nextToken();
           try {
              int thisX=Integer.parseInt(xAsString);
              int thisY=Integer.parseInt(yAsString);
              if (thisArea==null)
                 thisArea=new Polygon();
              thisArea.addPoint(thisX,thisY);}
           catch (NumberFormatException e) {
           throw (new
              ConfigurationInvalidValueException
                 ("no numbers in pair: "+thisPair, false));
        }
     }

  }
  public boolean inside(int x, int y) {

     return
   (thisArea!=null?thisArea.inside(x,y):false);}
```

```
public boolean mouseMove(int x, int y,Graphics g) {
   motherApplet.showStatus
  ("mouse moved: "+x+","+y);
   return false;
}

public boolean mouseDown(int x, int y,Graphics g) {
   motherApplet.showStatus
   ("mouse down: "+x+","+y);
   return false;}

public boolean mouseUp(int x, int y,Graphics g) {
   motherApplet.showStatus
   ("mouse up: "+x+","+y);
   return false;}

public boolean mouseDrag(int x, int y,Graphics g) {
   motherApplet.showStatus
   ("mouse drag: "+x+","+y);
   return false;}
}
```

We have now fleshed out all of the base classes in our system. As we've said, any of the classes can be subclassed to incorporate new functionality—what we have written are the classes that know about each other.

It's time to start putting together the basic running system. Our first step will be to create the exception hierarchy. You'll remember from Chapter 10 that we simply override the constructor and pass the exception a message explaining what happened. We won't discuss the coding of the exceptions here—you can find the code on the CD and the Online Companion. With exceptions covered, our first step is creating the parser. Then, we will implement the actionArea subclasses.

Creating the Parser

Before we can start using the applet at all, we need to create the parser. As we discussed when we wrote the Configuration class, the parser is responsible for making sure the configuration file is syntactically correct and for passing the information to the Configuration object. Also, the parser needs to interpret the exceptions that may be tossed by the Configuration object and create comprehensible messages.

Because of the structure of our language, the parser only needs to pass over the document once. Most of our challenge is translating the tags into variables that can be passed to the Configuration object. In addition, we need a few routines that will give a message that is more user-friendly than the exception messages are. The best way to ensure that the messages are easy to understand is to keep track of the line number. As we mentioned before, we also need to allow for comments and blank lines:

```java
package ventana.aia;

import java.util.*;
import java.net.*;
import java.io.*;
import ventana.util.*;

public class AIAnimParser extends ConfFileParser {

private DataInputStream conf;
private int lineNumber=1;
private Stack tokenStack=new Stack();
private final String packageName="ventana.aia.";

private final String beginClassToken="<";
private final String endClassToken=">";
private final String classNameDescript="type";
private final String closureToken="</";
private final String assignString="=";
```

```
private final String commentChar="#";
int hierarchyDepth=0;

final String
validClasses[]={"ActionAnimApplet","ActionImageCanvas",
"ActionImageAnimation","ActionImage","ActionArea"};

public AIAnimParser(URL U) throws IOException{
conf=new DataInputStream(U.openStream());}

public boolean start() {
   try {
      while(conf.available()>0) {
      String curLine=conf.readLine();
      if (!parseLine(curLine)) {
         messageError("Parsing stopped");
         return false;}
      lineNumber++;}
   } catch(IOException e) {
      messageError("Error reading configuration file",e); }
   return true; }

public boolean parseLine(String line) {

   line=line.trim();
   //trim white space off begin and end
   if (line.startsWith(commentChar) ||
      line.length()==0)
   return true;
   if (line.startsWith(closureToken))
      {return closeCurrentToken(line);}
   if (line.startsWith(beginClassToken))
      {return parseToken(line);
      }
   //if we got this far, pass as param/value
   //to current object
```

```
         passParam(line);
         return true;
         //if a value isn't understood, don't stop
         //parsing.
         //call to complete configuration at the
         //closure token will generate any errors
         }
   public void passParam(String line) {
      StringTokenizer splitter=new
      StringTokenizer(line,assignString);
      String param=splitter.nextToken();
      String value=splitter.nextToken();

   try {
      ConfigureObject.passToCurrent(param,value);}
      catch (ConfigurationInvalidParameterException e) {
      messageError("invalid parameter",e,curClass());

   }
      catch (ConfigurationInvalidValueException e)
      {messageError("invalid value",e,curClass());}
   }

   public boolean parseToken(String token) {
      int start=beginClassToken.length();
      int end=token.length()-endClassToken.length();
      token=token.substring(start,end);
      StringTokenizer splitter=new StringTokenizer(token,"=");
      String baseClassName=splitter.nextToken();

      String subClassName=splitter.nextToken();
      if (subClassName==null) {
      subClassName=baseClassName;}

      if (baseClassName==null){
         messageError("No class specified");
      return false;}
```

```
        else return configureNewClass(baseClassName,subClassName);
}

private boolean configureNewClass(String base, String sub) {
    if (hierarchyDepth==validClasses.length)
       {messageError("Can't attach to "+base);
    return false;}

    String nextBase=validClasses[hierarchyDepth+1];
    if (!nextBase.equals(base))
       {messageError("Can't deal with "+base);
    return false;}

try {
    sub=packageName+sub;

    ConfigureObject.attach(sub);
    hierarchyDepth++;
    return true;
    }catch (ConfigurationAttachmentException e){
    messageError("Attachment not allowed",e,base);
    }catch (IllegalAccessException e) {messageError
    ("access to class not allowed,",e,base);}
    catch (InstantiationException e) {messageError
    ("class didn't instantiate",e,base);}
    catch (NotConfigurableException e) {messageError
    ("invalid class for AIA",e,base);}
    catch (ClassNotFoundException e) {messageError
    ("class wasn't found",e,base);}
    return false;}

public boolean closeCurrentToken(String token)
{
    if (token.indexOf(curClass())==-1) {
    messageError(token+" doesn't match "+curClass());
    return false;}
```

```
        try {
            ConfigureObject.configureCurrent();}
        catch (ConfigurationFailedException e) {
        if (e.isTerminal()) {
            messageError("configuration not completed",e,curClass());
        return false;}
        else
            messageError("parameter was ignored",e,curClass());
        }
        hierarchyDepth--;
        if (hierarchyDepth<0) {
            messageError("Internal parser error");
        return false;}

        else return true;

    }

    private String curClass() {
        return validClasses[hierarchyDepth];}

    public void messageError(String mesg) {
        System.out.println("Error at line "+lineNumber+": "+mesg);}

    public void messageError(String mesg,Exception e) {
        messageError(mesg);
        System.out.print("details: ");
        System.out.println(e.getMessage());

        System.out.println("\n\n*** Java's error message *****");
        System.out.println("(Non programmers should ignore)");

        e.printStackTrace();
        System.out.println("------\n\n");}

    public void messageError(String mesg, Exception e, String
className) {
        System.out.println(className+" reports:");
        messageError(mesg,e);}

    }
```

Defining Action Areas

We have the parser built, and we are ready to finish the system with some action areas. All we have to do is define how they will be configured and what action they will perform. The latter is accomplished by overriding the mouse event handling methods in the ActionArea class—mouseDown,mouseUp,mouseDrag, and mouseMove. Configuration just requires the overriding of the configureObject method. The first class that we override will simply show a new page given by a specified URL:

```
package ventana.aia;
import java.applet.*;
import java.awt.*;
import java.util.*;
import java.net.*;

import ventana.util.*;

public class ShowDocArea extends ActionArea implements
Configurable {

URL doc;

public void configureObject(String param, String value)
throws ConfigurationInvalidParameterException,
ConfigurationInvalidValueException {

    param=param.toLowerCase();
    if (param.equals("doc"))
       parseDocURL(value);
    else
       super.configureObject(param,value);}

public void  parseDocURL(String value) throws
    ConfigurationInvalidValueException {
    try {
       doc=new URL(value);
    }catch (MalformedURLException e) {
```

```
        throw new ConfigurationInvalidValueException(value+
        " not a URL");}}

public String toString() {
   String S="SoundActionArea\n";
   S=S+doc.toString()+"\n";
   return S;}

public void completeConfiguration() throws
   ConfigurationFailedException {
  if (doc==null)
     throw (new ConfigurationFailedException
        ("no doc described"));}

public boolean mouseUp(int x, int y,Graphics g) {
   motherApplet.getAppletContext().showDocument(doc);
   motherApplet.showStatus("going to ");
   return false;}

public boolean mouseMove(int x, int y,Graphics g) {
   motherApplet.showStatus("Go to: "+doc.toExternalForm());
   return false;}
}
```

Now, let's write an ActionArea that will create a sound:

```
package ventana.aia;
import java.applet.*;
import java.awt.*;
import java.util.*;
import java.net.*;
import ventana.util.*;

public class SoundActionArea extends ActionArea implements
Configurable {

AudioClip sound;
```

```
public void configureObject(String param, String value)
throws ConfigurationInvalidParameterException,
ConfigurationInvalidValueException {
  param=param.toLowerCase();
  if(param.equals("sound"))
    parseSound(value);
  super.configureObject(param,value);}

  public void parseSound(String value) throws
    ConfigurationInvalidValueException {
  try {
    URL U=new URL(value);
    sound=motherApplet.getAudioClip(U);
    if (sound==null)
      throw new ConfigurationInvalidValueException(value+
      " not a valid file");
    }catch (MalformedURLException e) {
    throw new ConfigurationInvalidValueException(value+
    " not a URL");}
  }

  public String toString() {
    String S="SoundActionArea\n";
    S=S+sound.toString()+"\n";
    return S;}

  public void completeConfiguration() throws
    ConfigurationFailedException {
    if (sound==null)
      throw (new ConfigurationFailedException
        ("no sound described"));}

  public boolean mouseMove(int x, int y,Graphics g) {
    sound.play();
    return super.mouseMove(x,y,g);}
}
```

Possible Improvements

Because of the way we have structured the applet, we can extend it in many different directions. The simplest way is to add new ActionAreas, but we can also subclass the ActionImageAnimation class to add new functionality, such as the morphing of images, and lend support for background images on the canvas itself. Without any added work, we can have multiple canvases within an applet and multiple animations within a canvas.

17 |

Interfacing With CGI: The Java Store

What You'll Learn

In this tutorial, we create the Java Store Applet, a "shopping cart" program that gives users an intuitive way to browse products and select products for purchase. Here are some techniques we'll cover:

- Using HTTP to retrieve data for your applets.
- Interfacing with CGI programs that run on the Web server.
- Designing a slick user interface.
- Dynamic generation of the user interface.
- Creating reusable components.

The full source code for classes discussed in this chapter is available on the Companion CD-ROM (for Windows 95/NT and Macintosh users) and the Online Companion (for UNIX users). Visit the Online Companion at http://www.vmedia.com/java.html.

The Contract

A client wants to expand its online bookstore. Currently, the bookstore features snazzy graphics, the latest HTML tricks, and a "shopping cart" system in which to select books for purchase. A shopping cart system keeps track of what the user has selected for purchase while browsing the store's online catalog. While viewing

a specific product, the user clicks a button to add that product to his or her list of products for purchase. The bookstore's current shopping cart system is implemented as a series of CGI scripts that produce HTML forms from the store's online catalog and handle the selection of products for purchase. However, the staff complains of the following limitations of the HTML-based forms:

- No real interactivity with the user. The user can only click a button to add a product, and removing a product from the shopping cart is not as user-friendly as it should be.

- The client's Web server is heavily loaded by the constant requests that the current shopping cart program requires as the user browses the many products. Every action that a user takes, such as choosing a product for purchase, must call a CGI program on the Web server, which in turn must keep track of previous selections, adding a great deal of overhead. They even tried a "Cookies"-based shopping cart program, but discovered that it also requires a CGI call every time a user interacts with the Web page.

- Updating the Web pages of the online store is a painstaking task. New products require many links from various pages, and moving products from page to page requires changing many links; this becomes complicated as the store grows, and it's difficult and time consuming to manage.

The growth of the online store is essential to our client's Web presence, so the current limitations need to be addressed. We propose a Java applet that can tackle these problems. We also propose that the Java applet work with the existing online store so the transition from the HTML-based store to the Java-based store can be made smoothly. Additionally, users who do not have the ability to run Java-enabled Web browsers can still access the company's products. The origin of the orders, from either the current online store or the new Java-based online store, will be indistinguishable to the staff that handles the orders, so no additional training will be required.

Features

The Java Store Applet will allow the user to navigate the store using menus. Each menu item will be a different "section." Nested menus will allow the staff to organize the store into subsections. For example, under a Programming Books section, there may be subsections on Java Books, C++ Books, and Visual Basic Books. The Java Store will have a "shopping basket." In addition to containing a list of the user's current selections for purchase, the shopping basket will allow the user to remove items from the purchase list.

The Java Store will also have a Help menu so that users can select from options such as sending e-mail to the store owners to ask questions and obtaining detailed ordering information. The Java Store will consist of two main panels—the one on the left will contain an image of the products in the current store section, and the one on the right will contain a detailed description of the product that is currently selected in the panel on the left.

When the users are finished making selections, they can click on the "Check out of Store" button, which will take their purchase list and send it to a CGI script on the Web server. This information can be packaged so that it's identical to the current online store data, which is based on HTML forms. This allows us to call the same CGI program that processes the current online store's orders.

The internal engine of the Java Store is even more sophisticated than the external user interface we described above. The menus are built dynamically—they are built based on files residing on the Web server. This allows the Java Store to be customized without any programming! The store staff can change the products offered, product descriptions, and organization of the sections by changing simple text files. The Java Store reads these formatted files and builds the user interface according to the directions in the text files.

Design

First, we sketch out a rough diagram of the user interface. The front end must be carefully designed to be compact and intuitive. We've decided to use a help menu and menus that will let the user navigate between store sections. The frame will include a large panel containing the product images in the current store section, a panel in which a product's description can be shown, and a panel for the selected products list (or shopping basket). Figure 17-1 shows the general appearance and layout we would like to achieve.

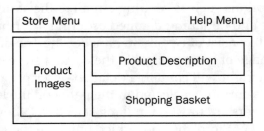

Figure 17-1: *Sketch of Java Store.*

We use direct interaction between the Web server and the Java applet. As you have seen, Java applets can open connections to ports other than the Web server's HTTP port. However, we want to reach people behind Internet firewalls because some users may have to go through them to access Web resources. We use the Web browser's built-in HTTP accessing ability to ensure than anyone who can access the Web page from which our Java Store is called can also access the information retrieved by the Java Store, such as the product images and descriptions. Additionally, we may want to call an existing CGI program that the current online store uses, so we must use the standard HTTP connection. The Java API facilitates this by giving us two classes to work with—URL and URLConnection. We make requests directly to the Web server to retrieve all the data we need to build the Java Store.

The store data files we'll use to build the user interface need to be organized so that it will be easy for the staff to make changes. We decide to use a base Store.idx file, which would contain the base menu items. This file will comprise directory names, followed by a menu name. Here is the Store.idx file used in this tutorial:

```
Internet/
Internet Books
Windows/
Windows Books
Programming/
Programming Books
```

The directories will be the store's "sections." Inside the directories will be a file named "directoryname".idx, which will contain an image filename, a description filename, and unique name to add to the shopping basket when the user selects it. If a trailing "/" appears in the name, it signifies a nested menu and corresponding store subsection! Again, store sections are physically manifested as directories; each will contain another .idx file. Here is a sample .idx file for the Internet section of the store:

```
webserver.gif
webserver.txt
Web Server Book
java.gif
java.txt
Java Programming for the Internet
```

By using this directory-enforced structure, we establish a rigid organization that is easy to follow. It's easy to make pinpoint changes now—you need only identify which section a product is to be added to or removed from, go to the corresponding directory, and modify the .idx file in the directory. Wholesale changes will be more difficult to do, but this is a compromise we are willing to make, since minor updates will be more frequent than the removal of entire sections of the store. The retrieval of all the .idx files is done in the base Store class, and the user interface from the data retrieved in the Store class is generated in the StoreWindow class.

We'll implement the Java Store in two main classes. The first is simply called Store. This module will fetch the store data, discussed above, for building the user interface. It also calls the second main class, StoreWindow. The StoreWindow is a frame that pops up after the user interface data has been retrieved. The StoreWindow contains the shopping basket, the product images, the store menus, and the product descriptions. It also calls other modules to do lower-level tasks that are needed to build the user interface. Figure 17-2 shows the complete class hierarchy for our Java Store.

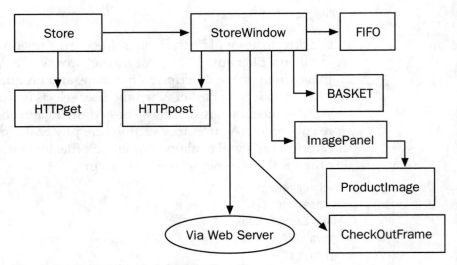

Figure 17-2: *Class hierarchy for the Java Store.*

We'll divide the Java Store into several key modules, each designed to do specific tasks. The tasks we'll build into classes are:

- **HTTPget and HTTPpost:** Low-level HTTP "GET" and "POST" routines that are used to fetch the .idx files and the description files.

- **ProductImage:** A special canvas class that holds product images.

- ◈ **FIFO:** A generic FIFO (First In First Out) class that facilitates building the user interface.

- ◈ **ImagePanel:** A Panel class that retrieves the product images and puts them into one panel, along with retrieving the product descriptions.

- ◈ **Basket:** Another Panel class that contains the entire selected products list with its method.

- ◈ **Store:** The base applet class that retrieves the aforementioned configuration files.

- ◈ **StoreWindow:** A Frame class that brings together the components and adds top-level functionality.

- ◈ **CheckOutFrame:** A Frame class that is called when the user exits the Store. It gets some user information and passes it to CGI program via the HTTPpost class.

With the exception of the base Store and StoreWindow modules, the classes are designed to be as generic as possible so that they are reusable. Indeed, the HTTPget class is used in both the Store and ImagePanel classes, and the ProductImage object is instantiated multiple times in the ImagePanel class.

Our applet doesn't need complicated event trapping. We want to allow users to choose menu items, for which we must look first in either a handleEvent or action method and then respond accordingly. We also want to show a description of a product when the user clicks on the product's image. When the user double-clicks on a product's image, we want to add it to the shopping basket. As you can see, there are only two main classes that handle specific high-level events. The StoreWindow module handles the events listed above. The Basket class handles three buttons that are labeled according to their operation: Remove, Clear all items, and Check out of Store. In reality, the event created when the user clicks on the Check out of Store button is passed up to the parent StoreWindow class, as shown in Figure 17-3.

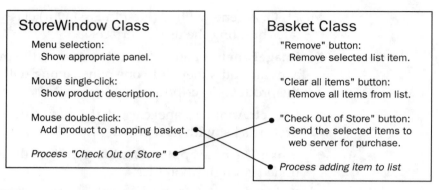

StoreWindow Class

Menu selection:
Show appropriate panel.

Mouse single-click:
Show product description.

Mouse double-click:
Add product to shopping basket.

Process "Check Out of Store"

Basket Class

"Remove" button:
Remove selected list item.

"Clear all items" button:
Remove all items from list.

"Check Out of Store" button:
Send the selected items to
web server for purchase.

Process adding item to list

Figure 17-3: *Required event handlers.*

Implementation

Let's start our implementation from the helper classes and work our way up. You will find that the classes fit together nicely as we discuss the top-level StoreWindow class.

Each helper class will be built and tested before we even start on the StoreWindow class. The extra time we'll spend to rigorously and independently test each module will make it possible to put together the components quickly and with no surprises. Figure 17-4 shows the Java Store as customers will see it.

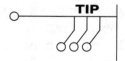 **TIP**

In the next section, we assume the reader has some knowledge of HTTP POST and GET, and the role of CGI programs. If you don't, consult The Web Server Book *(Ventana Press) or the Online Companion to get more information on the topic.*

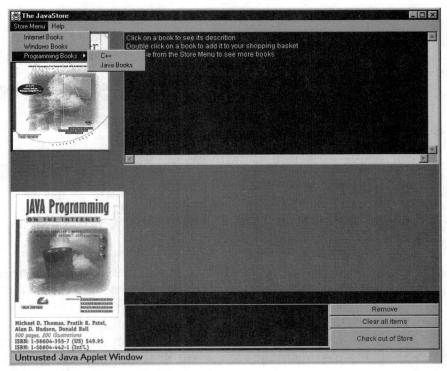

Figure 17-4: *The Java Store.*

Performing HTTP Requests

The first modules we need are the ones to retrieve the store setup data so that we can build the menus and product panels. We decide to use HTTP requests to get the setup .idx files. We'll make two generic classes—one for performing HTTP 'GET' requests and one for interfacing with Web server CGIs or HTTP 'POST.' We present a full discussion of the HTTPpost class below. We also present a variant HTTPget class to show how direct network sockets can be used to communicate with the Web server. The full source for both is available on the Companion CD-ROM (for Windows 95/NT and Macintosh) or the Online Companion (for UNIX).

The Java API provides us with a nice set of classes that do the hard work for us when we are creating a URL and its connection: The URL, URLconnection, and URLencoder classes. Chapter 14, "Networking With URLs," explains these classes in greater detail. Let's have a look at the HTTPpost class we use in the Java Store.

```java
import java.net.*;
import java.io.*;

public class HTTPpost {
  String CGIresults="";

    public HTTPpost(String URLline , String PostData){
    String inputLine;String PostDataEncoded = "result=" +
URLEncoder.encode(PostData);
```

We set up the HTTPpost to take two parameters—first, a string parameter, URLline, which includes the name of the CGI program we wish to run on the Web server, and the complete URL to the CGI program. The PostData parameter is the data we wish to pass to the CGI. We want to make sure it's in the proper format for passing to the Web server, so we encode it in the standardized x-www-form-urlencoded format using the URLencoder.encode method. We assign it the name "result". The CGI will see the data as "result=(PostData)" so that it appears that the name "result" has the value that is in PostData. This is important to remember when we are constructing a CGI program, as we will want to pull this name-value pair out for processing. The following section of code establishes the output connection to the Web server:

```java
    try {
      URL url = new URL(URLline);
      URLConnection connection = url.openConnection();
      PrintStream outStream = new
  PrintStream(connection.getOutputStream());
      DataInputStream inStream;
```

We first construct a new instance of URL using the URLline parameter. Then we construct a new URLconnection instance using the return object of the url.connection method. This gives us a basis on which to form an input and output stream. We construct a PrintStream for the output of the PostData to the CGI using the URLconnection as the conduit for the actual connection. Similarly, below we create an inputStream from the URLconnection instance to receive data from the Web server/CGI program:

```
        outStream.println(PostDataEncoded);
        outStream.close();
        inStream = new
DataInputStream(connection.getInputStream());
        while (null != (inputLine = inStream.readLine())) {
           CGIresults = CGIresults + inputLine +"\n";
        }
        inStream.close();
      } catch (MalformedURLException me) {
    System.err.println("MalformedURLException: " + me);
      } catch (IOException ioe) {
        System.err.println("IOException: " + ioe);
      }
    }
```

We are now ready to get down to business. Above, we send the PostData to the Web server, which passes it to the CGI program. We then start receiving data from the CGI, until the buffer returns null and is finished. This data is stored in the global variable, CGIresults. We have to catch all the exceptions generated by the creation of a new URL instance and created by the URL.openConnection method. Below is the method that we call to return the result of the HTTP post:

```
public String results() {
return CGIresults;
};
}
```

The results method simply returns the output from the CGI. This result is used to verify that the CGI program received the data we sent it and that it was processed properly. We can also use it to show a message to the user in our applet. Additionally, we can pass back a URL from the CGI program and then do a showDocument to make the Web browser show a page. This can be applied in our Java Store by sending a URL containing a "Thank You for Ordering" page, or an error page, or just about anything we want.

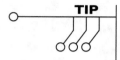

TIP

The HTTPget class does not take a POST parameter; instead it takes a QUERY LINE parameter. It fetches data from the Web server as well. We want to use it to get the Store.idx and other .idx files that contain the structure of the store. If we were to get an HTML file, we would see all the HTML tags. Since the .idx files are plain text files, we do not have to worry about the formatting of HTML files. Theoretically, we could even get binary data, but this would require modifying the input stream to read bytes instead of lines. This is not particularly useful since we already have methods like getImage.

Below, we present a different way of performing HTTP requests in the HTTPget class. It is analogous to the HTTPpost and is almost identical except that we use socket connections directly to perform the communication. You can skip reading the code if you feel comfortable with the HTTPpost discussion above.

```java
import java.awt.*;
import java.net.*;
import java.io.*;
import java.util.*;

public class HTTPget
    {
    private final String CONTENTtype  =
    "application/octet-stream";
    private String Recievedata  = "";
    private String home;
    private int port;
```

```
public HTTPget(String URLbase, int URLport) {
//Our constructor is a bit different here. We
//pass the URL as the machine name in URLbase
//and the Web server port in URLport.
//The path to the script is passed in via the
//submit method below as the Script parameter.

   home = URLbase;
   port = URLport;
   if (port == -1)  port = 80;
}


public void submit(String Script, String QData)
   {

   Socket sock;
   OutputStream outp;
   InputStream inp;
   DataOutputStream dataout;
   DataInputStream datain;
   String URLline;
   Recievedata = "";
   URLline = Script+"?"+QData;
   //create a client socket
      try
      sock = new Socket(home, port);
   catch (Exception e)
      {
      System.out.println("Error with HTTP GET "+e);
      }

//Obtain output stream to communicate with
//the server
```

```
            try
            {
                outp = sock.getOutputStream();
                inp  = sock.getInputStream();
            }
            catch (Exception e)
                {
                Recievedata = e+" (getstream)";
                try sock.close();
                catch (IOException ee) ;
                return;
                }

                try
                {
                    dataout = new DataOutputStream(outp);
                    datain  = new DataInputStream(inp);
                }
                catch (Exception e)
                {
                    Recievedata = e+" (Dstream)";
                    try sock.close();
                    catch (IOException ee) ;
                    return;
                }

    // Send http request to server and get return data

            try
            {
                dataout.writeBytes("GET "+URLline+" HTTP/1.0\r\n");
                dataout.writeBytes("Content-type: "+CONTENTtype+
                "\r\n");
                dataout.writeBytes("Content-length: 0 \r\n");
                dataout.writeBytes("\r\n");
                dataout.flush();
```

```
        boolean body = false;
        String line;
        while ((line = datain.readLine()) != null)
        {
            if (body)
                Recievedata += "\n" + line;
            else if (line.equals(""))
            // end of header
                body = true;
        }
    }
    catch (Exception e)
    {
        Recievedata = e+" (write)";
        try sock.close();
        catch (IOException e);
        return;
    }

    // close the streams

    try
    {
        dataout.close();
        datain.close();
    }
    catch (IOException e);
    try sock.close();
    catch (IOException e);
}

public String Results() {
    return Recievedata;
}

}
```

Storing Product Data

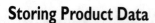

The ProductImage class stores not only the product's image within itself, but also a label and the description of the product. The class is implemented as an extension of Canvas, so we can instantiate it and keep the product specific data contained in its own object. We use it in the ImagePanel class as we add product images to it. The description and label can be accessed directly by creating a reference to a specific ProductImage and then accessing the description and label via this reference. This is done in the StoreWindow class, so we don't have to go through the ImagePanel class to get to the data. We also add height and width public variables to allow ImagePanel to properly set its size for all the ProductImages it adds to the specific ImagePanel. Let's look at the ProductImage class:

```java
import java.awt.*;

public class ProductImage extends Canvas {
private Image piece;
public String label;
public int height;
public int width;
public String Description;

public void setLabel(String s) {
   label = s;
}

public void setImage(Image i) {
   if (piece !=i) {
      piece = i;
      height= piece.getHeight(this);
      width= piece.getWidth(this);
   }
}
```

We do not hide the label, height, width, and description, but we do want to hide the Image piece. The setLabel and setImage methods are called with their respective object parameters, and the instance of ProductImage keeps them for future use. The description is set directly by referencing the Description variable in the instance of ProductImage. Again, we are basing this object on a Canvas class so we can add it directly to a panel that would show the product images:

```
public void paint(Graphics g) {
    Rectangle r = bounds();
    g.setColor(getBackground());
    g.fillRect(0,0,r.width,r.height);
    if (piece!=null) {
        g.drawImage(piece,0,0,this);
    }
}
```

Now we paint the image passed to us in the setImage method to the instance of ProductImage so it will be ready to be added to the panel that shows the product pictures.

FIFO class

The FIFO class is an extension of the handy Vector class available in the API. Vector is a growable array class in the java.util package. We add some methods to correspond to a FIFO data structure. We use the FIFO in building the user interface, and it does a great deal to facilitate the tracking of the user interface data. We can push stuff into the FIFO in a specific order, and get it back in the same order by using the corresponding push and pop methods. We also have an isEmpty method that tests to see if the list is empty:

```
import java.util.Vector;
import java.util.*;

public class FIFO extends Vector {
```

```
public String pop() {
    String s="";
    // Get the first element
    try{ s= (String)firstElement(); }
    catch (NoSuchElementException e )
      {System.out.println("FIFO EMPTY!!!!!");
       s="";
    }
    // and remove the first element
    try{ removeElement(s);}
    catch(ArrayIndexOutOfBoundsException e)
      {System.out.println("FIFO EMPTY!!!");}
    return s;
}

// Add an element to the top of the list
public void push(String s) {
    addElement(s);
}

// Check to see if the list is empty
public boolean empty() {
    return isEmpty();
}
}
```

We use the methods available in the Vector class to do the real work for us. They do generate exceptions, which we must catch. We've specified a String type as the elements to keep in the vector, but with some nominal modification, we can make the FIFO accept any object. We choose to make it String specific in nature because the FIFO is used only with Strings in the applet.

Getting the Images & Descriptions

The ImagePanel class actually calls the getImage method and the HTTPget method to get the data for each product in the specific panel. Each section of the store has its own ImagePanel. This is how we separate the sections, so that we can readily change the store section by displaying a different panel. It is covered in the StoreWindow class. We have one main loop, which loops until the FIFO list containing the data for the specific section of the store is completely processed:

```java
import java.awt.*;
import java.net.*;
import java.util.*;
import java.io.*;
import ProductImage;
import FIFO;
import HTTPget;

public class ImagePanel extends Panel {

    private ProductImage ImageCanvas;
    private URL ImageURL;
    protected Toolkit Tools;
    public int width;
    public int height;
    private  MediaTracker tracker;
    private Image i;
    public String label;
    private HTTPget DescText;
```

Note that we call the MediaTracker in this class. It is used to ensure that the images are retrieved before we do a ProductImage.setImage. Doing this with an image that has not yet been retrieved results in a nasty NullPointerException! The Toolkit is needed to be able to call getImage, since we are not directly in the applet panel, but rather in the StoreWindow frame:

```java
public ImagePanel(String ImageURLBase, FIFO FileList, String
PanelLabel) {
    String s;
    String Desc;
    Toolkit Tools;
    String Name;
```

```
label=PanelLabel;
Tools = getToolkit();
tracker= new MediaTracker(this);
width=0;
height=0;
setLayout(new GridLayout(0,1));
while (!FileList.empty()) {
   s = FileList.pop();
   try {
      ImageURL = new URL(ImageURLBase + s );
   }
   catch (MalformedURLException e) {
      System.out.println("Error retrieving " + ImageURL);
   }
   Desc = FileList.pop();
   DescText = new HTTPget(ImageURL.getHost(),
   ImageURL.getPort());
   DescText.submit( Desc, "");

   //Download the picture
   ImageCanvas = new ProductImage();
   i = Tools.getImage(ImageURL);
   tracker.addImage(i, 0);
   try {
      tracker.waitForID(0);
   }
   catch (InterruptedException e) {
      return;
   }
```

We use a GridLayout with one column and an unspecified number of rows. Since different store sections can have different numbers of products, we choose to do this instead of limiting the number of products that can belong in a store section. The pop method for the FIFO FileList returns the first item in its list and removes it. The three components that are grouped for each product are the product's image file name, description filename, and actual name. This data is parsed in the StoreWindow class and passed when each ImagePanel for each store section is created.

The image file is fetched first. We build the URL from the parameter passed as the base URL and add the path and filename from the FileList. Similarly, we use the HTTPget to retrieve the description file. We create a new ProductImage instantiation, called ImageCanvas, in the loop for each product. A ProductImage is created for every product in the section. The ProductImage also holds the description and name information, even though it is a Canvas object. Again, this is done to keep individual product data in one object. We assign the fetched image to the image *I* object and prod the applet to get the image immediately by using the MediaTracker via its tracker instantiation. Of course, with the tracker.waitForID(0), we must catch the InterruptedException.

```
ImageCanvas.setImage(i);
ImageCanvas.setLabel(s);
ImageCanvas.Description=DescText.Results();

Name= FileList.pop();
ImageCanvas.setLabel(Name);

ImageCanvas.resize(ImageCanvas.width,ImageCanvas.height);
    add(ImageCanvas);
    ImageCanvas.show();
    height += ImageCanvas.height;
    width += ImageCanvas.width;
    }
  }
} // ImagePanel
```

Now that we have fetched all the data on this product from the Web server, let's put it into the proper place. We use the instances of the ProductImage class to hold this data; in the section of code above, it is repeatedly instantiated as "ImageCanvas." We set the image *i* we retrieved above using the setImage method, use the setLabel method to set the label, and set the description directly,

using the Description variable in the ProductImage class (all via ImageCanvas). The label, or Name, is the last item from the group of three items we pop off the FIFO FileList for a specific product. We use the height and width of the product image to resize the ImageCanvas before we add it to the ImagePanel panel. Finally, we set the overall size of the ImagePanel so that we can use it in the StoreWindow class. The instances of ImagePanel, representing different store sections, are added as a panel component directly to the StoreWindow frame.

Managing User Selections

The Basket class is our implementation of the "shopping basket." In addition to a list of the products the user has selected for purchase, the Basket has features for removing items. The Basket consists of four basic elements—List and three Buttons. It extends Panel, so that we can add it directly to the StoreWindow frame. We handle the functions that deal directly with the list within this class (the "Remove" and "Clear all items" buttons) and pass the event of the "Check out of Store" button up to the parent StoreWindow:

```java
import java.awt.*;

public class Basket extends Panel {
    private List ItemList;
    private Button Remove;
    private Button Clear;
    public Button Checkout;

public Basket(String Name) {
    Label BasketLabel = new Label(Name, Label.CENTER);
    GridBagConstraints Con = new GridBagConstraints();
    GridBagLayout gridBag = new GridBagLayout();
    ItemList = new List(5, false);
    Remove = new Button("Remove");
    Clear = new Button("Clear all items");
    Checkout = new Button("Check out of store");
```

```java
setLayout(gridBag);
setFont(new Font("Helvetica", Font.PLAIN, 12));
setBackground(Color.blue);

Con.anchor = GridBagConstraints.CENTER;
Con.fill = GridBagConstraints.NONE;

Con.weighty = 1.0;
Con.weightx=0.0;
Con.gridwidth = GridBagConstraints.REMAINDER;
gridBag.setConstraints(BasketLabel, Con);
add(BasketLabel);

Con.fill = GridBagConstraints.BOTH;
Con.gridheight=3;
Con.gridwidth=GridBagConstraints.RELATIVE;
Con.weighty = 1.0;
Con.weightx=3.0;
gridBag.setConstraints(ItemList, Con);
add(ItemList);

Con.weightx=1.0;
Con.weighty = 0.0;
Con.gridheight=1;
Con.gridwidth=GridBagConstraints.REMAINDER;
Con.fill = GridBagConstraints.HORIZONTAL;
gridBag.setConstraints(Remove, Con);
add(Remove);

gridBag.setConstraints(Clear, Con);
add(Clear);

Con.fill = GridBagConstraints.BOTH;
gridBag.setConstraints(Checkout, Con);
add(Checkout);
}
```

We'll make three Buttons and a List, but hide, or declare private, all of them except the "Check out of Store" button. This is done because we want the parent, StoreWindow, to be able to access it. We deal with functions involving the other buttons in this class. Note that the list is set up to allow only one list item to be selectable. We use GridBagLayout to set up the ItemList to take up most of the space in the panel. The "Check out of Store" button is used to occupy the remaining space we set aside for the Buttons after the "Remove" and "Clear all items" Buttons have been added. See Chapter 8, "Advanced User Interface," for a detailed discussion on GridBagLayout:

```java
public void addItem( String ItemName ) {

ItemList.addItem(ItemName);
ItemList.select(ItemList.countItems()-1);
}

public String getItems() {
   String s = "";
   for (int i=0; i<ItemList.countItems(); i++ ) {
      s += ItemList.getItem(i)+"\n";
   }
return s;
}

public boolean action( Event evt, Object obj)
   {
   if ("Remove".equals(obj))
      {
      if (ItemList.getSelectedIndex()!=-1)
         {
         ItemList.delItem(ItemList.getSelectedIndex());
         }
      return true;
      }
```

```
    else if ("Clear all items".equals(obj))
       {
           ItemList.clear();
           return true;
       }
    return super.action(evt, obj);
    } // action
}
```

We make two methods, addItem and getItems, to allow adding items to the list and to fetch the list, respectively. These methods are used in StoreWindow when the user double-clicks on a product's image or when the user wants to exit the store (we'll discuss this further when we get to the section on the StoreWindow class). We'll make the appropriate method calls to ItemList to do the operations.

The button events for "Remove" and "Clear all items" are handled within the class by overriding the action method for the class. We look for the object obj parameter passed in to match one of the button labels so that we don't pass up the event to the parent via the super.action(evt, obj) statement. Again, this is primarily because we want to send the "Check out of Store" event to the parent. The ItemList handles the selection of list items within itself, so we don't have to deal with it.

Fetching Configuration Data & Initialization

The Store class is the base applet. It calls the StoreWindow class, which is a frame outside of the Web browser. Store is called from a Web page with the APPLET HTML tag. The primary purpose of the Store class is to retrieve and parse the Java Store configuration files for use by the StoreWindow class. We'll fetch the .idx files, starting with the Store.idx file, and then recursively fetch the specific .idx file from the referenced directories:

```
import java.awt.*;
import java.applet.Applet;
import StoreWindow;
import java.util.StringTokenizer;

public class Store extends Applet {
    StoreWindow f;
    String ProductDir;
    String CheckOutCGI;
// WE WANT TO PUT THIS IN A PARAM TAG!
    String Tree = "";

    public void init(){
        ProductDir = getParameter("index_location");
        CheckOutCGI = getParameter("CGI");
        ParseIndex( ProductDir, "Store.idx");

        f = new StoreWindow(getDocumentBase(), Tree, CheckOutCGI );
    }
```

We create a new instance of StoreWindow, and get the location of the first configuration file, Store.idx (from the parameter "index_location") from the HTML code from which the applet was called. We also get the URL of the CGI program to run when the user exits the store. We'll pass the path to the ParseIndex method, which gets and parses all the .idx files. Also, we'll pass the "Store.idx" as the default index file name:

```
private void ParseIndex ( String ProductDir, String s )
{
    HTTPget Index;
    String next;
    String nextDESCRIPTION;
    String nextNAME;
    String Params =   "";
    String ProductIndex = ProductDir + s;
```

```
Index = new HTTPget(getDocumentBase().getHost(),
getDocumentBase().getPort());
Index.submit( ProductIndex, "" );
//get the idx file from the web server
StringTokenizer LoadINDEX = new
StringTokenizer(Index.Results(), "\n");
// break the idx file by "\n"

while (LoadINDEX.hasMoreTokens()) {
//loop until we have no more in this idx file
   next= LoadINDEX.nextToken();
   //if it's a new dir, parse it, and
   //recurse, or call ParseIndex on its
   //idx file!
   if (next.endsWith("/")) {
      nextDESCRIPTION=LoadINDEX.nextToken();
      Tree += ("Menu:" + nextDESCRIPTION +"\n");
      //chop off trailing / and add .idx
      ParseIndex(ProductDir + next, next.substring(0,
      (next.length()-1)) + ".idx");
      // we are using recursion, so be careful!

   }
   else if (! next.equalsIgnoreCase("<none>") )
      {
      nextDESCRIPTION = LoadINDEX.nextToken();
      nextNAME = LoadINDEX.nextToken();
      Tree+= ("GIF:" + ProductDir+next + "\nTXT:" + ProductDir
      +nextDESCRIPTION + " \n"+"NAME:"+nextNAME+"\n");
      }
   else {
      Tree+=("Encountered a " + next+"\n" );
      }
   }
   Tree += "END:MENU\n";
}
```

We begin by using the applet's URL methods, getDocumentBase.getHost and getDocumentBase.getPort, to use the HTTPget class to get the index file from the Web server. The HTTPget Index object now allows us to get to the idx file via its Results method. The HTTPget is called repeatedly on different .idx files until all of them have been retrieved.

We then use the StringTokenizer to break the .idx files that have been retrieved. We'll break them by the newline character, \n. Since we structured our .idx files by placing data on consecutive lines, this breaking them with the newline character works well for us. Now it's possible that there is one of four items in the .idx file: it can be a menu or submenu, in which case we'd have to get another .idx file, or it can be the GIF filename, description filename, or a name. We know the order of the items, so we need to look for a trailing "/" to signify a menu/submenu. If it is a menu/submenu, we call ParseIndex with the path of the directory, which is simply the current token, and we add a label that we get from the next line in the .idx file, delimiting it using the "Menu:" tag. We add this to our Tree String variable, which is what we pass to the StoreWindow, which then parses this preformatted list to build the user interface. The recursive call to ParseIndex will parse through this branch of the menu using the same ParseIndex method, but with different parameters. This use of recursion saves us the work of having to run repeated loops with check-pointing.

If the token is not a directory/menu, we know it's a product. We make a tag identifying the item we're adding to Tree—"GIF:", "TXT:", and "NAME:". We will always add these three items for each product, but we add the tags to debug problems with the .idx files or the building of the Tree list. We loop within each .idx file until it has been completed, but we fork several times when we recurse for menus and submenus. The resultant Tree string variable may look jumbled, but there is a method to our madness: we use a similar recursive method in StoreWindow to build the user interface that benefits from this inlined form of the configuration Tree we have made here.

When the configuration files have been parsed and placed in our formatted form in Tree, we do a new StoreWindow(getDocumentBase, Tree), which passes it the configuration Tree variable. We also pass it the URL base, so that it can use it to retrieve the .gif image files and description files for the specific products from the Web server.

Putting It All Together

We bring together the components and add top-level functionality in the StoreWindow class. We have preformatted store configuration data in the Tree variable that we have been given and have all the necessary classes to begin building the user interface. We first set the proper base URL needed to get the image and description files from the Web server. We then create the screen elements we need, such as the shopping basket and the CardLayout based product image panel. Later, when we build the user interface and menus, we'll add panels to the product image panel.

```
import java.awt.*;
import java.applet.Applet;
import java.net.URL;
import java.util.*;

class StoreWindow extends Frame {

    Panel ProductPicPanel;
    String Params =  "";
    Panel DescriptionPanel;
    String BaseURL;
    Panel MainPanel;
    TextArea DescArea;
    Basket ShoppingBasket;
    String NewPickMessage;
    String CGI;
```

```java
public StoreWindow(URL BURL, String Tree , String
CGIprogram ) {
this.CGI=CGIprogram;

    if (BURL.getPort()==-1) {
       BaseURL = BURL.getProtocol() +"://" + BURL.getHost();
    }
    else {
       BaseURL = BURL.getProtocol() +"://" + BURL.getHost()
       +":"+BURL.getPort() ;
    }


ShoppingBasket = new Basket("Shopping Basket");
setTitle("The JavaStore");
MainPanel = new Panel();
MainPanel.setLayout(new BorderLayout());
setLayout(new BorderLayout());
DescArea = new TextArea(15, 30);
DescArea.setEditable(false);
DescArea.setBackground(Color.black);
DescArea.setForeground(Color.white);
DescArea.setFont(new Font("Helvetica", Font.PLAIN, 12));
NewPickMessage="Click on a book to see its description\n
Double click on a book to add it to your shopping basket\n
Choose from the Store Menu to see more books\n";
MainPanel.add("North", DescArea);
MainPanel.add("South", ShoppingBasket);
MenuBar Bar = new MenuBar();
ProductPicPanel = new Panel();
ProductPicPanel.setLayout(new CardLayout());
```

The code above mainly initializes the frame and creates some of the AWT objects we need. We set the LayoutManagers for the main area and the ProductPicPanel. We use CardLayout for ProductPicPanel, since we want to change the displayed panel when the menu selection changes. We add a menu bar to which we'll add menus and menu items later. Below, we call the BuildUI method, which builds the menus and adds panels to the ProductPicPanel. Note that we have already added the objects that need to be in the MainPanel. Later, we will add the MainPanel and the ProductPicPanel to the StoreWindow frame.

```
Bar.add(BuildUI(Tree));
Menu Help = new Menu("Help");
Help.add(new MenuItem("About us"));
Help.add(new MenuItem("Ordering information"));
Help.add(new MenuItem("-"));
Help.add(new MenuItem("Email us"));
Bar.setHelpMenu(Help);
Bar.add(Help);   .
setMenuBar(Bar);
setFont(new Font("Helvetica", Font.PLAIN, 12));
setBackground(Color.gray);
add("Center", MainPanel);
add("West", ProductPicPanel);
resize(700,500);
show();
} // StoreWindow
```

BuildUI returns a Menu that we add directly to the frame's menu bar. We also add a 'Help' menu and create its menu items. We are now ready to add the ProductPicPanel and the MainPanel to the StoreWindow frame. The BuildUI method has been called at this point, so the user interface is complete. We list the code for the BuildUI method below, as well as cover the event handling we wish to track:

```java
public boolean handleEvent(Event evt) {

    if (evt.id == Event.WINDOW_DESTROY) {
        dispose();
        return true;
    }
    if (evt.target instanceof ProductImage) {
        if (evt.id==Event.MOUSE_DOWN) {
            ProductImage p = (ProductImage)evt.target;
        if (evt.clickCount==2) {
            ShoppingBasket.addItem(p.label);
            }
        else {
            DescArea.setText(p.Description);
            }
        }
        return true;
    }
    return super.handleEvent(evt);
}

public boolean action(Event evt, Object arg) {
    if ( evt.target instanceof MenuItem) {
        ((CardLayout)ProductPicPanel.getLayout()).show
        (ProductPicPanel, (String)arg);
    DescArea.setText(NewPickMessage);
    return true;
    }
    if ("Check out of Store".equals(arg))
        {
        System.out.println(ShoppingBasket.getItems());
        dispose();
        SubmitItemList(ShoppingBasket.getItems());
```

```
        // Call the method to call the CGI
        return true;
        }
    return false;
    }
private void SubmitItemList(String ItemList) {
// send the ItemList to a CGI program
    CheckOutFrame Exit = new CheckOutFrame("Check Out of Java
    Store", ItemList, CGI);
}
```

The handleEvent method is created to look for two specific events—the clicking of the mouse on a product image or the double-clicking of the mouse on a product image. We use the argument clickCount to count the number of times the user has clicked on an image and then proceed to handle it accordingly. If the user has double-clicked on an image, as we have instructed them to do if they wish to put the product in their shopping basket, we call the Basket.addItem(ItemName) method. As you recall, we made a method called addItem in the Basket class that allowed users to add items to the selected products list. If mouse clicking that is not a double-click is detected, we show the product's description, which we fetch in the ImagePanel class. We finish the handleEvent by passing remaining events back, so that the following action event handler is allowed to deal with remaining events.

The action event first looks for user interaction with the menus. If the user has selected a new menu item or store section, we show the panel that corresponds to the store section they selected. This also triggers the generic instruction message to be displayed in the text area DescArea. The second part of the action handler looks for the clicking of the "Check out of Store" button event, which is passed up from the ShoppingBasket. We get the list of products the user has selected and pass it to the SubmitItemList method, which calls the CheckOutofFrame method and sends the item list to the CGI shown on the Web server. After the user has done this, there is no longer a need to remain in the Store, so we dispose of the StoreWindow frame. The CGI program processes the data.

```java
private Menu BuildUI(String Tree) {
    FIFO PanelAdd = new FIFO();

    Menu StoreMenu = new Menu("Store Menu");

    StringTokenizer SplitTree = new StringTokenizer(Tree, "\n");

    ParseTree( SplitTree, StoreMenu, "", PanelAdd);

    return StoreMenu;

} // StoreWindow

private void ParseTree(StringTokenizer TreeBranch, Menu
MenuIn, String PreviousToken, FIFO PanelAdd)
    {
    StringTokenizer Leaf;
    Menu subMenu;
    String next;
    //ImagePanel MenuPanel;

    while (TreeBranch.hasMoreTokens()) {

        Leaf = new StringTokenizer(TreeBranch.nextToken(), ":");
        next = Leaf.nextToken();

        // Look for "Menu", add a new menu item..
        if (!PreviousToken.equals("")) {
```

```java
                    if (next.equalsIgnoreCase("Menu")) {
                        subMenu = new Menu(PreviousToken);

                    MenuIn.add(subMenu);
                    // Now recurse this new sub-menu!
                    PreviousToken="";
                    MenuIn=subMenu;
                }
                else {
                    MenuIn.add(PreviousToken);
                    PanelAdd.push(PreviousToken);
                }
            }

            // Look for "Menu", add a new menu item..
            if (next.equalsIgnoreCase("Menu")) {

                ParseTree(TreeBranch, MenuIn, Leaf.nextToken(), PanelAdd);
            }

            else if (next.equalsIgnoreCase("GIF")) {
                PanelAdd.push(Leaf.nextToken());
                ParseTree(TreeBranch, MenuIn, "", PanelAdd);
            }

            else if (next.equalsIgnoreCase("TXT")) {
                PanelAdd.push(Leaf.nextToken());
                ParseTree(TreeBranch, MenuIn, "", PanelAdd);
            }

            else if (next.equalsIgnoreCase("NAME")) {
                PanelAdd.push(Leaf.nextToken());
                ParseTree(TreeBranch, MenuIn, "", PanelAdd);
            }
```

```
        else if (next.equalsIgnoreCase("END")) {
          if (!PanelAdd.empty())
            {
            String PanelName =(String)PanelAdd.pop();
            Leaf.nextToken();
            ProductPicPanel.add(PanelName, new ImagePanel(BaseURL,
            PanelAdd, PanelName));
            }
          }
        }
      }
    } // end StoreWindow
```

The BuildUI method is really an initializer for the ParseTree method. We create a new FIFO object, a new Menu. Then we StringTokenize the Tree on the newline character. The Tree is the one we created in the Store class from the configuration data fetched from the Web server. It has been preformatted and ordered so that the recursive ParseTree method can use it inline. Most of the work done in the BuildUI method is to start the recursion of the ParseTree properly.

ParseTree, as we have said, works recursively. Specifically, it calls itself when it encounters a new menu. This way, nested menus can be handled without complex nested loops. We call ParseTree with a StringTokenizer containing the tree branch that is to be traversed, the parent Menu, a string containing the previous token, and the FIFO list containing the data for the ImagePanel that is to be built with the configuration data. The parent Menu and previous token are required for submenus. We generally follow this path in the ParseTree method: process the current leaf and get the next leaf, which is the label for the previous leaf, then ParseTree with the remaining portion of the tree. We stop going down a tree branch when we have reached the end, signified by an "END" tag. While we are traversing the tree, we push items onto the PanelAdd FIFO. This FIFO is passed to the ImagePanel, which uses the data in the FIFO to fetch the product images and product description.

Sending the User's Selection to the Web Server

We call the CheckOutFrame class in the SubmitItemList method.
The CheckOutFrame consists of two TextFields and a Button
labeled "Done," as shown in Figure 7-5. The user fills in his or her
Name and Phone number in the TextFields. This data, along with
the list of products the user has selected, is passed to a CGI running
on the Web server with the HTTPpost class. The CheckOutFrame
code is shown below. Note that we destroy the StoreWindow
before opening the CheckOutFrame so the user does not get
confused, and by doing so, we immediately get the user's attention. We use GridBagLayout again to position the components.
The action event handler is coded to watch for the "Done" button's
click, which is when we wrap up the selected products list, the
user's name, and phone number and send it to the CGI program:

Figure 17-5: *The CheckOutFrame.*

```java
import java.awt.*;
import HTTPpost;

public class CheckOutFrame extends Frame {
TextField Name;
```

```
TextField Phone;
Button Done;
String ItemList;
GridBagLayout gridbag = new GridBagLayout();
GridBagConstraints Con = new GridBagConstraints();
Label LName;
Label LPhone;
Label Message1;
Label Message2;
HTTPpost CGIpost;
String CGI;

public CheckOutFrame( String Title, String ItemList, String CGI )
{
super(Title);
this.ItemList = ItemList;
this.CGI = CGI;
setLayout(gridbag);
Name = new TextField(25);
Phone = new TextField(25);
Done = new Button("Done");
LName = new Label("Your Name");
LPhone= new Label("Phone number");
Message1=new Label("Please enter in the above information and a");
Message2=new Label("sales agent will call to confirm your order");

Con.weightx=.2;
Con.weighty=.2;

Con.anchor = GridBagConstraints.CENTER;
Con.fill = GridBagConstraints.NONE;
Con.gridwidth = GridBagConstraints.REMAINDER;
gridbag.setConstraints(Name, Con);
gridbag.setConstraints(LName, Con);

add(LName);
add(Name);
```

```
gridbag.setConstraints(Phone, Con);
gridbag.setConstraints(LPhone, Con);

add(LPhone);
add(Phone);
gridbag.setConstraints(Done, Con);
gridbag.setConstraints(Message1, Con);
gridbag.setConstraints(Message2, Con);

add(Message1);
add(Message2);
add(Done);
pack();
resize(300,300);
show();
}

public boolean action(Event evt, Object arg) {
    if ("Done".equals(arg))
    {
        System.out.println(CGI);
        CGIpost = new HTTPpost(CGI, "NAME: " + Name.getText() +
        "\nPHONE: " + Phone.getText() +"\nPURCHASES:\n" +
        ItemList + "\n");
        System.out.println(CGIpost.results());
        dispose();
        return true;
    }
    return false;
}
} //CheckOutFrame
```

When the user clicks the Done button, we call the HTTPpost and pass the CGI's URL along with the data the user has entered. The program then effectively terminates. The CGI program handles the data it received by storing it to a file or by e-mailing it to the ordering department.

Processing Return Data With a CGI Program

We want to use a CGI program on the Web server to either save the user's ordering information or e-mail it to the ordering department. Remember that this CGI program is specified in the PARAM tag in the HTML document from which the Store class is first called. The implementation of the CGI can be platform specific, and is currently not well suited for Java. Consult *The Web Server Book* or a book that is specifically about CGI programming for more information about this processing. There are several freely available CGI libraries that can facilitate the task of writing a CGI program to do what you want. The Online Companion has links to CGI programming resources if you don't know where to start!

Possible Improvements

Many features can be added to the Java Store. Use what you now know about Java's programming potential to do some creative thinking about the possibilities. Here are some ideas we thought of that you may want to implement as an exercise:

- Make the Product Images drag and drop: make an icon of a shopping basket, so that when the user wishes to select a product for purchase, he can drag it onto the icon. It will automatically be added to the product list (or shopping basket).

- Add additional text fields in which the user can enter his or her address and possibly, a credit card number. This must be done with care, using encryption to protect the user's personal information. This feature would greatly facilitate order processing and eliminate the need for a sales agent to call for this information.

- Implement the Help menus! We have demonstrated how menus are handled in the code, and implementing a series of event handlers for the Help menus would be a straightforward task.

18 | Interfacing With Non-HTTP Servers: Chess Client

What You'll Learn
In this tutorial, we create a graphical client for the Internet Chess Server in Java. We'll be covering these topics in detail:

- Socket programming.
- Handling asynchronous data transfer.
- Multithreading.
- Creating a complex user interface.

The Contract

An Internet startup company wants to provide free high-quality entertainment to the Internet community as a means of drawing users to their site and has contracted us to do the job. We decide that a chess program that allows people to play against one another would be suitable for the task. We'll use the Internet Chess Server (ICS) for the back end because it can handle such tasks as accepting connections, matching players, keeping score, and checking for valid moves. It is, however, somewhat limited in that its interface is character-based. Figure 18-1 contains a picture of the text chessboard supplied by the server.

The ICS is released for free under the GNU Public License, and can be found at ftp://chess.onenet.net/pub/chess/Unix.

```
Telnet - ics.onenet.net
Connect  Edit  Terminal  Help
   8 |   |   |*R|   |*Q|   |*K|   |*R|       Move # : 18 (White)
     |---+---+---+---+---+---+---+---|
   7 |*P|*P|*P|*B|*N| B |*P|   |       Black Moves : 'Kf8      (0:02)'
     |---+---+---+---+---+---+---+---|
   6 |   |   |   |   |*P|   | P |*P|
     |---+---+---+---+---+---+---+---|
   5 |   | B |   |*P| P |   |   |   |       Black Clock : 2 : 34
     |---+---+---+---+---+---+---+---|
   4 |   |   |   | P |   |   |   |   |       White Clock : 2 : 15
     |---+---+---+---+---+---+---+---|
   3 |   |   | P |   | Q |   |   | P |       Black Strength : 39
     |---+---+---+---+---+---+---+---|
   2 | P |   | P |   |   | P | P |   |       White Strength : 34
     |---+---+---+---+---+---+---+---|
   1 |   | R |   |   | K |   |   | R |
     |---+---+---+---+---+---+---+---|
       a   b   c   d   e   f   g   h
White holding: []
fics%
```

Figure 18-1: *The text chessboard used by the ICS.*

Graphical front ends already exist for the ICS for some platforms, but they must be installed on the user's machine, which can be difficult or impossible for many users. We agreed to develop a Java applet to act as a graphical front end to the ICS. By writing the front end as an applet, we solve two problems simultaneously: the client can run on any machine with a Java-capable Web browser, and it requires no installation by the user. The security restrictions imposed on untrusted applets by Netscape Navigator 2.0 will not hamper us in this situation, since we can arrange for the ICS and the applet code to reside on the same computer.

Features

The most important feature the graphical front end adds to the ICS is a graphical chessboard that accepts mouse input. We must also have a text input line to allow the user to issue ICS commands that our client does not generate. The ICS supports timed chess games, so we'll add dynamic clocks to the board that count down the seconds for the active player. Players are allowed to chat with other players who are currently on the server, so we'll also add a text window to accommodate that output. Incoming match requests can sometimes get lost in the jumble of chatting; we'll have the client check for those and display them to the user in a separate window. As a final touch, we'll add a dynamically updated listing of the players on the server who are currently accepting match requests. From this listing, our user can select a potential opponent.

Design & Implementation

We'll describe our development process more or less chronologically. We'll start with the most fundamental problems, develop solutions to them, and flesh out the skeleton with a functional ICS client. Later on, we'll develop some enhancements to our applet and suggest exercises for the reader.

The task is essentially to develop a graphical front end to an ICS in an applet. To build an applet of this complexity, we'll need to break the task down into several manageable chunks, as follows:

- Develop procedures to communicate with a server.
- Create a generic chessboard.
- Create a class connecting a chessboard to an ICS.

The client is a translator between the ICS and the user; we must take the user's desires and translate them into ICS commands. Similarly, we must take the ICS output and translate it into a user-friendly format.

Communicating With an Asynchronous Server

We already know from Chapter 13, "Networking With Sockets & Streams," how to achieve a socket-based communication between our applet and a server. However, we did not touch upon asynchronous data transfer. For a simple server like the finger server, handling data transfer is easy because it is *synchronous*—the server waits to receive our command before issuing its output. Many servers are *asynchronous*—they can send data with no warning. The ICS is of this type. For instance, if another user sends a message to our user, the ICS will send the message to our client with no warning.

We decide to implement a data receptionist that runs on its own thread. By threading it, we ensure that asynchronous data will be received in the background while our applet is busy elsewhere. Given an InputStream, it will read Strings terminated by EOL characters or an EOF. Having read the Strings, it will need some way to transfer them to the ICS client. We describe an interface, Listener, that allows this. The code for Listener is:

```
package ventana.io;

public interface Listener {
    public void receiveInput(InputStreamHandler i, Object o);
}
```

This method allows the data receptionist, the InputStreamHandler class, to transfer the Strings it reads from the InputStream to another object via the receiveInput method. Although we will use it only to pass Strings, we allow the Listener to receive any Object using this method. In the future, we may want to develop a specialized InputStreamHandler that passes some other class. We also return a reference to the InputStreamHandler itself in case the Listener object is using several different InputStreamHandlers and needs to distinguish between them:

```
package ventana.io;

import java.io.*;
```

```
public class InputStreamHandler implements Runnable {
<Com private Thread engine;
   private DataInputStream in;
   private Listener client;

   public InputStreamHandler(InputStream in,
   Listener client) {
      this.in = new DataInputStream(in);
      this.client = client;
      engine = new Thread(this);
      engine.start();
   }

   public void close() {
      if (in!=null) {
         try {in.close();}
         catch (IOException e) {}
      }
      engine.stop();
   }

   public void run() {
      if (in==null) {return;}
         String s;
      try {s = in.readLine();}

      catch (IOException e) {
         return;
      }}
      while (s!=null && engine.isAlive()) {

         client.receiveInput(this,s);
         try {s = in.readLine();}

         catch (IOException e) {s = null;}
      }
   }
}
```

When the InputStreamHandler is constructed, it creates a DataInputStream on top of the InputStream it is passed and starts the thread running. The run method reads lines from the DataInputStream and passes them to the Listener client with the receiveInput method. The InputStreamHandler will simply stop reading from the InputStream if an IOException occurs.

Creating a Generic Chessboard

We'd like to keep the code for the chessboard separate from the code that interacts with the ICS. The chessboard we develop here might have several uses: as part of a standalone computer chess program, for instance, or as a board for playing checkers. Our board will be rather dumb— it will essentially be an 8 X 8 grid that contains pictures and responds to mouse clicks. We don't need to program the board to understand chess moves and generate them properly. That task is left to the ICS server.

Our generic chessboard is an extension of the Canvas class, which is more or less a usable implementation of the abstract Component class. We decided not to use a Container for our chessboard for two reasons. Images, which are what we'll use to hold the graphics data for the chess pieces, are not Components and thus cannot be added to a Container directly. In addition, the current implementation of the Java API for Microsoft Windows systems has some problems with Containers that contain lots of Components.

The ChessBoard class is responsible for drawing the board and generating moves if appropriate. The public methods of the ChessBoard class are listed in Table 18-1.

Method	Description
setImage(Image, String)	Sets the square indicated by the given String to contain the given Image and redraws the square. The String should be in chess notation, that is, "A1".
endGame()	Ends the chess game.
setGenerateMoves(boolean)	Tells the board whether it should allow the user to generate moves or not.
setOrientation(boolean)	Tells the board if it should be oriented white down (true) or white up (false).
boolean getOrientation()	Returns the current orientation of the board.

Table 18-1: *Public methods of the ChessBoard class.*

The ChessBoard class contains a two-dimensional array of Images. These are the game squares. The ChessBoard allows access to the array of squares by means of the setImage method. The setImage method doesn't specify the array indices directly, but relies on a String in chess notation to tell it which square to modify. The mapping from chess notation to array indices is done internally. This allows us do the mapping differently depending on whether the board is oriented white down or white up. For instance, the square "A1" should be in the lower left-hand corner if our user is playing white, but should be in the upper right-hand corner if our user is playing black.

When the user clicks on a square, it becomes selected and a red circle is drawn on the square to indicate its selection. If the user clicks on that square again, the square becomes unselected and the circle disappears. If the user clicks on a different square while the first is still selected, the move is generated and passed to the ChessBoard's parent, and the first square becomes unselected. This behavior can be inhibited by the setGenerateMoves method—we don't want a user generating moves when it's not his or her turn!

Here is the code for our ChessBoard class:

```java
import java.awt.*;
import java.util.*;

public class ChessBoard extends Canvas {
   private Image[][] squares;
   private boolean up = true;
   private boolean generate = false;
   private Point selected;
   private Color dark;
   private Color light;

   public ChessBoard() {
      squares = new Image[8][8];
      dark = Color.gray;
      light = Color.lightGray;
      resize(320,320);
      repaint();
   }
```

The endGame method is called when the chess game is over. It darkens all of the squares to indicate to the user that the game is complete and then repaints the board. Finally, it prevents the user from trying to generate any more moves:

```java
   public void endGame() {
      dark = Color.darkGray;
      light = Color.gray;
      repaint();
      setGenerateMoves(false);
   }

   public void setGenerateMoves(boolean b) {
      generate = b;
   }

   public void setOrientation(boolean b) {
      up = b;
   }
```

```
public boolean getOrientation() {
   return up;
}
```

The getSquare method is used internally to map between chess notation and array indices. Given two integers indicating a position in the array of squares, it returns a String in chess notation corresponding to that square:

```
private String getSquare(int x, int y) {
   char ary[] = new char[2];
   if (up) {
      ary[0] = (char)('a'+x);
      ary[1] = (char)('1'+(7-y));
   } else {
      ary[0] = (char)('a'+(7-x));
      ary[1] = (char)('1'+y);
   }
   return new String(ary);
}
```

The class in charge of overseeing the actual chess game will use the setImage method to put pieces into squares. The setImage method takes an Image, presumably of a chess piece, and a String in chess notation indicating which square to put the Image into. If the new Image differs from the square's old Image, the square is updated and redrawn. The setImage method can be used to remove a piece from a square simply by sending it a null pointer for the Image:

```
public void setImage(Image i, String s) {
   int x = (int)(s.charAt(0)-'a');
   int y = (int)(s.charAt(1)-1-'0');
   if (up) {
      y = 7-y;
   } else {
      x = 7-x;
   }
   if (squares[x][y]!=i) {
      squares[x][y] = i;
```

```
            paintSquare(x,y,false,getGraphics());
        }
    }

    public boolean mouseDown(Event evt, int px, int py) {
        if (!generate) {
            return false;
        }
        int x = px/40;
        int y = py/40;
        if (selected==null) {
            selected = new Point(x,y);
            paintSquare(x,y,true,getGraphics());
        } else if (selected.x==x && selected.y==y) {
            selected = null;
            paintSquare(x,y,false,getGraphics());
        } else {
            String move = getSquare(selected.x,selected.y);
            move = move+"-"+getSquare(x,y);
            Event e = new
Event(getParent(),Event.ACTION_EVENT,move);
            getParent().deliverEvent(e);

paintSquare(selected.x,selected.y,false,getGraphics());
            selected = null;
        }
        return true;
    }

    public synchronized Dimension preferredSize() {
        return new Dimension(320,320);
    }

    public synchronized Dimension minimumSize() {
        return new Dimension(320,320);
    }
```

The paintSquare method is in charge of drawing the individual squares. Given the array indices of a square, it draws the square's background either light or dark, as appropriate (the lower left-hand square is always light), and draws the square's piece Image into the square if there is one. The boolean argument indicates whether or not the red circle (indicating a selected square) should be drawn:

```
public void paintSquare(int x, int y, boolean b, Graphics
g) {
    if ((x%2==0 && y%2==0)||(x%2==1 && y%2==1)) {
      g.setColor(light);
    } else {
      g.setColor(dark);
    }
    g.fillRect(x*40,y*40,40,40);
    if (squares[x][y]!=null) {
      g.drawImage(squares[x][y],x*40,y*40,this);
    }
    if (b) {
      g.setColor(Color.red);
      g.fillOval(x*40+15,y*40+15,10,10);
    }
  }

  public void paint(Graphics g) {
    for (int y=0; y<8; y++) {
      for (int x=0; x<8; x++) {
        paintSquare(x,y,false,g);
      }
    }
  }

}
```

Connecting the Chessboard to the ICS

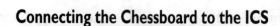

We'll implement an applet that uses both the chessboard we have developed and the asynchronous data receptionist to implement an ICS client. The code dealing with parsing ICS output and generating ICS commands will go here. If we design our applet well, this should be the only section that contains code specific to the ICS.

We don't want to put the chessboard in the applet itself because ICS allows users to observe or even play multiple games simultaneously. Our client should not limit the functionality of the ICS, but should instead enhance it. The ICS keeps track of games by number, and when it sends out a board update message, it includes that number. We designed our main applet to contain a hashtable of chessboards indexed by game number. Each chessboard is dedicated to a single game and resides in a frame of its own.

There should be a few other things in that frame as well. To help the user keep track of which board is which, we should indicate the name of each player. The ICS allows players to set time limits on their games. Each player starts off with a fixed amount of time on the clock. After each move, another fixed amount of time is added to the player's remaining time. For instance, suppose a player started a game with 90 seconds on the clock and a 10-second increment. If he took 2 seconds to make his first move, he would end up with 98 seconds remaining. If a player's clock drops below zero, the other player can win the game. We'll display the current time on each player's clock below their names in the frame.

Setting Up the StopWatch

Instead of simply displaying the time remaining, we use the threading capabilities of Java to allow the clocks to count down the seconds for the currently active player. The Label class provides us with a generic non-editable text output field. We'll extend that in a StopWatch class to produce a label that prints out its time variable in clock notation and decrements the variable every second. The public methods of the StopWatch class are in Table 18-2.

Method	Description
set(int)	Sets the current time remaining and displays it in clock notation.
start()	Starts the clock countdown.
stop()	Stops the clock countdown.
clear()	Stops the clock's thread entirely.

Table 18-2: *Public methods of the StopWatch class.*

Here is the code for the StopWatch:

```java
import java.awt.*;

public class StopWatch extends Label implements Runnable {
   private Thread engine;
   private int time = 0;

   public StopWatch() {
      super();
      engine = new Thread(this);
      engine.setPriority(3);
   }

   public StopWatch(int i) {
      this();
      set(i);
   }
```

The set method sets the time remaining on the StopWatch. This method must be synchronized because another thread and ours might try to set the time simultaneously. If the time is not negative, we reset the label output to display the time in clock notation:

```java
   public synchronized void set(int i) {
      time = i;
      if (time>0) {
         int min = time/60;
         int sec = time%60;
         if (sec>9) {
            setText(""+min+":"+sec);
```

```java
        } else {
          setText(""+min+":0"+sec);
        }
      } else {
        setText("0:00");
      }
    }

    public void start() {
      if (engine!=null) {
        if (!engine.isAlive()) {
          engine.start();
        } else {
          engine.resume();
        }
      }
    }

    public void stop() {
      if (engine!=null) {
        engine.suspend();
      }
    }

    public void clear() {
      if (engine!=null) {
        engine.stop();
        engine = null;
      }
    }

    public void run() {
      while (engine!=null && engine.isAlive()) {
        set(time-1);
        try {
          engine.sleep(1000);
        } catch (InterruptedException e) {}
      }
    }
  }
```

Implementing the ChessFrame

Now we are ready to implement a ChessFrame that has the functionality we have just described. Table 18-3 contains the public methods of the ChessFrame.

Method	Description
updateGame(String)	Updates the frame's status to reflect that of the given game.
endGame()	Ends the current game.

Table 18-3: *ChessFrame methods.*

The ChessFrame is primarily responsible for parsing the board update messages and displaying the relevant information. The default board update message was shown in Figure 18-1. This can be somewhat difficult to parse; fortunately, the ICS lets users select from a variety of different board styles. The style we choose, style 12, sends a board update message as a single string containing fields delimited by spaces:

```
<12> rnbqkbnr pppppppp ---- ---- ---- ---- PPPPPPPP RNBQKBNR
W -1 1 1 1 1 0 1 donald donald 2 0 0 39 39 0 0 1 none (0:00)
none 0
```

The first field is an indicator that the string contains board update information in style 12 format. The parent of the ChessFrame will use this field to determine when to call the updateGame method. The next eight fields contain the current state of the board. Each piece is indicated by a letter; white pieces are uppercase and black pieces are lowercase. A dash represents a square containing no piece. We'll detail what the rest of the fields are used for in the code for the updateGame method.

THE PACKERLAYOUT

The layout managers supplied with the Java API, while much more sophisticated than the layout management support of many other programming languages, cannot easily give us the type of layout we want for the chess client. Documentation for the PackerLayout class can be found at http://www.geom.umn.edu/~daeron/apps/ui/pack/gui.html. The PackerLayout source and class files are included on the Companion CD-ROM and the Online Companion.

Here is the code for our ChessFrame:

```java
import ChessBoard;
import ChessClient;
import PackerLayout;
import java.awt.*;
import java.util.*;
import ventana.awt.*;

public class ChessFrame extends Frame {

    private ChessBoard board;
    private ChessClient parent;
    private String user;

    private Panel players;
    private Panel whitePlayer;
    private Panel blackPlayer;
    private Label whiteName;
    private Label blackName;
    private StopWatch whiteTime;
    private StopWatch blackTime;
```

The frame contains two main components; the ChessBoard itself and a panel of player information. The player panel is subdivided into a panel for the white player and a panel for the black player. Each player's panel contains the player's name and a StopWatch that displays his or her remaining time.

```java
public ChessFrame(ChessClient parent, String user,
  Font fixed) {

  super("Chess Game");
  this.user = user;
  this.parent = parent;
  setLayout(new PackerLayout());

  whitePlayer = new Panel();
  whitePlayer.setLayout(new PackerLayout());
  whiteName = new Label("--------");
  whiteName.setFont(fixed);
  whiteName.setAlignment(Label.CENTER);
  whiteTime = new StopWatch();
  whiteTime.setFont(fixed);
  whiteTime.setAlignment(Label.CENTER);
  whitePlayer.add("whitename;fill=x;pady=5",whiteName);
  whitePlayer.add("whitetime;fill=x;pady=5",whiteTime);

  blackPlayer = new Panel();
  blackPlayer.setLayout(new PackerLayout());
  blackName = new Label("--------");
  blackName.setFont(fixed);
  blackName.setAlignment(Label.CENTER);
  blackTime = new StopWatch();
  blackTime.setFont(fixed);
  blackTime.setAlignment(Label.CENTER);
  blackPlayer.add("blackname;fill=x;pady=5",blackName);
  blackPlayer.add("blacktime;fill=x;pady=5",blackTime);

  players = new Panel();
  players.setLayout(new PackerLayout());
  players.add("wplayer;side=bottom;fill=x",whitePlayer);
  players.add("bplayer;side=top;fill=x",blackPlayer);
  add("panel1;side=left",players);

  board = new ChessBoard();
  add("panel2;side=left",board);
```

```
        pack();
        resize(size());
        show();
    }
```

The only event that the frame itself is concerned with is the
WINDOW_DESTROY event. If any other event occurs, we pass it
to the frame's parent. This allows the move events generated by
the ChessBoard to be passed upward to the applet for eventual
delivery to the ICS:

```
public boolean handleEvent(Event evt) {
    if (evt.id==Event.WINDOW_DESTROY) {
        dispose();
        return true;
    } else {
        parent.deliverEvent(evt);
        return true;
    }
}
```

During the first time the board is updated, we'll find out whether
or not our user is playing black. If so, the flipPlayers method
reverses the players' labels and flips the chessboard upside down:

```
protected void flipPlayers() {
    players.remove(whitePlayer);
    players.remove(blackPlayer);
    players.add("wplayer;side=top;fill=x",whitePlayer);
    players.add("bplayer;side=bottom;fill=x",blackPlayer);
    board.setOrientation(false);
}
```

The next method is the heart of the ChessFrame; this method
parses the ICS's board update message. First, we read the eight
board status lines from the update message by using a
StringTokenizer. Then, we find out whose move it is; we'll use that
information a little later in the method when we find out how
much time each player has left. The code is as follows:

```
public void updateGame(String s) {
   System.out.println(s);
   StringTokenizer st = new StringTokenizer(s);
   st.nextToken(); //The <12> board indicator
   String lines[] = new String[8];
   for (int i=0; i<8; i++) {
      lines[i] = st.nextToken();
   }
   String token = st.nextToken(); //Whose move it is (W,B)
   System.out.println(token);
   boolean whiteMove = true;
   if (token.equals("B")) {
      whiteMove = false;
   }
   st.nextToken(); //-1 if not double pawn push, else
         //column number
   st.nextToken(); //Can white still castle short?
   st.nextToken(); //Can white still castle long?
   st.nextToken(); //Can black still castle short?
   st.nextToken(); //Can black still castle long?
   st.nextToken(); //Number of moves since last
                   //irreversible one
   st.nextToken(); //The game number
```

The next tokens contain the names of the players. If the names don't match the text of the player name labels, we assume the ICS knows what it's doing. If the new black player name is the same as our user and the type variable does not equal two, we flip the board so that black is down. The type variable contains a number indicating the user's relation to the game. If this variable is set to two, the user is playing a game in examine mode—that is, playing against himself. If this variable is set to one, the user is playing against a real opponent and it's the user's turn. Either way, we want the chessboard to generate moves:

```
token = st.nextToken(); //The white player's name
if (! whiteName.getText().equals(token)) {
   whiteName.setText(token);
}
token = st.nextToken(); //The black player's name
String type = st.nextToken();
```

```
if (! blackName.getText().equals(token)) {
  blackName.setText(token);
  if (user.equals(token) && ! type.equals("2")) {
    board.setOrientation(false);
    flipPlayers();
    System.out.println("Tried to anyway");
  }
  layout();
}
if (type.equals("1") || type.equals("2")) {
  board.setGenerateMoves(true);
} else {
  board.setGenerateMoves(false);
}
token = st.nextToken(); //Initial time of match
token = st.nextToken(); //Increment of match
token = st.nextToken(); //White's strength
token = st.nextToken(); //black's strength
```

The next two tokens contain the number of seconds left for each player. We set the StopWatches to the new proper time, stop the countdown for the player who just moved, and start the countdown for the player who's about to move:

```
token = st.nextToken(); //white's remaining time
try {
  Integer i = new Integer(token);
  whiteTime.set(i.intValue());
} catch (NumberFormatException e) {}
token = st.nextToken(); //black's remaining time
try {
  Integer i = new Integer(token);
  blackTime.set(i.intValue());
} catch (NumberFormatException e) {}
if (whiteMove) {
  blackTime.stop();
  whiteTime.start();
} else {
  whiteTime.stop();
  blackTime.start();
}
```

Finally, we parse the board tokens we set aside earlier. We wait until the end to update the board because the board might have been reversed by the previous section of code. If we had drawn the board at the beginning and then flipped it, the flipping would be apparent to the user. We read each line one character at a time. If the character is a hyphen, we set the square corresponding to that character to contain no picture; otherwise, we request the picture from our parent:

```
for (int i=0; i<8; i++) {
   String line = lines[i];
   char ary[] = new char[8];
   line.getChars(0,8,ary,0);
   for (int j=0; j<8; j++) {
      char row = (char)('8'-i);
      char column = (char)('a'+j);
      Image piece;
      if (ary[j]!='-') {
         piece = parent.getPieceImage(""+ary[j]);
      } else {
         piece = null;
      }
      board.setImage(piece,""+column+row);
   }
 }
}
```

Writing the Applet

We have created a stand-alone frame that contains a generic chessboard and the necessary player information. Now we can start writing the applet itself. We'll start small and add features later on. The first implementation of the applet should connect to an ICS and offer up a chat-style window to allow the user to interact with other players. Whenever a line is received that begins with <12>, the applet recognizes the line as containing board update information and passes that line to the appropriate ChessFrame, constructing one if necessary. The applet must also

recognize the server output that indicates the end of a game and pass that information on to the ChessFrame. The following code implements our ChessClient Applet:

```java
import ChessFrame;
import PackerLayout;
import java.applet.*;
import java.awt.*;
import java.net.*;
import java.util.*;
import java.io.*;
import ventana.io.*;

public class ChessClient extends Applet implements Listener {

    private String user;
    private Label title;
    private TextArea output;
    private TextField input;
    private Hashtable games;
    private Hashtable pieceImages;
    private Socket ChessSocket;
    private InputStream ChessInput;
    private OutputStream ChessOutput;
    private InputStreamHandler ChessInputHandler;
    private MediaTracker tracker;
    private Font fixed;
    private Font pretty;
```

The first thing we do in the applet's init procedure is set the pretty and fixed fonts for the entire applet. Since monitor resolutions vary widely, a 10-point font that looks large on an older monitor may be unreadable on a high-resolution monitor. For this reason, we allow the HTML designer to choose the font type and size. We use the following code to set the fonts:

```java
public void init() {
    String fixedName = getParameter("FIXEDFONTNAME");
    if (fixedName==null) {
        fixedName = "Courier";
    }
```

```
int fixedSize = 12;
String fixedSizestr = getParameter("FIXEDFONTSIZE");
if (fixedSizestr!=null) {
  try {
    Integer i = new Integer(fixedSizestr);
    fixedSize = i.intValue();
  } catch (NumberFormatException e) {}
}
fixed = new Font(fixedName,Font.PLAIN,fixedSize);
String prettyName = getParameter("PRETTYFONTNAME");
if (prettyName==null) {
  prettyName = "Courier";
}
int prettySize = 12;
String prettySizestr = getParameter("PRETTYFONTSIZE");
if (prettySizestr!=null) {
  try {
    Integer i = new Integer(prettySizestr);
    prettySize = i.intValue();
  } catch (NumberFormatException e) {}
}
pretty = new Font(prettyName,Font.PLAIN,prettySize);
```

Now that we've set the font information, it's time to lay out the applet. We add a title label, a TextArea to display output from the server, and a TextField to receive text input from the user. Finally, we load the piece pictures into a hashtable:

```
setLayout(new PackerLayout());
title = new Label("Internet Chess Server");
title.setFont(
  new Font(prettyName,Font.PLAIN,prettySize+12));
title.setAlignment(Label.CENTER);
add("title;side=top;fill=x",title);
output = new TextArea(20,80);
output.setEditable(false);
output.setFont(fixed);
add("output;side=top;fill=x",output);
input = new TextField(80);
input.setFont(fixed);
```

```
        add("input;side=top;fill=x",input);
    show();

    pieceImages = new Hashtable(10);
    initPieceImages();
}
```

This procedure builds a hashtable of Images indexed by character. The character indicates the type of piece to which the Image corresponds. We build an initial hashtable indexed by characters of relative URLs (in String format) to the pictures. Then we run through the hashtable, get the Images pointed to by the URLs, and build a new hashtable from them. We use a MediaTracker to ensure that all of the images have been downloaded and are ready to be displayed before exiting. The code is:

```
protected void initPieceImages() {
    tracker = new MediaTracker(this);
    Hashtable h = new Hashtable(10);
    h.put("r","pics/br.gif");
    h.put("n","pics/bn.gif");
    h.put("b","pics/bb.gif");
    h.put("q","pics/bq.gif");
    h.put("k","pics/bk.gif");
    h.put("p","pics/bp.gif");
    h.put("P","pics/wp.gif");
    h.put("R","pics/wr.gif");
    h.put("N","pics/wn.gif");
    h.put("B","pics/wb.gif");
    h.put("Q","pics/wq.gif");
    h.put("K","pics/wk.gif");
    Enumeration e = h.keys();
    while(e.hasMoreElements()) {
        try {
            String key = (String)e.nextElement();
            String s = (String)h.get(key);
            URL u = new URL(getCodeBase(),s);
            Image i  = getImage(u);
            tracker.addImage(i,0);
            pieceImages.put(key,i);
```

```
      } catch (Exception ex) {
        handleException(ex);
      }
    }
    try {tracker.waitForAll();} catch (InterruptedException
ex) {}
  }
```

The getPieceImage method returns the Image referred to by the piece String. For instance, getPieceImage("P") would return an Image of a white pawn:

```
public Image getPieceImage(String piece) {
  return (Image)pieceImages.get(piece);
}
```

When the applet starts, we open a connection to the ICS and build streams on the socket. We create a new InputStreamHandler on our InputStream. Remember that this class reads Strings from the stream and returns them to us via the receiveInput method. Finally, we create a new hashtable for storing ChessFrames. Most users will only want to play or view one game at a time, so we initialize this hashtable to have space for only one element:

```
public void start() {
  try {
    String ChessHost = getParameter("HOST");
    if (ChessHost==null) {
      ChessHost = getCodeBase().getHost();
    }
    ChessSocket = new Socket(ChessHost,5000);
    ChessInput = ChessSocket.getInputStream();
    ChessOutput = ChessSocket.getOutputStream();
    ChessInputHandler = new
InputStreamHandler(ChessInput,this);
  } catch (Exception e) {
    handleException(e);
  }
  games = new Hashtable(1);
}
```

When the applet stops, we close down the InputStreamHandler, the streams, and the socket, and we clear the input and output windows:

```
public void stop() {
  try {
    ChessInputHandler.close();
    ChessOutput.close();
    ChessInput.close();
    ChessSocket.close();
  } catch (IOException e) {
    handleException(e);
  }
  output.setText("");
  input.setText("");
}

public void handleException(Exception e) {
  e.printStackTrace();
}
```

Any time we need to send output to the ICS, we do it through the writeOutput. Using a single method gives us two advantages here: we don't have to replicate all of the code every time we want to send output, and by using the *synchronized* keyword, we guarantee that two threads cannot try to send output to the server simultaneously. Since we have not set the user String yet, the first time the writeOutput method is called, the user will be set to the String. This works because the first command issued to the ICS is the user's name:

```
protected synchronized void writeOutput(String s) {
  if (user==null) {
    user = s.trim();
  }
  byte b[] = new byte[s.length()];
  s.getBytes(0,s.length(),b,0);
  try {
    ChessOutput.write(b);
```

```
    } catch (IOException e) {
      handleException(e);
    }
  }
```

The receiveInput method is called by the InputStreamHandler every time a complete new line is received. If the line is blank or contains the ICS prompt, we ignore it entirely. If the line starts with <12>, we recognize that it indicates a board update message and call the parseBoard method. If the line looks like it indicates the end of a game, we parse the line for the game number. If the game number is in our hashtable of games, we call the ChessFrame's endGame method and remove the frame from the hashtable. If none of these is the case, then the line is an ordinary server output line, and we append it to our output window:

```java
public void receiveInput(InputStreamHandler ish, Object o) {
  String s = (String)o;
  if (s.trim().equals("") || s.trim().equals("fics%")) {
    return;
  }
  if (s.trim().startsWith("<12>")) {
    parseBoard(s.trim());
  } else if (s.trim().startsWith("{Game")) {
    StringTokenizer st = new StringTokenizer(s);
    String token = st.nextToken(); //{Game
    String number = st.nextToken(); //number
    ChessFrame frame = (ChessFrame)games.get(number);
    if (frame!=null) {
      token = st.nextToken(); //(player1
      token = st.nextToken(); //vs.
      token = st.nextToken(); //player2
      token = st.nextToken(); //loser
      frame.endGame(token);
      games.remove(number);
    }
  } else {
    output.appendText(s+"\n");
  }
}
```

This method is called when the receiveInput method finds a board update message. We parse the line for the game number, which is the 16th field in the line. If that game does not already exist in our hashtable of games, we create a new ChessFrame for that game and add it to the hashtable. Finally, we update the frame via the updateGame method:

```java
protected void parseBoard(String s) {
    StringTokenizer st = new StringTokenizer(s);
    String token = st.nextToken();
    if (! token.equals("<12>")) {
        output.appendText("oops... "+token);
        return;
    }
    for (int i=0; i<16; i++) {
        token = st.nextToken();
    }
    ChessFrame frame = (ChessFrame)games.get(token);
    if (frame==null) {
        frame = new ChessFrame(this,user,fixed);
        games.put(token,frame);
    }
    frame.updateGame(s);
}
```

All action events that have been passed upward are dealt with here. If the target of the event is a ChessFrame, the event must be a move generated by a board, so we send the move to the ICS. If the target is our input window, we send the message to the ICS and clear the input window:

```java
public boolean action(Event evt, Object arg) {
    if (evt.target instanceof ChessFrame) {
        writeOutput((String)arg+"\n");
        return true;
    } else if (evt.target==input) {
        writeOutput((String)arg+"\n");
        input.setText("");
        return true;
```

```
        } else {
          return false;
        }
     }


  }
```

Our Java ICS client is now complete. The applet displays its title, an output window from the server, and an input field for the user to issue ICS commands. When the user starts a new game with someone, a new ChessFrame is created, and the user can play chess using a graphical interface. A screen shot of this applet is in Figure 18-2.

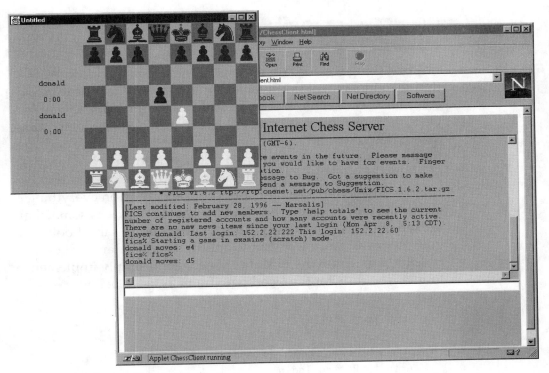

Figure 18-2: *The functional ICS client.*

Possible Improvements

Our chess applet has been released to the community, and every-one loves it. The company we created it for has come back and requested several new features. First of all, they note that the login procedure does not mask out the password; a user's password can be seen by anyone who happens to be watching. Also, the client doesn't set the chessboard to use style 12 rather than style 1 (see Figure 18-1), but relies on the user to set it. They also note that many users have trouble keeping track of which players are online and available for games. They want a current player listing in a separate window. We've agreed to work on these problems in the next version of the applet.

Improving the Login Window

The first thing we need to tackle is the new login window. We decide to implement this as an external frame. When the user connects to the server, the applet watches for the login screen. Once the login screen is complete, we launch our user login frame. This frame contains two text fields, one for the username and one for the password, and a button to initiate the login procedure. It would be more proper to implement this as a Dialog, because Dialogs are modal—they inhibit event generation on everything else while they're displayed—but the Dialog class was somewhat broken under Netscape Navigator 2.0 for Solaris as this book was going to press. Since we want to appeal to as large an audience as possible, we ignore the modality concern and simply implement a Frame. The code for the UserLogin frame is listed below:

```java
import java.awt.*;
import java.util.*;

public class UserLogin extends Frame {
    private Button login;
    private TextField user;
    private TextField password;
    private Component target;
```

In the constructor for the UserLogin class, we specify the target Component for events to be sent to and the font for the login window. We add two TextFields; one for the user name and one for the password. In the password TextField, we specify an asterisk as our echo character; this method causes any input to the TextField to be echoed as asterisks. We also add a login button that will generate a login event and close this window:

```
public UserLogin(Component target, Font f) {
    super("Internet Chess Server Login");
    this.target = target;
    setBackground(Color.gray);
    setLayout(new FlowLayout());

    Panel p = new Panel();
    p.setLayout(new FlowLayout());
    Label l = new Label("Username:");
    p.add(l);
    user = new TextField(16);
    user.setFont(f);
    user.setEditable(true);
    p.add(user);
    l = new Label("Password:");
    p.add(l);
    password = new TextField(16);
    password.setFont(f);
    password.setEditable(true);
    password.setEchoCharacter('*');
    p.add(password);
    login = new Button("Login");
    login.setFont(f);
    p.add(login);
    add(p);
    pack();
    show();
}
```

When the login button is clicked, we first check to see if the user has typed anything in the username field. If not, we assume that he or she pushed the login button erroneously, and we return.

We don't check the password field because most ICSes allow guests to log in with no password. If the user entered something in the name field, we generate a new action event and pass it to the target specified in the constructor. The event's argument is a Vector with two elements: the user name and the password. After generating the event, we dispose of the frame:

```java
public boolean action(Event evt, Object arg) {
    if (evt.target==login) {
        if (user.getText().trim().equals("")) {
            return true;
        }
        Vector v = new Vector(2);
        v.addElement(user.getText());
        v.addElement(password.getText());
        Event e = new Event(this,Event.ACTION_EVENT,v);
        target.deliverEvent(e);
        dispose();
        return true;
    }
    return false;
}
```

Now that we have our UserLogin frame, it's time to add it to the main applet. We need to decide when to construct (and display) the frame and then add code to handle the login event generated by the frame. We'll construct the UserLogin frame in the applet's start method by adding the following line to the end:

```java
UserLogin ul = new UserLogin(this,pretty);
```

To revise the action method so that the server generates the proper input when it receives a login event, we'll add the following conditional:

```java
} else if (evt.target instanceof UserLogin) {
    Vector v = (Vector)evt.arg;
    user = (String)v.elementAt(0);
    String pass = (String)v.elementAt(1);
    writeOutput(user+"\n"+pass+"\n");
    writeOutput("set style 12\n");
    return true;
}
```

We decide to set the user here instead of in the writeOutput method because this is safer. After deleting the code that sets the user variable in that method, we're done with this improvement. Figure 18-3 contains a screen shot of our applet with its login frame.

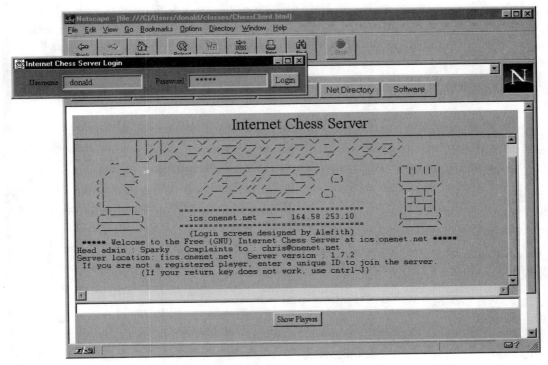

Figure 18-3: *ChessClient with LoginFrame.*

Adding a Current Player Listing

The other improvement the company requested, a current player listing in a separate window, is a bit more challenging and fun. We decide to display the current available users and their scores in an external frame with three columns. The players' names will in fact be buttons that, when pressed, generate a match request to the corresponding player.

One problem with displaying such a listing is its dynamic nature; as players log in and out of the ICS, the listing will change. Since the number of users on the ICS can be quite large at times, we decide to restrict the listing to the players who are currently available to play games. We'll create a new Thread that updates the listing every minute, and we'll add a way for the user to request an immediate refresh of the player listing. For convenience and to allow for future enhancement, we'll create a simple class, Player, to contain data on a single ICS player. The Player class currently keeps track of the user's name and blitz rating. Here is the code for the Player class:

```
public class Player {
    public String name;
    public String blitz;

    public Player(String name, String blitz) {
        this.name = name;
        this.blitz = blitz;
    }
}
```

The PlayerFrame class implements a frame that contains the columns of player buttons and score labels. It takes input via the updatePlayerListing method:

```
import java.awt.*;
import java.util.*;
import PackerLayout;
import Player;
import ChessClient;

public class PlayerFrame extends Frame {

    private ChessClient parent;
    private Vector playerList;
    private Panel topplayers;
    private Panel topscores;
    private Panel midplayers;
    private Panel midscores;
```

```
    private Panel lowplayers;
    private Panel lowscores;

    public PlayerFrame(ChessClient parent) {
      this(parent,new Vector(0));
    }
```

Our main constructor takes two arguments: the ChessClient that created it and a listing of the current players in Vector format. We construct three panels for player names and three panels for player blitz ratings:

```
    public PlayerFrame(ChessClient parent,Vector v) {
      super("Chess Players");
      this.parent = parent;
      topplayers = new Panel();
      topscores = new Panel();
      midplayers = new Panel();
      midscores = new Panel();
      lowplayers = new Panel();
      lowscores = new Panel();
      setLayout(new PackerLayout());
      setBackground(Color.gray);
      add("topplayers;side=left",topplayers);
      add("topscores;side=left",topscores);
      add("midplayers;side=left",midplayers);
      add("midscores;side=left",midscores);
      add("lowplayers;side=left",lowplayers);
      add("lowscores;side=left",lowscores);
      updatePlayerList(v);
      pack();
    }
```

The frame updates its display whenever the updatePlayerList method is called. We remove all elements from the player and score panels, construct new layout managers of the proper size for each of them, and add players from the vector to the panels; the first player goes in the first panel, the second goes in the second panel, and the third goes in the third panel:

```java
public void updatePlayerList(Vector v) {
    playerList = v;
    topplayers.removeAll();
    topscores.removeAll();
    midplayers.removeAll();
    midscores.removeAll();
    lowplayers.removeAll();
    lowscores.removeAll();
    int length = 2+playerList.size()/3;
    topplayers.setLayout(new GridLayout(length,1));
    topscores.setLayout(new GridLayout(length,1));
    midplayers.setLayout(new GridLayout(length,1));
    midscores.setLayout(new GridLayout(length,1));
    lowplayers.setLayout(new GridLayout(length,1));
    lowscores.setLayout(new GridLayout(length,1));

    topplayers.add(new Label("Player Name"));
    topscores.add(new Label("Score"));
    midplayers.add(new Label("Player Name"));
    midscores.add(new Label("Score"));
    lowplayers.add(new Label("Player Name"));
    lowscores.add(new Label("Score"));
    Enumeration e = playerList.elements();
    Player p;
    int count = 0;
    while (e.hasMoreElements()) {
        p = (Player)e.nextElement();
        Button b = new Button(p.name);
        Label l = new Label(p.blitz);
        switch(count%3) {
            case 0:
                topplayers.add(b);
                topscores.add(l);
                break;
            case 1:
                midplayers.add(b);
                midscores.add(l);
                break;
            case 2:
                lowplayers.add(b);
```

```
            lowscores.add(1);
            break;
        }
        count++;
    }
    layout();
    pack();
}
```

If the user presses one of the player buttons, we generate a new event with the PlayerFrame as the target and pass the event to the ChessClient with the match request string as the event's argument. We construct a new event instead of simply passing on the existing button event because the applet doesn't know or care that we're creating buttons from the player names; all it needs to know is that the user wants a match with the specified player. We'll be adding a MenuBar to the frame in the ChessClient, so we need to watch for menu events and pass them to the applet as well. We pass those intact because the MenuItems will be created by the applet, which will distinguish between them by looking at the event's target:

```
public boolean handleEvent(Event evt) {
    if (evt.target instanceof Button) {
        String s = "match "+(String)evt.arg;
        Event e = new Event(this,Event.ACTION_EVENT,s);
        parent.deliverEvent(e);
        return true;
    } else if (evt.target instanceof MenuItem) {
        parent.deliverEvent(evt);
        return true;
    }
    return false;
    }
}
```

Now that we have a frame that can contain a list of ICS players, it's time to fill it with some data. We'll add the PlayerFrame to the applet and give it a menu bar with two options—a request to refresh the listing immediately and a request to start automatic refreshing. We'll need to add some variables to the applet:

```
private MenuBar whobar;
private PlayerFrame players;
private MenuItem whoRefresh;
private MenuItem whoStopStart;
private Button showhidePlayers;
private String whoCommand;
private Vector playerList;
private boolean waitingforwho = false;
```

The menu items are associated with the PlayerFrame; the button will go below the input text field in the main applet and will control the visibility of the player window. The command string contains the player listing update request to be passed to the server, the vector will contain a list of the players, and the waitingforwho variable will let the receiveInput method know that we are expecting a list of players from the server. The following code will be appended to the applet's init method:

```
whoCommand = "who an";
whobar = new MenuBar();
whobar.setFont(pretty);
Menu m = new Menu("Update Listing");
whoRefresh = new MenuItem("Refresh now");
whoStopStart = new MenuItem("Start updating");
m.add(whoRefresh);
m.add(whoStopStart);
whobar.add(m);
players = new PlayerFrame(this);
players.setFont(fixed);
players.setMenuBar(whobar);
showhidePlayers = new Button("Show Players");
add("showhideplayers;side=top",showhidePlayers);
```

First, we initialize the player request command to "who an". The *a* indicates to the ICS that we are only interested in players who are available for matches, and the *n* indicates that we want the listing to appear in a verbose fashion, to make it easy to parse the output. We then create a new menu and add it to the new PlayerFrame. Finally, we create a new button to control the window and add it to the applet. We need to add the following to the start method to create a new player list:

```
        playerList = new Vector(32);
        players.updatePlayerList(playerList);
```

We'll modify the action event by adding the following condition-als to it:

```
    } else if (evt.target==whoRefresh) {
      writeOutput(whoCommand+"\n");
      playerList = new Vector(32);
      waitingforwho = true;
      return true;
    } else if (evt.target==showhidePlayers) {
      if (players.isShowing()) {
        players.hide();
        showhidePlayers.setLabel("Show Players");
      } else {
        players.show();
        showhidePlayers.setLabel("Hide Players");
      }
      return true;
    } else if (evt.target==players) {
      writeOutput((String)arg+"\n");
      return true;
    }
```

Remember that the PlayerFrame passes on MenuItem events to the applet intact. Here we catch the user's request to refresh the player listing, send the update command to the ICS, create a new Vector to hold the listing, and set the waitingforwho variable to be true. We also check to see if the user is pushing the player listing visibility button. If so, we toggle the visibility of the PlayerFrame and the text of the button. If the event comes from the PlayerFrame, we send the match request on to the ICS.

Now we have to modify the receiveInput method to try to parse the server's who listing when waitingforwho is true. The output from the "who an" listing looks like this:

Name	Stand	win	loss	draw	Blitz	win	loss	draw	idle
MchessPro(C)	2337	20	7	8	2474	145	53	22	9
jocelyn	1970	1	0	1	1985	12	11	2	
StIdes	1820	5	5	1	1906	28	22	2	13

3 Players Displayed.

For our purposes, we are only interested in the Name and Blitz fields. We can detect the start of a who listing by a String that starts with "Name" followed by "Stand". We should ignore the hyphenated line. We can recognize the end of the who listing by checking to see if the line ends with "Players Displayed." Here is the new receiveInput method:

```java
public void receiveInput(InputStreamHandler ish, Object o) {
   String s = (String)o;
   if (s.trim().equals("") || s.trim().equals("fics%")) {
     return;
   }
   if (s.trim().startsWith("<12>")) {
     parseBoard(s.trim());
   } else if (s.trim().startsWith("{Game")) {
     StringTokenizer st = new StringTokenizer(s);
     String token = st.nextToken(); //{Game
     String number = st.nextToken(); //number
     ChessFrame frame = (ChessFrame)games.get(number);
     if (frame!=null) {
       token = st.nextToken(); //(player1
       token = st.nextToken(); //vs.
       token = st.nextToken(); //player2)
       token = st.nextToken(); //loser
       frame.endGame(token);
       games.remove(number);
     }
```

Here's where the modified section begins. If we are waiting for a who listing, we create a new StringTokenizer on the input string. If it starts with the ICS prompt, we aren't interested in it at all. But if it starts with "Name", we might be interested. If the next token is "Stand", we can simply ignore the line. Otherwise, it's probably some other server output and we append it to the output TextArea.

Next, we check to see if the first token is a series of hyphens of the proper length to appear in a who listing. If so, we ignore the line as well. If not, we check to see if the line starts with a number followed by "Players". If it does, the line must be the end of the player listing, so we update the PlayerFrame and set waitingforwho

to be false. If none of these is the case, the line must be part of the
who listing and we parse it for the player's name and blitz rating.
We create a new Player from that information and add it to the
Vector of players:

```
  } else if (waitingforwho) {
    StringTokenizer st = new StringTokenizer(s);
    String token = st.nextToken();
    if (token.equals("fics%")) {
      return;
    }
    if (token.equals("Name")) {
      if (st.nextToken().equals("Stand")) {
        return;
      } else {
        output.appendText(s+"\n");
        return;
      }
    } else if (token.equals("---------")) {
      return;
    } else {
      try {
        Integer i = new Integer(token);
        if (st.nextToken().equals("Players")) {
          waitingforwho = false;
          players.updatePlayerList(playerList);
        }
        return;
      } catch (NumberFormatException e) {}
      String name = token;
      st.nextToken(); //standard rating
      st.nextToken(); //standard win total
      st.nextToken(); //standard loss total
      st.nextToken(); //standard draw total
      String blitz = st.nextToken();
      Player p = new Player(name,blitz);
      playerList.addElement(p);
      return;
    }
```

```
      } else {
        output.appendText(s+"\n");
      }
    }
```

The applet now has a working PlayerFrame. The frame's visibility can be toggled with the Show/Hide Players button. The user can request an immediate refresh of the player listing from the menu in the PlayerFrame. We have one more feature to add; the automatic update. We'll accomplish this by threading the applet. Once every minute, the thread will wake up and generate an event requesting a refresh. We'll add the following variable to the applet:

```
private Thread engine;
```

In the applet's start method, we add:

```
engine = new Thread(this);
```

And in the applet's stop method we add:

```
engine.stop();
```

The applet's run method consists of the following:

```
public void run() {
  while (engine!=null && engine.isAlive()) {
    Event e = new Event(whoRefresh,Event.ACTION_EVENT,
      "Refresh now");
    handleEvent(e);
    try {
      engine.sleep(60000);
    } catch (InterruptedException ex) {}
  }
}
```

Because the automatic refresh may be somewhat time-consuming when the ICS is heavily loaded, we give the user the ability to turn it off and on via the whoStopStart menu item we added to the PlayerFrame earlier. We add the following conditional to the applet's action method:

```
        } else if (evt.target==whoStopStart) {
          if (!engine.isAlive()) {
            engine.start();
            whoStopStart.setLabel("Stop updating");
            running = true;
          } else if (running) {
            engine.suspend();
            whoStopStart.setLabel("Start updating");
            running = false;
          } else {
            engine.resume();
            whoStopStart.setLabel("Stop updating");
            running = true;
          }
        return true;
```

We are now finished with the requested enhancements to the
ICS applet. Figure 18-4 contains a screen shot of the final applet
with the player listing window.

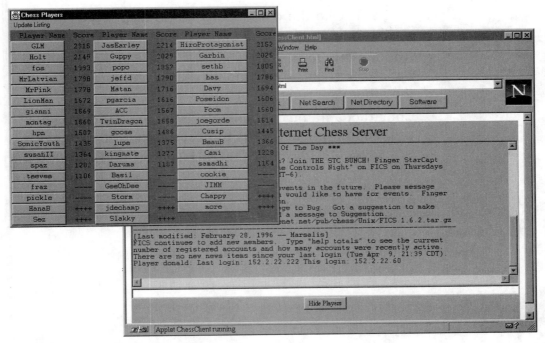

Figure 18-4: *ChessClient with PlayerFrame.*

ADDITIONAL IMPROVEMENTS

We've only begun to scratch the surface in terms of adding features to this applet. Here are a few ideas for future improvements:

- Add the ability to set upper and lower bounds to the player listing.

- Change the player listing window to display standard rating instead of blitz rating (or to display both!).

- Allow the user to specify a different match type when requesting matches via the player listing window.

- Allow the user to open chat windows devoted to a single other player or a channel.

- Modify the chessboard so that when the user double-clicks on a square containing a piece, the board highlights the squares that piece could attack.

- Add a field to the chessboard frame displaying the last move made.

- Add a menu to the chessboard frame allowing the user options such as requesting takebacks and forcing wins if the other user runs out of time.

- Construct a frame containing a list of the current games; users could select games to observe from the list in the same way that they select players to match from the player listing.

19

Writing Your Own Servers: A Meeting Scheduler

What You'll Learn
In this tutorial, we create a meeting scheduler in Java. We cover these topics in detail:

- Server design.
- Exception handling.
- Object-oriented design.
- File handling.

The easiest way to see this tutorial is to use the appletviewer and run the code from the CD, examples/ch19/ui.html. This method requires that you have a network connection. If you do not have a network connection, you'll need to set up a local server. See "User's Guide" and "Setting Up Your Own Server" below for details on how this is done.

The Contract

A small virtual company has asked us to create a system that will allow it to schedule meetings for its employees. The employees generally work at other companies but are looking to join this one full-time once the company gains some revenue. They all live in the same area, with the exception of one employee who moved to another country. The scheduler will be used to manage each employee's unique schedule and to make communication with the international member easier.

We can write this in any language, but it must support a variety of hardware because the members of the group will most likely be using their current employers' hardware on the sly. Most of the users of the system will be on incompatible networks, so current commercial schedulers will not work.

We can simplify the task by using Java and the Internet. We'll only have to write one program that will run on many different platforms. The Internet will give the client access to international communications at very little cost. The company gives us the go-ahead—they want a demo in two weeks!

Features

The principal focus of the meeting scheduler will be to help people manage their time. It will facilitate the planning of group meetings by making sure all members are available for a selected time slot. This program is a small implementation of popular scheduling software such as Meeting Maker, or the scheduler that comes with Lotus Notes. The difference is that our meeting scheduler will work over the Internet. Most schedulers work only on local area networks (LANs) such as a Novell network. Using the Internet will allow a group spanning international borders to use the software as easily as a local group could.

The primary feature of the scheduler is its ability to schedule (add) and cancel (delete) meetings. This will involve the creation of a server application and a client. Both the server and the client are to be written in Java. This tutorial will focus on the issues surrounding the creation of a Java server.

User's Guide

Before we dig into the scheduler's design, you might like to see it in action. To try out the program, you need to first log in to a scheduling server. The program defaults to a sample server residing on the Online Companion. Just select login from the File menu and you'll be on your way.

Using the program is fairly simple. After the program is started and you're logged in, your schedule for the current day automatically comes up. You can scroll through the day, move on to other days, or change your schedule for any day you choose. The Add button lets you make additions to your schedule.

The main function of the scheduler is to schedule meetings with other people. The following is a list of the employees in our sample company. You will be logged in initially as Bart, but you can use the Change User command to select a different user.

- Bart
- Lisa
- Maggie
- Homer
- Marge
- Mel
- Krusty

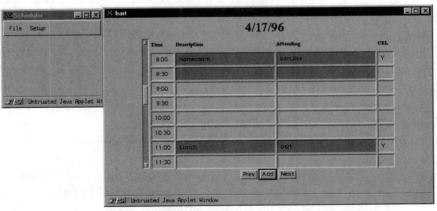

Figure 19-1: *Netscape Navigator with Scheduler running from Ventana.*

When you use the add function, you are automatically selected to be in the meeting. If you wish to include others, just type in their names. This list is comma delimited and can include only valid employees. Have fun scheduling your fellow virtual employees for some crazy meetings!

Setting Up Your Own Server

Setting up your own server is not difficult, but you must address a few issues. The server program is a stand-alone application. You will need to copy over the code from the CD-ROM to your hard drive. To set up a server:

1. Make a directory (we'll call it "server" for demonstration).
2. Copy files from the CD: examples/ch19 to this directory.
3. Make sure all .dat and .idx files have read and write permissions.
4. To run the server, just type **java server**.

You should see a message stating that the server is waiting for connections. If you don't see this message, you're probably having problems with the server sockets. This server uses socket 1666. You will need to set up your system to allow the program to use this socket. For instructions, look up TCP/IP services in your system reference manual.

Design

Most networked applications can be broken down into three basic modules: the user interface, the network interface, and an application-specific module. This type of organization lends itself to reuse. Later projects can use certain parts—the network interface, for instance—without having to use or understand the other modules. As time goes by, you will develop a group of objects that make future projects a snap.

In order for these objects to work as a whole, they must have well-defined interrelationships. The user interface code should excel in handling user interface issues and should pass on any other actions to an appropriate program component. Suppose we had a button that was marked login. The user interface would detect it being pressed and then pass the action on to the network module.

Network Interface Module

Communication across the Internet is a breeze compared to writing our own protocols. By using TCP/IP, we need not worry about messy communication issues such as corrupted data and packet overruns. It's still not a walk in the park, but a good design will allow you to *almost* forget the underlying complications.

On the lowest level, communication between two machines is a sequence of 0s and 1s, which is not very useful for our scheduler. By structuring this stream of bits into known data types, we can make our creation and parsing jobs much easier. Java has a class made for the job. Remember in Chapter 13, "Networking With Sockets & Streams," when we discussed the DataInput and DataOutput streams? These streams will be of great value to us here. They allow us to send Java data types across a stream. The server can put an integer on the stream, and the client will easily be able to read it—no conversions, no fuss. We just need to agree on some structure for the data.

We have chosen to use a fairly simple model for our messages. Each message will contain a byte describing the message type and then a variable-length message body. Each message type will have a routine that knows how to parse the data. This design allows for easier creation of more messages. More important, it greatly simplifies parsing. If you have ever converted a stream of bits into real data, you'll appreciate this feature.

This method will not generate the smallest possible network traffic. The smallest item we can send is a byte. This protocol is not a good choice if transmission speed is your major concern. On the other hand, if coding speed and easy maintenance are your primary concerns, you have a winner. This method would not be efficient for sending large data files, but it suits our purposes for now.

Once we have the underlying network model, we can start to design the client and server. Generally, they will have complementary methods. When one produces a message, the other will have to know how to parse it. We can get fancy and create a definition file for each message, basically specifying each data element and creating a routine that parses each message. This is not a bad method, but there's an easier way: just write one method to create and one to parse for each message. If this gets out of synch, then you have a problem. Anything that a producer puts on the wire must be used by the consumer.

In addition to handling network traffic, there are some special considerations concerning the server. In the following section, we'll go over the details of creating an Internet server.

The Server

If I asked you to write a simple server right now, you might respond with a perl script using CGI (Common Gateway Interface), which has been the standard response for quite some time. If I then told you it must be really fast, you might write a program in C instead, again interfacing by CGI.

CGI is a protocol that is used to provide dynamic content to the Web. It takes some inputs, processes them, and then creates a MIME (Multimedia Internet Mail Extensions) document in response. It's powerful, but it has its limits. CGI is basically talking to a Web browser. The Web browser understands MIME documents and will display them, but that's it. What if you wanted it to take the data, process it some more, and then display it?

Having a server written in Java will give us some extra features, but having the client running in Java will make a world of difference. The client can process the incoming data and then present it in a pretty fashion. Not only will we take some load off the server, we'll also put more power back into the client, resulting in a nicer presentation of the data. For instance, the user can change items such as fonts, and the system can adjust data for the size of the monitor.

Using Java to write the server is a matter of preference—it has certain strengths and weaknesses. As always, you have to evaluate the needs of each project to determine the correct language to use. Let's look at some of the issues to consider when using Java to write a server.

Security

Writing a server program entails a certain amount of responsibility because a server is probably the weakest point in your Internet armor. A badly written server program can crash the machine, or worse yet, destroy data. A fair amount of publicity has been given to Internet hacks that involve the exploitation of holes in server programs. Servers are written to dispense information or perform tasks; you want to make sure the information is not private and the task is not destructive.

Using Java for a server language is rather ideal from a security viewpoint, since it was designed with security in mind. No simple pointer error is going to expose your system to attack. It's important to remember that a Java application has fewer restrictions than an applet. In particular, a Java application can access the disk drive, so your permissions on the server must be set correctly. It is unwise to have a server that has permission to write to important files. A good rule of thumb is to allow a server access to only the files it needs.

Internet security is such a critical issue, we could write a whole book on the subject—in fact, there have already been several published. *Internet Firewalls* by O'Reilly & Associates is required reading for those interested in Internet security. *The Web Server Book* (Ventana) also has a good section on security, as well as issues surrounding Internet servers in general. A Java program is less likely to present a security hole than a C program, or possibly a perl script, but no language can remove all security issues.

Speed & Memory Considerations

Regarding speed, Java code generally performs on par with a perl script. Perl is better at processing raw text, but for most operations, Java holds its own. Java will run faster with the help of the soon-to-be-released Just in Time (JIT) modules, which will convert Java byte code to machine code. Nevertheless, it will probably not be the deciding factor when deciding which language to use for a project. Speed is important, but most often when it's an order of magnitude difference. Java code will not be that much slower than other languages.

Java is object-oriented, and it has garbage collection. Both these factors may make Java use more memory than other server languages, such as perl or C. Object-oriented languages typically use up more memory; each object needs some extra space to provide its OOP advantages. Since Java has garbage collection, it also will do sporadic memory cleanups. The system might wait to clean up memory until you need it, not when other programs need it. This means that your Java server might be holding more memory than it needs. For the most part, you need to weigh your priorities. The fact that Java is interpreted and object-oriented means that it will always use more memory than comparable C code. When comparing Java to perl, you will have to consider that perl 5 will include object-oriented extensions and will suffer accordingly. And different projects will have different considerations.

Server Design

Designing the server itself is fairly straightforward. When a connection is established through a socket, it creates a new thread to handle the requests. This thread uses a Schedule object to answer requests from the client. That's all there is to it. It's rather eloquent and easy to code. We'll go over particular implementation issues in "The Implementation: Network Interface Module" later in this chapter.

The Client

Using Java to write the client is certainly a win. The pain of writing multiple CGI programs and having to pass data all over the place was getting old. Web developers quickly ran into problems using CGI. Even if the server was a CGI program, using Java as the client would still be helpful. Chapter 17, "Interfacing With CGI: The Widget Store," shows how you can communicate with a CGI program while using Java.

The client is actually just a thread that handles incoming network traffic. It acts as a dispatch for incoming packets. It decodes the packet and then calls the appropriate code to handle the packet. And it runs as its own thread so that we don't have to worry about networking in our other code.

Messages coming from the server can be treated just like any other event. When we request something from the server, it will send the data to the network module. Once the packet is decoded, it can be handled just like a user event. We have managed to make the network a simple message passer. This solution works very smoothly with the event-driven nature of graphical user interfaces.

With the network taken care of, we can now concentrate on some low level routines, which will form the core of the functionality for our program. After that, we will create the user interface, and the project will be completed.

Project-Specific Module

The heart of the scheduler is a data structure that contains all of the scheduled meetings. Both the client and server will need access to this information. The implementation of the structure may be different for each side, but the interface should be the same. This is a perfect place to use Java's interface mechanism.

We've created an interface called schedule. Conceptually, a schedule is an object that contains the data about a person's scheduled meetings, along with routines to modify this data. An interface allows us to define the methods that all objects that implement the schedule interface will have. We'll define how and what will be passed to each routine. We'll leave the actual coding till later, but the design is done at this stage of the development.

Using an interface allows us to change how we implement a schedule, which is very useful for our scheduling application. On the server side, we'll save the schedules on disk, allowing them to be saved in a permanent manner. On the client side, we'll save the schedules in memory for two reasons: one, Java does not allow a user to access local files, and two, we would like the access to be as fast as possible. Storing the schedule in memory is fine for the client, but imagine if the server machine had everyone's schedules in memory! An active server can have thousands of people on it at one time and having that many schedules would quickly overfill the main memory. Figure 19-2 shows the object hierarchy for the schedule classes.

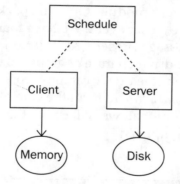

Figure 19-2: *Schedule object hierarchy.*

The illustration of the object hierarchy is pretty simple, but it makes a few good points. Notice that the client and server implement the schedule interface (implementation is denoted by dashed lines). They, in turn, each use a different internal data structure to save the data. Later, we can create another type of schedule—a distributed schedule, for example, in which each person's schedule resides on his or her home machine. In our disk-based system, on the other hand, we'll store everyone's schedule on the server machine. Each method has its pros and cons.

Regardless of how we implement the schedule, we can simply plug it directly into our code and voilà—it works! The Interface is a powerful design tool and a nifty way to support open systems development. Once a standard is developed, everyone can create his or her own implementation. Table 19-1 contains a description of each of the schedule methods.

Method	Description
add(scheduleStruct)	Add a meeting to the schedule.
del(scheduleStruct)	Delete a meeting from the schedule.
find(Date)	Find a meeting at a certain date/time.
findRange(Date, Date)	Return all meetings for a date range.
getUser()	Return the owner of this schedule.

Table 19-1: *Schedule methods.*

Let's take a look at the code to define this interface:

```
package ventana.scheduler;

import java.io.*;
import java.util.*;
import ventana.util.*;
import ventana.scheduler.*;

public interface schedule {
    // Maintenance Routines

    public void add(scheduleStruct newSchedule)
        throws DuplicateException, IOException;
        /* Description:
         *      Adds a new meeting to the schedule
         *
         * Exceptions:
         *          DuplicateException - Time slot not available
         *          ServerException - Could not contact server
```

```
 *          IOException - Unhandled IO exception
 */
public void del(scheduleStruct del)
    throws NotFoundException, IOException;
    /* Description:
     *    Deletes a meeting
     *
     * Exceptions:
     *        NotFoundException - Meeting doesn't exist
     *        ServerException - Could not contact server
     *        IOException - Unhandled IO exception
     */


// Search/Retrieval Routines

public scheduleStruct find(Date date)
    throws NotFoundException, IOException;
    /* Description:
     *    Find a scheduleStruct for a specific date/time
     *
     * Exceptions:
     *    NotFoundException - No meeting was found
     *    IOException - Unhandled IO Exception
     */
public scheduleStruct[] findRange(Date start, Date end)
    throws IOException;
    /* Description:
     *    Return all scheduled items specified by a
     *    date/time range
     *
     * Exceptions:
     *    IOException - Unhandled IO Exception
     */
public String getUser();
    /* Description:
     *    Who is this schedule for?
     */
}
```

As we write the client and server, we will implement this interface. At that time, we can make decisions about how we wish to implement the memory and disk stores. By creating an interface, we can concentrate on design issues and leave the implementation particulars for later. The implementor might not even be the designer. Imagine you are some big shot "visionary." You might design the system, get paid, and then move on to other, more important projects. Someone who specializes in writing code could then come in and implement the system.

User Interface Module

At its best, designing a user interface can be an easy task using some tool to graphically lay out all your screens. At its worst, it involves laying out the design by hand. Screen layout in Java is accomplished by placing items on the screen using some layout manager. Typically you will use a combination of the layout managers provided with Java to accomplish what you want. Having your program resize correctly is essential in an environment as diverse as the Internet.

The AWT is slated for a bug release soon, followed by a major overhaul later in the summer of 1996. You can expect major improvements in Java's screen building. We also hope to see more documentation of the layout managers, as well as fixes for a few layout manager bugs. In this tutorial, we opted for the flexibility offered by the PackerLayout manager, which is provided for free on the Net by its creator, Daeron Meyer.

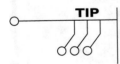

TIP

A word to the wise: double or triple the time you expect it will take to develop the user interface for your programs. Using a GUI screen builder will save you many hours and white hairs.

The scheduler starts with a main screen that sports a menu and nothing else. From this menu, the user can choose from important tasks such as logging in, opening schedules, and configuring the program. Any future functionality will need a spot on this menu.

Notice how simple it is. Both the program design and the Java design are responsible for the screen's simplicity. Java does not allow menus to be placed on an applet, so we had to create a separate frame to house the menu. This practice will tend to make your applets look like full-blown applications, although this is generally not a bad thing. Considering the scope of this project, it's closer to a real application than a Web-page enhancer such as an animator or billboard.

From the main menu, the user generally will open a schedule. This will bring up what hopefully looks like a common daily planner—well, sort of a daily planner. It doesn't have pretty floral patterns or pictures of your favorite wilderness scene. Instead, it's a functional screen with the ability to go to next and previous days and to add scheduled items. We can add pretty pictures, however, if the client wants it to be fancier. The daily planner is pictured in Figure 19-3.

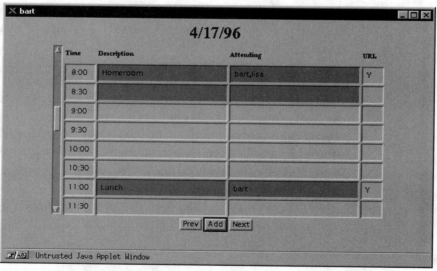

Figure 19-3: *The daily planner.*

The rest of the screens are small and contain only one function. We won't show them all here; you'll find them as you go through the application. One key thing to remember is that all the screens are separate frames, which is a double-edged sword: it gives us freedom, but it also requires more work. During the implementation, we'll point out a few details that are important when dealing with frames.

The Big Picture

Once all the components come together, we have something that is greater than its parts. Each module handles its own area of specialty and gives work to other specialists. After we have developed a module, it can be used in later projects. This way, we can focus more on the particulars of a project and worry less about common tasks such as network communications or creating data structures, which is one of the biggest advantages of using object-oriented techniques and languages. The work we put into design now will repay itself in full in later projects. Figure 19-4 is provided to solidify the relationships between the modules.

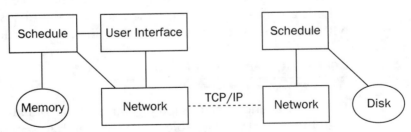

Figure 19-4: *Overall object hierarchy.*

Now that we have designed our system, we can move on to the task of writing the code. During the implementation phase, we may have to change the design (hopefully not, but it sometimes happens). As you get better at foreseeing problems, and your experience with Java and object-oriented design grows, you'll make fewer mistakes and generate cleaner designs. It's a good feeling to have someone look at your design and say, "Yeah, that's it."

Implementation

Once we have a solid design, we need to sit down and decide how we're going to implement each object. We'll need to make decisions about what data structures to use and what algorithms to employ. We may also decide to create a demo program that shows the concepts, although it won't be as efficient as the finished product. Using object-oriented techniques will allow us to create several implementations, and then use whichever one is right for the project.

It's not uncommon to write a program with little attention to speed and memory and then go back later and improve our algorithms. A working demo is almost as good as a working product in terms of sales. Vaporware, or products that are only screen based, are used frequently in sales. Our job is to make sure that what the sales team is selling will be possible to implement in a reasonable amount of time. You will notice many places in this code that could use improvement, such as speed and variety of features. The beauty of an object-based design is that it can be extended without much effort. If we don't like how something works, we can borrow the functionality we like and replace the rest.

Let's get into how we implemented the scheduler. We'll start with a tour of the directories and then look at the code itself.

Code Road Map

This tutorial encompasses a fairly large bit of code. In order to keep the project manageable, it was broken into separate directories. Each directory has its own makefiles and is generally a separate and useful entity. Using packages makes development of handy libraries pretty easy. We have followed Java's naming conventions and constructed our directories in a similar fashion.

Compiling the programs is simple. We edit the make-file to change the location of the class files. It stores all its files under the directory ventana. This path will need to be in our CLASSPATH, so it might make sense to place these directories wherever our Java classes are located. After modifying the file, we type **make**. The make program will compile the program for us.

Network Interface Module

The focus of this tutorial is server design and implementation. Writing a server in Java requires a good understanding of threads and exceptions. Since it is generally unacceptable for a server to crash, we must try to handle as many exceptions as possible. Exceptions should be logged, and the program should continue. The worst-case scenario should be that one session is lost, while all others continue unharmed.

We had an unfortunate limitation while writing this server. The database API for Java is slated for release soon, but is not available at the time of this writing. This means that issues such as file and record locking must be handled by our server. We have implemented a simple file-locking mechanism, but it is possible to write a much better system. Ideally, the server would access a database with record locking. We have not yet dealt with the issues of transaction rollback. It's possible for a partial transaction to be entered into the database. Hopefully, the database API will solve some of these problems.

Server Vocabulary

Here's some server terminology:

File locking   To make a file accessible to only one person at a time so that the file cannot be corrupted.

Record locking   To make a record accessible to one person at a time; better than file locking because more transactions can occur at the same time.

Transaction   A write operation performed on a file.

Transaction rollback   A recovery method to undo some number of transactions. Typically used to handle error conditions.

The actual server is a very simple loop. It listens to a socket port, accepts a connection, and then starts a thread to handle the requests. It is an application as opposed to an applet, so it has a main method. Here is the code for the main server loop:

```java
public class server {
  public static void main(String args[])
    throws IOException {

    ServerSocket session = new ServerSocket(1666,100);
    handleRequests handler;
    Hashtable users = new Hashtable();
    locks schedLocks = new locks();

    System.out.println("Waiting for connections");

    while(true) {
      Socket socket = null;

      try {
        socket = session.accept();
      }
      catch (SocketException e) {
        // Generally a timeout, keep trying
      }

      if (socket == null) {
        continue;
      }

      System.out.println("Connection made");

      // Create a seperate thread for connection
      handler  = new handleRequests(socket,users,
                                    schedLocks);

      // Set for non-premtive systems
      handler.setPriority(handler.getPriority() + 1);

      handler.start();
    }
  }
}
```

The server makes use of a class called serverSocket. A serverSocket listens to a port using the accept method and waits for a connection. We have chosen port 1666 to listen to and have specified a wait of 100 milliseconds. Notice the try block around the accept method. If a connection is not made in the allotted time, a SocketException is generated. In our case, we will just loop until we get a connection.

After a connection is made, we'll create a new thread and let it handle the requests for us. We have created a class called handleRequests to service each connection. Since it extends the Thread class, its main execution code is contained in the run method. This will act as our dispatch. When a packet comes in, the first byte will be used to determine what type of packet it is. Then the appropriate method will be called to parse the packet. That's it—except for parsing and handling requests, we are done. The handleRequest class will perform all client-requested operations:

```
class handleRequests extends Thread {

    DataInputStream in = null;
    DataOutputStream out = null;
    Socket socket = null;
    String user=null;
    Hashtable users;
    locks schedLocks;

    handleRequests(Socket s, Hashtable users,
        locks schedLocks) throws IOException {

        socket = s;

        in = new DataInputStream(
            new BufferedInputStream(socket.getInputStream()));
        out = new DataOutputStream(new BufferedOutputStream(
            socket.getOutputStream()));

        this.users = users;
        this.schedLocks = schedLocks;
    }
```

The constructor for this class is given a socket, a hashtable, and an object of the class locks. Let's examine each component and see what role it plays in the server. When a connection is made, the system creates a socket between the user and the server. This socket is a two-way pipe we can use to communicate with the user. It doesn't matter if the user is on the same machine or across the world; it works the same. The socket provides two streams, an input stream and an output stream. First, we'll add a buffer and a data filter to both the input and output streams.

Remember that we can layer different filters onto the streams to get desired results. Here, we have layered a buffered filter and a data filter. The buffered filter is used to make accessing streams more efficient. A buffer provides a space to store characters as they come across the pipe. This will allow us to read and write larger chunks of data more efficiently. Using a buffered stream lets us decouple the size of our data with the speed of the link. We might write out a 64 byte data packet, but it will be written one byte at a time. Our write command can write its data and then continue on instead of waiting for the whole packet to be written. This will make our Net traffic more compact and allow our program to run smoother.

The data filter is used to send primitive types across a stream, allowing us to write data elements such as integers and strings without parsing them. Using a data filter will make our code more readable and easier to write.

The second parameter to the constructor is the users' hashtable, which keeps track of all the users logged on to our server. This information is needed to notify users when a schedule has been changed. We're using a somewhat inefficient algorithm that tells everyone of any schedule change. It would be better to notify each user of changes relevant to only his or her schedule; the problem is keeping track of individual schedules. It would require the addition of a message that tells when each user has opened or closed a schedule. For the purpose of our tutorial, we'll use the easier implementation.

The last parameter is schedLocks object. This object is used to handle file locking. We cannot have two users modifying the file at the same time. In order to avoid this, we'll make the program lock a file before it uses it and then unlock it after it is done. Although this will stop our files from getting corrupted, it would be better to use a record-locking mechanism. See Chapter 11, "Advanced Threading," for a discussion on deadlock and corrupted data.

After we have created the thread, we'll call its start method. After we call the start method, the system will call the thread's run method. The run method for our handleRequests class is fairly simple. It will act as a dispatch. It is also responsible for handling any exceptions we get. The following code shows the parser for our messages:

```java
public void run() {
    byte b;
    boolean cont=true;

    try {
        loginRequest();
        while(cont) {
            b = in.readByte();

            switch(b) {
                case packetTypes.login :
                    loginParse(); break;
                case packetTypes.logoff :
                    cont=false; break;
                case packetTypes.reqSchedule :
                    reqSchedule(); break;
                case packetTypes.addMeeting :
                    addMeeting(); break;
                default : System.out.println("Unknown type");
            }
        }

        out.close();
        in.close();
        socket.close();
    }
    catch (IOException ignore) {
        System.out.println("IO Exception, thread stopped");
```

```
          stop();
      }
      catch (Exception e) {
        System.out.println("Unknown error, thread stopped");
        e.printStackTrace();
        stop();
      }
      finally {
        users.remove(user);
        schedLocks.unlock(users)
      }
    }
```

Let's look at how we handled the exceptions in this block of code. Our general premise is that a connection can be allowed to die, but we want the server to continue running. A problem in one thread should not be allowed to kill other threads. Our main concern is to clean up any locks or user entries left for this thread. Notice the finally block, which cleans up any leftover user or locks entries.

Since we can neither anticipate all the errors this program could generate nor program a fix for each one, we have taken a more general approach. We'll log any errors that happen and allow the administrator to fix any problems. Errors such as an out of memory error or a disk problem cannot be fixed by the program. Bugs in the program can be reported to the programmer, and general gee-whiz errors can just be admired. In any case, we will try and keep the system up and running.

The main meat of the server is how it handles each request. This is also the most tedious part of the program. We will skim over the boring parts and point out any interesting or difficult parts. This code shows how the server can send a message to a client:

```
public void loginRequest() throws IOException {
    System.out.println("Requesting login");
    out.writeByte(packetTypes.login);
    out.flush();
}
```

The loginRequest method exemplifies one important concept when dealing with buffered output: we don't know when the buffer will be emptied. By using the flush method, we can force the output to be written right then. This method is useful for debugging and also keeps things running smoothly. Some buffering systems wait until a certain number of bytes are queued before sending a message. Our one-byte message might be waiting a long time before it is sent. After a message is sent, we will force the system to send it along the pipe:

```java
public void loginParse() throws IOException {
    byte pakType;

    user = in.readLine();
    System.out.println("User " + user + " logged in");

    users.put(user, this);
}

public void reqSchedule() throws IOException {
    String user;
    Date start, end;
    scheduleStruct result[];

    user = in.readLine();
    start = new Date(in.readLong());
    end = new Date(in.readLong());

    System.out.println("Schedule Request for " + user);
    System.out.println("Start: " + start.toString());
    System.out.println("End: " + end.toString());

    try {
        schedLocks.lock(user);
        serverSchedule schedule = new serverSchedule(user);

        result = schedule.findRange(start, end);

        out.writeByte(packetTypes.getSchedule);
        out.writeBytes(user + "\n");
```

```
            if (result == null) {
                out.writeInt(0);
                out.flush();
                return;
            }

            out.writeInt(result.length);

            System.out.println("Recs to send: " + result.length);
            for(int i=0; i < result.length; i++) {
                System.out.println("Meeting: " + result[i].desc);
                out.writeLong(result[i].start.getTime());
                out.writeLong(result[i].end.getTime());
                out.writeBytes(result[i].desc + "\n");
                out.writeBytes(result[i].descURL + "\n");
                out.writeBytes(result[i].minutesURL + "\n");
                out.writeBytes(result[i].attending + "\n");
            }
            out.flush();

            System.out.println("Schedule Sent");
        }
        finally {
            schedLocks.unlock(user);
        }
    }
```

The reqSchedule method is the largest producer of data in the
server. Given a date range and a user, it will send over all meetings within that time frame. This routine is used by the client to
fill in its local schedule object. We use a serverSchedule object to
read in the data, and then we send over the data in message
format.

For this message, we needed a length field to tell the parser
how many records to expect. If a person has a busy schedule, this
message might become very large. The client should be designed
to request reasonable ranges. One day, or maybe a week, might be
a good range. We do not have a maximum range—it's just not a
good idea to send large chunks of data that might not be needed.

The next couple of routines handle the adding of new meetings. This is probably the hardest task for the system. We have implemented a good subset of the needed functionality, but plenty more could be done:

```
public void addNAK(String s) throws IOException {
    out.writeByte(packetTypes.addNAK);
    out.writeBytes("AddMeeting: " + s + "\n");
    out.flush();
}

public void addACK() throws IOException {
    out.writeByte(packetTypes.addACK);
    out.flush();
}

public void scheduleChange(String s, Date start)
    throws IOException {

    System.out.println("Schedule changed:" + s);
    out.writeByte(packetTypes.scheduleChange);
    out.writeBytes(s + "\n");
    out.writeLong(start.getTime());
    out.flush();
}
```

AddNAK, addACK, and scheduleChange are all notification routines. NAK, or negative acknowledge, is used to say that an add failed. It accepts a string that will be printed out to the user. Typical errors are invalid dates or times and trying to schedule a person who is busy. The ACK message, or acknowledge, is used to tell the system that the add was successful.

The scheduleChange message is sent to all current users whenever a person's schedule is updated. The client then looks at the schedule for that person and determines if it should be reloaded. Having current information on the client side will help prevent the user from creating scheduling conflicts. We'll now look at the code to add a meeting:

```java
public void addMeeting() throws IOException {
    String line;
    String dateLine;
    scheduleStruct ss = new scheduleStruct();

    dateLine = in.readLine();
    line = in.readLine();
    try {
        ss.start = new Date(dateLine + " " + line);
    } catch ( IllegalArgumentException e) {
        System.out.println("Illegal argument, aborting");
        in.readLine();
        in.readLine();
        in.readLine();
        in.readLine();
        addNAK("Error converting start date");
        return;
    }
    line = in.readLine();
    try {
        ss.end = new Date(dateLine + " " + line);
    } catch (IllegalArgumentException e) {
        System.out.println("Illegal argument, aborting");
        in.readLine();
        in.readLine();
        in.readLine();
        addNAK("Error converting end date");
        return;
    }
    ss.desc = in.readLine();
    ss.attending = in.readLine();
    ss.descURL = in.readLine();

    // Parse attending, its comma delimited
    int pos;
    String st,st2;
    handleRequests hr;
    Enumeration e;
```

```
        st = new String(ss.attending + ",");
        if (st == null) {
            addNAK("Attending field blank");
            return;
        }
        st = st.trim();
        while ((pos = st.indexOf(',')) != -1) {
            st2 = st.substring(0,pos);
            System.out.println("Attending: " + st2);
            st = st.substring(pos + 1);

            schedLocks.lock(st2);
            serverSchedule sched = new serverSchedule(st2);
            try {
                System.out.println("Adding: " + ss);
                sched.add(ss);
            } catch(DuplicateException bad) {
                addNAK(st2 + " already scheduled");
            }

            schedLocks.unlock(st2);
            e = users.elements();

            while(e.hasMoreElements()) {
                hr = (handleRequests) e.nextElement();
                hr.scheduleChange(st2,ss.start);
            }
        }
        addACK();
    }
```

The addMeeting method can be broken down into three parts:
(1) parsing and verification, (2) the actual addition to the database,
and (3) notification. Any time an error is generated, an addNAK
packet is sent. The client is expected to display this to the user to
indicate what went wrong. They can then adjust their input and
resend the packet.

The parsing and verification stage consists of making sure the dates and times are valid. We use the Dates constructor to parse the date. The constructor calls Date.parse to make sense of this string. It supports a host of date formats but has one unusual feature: the month starts at zero, not one. Consequently, if the date reads 07/27/1942, it will be June 27, 1942, not July. On the client side, we have changed it to send the correct date; that is, we subtract one from the month. If you're interested in how the Date class works, check the documentation or read the source code for the Java.util.Date class.

Adding the data to the database is a simple process using our schedule object. If a user is already scheduled for a particular time slot, we get a duplicateException. This can cause a problem if, for example, four people are scheduled for a meeting. There is no transaction rollback, so if we schedule four people, and one of them already has an entry in that time slot, the meeting will not be entered into that person's schedule. The moral is this: make sure each person is free to attend the meeting. Since that is often not the case, you might want to implement a function that finds open time slots for a group of people and then chooses from that list. Although it's functional, the addMeeting routine could certainly be improved.

The last step to adding a meeting is notifying all users that a person's schedule has changed. They can then request an updated schedule and display it. Each person might have multiple schedules, so we need to notify everyone of a change. Again, we can improve this design by keeping track of the availability of everyone in the group. We need to pay particular attention to keeping this list accurate.

That's the server in a nutshell. The code is fairly long, but most of it is parsing routines. Special attention was paid to exception handling and keeping the server from crashing. Issues such as file locking and transaction rollback are looked at, but generally not implemented completely. For a bullet-proof server, you will need to address these issues. Replacing the serverSchedule to use a database system would improve the system significantly.

Project-Specific Module

The client and server both make use of the schedule interface in ways best suited for their somewhat conflicting needs. The client has certain security issues, such as no local disk storage. This means that we'll have to request scheduling information over the Net. Once we get this information, we will want to store it in memory for later use.

Instead of requesting scheduling information in little chunks, it will be more efficient to request the data in a few large batches. While the user is viewing the screen, we can send the data in the background. We will need a place to store this data, and that's where the clientSchedule comes into play.

Client Schedule

The clientSchedule is implemented using a hashtable. A hashtable allows us a fast, compact method to store data. A hashtable will only have one entry for each meeting and will be indexed by the starting time. We could have used an array indexed by starting time, but it would be too large. Let's look at the code for the clientSchedule:

```
public class clientSchedule implements schedule {
    Hashtable memoryStore = new Hashtable();
```

The class clientSchedule implements the schedule interface. It will provide code for the previously declared interface. The beauty of interfaces is that if you don't like this implementation, you can just write your own. You can even borrow some parts of this code and override the parts you don't like:

```
public void add(scheduleStruct newSchedule)
    throws DuplicateException, IOException {

    if (memoryStore.put(newSchedule.start, newSchedule)
        != null) {

        throw new DuplicateException();
    }
}
```

The add method is used to add a new meeting. There are two important points to notice about this code. One is how you put items into a hashtable. We must provide the data and a key, in this case, the start date. Both items must be objects. Hashtables only store one object per key value. So, if we try to add two meetings at the same time, we'll get an error. This works well, since most people don't attend two meetings at once.

The second item of importance is the throws section of the method. Remember that we must declare all exceptions that a method can generate. The add method seems to only generate one exception, the DuplicateException. The IOException is generated by the hashtable method put. Since we don't handle the errors here, we must pass them on to the calling method. It's unlikely that we will get an IOException when dealing with an in-memory data structure, but it is possible. If this happens, we will let the programmer using this class deal with it.

The DuplicateException is generated instead of returning some error code. Here it makes little difference, but later we will be using the return value to provide needed information. In those cases, we will want to leave the return value free. Having a return value serves two purposes: returning a number and returning –1 for an error is bad. Exceptions allow you a clean way of circumventing this problem, as shown in the following code:

```java
public void del(scheduleStruct del)
    throws NotFoundException {

    if (memoryStore.remove(del.start) == null)
        throw new NotFoundException();
}

public scheduleStruct find(Date date)
    throws NotFoundException {

    scheduleStruct ss;

    ss = (scheduleStruct) memoryStore.get(date);
    if (ss == null) {
        throw new NotFoundException();
    }
```

```
        return ss;

    }
```

The delete and find methods are simple and need little discussion. Again, we have chosen to use exceptions to return error information. Both of the hashtable methods (get and remove) return a reference value to the requested information. If the key value is not found, a value of null is returned. On this condition, we will return a NotFoundException.

The last method is findRange. Here, we will use an enumeration to help return the data. The findRange method is given a date range and returns all meetings in that time period. Since a hashtable does not support ranges, we'll have to search it in a linear fashion. A hashtable does implement the enumeration interface. This allows us to traverse the hashtable in a linear fashion.

We'll make two passes through the table. The first pass will determine the number of items we will return, and the second will be used to fill in the result array. We have to do this because at least one dimension of an array must be specified at creation. Notice that we call the hashtable method elements twice. Every time you traverse an enumeration, it is consumed. You have to rebuild the enumeration for each use. Here is the code for the findRange method:

```
    public scheduleStruct[] findRange(Date start, Date end)
        throws IOException {

        Enumeration list = memoryStore.elements();
        scheduleStruct ss;
        int cnt=0;

        // Count the number of elements

        while (list.hasMoreElements()) {
            ss = (scheduleStruct) list.nextElement();
            if (start.getTime() <= ss.start.getTime() &&
                end.getTime() >= ss.end.getTime()) {
```

```
                cnt++;
            }
        }

        if (cnt < 1) return null;

        scheduleStruct result[] = new scheduleStruct[cnt];

        // Enum is consumed, re-build

        list = memoryStore.elements();

        // Create result array

        cnt=0;
        while (list.hasMoreElements()) {
            ss = (scheduleStruct) list.nextElement();
            if (start.getTime() <= ss.start.getTime() &&
                end.getTime() >= ss.end.getTime()) {

                result[cnt++] = ss;
            }
        }

        return result;
    }
}
```

That's all there is to the clientSchedule. By using a hashtable, we have given most of our work to an already created and debugged class. This type of reuse allows us to write code faster and with fewer bugs.

Server Schedule

The server schedule is a bit more complicated because we will be dealing with a disk-based data structure. In order to handle a fairly good-sized database, the server implementation will have to be fairly efficient. We will save the data in a flat-file but use an index file to allow faster searches. If you're interested in how the index file works, take a look at schedule/IndexFile.java. It's pretty straightforward, but contains a little too much code to include here. Here is the code for the serverSchedule:

```
public class serverSchedule implements schedule {
    IndexFile index;
    RandomAccessFile dataFile;
```

Again, we are implementing the schedule interface. This time, we'll use two files to save the data. The first is an index file, which is indexed by the start date and stores the position of the data in the datafile. The datafile will store the records in a variable-length format. The files are based on the user's name, with the index file ending in ".idx" and the datafile ending in ".dat":

```
public serverSchedule(String user)
    throws IOException {

    this.user = user;
    index = new IndexFile(user + ".idx","rw",Size,Size);
    dataFile = new RandomAccessFile(user + ".dat","rw");
}
```

The constructor for this class takes the a string specifying the user. This string is used to build a filename for both the index and datafile. Notice that this routine returns an IOException. This might happen if the server process didn't have write permission to the files—you need to catch this error in your code. We are using a RandomAccessFile in which to store the data. We are opening the file read-write,"rw", under the name *username* + ".dat". For user maggie, the data file would be "maggie.dat". This next piece of code adds a meeting to a schedule:

```
public void add(scheduleStruct newSchedule)
    throws DuplicateException, IOException {

    String key;
    String data;
    Long conv;
    long pos;
```

```
dataFile.seek(dataFile.length());
pos = dataFile.getFilePointer();
dataFile.writeLong(newSchedule.start.getTime());
dataFile.writeLong(newSchedule.end.getTime());
dataFile.writeBytes(newSchedule.desc + "\n");
dataFile.writeBytes(newSchedule.descURL + "\n");
dataFile.writeBytes(newSchedule.minutesURL + "\n");
dataFile.writeBytes(newSchedule.attending + "\n");

conv = new Long(newSchedule.start.getTime());
key = conv.toString();
key = StringUtil.padStringLeft(key,' ',Size);

conv = new Long(pos);
data = conv.toString();
data = StringUtil.padStringLeft(data,' ',Size);

index.addRecord(key,data);
}
```

The add method must add entries to both the datafile and the index file. A RandomAccessFile sits above a DataOutput and DataInput filter so we can read/write Java types directly. It would be nice to actually write an object, but alas, that is not supported. An important note: we have used the writeBytes routine. This writes data out as 8-bit bytes. If we had used the writeChars method, it would have been 16 bits per character. The writeUTF routine will write out 16-bit Unicode characters. If you plan to use the readLine method, you need to use the writeBytes routine. There is no corresponding read routine that reads the writeChars output.

Also notice that we put "\n" after each string. Later, we will use the readLine routine—it expects to find a return to indicate the end of a string. This allows the strings to be of variable length. It saves a little space and means we don't have to do any parsing.

The index file is composed of two entries, a key value and a data value. Both are of fixed length. The index entry is the start date. We have saved it as a long value. It is saved as a string to make the index file easier to read. The data is saved at the position offset into the datafile and is stored as a string. If we want to make the index file smaller, we can save these values as longs instead of strings:

```
public void del(scheduleStruct del)
    throws NotFoundException, IOException {

    Long conv;
    String key;
    String data;
    long pos;

    conv = new Long(del.start.getTime());
    key = conv.toString();
    key = StringUtil.padStringLeft(key,' ',Size);

    data = index.findRecord(key);

    conv = new Long(data.trim());
    pos = conv.longValue();

    // We could now delete the data at pos, but we won't

    index.delRecord(key);
}
```

The delete routine only deletes the index file entry. If we deleted
the datafile entry, we'd be left with a hole in the file. In order to
remove this hole, we would have to move all the data upward in
the file and change all the corresponding index file entries. This
type of operation is commonly in a compaction program and is
typically performed infrequently. Disk space is fairly cheap, so
we'll let our program run a little faster and periodically perform
maintenance on the database. This code fragment shows how we
implemented the find routine for our disk-based schedule:

```
public scheduleStruct find(Date date)
    throws NotFoundException, IOException {

    scheduleStruct result;
    long pos;
    Long conv;
    String key;
    String data;
```

```
            conv = new Long(date.getTime());
            key = conv.toString();
            key = StringUtil.padStringLeft(key,' ',Size);

            data = index.findRecord(key);

            conv = new Long(data.trim());
            pos = conv.longValue();

            return findPos(pos);
        }

    public scheduleStruct findPos(long pos)
        throws IOException {

        scheduleStruct result = new scheduleStruct();

        dataFile.seek(pos);
        result.start = new Date(dataFile.readLong());
        result.end = new Date(dataFile.readLong());
        result.desc = new String(dataFile.readLine());
        result.descURL = new String(dataFile.readLine());
        result.minutesURL = new String(dataFile.readLine());
        result.attending = new String(dataFile.readLine());

        return result;
    }
```

The find routine is composed of two routines. The first, the one defined by the schedule interface, looks in the index file and finds the position of the desired in the data file. The second, findPos, is used to retrieve the data from the datafile. Here, we are using the readLine routine. We seek for the position and then read each field from the datafile. This data is then returned to the calling method.

This brings us to the last, and hardest, routine in the serverSchedule. The findRange routine takes advantage of the sorted index file to make this routine run faster. We do two binary searches into the index to find the starting and ending entries. We then go through each entry to find its data in the datafile. For a large database and reasonable date range, this is much faster than searching the whole datafile. Now that we have a routine to find a specific schedule, we need a routine to return a range of schedules:

```java
public scheduleStruct[] findRange(Date start, Date end)
    throws IOException {

    searchStruct resultStart, resultEnd;
    Long conv;
    String key,data;
    int num;

    conv = new Long(start.getTime());
    key = conv.toString();
    key = StringUtil.padStringLeft(key,' ',Size);

    resultStart = index.binarySearch(key);

    conv = new Long(end.getTime());
    key = conv.toString();
    key = StringUtil.padStringLeft(key,' ',Size);

    resultEnd = index.binarySearch(key);

    num = (int) (resultEnd.pos - resultStart.pos) /
                index.getRecordSize();

    if (num < 1) return null;

    scheduleStruct result[] = new scheduleStruct[num];

    int cnt=0;

    for(long i=resultStart.pos; i < resultEnd.pos;) {

        data = index.findPos(i);

        // Data is an index into the .dat file
```

```
            conv = new Long(data.trim());
            result[cnt++] = findPos(conv.longValue());

            i += index.getRecordSize();
        }

        return result;
    }
}
```

That covers the implementation on the schedule interface. Each implementation is geared to solving the specific problems of each side. The client has no local file storage and needs to conserve memory. The server needs to be fast and able to handle large databases. By having a common interface, we can develop classes that perform the same function but in a fashion that can differ radically.

User Interface Module

We'll spare you a presentation of the complete user interface code. Suffice it to say that the process is currently more cumbersome than it will be when layout managers have had time to evolve. In this section, we show you only the highlights of the process we used and focus on the use of frames in Java.

A Java applet normally resides on the Web page it is run on. This is fine for a one-window applet, but suppose we want several windows open? Additionally, applet windows cannot have menus. Thus, if we want to use a menu, we will have to use a frame.

The first screen of the scheduler application is the menu screen. It contains a menubar that acts as a dispatch point for future operations. The user can log in, open and close schedules, and generally run the application. It will call many other routines to do its work:

```
class MenuFrame extends Frame {
    MenuBar mb = new MenuBar();
```

```
public MenuFrame(String s, ui applet) {
    super(s);
    owner = applet;
}

public void init() {
    createMainMenu();
}
```

The MenuFrame class extends the basic functionality of the Frame class. We would like to view frames and applets in a similar light. This means borrowing a few conventions from applets and applying those to frame. In order to do this, we've made a convention in which we create a routine called init. Its function will be similar to the applet: to set up variable and the screen space. Here, our init routine calls createMainMenu, which will set up the menu system. The code to set up the menu follows:

```
public void createMainMenu() {
    setMenuBar(mb);

    Menu m = new Menu("File");
    m.add(new MenuItem("Login"));
    m.add(new MenuItem("Open Schedule"));
    m.add(new MenuItem("-"));
    m.add(new MenuItem("Quit"));
    mb.add(m);

    m = new Menu("Setup");
    m.add(new MenuItem("User Name"));
    m.add(new MenuItem("Server Name"));
    mb.add(m);
}
```

Once the menu is displayed, we will need to know when a user has picked an item. We can do this by overriding the handleEvent method. Each time an event occurs for this frame, the handleEvent method will be called. We are only concerned with two events.

Our first concern is the WINDOW_DESTROYED event. It is generated whenever a user selects the destroy function of the window manager. The actual mechanism is system dependent, but most window managers allow the user to kill a window. When this happens, we need to exit gracefully. To clean up a frame, call its dispose method, which will free any system resources it has used and then exit. We also need to use this mechanism when we exit the application.

The ACTION_EVENT, which is associated with the menubar, is also an important consideration. We will use the instanceof operator to determine that the event happened on a MenuItem. Since we only have one menubar, we know this is the right one. From there, we can test the evt.arg to get the name of the button. We will then call a routine to handle that button.

One important aspect of event handling in frames is that they will not propagate up the event chain. Each frame is an independent entity and has no real parent. While you might think that an Unhandled event would be passed on to the creating window (the applet, for instance), it won't. You will have to handle all the events here or explicitly throw the event to the applet:

```java
public boolean handleEvent(Event evt) {
    if (evt.id == Event.WINDOW_MOVED) {
    }
    else if (evt.id == Event.WINDOW_DESTROY) {
        dispose();
    }
    else if (evt.id == Event.ACTION_EVENT) {
        if (evt.target instanceof MenuItem) {
            String st = (String) evt.arg;
            if (st.equals("Quit")) {
                quit();
                return true;
            }
            else if (st.equals("Login")) {
                login();
                return true;
            }
            else if (st.equals("Open Schedule")) {
```

```
            open();
            return true;
        }
        else if (st.equals("Server Name")) {
            snFrame sname = new snFrame("Change Server",owner);

            sname.init();
            sname.show();
            return true;
        }
        else if (st.equals("User Name")) {
            unFrame uname = new unFrame("User Name",owner);

            uname.init();
            uname.show();
            return true;
        }
        else System.out.println("Menu: " + (String) evt.arg);

        return true;
    }
}

return false;
    }
}
```

The acFrame is used to add meetings to the system. The code is shown here to demonstrate the use of a nonstandard layout manager. We are using the TK packer layout manager. If you don't like the way Java's layout managers work, you can write your own. Check out ventana/awt/PackerLayout.java for an example:

```
class acFrame extends Frame {

    ui owner;

    Panel datePanel = new Panel();
    Panel timePanel = new Panel();
```

```java
Label mdLabel = new Label("Meeting Date");
TextField mdField = new TextField(7);
Label tsLabel = new Label("Time     Start");
TextField tsField = new TextField(4);
Label endLabel = new Label("End");
TextField endField = new TextField(4);

Panel dataPanel = new Panel();
Panel labPanel = new Panel();
Panel fieldPanel = new Panel();
Label descLabel = new Label("Description");
TextField descField = new TextField(40);
Label attendLabel = new Label("Attending");
TextField attendField = new TextField(40);
Label urlLabel = new Label("URL");
TextField urlField = new TextField(40);

Panel buttonPanel = new Panel();
Button schedButton = new Button("Schedule");
Button cancelButton = new Button("Cancel");

public acFrame(String s, ui owner) {
    super(s);
    this.owner = owner;
}

public void init() {
    setLayout(new PackerLayout());
    datePanel.setLayout(new PackerLayout());
    timePanel.setLayout(new PackerLayout());

    datePanel.add("mdLabel;side=left",mdLabel);
    datePanel.add("mdField;side=left",mdField);

    timePanel.add("tsLabel;side=left",tsLabel);
    timePanel.add("tsField;side=left",tsField);
    timePanel.add("endLabel;side=left",endLabel);
    timePanel.add("endField;side=left",endField);
```

```
        dataPanel.setLayout(new PackerLayout());
        labPanel.setLayout(new PackerLayout());
        fieldPanel.setLayout(new PackerLayout());

        dataPanel.add("labPanel;side=left",labPanel);
        dataPanel.add("fieldPanel;side=left",fieldPanel);

        labPanel.add("descLabel;anchor=w;ipady=3",descLabel);
        labPanel.add("attendLabel;anchor=w;ipady=3",
                        attendLabel);
        labPanel.add("urlLabel;anchor=w;ipady=3",urlLabel);

        fieldPanel.add("descField",descField);
        fieldPanel.add("attendField",attendField);
        fieldPanel.add("urlField",urlField);

        buttonPanel.setLayout(new PackerLayout());
        buttonPanel.add("schedButton;side=left;padx=5",
                schedButton);
        buttonPanel.add("cancelButton;side=left",
                cancelButton);

        add("datePanel;anchor=w;pady=5",datePanel);
        add("timePanel;anchor=w;pady=5",timePanel);
        add("dataPanel;anchor=w;pady=5",dataPanel);
        add("buttonPanel",buttonPanel);
    }
}
```

The creation of this fairly simple form is a bit tedious. Using the PackerLayout made it easier, but coding screen layout code is never fun. New Integrated Development Environments (IDEs) will soon allow you to drag and drop components around on the screen. They will then generate the AWT code for you. You'll be responsible for handling the events and putting the glue code together.

Possible Improvements

Our meeting scheduler applet is pretty basic. It could take us weeks to add all of the features we'd like to see included in it. A full-blown scheduler would be really cool—it would also consist of a lot of code. If you are interested in extending this program, you might consider the following ideas:

- Add a weekly/monthly planner view.
- Allow the user or company to specify availability and holidays.
- Specify a group of people and have the computer find an available time slot of specified length.
- Handle issues of security, such as who is allowed to schedule a user.
- Some possible things to send by e-mail:
  - Notify the user when his or her schedule has changed.
  - Give a warning of important meetings or days (wedding anniversaries come to mind).
  - Allow scheduling of resources such as conference rooms and audio-visual supplies.

Appendices

APPENDIX A

About the Online Companion

Information is power! The *Java Programming for the Internet Online Companion* connects you to the best Internet information and Java programming resources.

You can access the Web site at http://www.vmedia.com/java.html. Some of the valuable features of this special site include links to useful Web sites, a database of up-to-date software, and information about other Ventana titles.

The *Java Programming for the Internet Online Companion* also links you to the Ventana bookshop, where you will find useful press and jacket information on a variety of Ventana Communications Group offerings. Plus, you have access to a wide selection of exciting new releases and coming attractions. Ventana's Online Library allows you to order online the books you want without leaving home.

The Online Companion represents Ventana Communications Group's ongoing commitment to offering the most dynamic and exciting products possible. And soon Ventana Online will be adding more services, including more multimedia supplements, searchable indexes, and sections of the book reproduced and hyperlinked to the Internet resources they reference.

Free voice technical support is offered but is limited to installation-related issues and is available for 30 days from the date you register your copy of the book. After the initial 30 days and for non-installation-related questions, please send all technical support questions via Internet e-mail to help@vmedia.com. Or point your browser to http://www.vmedia.com/support. Our technical support staff will research your question and respond promptly via e-mail.

APPENDIX B

About the Companion CD-ROM

The Companion CD-ROM included with your copy of *Java Programming for the Internet* contains a wealth of sample applets, example code from the book, and useful programs.

To install the CD-ROM, take these steps:

* **Windows 95/NT:** Double-click on the CD-ROM icon, and then double-click on viewer.exe from the Windows Explorer or File Manager.

* **Macintosh:** Double-click on the CD-ROM icon, and then double-click on the Viewer icon.

You'll see an opening screen offering several choices: You can exit from the CD, get help on navigating, view the code samples, learn more about Ventana, or view the Hot Picks.

To view Code Samples, select the Code Samples option from the main screen. You'll see a list of the code examples. Click on an item in the list and choose Read to bring up the example code in a text editor.

To view the sample applets, you must locate your Java-enabled Web browser and choose it. Then click on Launch to bring up the applet in your Web browser.

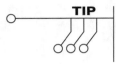

TIP

Note that once you have launched your Web browser, you must double-click on viewer. exe or viewer to return to the CD interface. If you only look at the source code files in the text editor, you can return to the Main Menu of the CD by clicking Main after you close the editor.

To view the programs on the CD, double-click on the Program folder, and then double-click on the Windows or Mac folder. Please copy the programs to your hard drive in order to use them.

You can view all of the sample applets and examples from the book by looking in the Applets folder on the CD. There is also an index.html file that provides a complete listing of all of the applets and samples.

Technical Support

Technical support is available for installation-related problems only. The technical support office is open from 8:00 A.M. to 6:00 P.M. Monday through Friday and can be reached via the following methods:

※ Phone: (919) 544-9404 extension 81

※ E-mail: help@vmedia.com

※ FAX: (919) 544-9472

※ World Wide Web: http://www.vmedia.com/support

※ America Online: keyword *Ventana*

Index

Symbols

! operator   41
!= operator   41, 140
+ (plus) operator   129–130
- (minus) operator   129–130
. (dot) operator   43
/* text */ comment   116
/** text */ comment   117
//text comment   116
= (equals) operator   129–130, 140
== operator   41, 140
    string comparisons   234–235
{} brackets, enclosing methods   47

A

abstract classes   103
abstract method   153, 222
Abstract Windowing Toolkit (AWT)   381
access modifier   80, 107
access rules, OOP   99–100
acFrame class   747–749
ActionArea class   610–613
ActionImage class   590–593
ActionImageAnimation base class   603–606
ActionImageCanvas base class   593–600
additive operators   134

addresses
  George Gilder "The Coming Software Shift"   10
  ICS (Internet Chess Server)   664
  MIME   535
  Online Companion   xxi, 3
  PackerLayout manager   678
  RFC 1738   530
  Sun World Online   10
  W3C (World Wide Web Consortium)   179
advanced user interface   305–348
ALIGN attribute   72
ALT attribute   72
Animated Cursor applet   204–208
animation, thread   201–212
ANSI C, platform independent language   4
API (Applications Programming Interface)   xvii, 213–270
  abstract method   222
  advantages   215
  basics   214–229
  class library   214–215
  copyInto method   250
  described   213–214
  exception catching   402–411
  exceptions   224–228
  final method   222
  hashtables   252–257
  importing packages   218–219
  interfaces   259–261

W

Y

Z

HTML Publishing on the Internet for Windows
HTML Publishing on the Internet for Macintosh

$49.95, 512 pages, illustrated
Windows part #: 229-1, Macintosh part #: 228-3

Successful publishing for the Internet requires an
understanding of "nonlinear" presentation as well as
specialized software. Both are here. Learn how HTML
builds the hot links that let readers choose their own
paths—and how to use effective design to drive your
message for them. The enclosed CD-ROM includes
Netscape Navigator, HoTMetaL LITE, graphic viewer,
templates conversion software and more!

The Web Server Book

$49.95, 680 pages, illustrated, part #: 234-8

The cornerstone of Internet publishing is a set of UNIX
tools, which transform a computer into a "server" that can
be accessed by networked "clients." This step-by-step in-
depth guide to the tools also features a look at key issues—
including content development, services and security. The
companion CD-ROM contains Linux™, Netscape
Navigator™, ready-to-run server software and more.

The Windows NT Web Server Book

$49.95, 500 pages, illustrated, part #: 342-5

A complete toolkit for providing services on the Internet
using the Windows NT operating system. This how-to guide
includes adding the necessary World Wide Web server
software, comparison of the major Windows NT server
packages for the Web, becoming a global product provider
and more! The CD-ROM features a hyperlinked, searchable
copy of the book, plus ready-to-run server software, support
programs, scripts, forms, utilities and demos.

 Books marked with this logo include a free Internet *Online
Companion*™, featuring archives of free utilities plus a
software archive and links to other Internet resources.

Web Pages Enhanced

Shockwave!

$49.95, 350 pages, illustrated, part #:441-3

Breathe new life into your Web pages with Macromedia Shockwave. Ventana's Shockwave! teaches how to enliven and animate your Web sites with online movies. Beginning with step-by-step exercises and examples, and ending with in-depth excursions into the use of Shockwave Lingo extensions, Shockwave! is a must-buy for both novices and experienced Director developers. Plus, tap into current Macromedia resources on the Internet with Ventana's *Online Companion.*

Java Programming for the Internet

$49.95, 500 pages, illustrated, part #: 355-7

Create dynamic, interactive Internet applications with Java Programming for the Internet. Expand the scope of your online development with this comprehensive, step-by-step guide to creating Java applets. Includes four real-world, start-to-finish tutorials. The CD-ROM has all the programs, samples and applets from the book, plus shareware. Continual updates on Ventana's *Online Companion* will keep this information on the cutting edge.

Exploring Moving Worlds

$19.99, 300 pages, illustrated, part #:467-7

Moving Worlds—a newly accepted standard that uses Java and JavaScript for animating objects in three dimensions—is billed as the next-generation implementation of VRML. Exploring Moving Worlds includes an overview of the Moving Worlds standard, detailed specifications on design and architecture, and software examples to help advanced Web developers create live content, animation and full motion on the Web.

Macromedia Director 5 Power Toolkit

$49.95, 800 pages, illustrated, part #: 289-5

Macromedia Director 5 Power Toolkit views the industry's hottest multimedia authoring environment from the inside out. Features tools, tips and professional tricks for producing power-packed projects for CD-ROM and Internet distribution. Dozens of exercises detail the principles behind successful multimedia presentations and the steps to achieve professional results. The companion CD-ROM includes utilities, sample presentations, animations, scripts and files.

Internet Power Toolkit

$49.95, 800 pages, illustrated, part #: 329-8

Plunge deeper into cyberspace with *Internet Power Toolkit*, the advanced guide to Internet tools, techniques and possibilities. Channel its array of Internet utilities and advice into increased productivity and profitability on the Internet. The CD-ROM features an extensive set of TCP/IP tools including Web USENET, e-mail, IRC, MUD and MOO, and more.

The 10 Secrets for Web Success

$19.95, 350 pages, illustrated, part #: 370-0

Create a winning Web site—by discovering what the visionaries behind some of the hottest sites on the Web know instinctively. Meet the people behind Yahoo, IUMA, Word and more, and learn the 10 key principles that set their sites apart from the masses. Discover a whole new way of thinking that will inspire and enhance your own efforts as a Web publisher.

TO ORDER ANY VENTANA TITLE, COMPLETE THIS ORDER FORM AND MAIL OR FAX IT TO US, WITH PAYMENT, FOR QUICK SHIPMENT.

TITLE	PART #	QTY	PRICE	TOTAL

SHIPPING

For all standard orders, please ADD $4.50/first book, $1.35/each additional.
For software kit orders, ADD $6.50/first kit, $2.00/each additional.
For "two-day air," ADD $8.25/first book, $2.25/each additional.
For "two-day air" on the kits, ADD $10.50/first kit, $4.00/each additional.
For orders to Canada, ADD $6.50/book.
For orders sent C.O.D., ADD $4.50 to your shipping rate.
North Carolina residents must ADD 6% sales tax.
International orders require additional shipping charges.

SUBTOTAL = $ _____

SHIPPING = $ _____

TOTAL = $ _____

Name _____

E-mail_____ Daytime phone _____

Company _____

Address (No PO Box) _____

City_____ State_____ Zip_____

Payment enclosed ____VISA ____MC ____ Acc't # _____Exp. date_____

Signature _____ Exact name on card _____

Mail to: Ventana • PO Box 13964 • Research Triangle Park, NC 27709-3964 ☎ 800/743-5369 • Fax 919/544-9472

Check your local bookstore or software retailer for these and other bestselling titles, or call toll free: **800/743-5369**